Studies in National Policy

V. O. KEY, KENT T. HEALY,
HAROLD D. LASSWELL, JOHN P. MILLER,
EUGENE V. ROSTOW,

Editorial Committee

This series is designed to present the result of studies made in the course of an interdepartmental program of research in national policy, organized at Yale University in 1946, by members of the Departments of Economics and Political Science, and the School of Law.

STUDIES IN NATIONAL POLICY

THE
Lonely Crowd

A Study of the
Changing American Character

By

DAVID RIESMAN

IN COLLABORATION WITH

Reuel Denney and Nathan Glazer

NEW HAVEN : YALE UNIVERSITY PRESS

LONDON : GEOFFREY CUMBERLEGE : OXFORD UNIVERSITY PRESS

Preface

I speak of the American in the singular, as if there were not millions of them, north and south, east and west, of both sexes, of all ages, and of various races, professions, and religions. Of course the one American I speak of is mythical; but to speak in parables is inevitable in such a subject, and it is perhaps as well to do so frankly.

Santayana, *Character and Opinion in the United States*

THIS is a book about "character" in the contemporary scientific sense of "social character"—the patterned uniformities of learned response that distinguish men of different regions, eras, and groups. It is a book about the nature of the processes that produce the differences in character of Americans, Frenchmen, Pueblo Indians, and so on; of northern Americans and southern Americans; of middle-class Americans and lower-class Americans. Furthermore, it is a book about the way in which certain social character types, once they are formed at the knee of society, are then deployed in the work, play, politics, and child-rearing activities of adult life.

The first few chapters deal with the hypothesis that changes in population and technology everywhere are the chief correlates of changes in the social character. Then the character and destiny of the middle- and upper middle-class American of yesterday and today are scrutinized. My major thesis in these opening chapters is that the conformity of earlier generations of Americans of the type I term "inner-directed" was mainly assured by their internalization of adult authority. The middle-class urban American of today, the "other-directed," is, by contrast, in a characterological sense more the product of his peers—that is, in sociological terms, his "peer-groups," the other kids at school or in the block. In adult life he continues to respond to these peers, not only with overt conformity, as do people in all times and places, but also in a deeper sense, in the very quality of his feeling. Yet, paradoxically, he remains a lonely member of the crowd because he never comes really close to the others or to himself; his inner-directed predecessor was lonely too, but in a different way: his chief company being the ancestors within—the parents whom he had internalized.

To the reader who is familiar with Erich Fromm's treatment of the role of social character types in the historical process, this approach will not present difficulties; our principal reliance has been on the concepts he has done so much to develop. On the other hand, it should present no great difficulties to the everyday reader, especially perhaps the reader of novels and drama, who is aware of salient differences between his generation and that of his father and grandfather.

The terms I use for these "ideal" types (in Max Weber's sense) will be defined in their proper place, but I should like to warn the reader lest his judgment be prejudiced by the term "inner-directed," which apart from the definition, *sounds* like a more autonomous and therefore better type than "other-directed." This inference would not be warranted; more should not be read into the terms than is intended. At every step of theory making the investigator remains in the grip of his terms, and the modification of terms throughout the progress of the study was evidence of a constant dialectic between the urge to simplify and the urge to take account of everything.

The urge to simplify won out most of the time. But even when the writer and his collaborators made a plunging commitment to this or that answer to the as yet unanswered questions we were asking of history, difficulties of expression and communication remained. An expository rhetoric of shorthand and slogans—as in the chapter title "The Other-directed Round of Life: from Invisible Hand to Glad Hand"—raised many problems. Might the reference to an "invisible hand," recalling Adam Smith's metaphorical view of society and character, disappoint the specialist (who includes Smith's *Moral Sentiments* as well as *Wealth of Nations* in his purview) and at the same time mystify the nonspecialist? Perhaps so. Yet these are the chances communication must take.

The study should be accepted, then, as a "model construction" of the interaction of certain conformity patterns in middle-class character and certain elements in American productivity, politics, and leisure. No attempt is made at completeness. No satisfactory answer is given, for instance, to the question whether there is such a thing as "the" American, persistent through time, from Crevecoeur's day and Tocqueville's day and before down to the present. I have found it more useful to frame my character types in such a fashion as to give them the run of the world; to speak of the nineteenth-century American as a subtype of a generalized western European industrial type; and to assume that the other-directed American of our day represents nothing necessarily unique about America but is rather the forerunner of a type of whom we shall see more. For he bespeaks a western urban world in which, with growing economic abundance, work has lost its former importance and one's peers educate one in the proper attitudes toward leisure and consumption—indeed, in which politics and work become, in a sense, consumables.

This book was written in the course of researches into specific problems of American character and politics. But these researches contributed very little in any direct way to the building, let alone the testing, of the model. Indeed, quite the other way around: the model put forward here (and earlier circulated in draft form to collaborators and colleagues) was used and is now being used to orient our speculations, to guide our research, and to pose questions for further investigation. In later publications we expect to present some of our more empirical material: a community study or two, a number of "profiles" or character studies of individuals, an analysis of a group of interviews with teen-agers. There will then be time and space to comment on the relationships between hypothesis, evidence, and new hypothesis.[1]

In the present volume three planes of social life are explored. Part I, in essence, is a description and revaluation of the modes of conformity in the several successive stages of our western society: the medieval, the near-contemporary industrial, and the modern. This part of the book culminates in an extended comparison and contrast, setting the inner-directed man of the "age of production" who is still very much with us over against the other-directed man of the coming (to paraphrase Leo Lowenthal) "age of consumption."

Part II is a reassessment of the sphere of politics insofar as this represents a characteristic field of emotional commitment for the

1. Some of these methodological problems are discussed in a long monograph (with Nathan Glazer), "Criteria for Political Apathy," *Studies in Leadership*, ed. Alvin W. Gouldner (New York, Harper, forthcoming); and in two articles (also with Nathan Glazer), "The Meaning of Opinion," *Public Opinion Quarterly*, XII (1948–49), 633–648, and "Social Structure, Character Structure, and Opinion," *International Journal of Opinion and Attitude Research*, II (1949), 512–527. On the "profiles" see my remarks at the 1949 meeting of the American Association for Public Opinion Research, abstracted in *Public Opinion Quarterly*, XIII (1949–50), 741–745.

American middle- and upper middle-class man. Does politics have meaning for him in the inherited terms in which we are accustomed to define politics? Or is he beginning to define it in new ways? Perhaps his orientation toward consumption, resting on historical, technological, and eventually characterological foundations of which he himself is only dimly aware, causes him to use politics as a commodity like other commodities. If so, what prevents him from seeing that politics by that very fact is altered and that his assumptions of a "ruling class" based on pelf or power may be quite as mythical as the belief of residual capitalists in the "invisible hand"? Is it possible that the middle- and upper middle-class man of our day goes out of his way to create a series of political demons that exist only because his obsolete belief confirms their existence?

Part II suggests that for the more privileged classes in America it is probably as important to feel free as to be free. Part III attempts to come to grips with the practical implications and limitations of that approach to life and politics. It begins with the essentially psychological and philosophical postulate that "adjustment," no matter how comfortable it appears to be, is never freedom. Beyond adjustment to the prevailing mode of conformity, beyond obedience to or fascination by the peers, lies the possibility of autonomy. Autonomy arises when men use the opportunity presented by the "loose fit" of social character, which is never all of character.

But the quality of autonomy in a particular age depends very much on the social character typical for that age. Thus, with the change in social character from inner-direction to other-direction, new problems inevitably arise for those who seek autonomy. They can no longer, in an age of consumption, so easily find autonomy in the way they make a living. Leisure, however, presents them with new potentialities—and new hazards. My analysis does little more than open up the very difficult problem of the demands that the individual today can make on himself, on his peers, and on his society for a more creative use of his leisure.

ACKNOWLEDGMENTS

This book could not have been written but for the support given by the Committee on National Policy of Yale University. The committee is a group drawn from various social sciences; its members are "located" in law, economics, and political science, but not confined there. The committee invited me to Yale, gave me a completely free hand as to what I wanted to do and with whom I should do it, and generously supported the work from its time-limited funding by the Carnegie Corporation, to which my thanks are also due. I am particularly grateful to Professors Harold D. Lasswell and Eugene V. Rostow, of the Yale Law School, the committee members most closely concerned with the work, to the committee's chairman, Kent Healy, and to Professor John P. Miller, of the Yale Economics Department, who gave me helpful advice concerning Chapter VI.

My extended leaves of absence from the University of Chicago were made possible by the cooperation of Dean F. Champion Ward and Milton Singer of the College. I am deeply indebted to Professor Singer for incisive criticisms of and decisive suggestions toward the theory of character developed in the book and, beyond these specific aids, for the continuous encouragement of his own kind of thinking and research that cuts across departmental lines.

My indebtedness to my two collaborators is very great indeed. Reuel Denney has been my friend for many years, and my colleague at Chicago since 1947. It was in his company that I first began to try to cross the line that separates the culture of the adult world from that of the teen-ager and to explore young people's tastes in music, literature, movies, and other leisure pursuits. The discussion of the socializing and "escapist" functions of literature in Chapters IV, V, VII, and X draws heavily on memoranda written by him; and the treatment of work and play in the contemporary American middle class in Chapters XV through XVII draws not only on his memoranda but on the work of students whom we have jointly introduced to or encouraged in the study of these problems. Indeed, our collaboration in the investigation of American leisure has been so close that it is often hard to separate our ideas. In 1949 Mr. Denney worked with me in the task of revising and recasting the final manuscript. His efforts were indispensable in the organization of the book.

Mr. Nathan Glazer worked with me in the first half year of research at Yale, assuming coresponsibility for the planning and carrying out of the project and coauthorship of our earlier reports, published and unpublished. He brought to the work not only great intellectual gifts and excellent training in anthropology, linguistics, and social research generally but also a curiosity of mind and generosity of spirit which enriched our colleagueship. Since leaving Yale he has continued to act as consultant and to use his editing skill in making suggestions concerning the manuscript. The treatment of the role of character structure in history in Chapter I, of the relation between character and politics in Part II, and of the concept of autonomy in Chapter XIV owes much to drafts written by him.

The study of a community in Vermont was made under the direction of Martin and Margy Meyerson. They were assisted by Rosalie Hankey, who provided us with some fine examples of the interviewer's art, and by David Miller. In collaboration with Mr. and Mrs. Meyerson, Dr. Genevieve Knupfer undertook a group of interviews in East Harlem, New York, and elsewhere. Coding of the interviews has been in the capable hands of Rose Laub Coser and, in time spared from her duties at the University of Rochester Medical School, of Dr. Knupfer. Erika Eichhorn gathered and analyzed a group of Rorschach tests in the Vermont community, and Albert Halasi analyzed several handwriting specimens from our interviewees; both joined by correspondence the continuing "seminar" among my collaborators from which this book, as well as our more specialized publications, has benefited. Sheila Spaulding assisted with research on American history, on the theory of the population cycle, on the problems of "utopian" thinking, and in preparing the manuscript for the press. Mollie Mansfield did some of our first interviews and made many suggestions for improvement of the interview guide. Janice Feldstein typed drafts and memoranda and helped build up our meager store of data on contemporary leisure activities. Betty Martin of the Yale University Press took great pains with the final styling of the manuscript.

Much of the work was done at the Yale Law School, where I held a research appointment. Its dean, Wesley A. Sturges, and its library, secretarial, and administrative staffs are to be thanked for their cooperation. I am also indebted to the College and to the Social Science Research Committee of the University of Chicago for grants which aided me in the completion of the manuscript.

Since my purpose in this volume has not been bibliographic, I have only cited either those works from which we have knowingly taken a great deal or those which happened to serve as illustrations or allusions to our themes. Here I would like to acknowledge the help of some of those who read the manuscript or portions of it: Lewis Dexter, Herman Finer, Erich Fromm, Everett Hughes, Nathan Leites, John R. Seeley, M. Brewster Smith, and Martha Wolfenstein. Their willingness and that of others mentioned later on, to go to great pains in such a task—often, when they did not share my preconceptions—is testimony to the strength of a tradition of cooperative inquiry in social research. I also owe much to my wife's encouragement and specifically to her novel concerning children and to her criticism of this book through its various stages.

I want to thank Alfred Knopf, publisher of Tocqueville's *Democracy in America,* for permission to quote from that book.

I also want to thank the *Public Opinion Quarterly;* the Graduate School of Public Administration, Cambridge, Massachusetts; and Longmans, Green, for permission to draw on articles of mine published by them.

D. R.

Chicago, Illinois
February 20, 1950

Contents

PART I
CHARACTER

Some Types of Character
and Society

. . . nor can the learned reader be ignorant, that in human nature, though here collected under one general name, is such prodigious variety, that a cook will sooner have gone through all the several species of animal and vegetable food in the world, than an author will be able to exhaust so extensive a subject.

Fielding, *Tom Jones*

SOCIAL CHARACTER is the product of social forms; in that sense, man is made by his society. Yet we know that social forms change; sometimes men change them; and character changes with them. What part does character play, then, in the initiation of change?

Let us take political apathy as an illustration. The complexity of society, its segmentation, the difficulty of comprehending it, the consistent failure to have it act the way people say they would like it to act—all these factors induce political apathy. At the same time general political apathy is itself one of the main factors "causing" the apparent inelasticity of society.

The relations between political apathy and social change are actually more complicated even than this, once unconscious interconnections are recognized. For example, uncertainty as to social position, combined with the possibility or hope of rapid social advance, leads parents in certain middle social strata to largely unconscious changes in their child-rearing practices. The child is no longer trained to an unquestioned ideal as perhaps his parents were; he is trained to do the "best possible" in any situation. The decline of specifically defined goals and clear purposes, for this and other reasons, can easily have the effect of making the person more vulnerable to apathy. This in turn may lead him to interpret the world in such a way as to justify his apathy and to mold it into a political style. He says, "No one can do anything in politics anyway," when the point is, "I cannot imagine myself doing anything, in politics or elsewhere."

The complexity of such interconnections is so great that we must recognize very clearly the limitations of historical analysis pursued according to *any* method we now have; the *Kulturkampf* aroused by Max Weber's magnificent essay on *The Protestant Ethic and the Spirit of Capitalism* indicates both the controversiality and the possible fruitfulness of pursuing a typological method to see where it leads. Hence the place given to character in this book is heuristic; it is an effort to find something out, not a conviction as to *the* road for overcoming the elusiveness of history.

Let us begin by defining character structure as the more or less permanent, socially and historically conditioned organization of an individual's drives and satisfactions. The term as thus defined is less inclusive than "personality," the word which in current usage denotes the total self, with its inherited temperament and talents, its biological as well as psychological components, its evanescent as well as more or less permanent attributes.[1] My reason for selecting from this complex the abstraction called "character" is that in this book I propose to deal with those components of personality that also play the principal role in the maintenance of social forms—those that are *learned* in the lifelong process of socialization.

As soon as we begin to speak of character as related to social forms we make, in effect, a still further selection from the matrix of personality. For we begin to isolate for inspection those components of character that are shared among significant social groups. And to speak of character in these terms is to speak of character as "social character." This notion of social character, the character that is clearly generalized in a society, permits us to speak elliptically but meaningfully of the character of classes, groups, regions, and nations.

The assumption that a social character exists has always been a

---

1. See Erich Fromm, *Man for Himself* (New York, Rinehart, 1947), pp. 50–61; see also, Gardner Murphy, *Personality: A Biosocial Approach to Origins and Structure* (New York, Harper, 1947), pp. 1–11; *Culture and Personality,* ed. S. Stansfeld Sargent and Marian W. Smith (Viking Fund, 1949).

more or less invisible premise in ordinary parlance; and it is becoming a more or less visible premise in the language of the social sciences. Its importance as a premise in the social sciences stands in direct proportion to the uncertainty that the social sciences feel about the nonsocial, or less obviously social, aspects of personality that are rooted in temperament. Under "temperament" we may lump together the constitutional or physiological determinants of behavior—such matters as hormones, metabolism, blood pressure as well as "temperament" in the sense of cheerfulness, dourness, peppiness, etc. We know little about the causes or consequences of differences of temperament in individuals and groups; and hence they are excluded from the scope of this study, although this is not intended to deny their importance.

Why should there be a social character? Psychoanalysts have given an answer explaining it on the basis of the society's needs. Thus Erik H. Erikson writes, speaking of child socialization in preliterate groups: ". . . systems of child training . . . represent unconscious attempts at creating out of human raw material that configuration of attitudes which is (or once was) the optimum under the tribe's particular natural conditions and economic-historic necessities." [2]

Likewise, Erich Fromm declares:

In order that any society may function well, its members must acquire the kind of character which makes them *want* to act in the way they *have* to act as members of the society or of a special class within it. They have to *desire* what objectively is *necessary* for them to do. *Outer force* is replaced by *inner compulsion,* and by the particular kind of human energy which is channeled into character traits.[3]

By implication these writers are saying that if human beings lived at random—in an inconceivable pure contingency—their drives could not be harnessed to perform the culturally required tasks.

The individual undoubtedly gets some benefit out of living in the more or less confining strait jacket of the social character which is imposed on him. It is one of the ambiguities of human existence, as it is of art, that personal life flourishes within the forms provided for it

2. "Observations on the Yurok: Childhood and World Image," *University of California Publications in American Archaeology and Ethnology,* XXXV (1943), iv.

3. "Individual and Social Origins of Neurosis," *American Sociological Review,* IX (1944), 380; reprinted in *Personality in Nature, Society, and Culture,* ed. Clyde Kluckhohn and Henry Murray (New York, Alfred A. Knopf, 1948), pp. 407, 409–410.

by tradition and necessity. Character structure, like social structure, serves not only to limit choice but also to channel action by foreclosing some of the otherwise limitless behavior choices of human beings. We are familiar enough with the compulsive person, who feels he must decide, without the aid of habitual conformity, which shoe to put on first, whether to take the local or the express, whether to order eggs boiled or scrambled. Since life is too short for such overworked elaboration of choice, the social character permits it to be lived in some sort of working harness.

The danger is not of having too much leeway but of having too little. This is the constriction of choice range against which Freud eloquently warned mankind—character and culture can overreach themselves and thus swallow up all of life in enterprises whose only virtue is that they are shared.

I. CHARACTER AND SOCIETY

Since this study assumes that character is socially conditioned, it also takes for granted that there is some observable relation between a particular society and the kind of social character it produces. What is the best way to define this relation? Since the social function of character is to insure or permit conformity, it appears that the various types of social character can be defined most appropriately in terms of the modes of conformity that are developed in them. Finally, any prevalent mode of conformity may itself be used as an index to characterize a whole society.

Having said this, we must not overestimate the role of character in the social process. It is not a sufficient explanation, for instance, to say, as some students have said, that the German army held together because "the Germans" had an authoritarian character, since armies of very diverse character type do in fact hold together under given conditions of battle and supply. Nor will it do to assume, as American aptitude-testers sometimes do, that certain jobs can be successfully handled only by a narrowly limited range of character types: that we need "extrovert" or "oral" salesmen and administrators, and "introvert" or "anal" chemists and accountants. Our conventions on this score may make an introvert administrator feel inadequate because he does not fit the stereotype that patterns the narrow judgment passed on him by others and, through their eyes, by himself.

Actually, people of radically different types can adapt themselves to perform, adequately enough, a wide variety of complex tasks. Or, to put the same thing in another way, social institutions can harness a gamut of different motivations, springing from different character types, to perform very much the same kinds of socially demanded jobs. And yet, of course, this is not to say that character is merely a shadowy factor in history, like some Hegelian spirit. Character will affect the style and psychic costs of job performances that, in economic or political analysis, look almost identical.

Thus we are forced to take account of the possibility that people may be compelled to behave in one way although their character structure presses them to behave in the opposite way. Society may change more rapidly than character, or vice versa. Indeed, this disparity between socially required behavior and characterologically compatible behavior is one of the great levers of change. Fortunately we know of no society like the one glumly envisaged by Aldous Huxley in *Brave New World,* where the social character types have been completely content in their social roles and where consequently, barring accident, no social change exists. Thus while we shall be talking hereafter of social character types we must try to remember that these types are constructions and that the richness of human potentiality, human discontent, and human variety cannot be imprisoned within a typology.

As there are numberless ways of classifying people, none of them definitive, none of them more than approximations, none of them useful for more than a limited range of analytic purposes, so there exists in the social science literature an enormous number of different ways of classifying societies. I myself have chosen to emphasize some possible relationships between the population growth of a society and the historical sequence of character types. For I think it fruitful in developing a historical characterology to explore the correlations between the conformity demands put on people in a society and the broadest of the social indexes that connect men with their environment—the demographic indexes. A useful key to those indexes is the theory developed by modern students of population who see all societies as located in and moving along a *curve of population growth and distribution.*

Actually there is no single curve of population, but a variety. We are interested here in a particular kind of S-shaped curve that appears in the history of the long-industrialized countries, as well as in the projected populations of certain other countries as they are expected to take shape in the future. The S-shaped curve begins at a point where the number of births and deaths are fairly equal (both birth rates and death rates being high) and moves through a period of rapid population increase to a new plateau where births and deaths are again equal (both rates being low).

As Malthus gloomily observed one hundred and fifty years ago, populations are capable of growing at a geometric rate. A slight rate of increase of births over deaths per annum means that in fifteen or twenty years there will be more women of childbearing age who are able in turn to swell the birth rate in comparison with the death rate. In a short time, moreover, such a development can change the age composition of a society—just as in the postwar years in America some of the consequences of an upward spurt in births are visible.

Societies at an early place on the S-curve are heavily weighted toward the younger age groups, which means that birth rates and death rates are high: the turnover of generations is rapid. Societies at a late place on the curve are weighted toward the middle-aged groups, which ordinarily means that birth rates and death rates are low. These vital statistics (we are ignoring the many technical indeterminates that haunt work with population figures) are in their turn dependent on many subtle social and psychological factors: attitudes toward sanitation and toward children, cultural beliefs about the standard of living apppropriate to different classes, food and sex taboos—these merely begin the list.

Population theorists [4] distinguish three phases on the population S-curve. Societies of high birth rate and equally high death rate are said to be in the phase of "high growth potential": their population would increase with great rapidity if the death rate were lowered by, say, a sudden advance in hygiene. Societies which have passed into the phase of decreased death rate are said to be in the phase of "transitional growth." Finally, societies which have passed through both these earlier phases and are beginning to move toward a net decrease in population are said to be in the phase of "incipient population decline." (It should be noted that all references to the population phase of a society are to averages which do not take account of the very different rates that may characterize classes or ethnic groups within the society—our treatment is highly generalized.)

4. We have relied here chiefly on the terminology and theory of Frank W. Notestein.

It would be very surprising if variations in the basic conditions of reproduction, livelihood, and survival chances, that is, in the supply of and demand for human beings, failed to influence character. My thesis is, in fact, that each of these three different phases on the population curve appears to be occupied by a society that enforces conformity and molds social character in a definably different way.

The society of high growth potential develops in its typical members a social character whose conformity is insured by their tendency to follow tradition: these I shall term *tradition-directed* people and the society in which they live *a society dependent on tradition-direction*.

The society of transitional population growth develops in its typical members a social character whose conformity is insured by their tendency to acquire early in life an internalized set of goals. These I shall term *inner-directed* people and the society in which they live *a society dependent on inner-direction*.

Finally, the society of incipient population decline develops in its typical members a social character whose conformity is insured by their tendency to be sensitized to the expectations and preferences of others. These I shall term *other-directed* people and the society in which they live one *dependent on other-direction*.

Let me point out, however, before embarking on a description of these three "ideal types" of character and society, that I am not concerned here with making a detailed demographic analysis such as would be necessary before one could prove that a link exists between population phase and character type. Rather, the theory of the curve of population provides me with a kind of shorthand for referring to the myriad institutional elements that are also—though usually more heatedly—symbolized by such words as "industrialism," "folk society," "monopoly capitalism," "urbanization," "rationalization," and so on. Hence when I speak here of transitional growth or incipient decline of population in conjunction with shifts in character and conformity, these phrases should not be taken as magical and comprehensive explanations.[5]

I am sure that change in the population age distribution, even with all it implies in change of the spacing of people, the size of markets, the role of children, the society's feeling of vitality or senescence, and

5. See the incisive discussion of the psychological appeal and social menace of deterministic theories of history by Jerome Frank, *Fate and Freedom* (New York, Simon & Schuster, 1945). I am indebted to Judge Frank for a number of helpful suggestions.

many other intangibles, cannot determine character all by itself. It is a necessary but not a sufficient condition. What matters, too, is the *rate* of change, the size of the country or other unit of organization, the distribution of the change among social classes, a group's reaction to its density, the persistence of traditions because (as in the case of Japan) they can be made compatible with industrialization.

HIGH GROWTH POTENTIAL: TRADITION-DIRECTED TYPES

It has already been stated that a society characterized by high birth rates and high death rates is in the stage of high growth potential. The mortality rates are so high that any decline in them permits a very rapid expansion of the population. This is the situation of more than half the world's population: in India, Egypt, and China (which have already grown immensely in recent generations), for most pre-literate peoples in Central Africa, parts of Central and South America, in fact in most areas of the world relatively untouched by industrialization. Here death rates are so high that if birth rates were not also high the populations would die out.

Regions where the population is in this stage of growth may be sparsely populated, as in the areas occupied by many primitive tribes and as in parts of Central and South America. They may be densely populated, as in India, China, and Egypt. In either case, the society achieves a Malthusian bargain with the limited food supply by killing off, in one way or another, some of the potential surplus of births over deaths—the enormous trap which, in Malthus' view, nature sets for man and which can be peaceably escaped only by prudent cultivation of the soil and prudent uncultivation of the species through the delay of marriage. Without the prevention of childbirth by means of marriage postponement or other contraceptive measures, the population must be limited by taking the life of living beings. And so other societies have "invented" cannibalism, induced abortion, organized wars, made human sacrifice, and practiced infanticide (especially female) as means of avoiding periodic famine and epidemics.

Though this settling of accounts with the contradictory impulses of hunger and sex is accompanied often enough by upheaval and distress, these societies in the stage of high growth potential tend to be stable at least in the sense that their social practices, including the "crimes" that keep population down, are institutionalized and patterned. Generation after generation people are born, are weeded out, and die to make room for others. The net rate of natural increase fluctuates only within narrow limits, as is true also of societies in the stage of incipient decline. But unlike the latter, the average life expectancy in the former is characteristically low: the population is heavily weighted on the side of the young, and generation replaces generation far more rapidly and less "efficiently" than in those industrialized societies of incipient population decline.

In viewing such a society we inevitably associate the relative stability of the man-land ratio, whether high or low, with the tenacity of custom and social structure. However, we must not equate stability of social structure over historical time with psychic stability in the life span of an individual: the latter may subjectively experience much violence and disorganization. In the last analysis, however, he learns to deal with life by adaptation, not by innovation. With certain exceptions conformity is largely given in the "self-evident" social situation. Of course nothing in human life is ever really self-evident; where it so appears it is because perceptions have been narrowed by cultural conditioning. As the precarious relation to the food supply is built into the going culture, it helps create a pattern of conventional conformity which is reflected in many, if not in all, societies in the stage of high growth potential. This is what we mean when we speak of tradition-direction.

A definition of tradition-direction. Since the type of social order we have been discussing is relatively unchanging, the conformity of the individual tends to be dictated to a very large degree by power relations among the various age and sex groups, the clans, castes, professions, and so forth—relations which have endured for centuries and are modified but slightly, if at all, by successive generations. The culture controls behavior minutely, and, while the rules are not so complicated that the young cannot learn them during the period of intensive socialization, careful and rigid etiquette governs the fundamentally influential sphere of kin relationships. Moreover, the culture, in addition to its economic tasks, or as part of them, provides ritual, routine, and religion to occupy and to orient everyone. Little energy is directed toward finding new solutions of the age-old problems, let us say, of agricultural technique or "medicine," the problems to which people are acculturated.

It is not to be thought, however, that in these societies, where the activity of the individual member is determined by characterologically grounded obedience to traditions, the individual may not be highly prized and, in many instances, encouraged to develop his capabilities, his initiative, and even, within very narrow time limits, his aspirations. Indeed, the individual in some primitive societies is far more appreciated and respected than in some sectors of modern society. For the individual in a society dependent on tradition-direction has a well-defined functional relationship to other members of the group. If he is not killed off, he "belongs"—he is not "surplus," as the modern unemployed are surplus, nor is he expendable as the unskilled are expendable in modern society. But by very virtue of his "belonging," life goals that are *his* in terms of conscious choice appear to shape his destiny only to a very limited extent, just as only to a limited extent is there any concept of progress for the group.

In societies in which tradition-direction is the dominant mode of insuring conformity, relative stability is preserved in part by the infrequent but highly important process of fitting such deviants as there are into institutionalized roles. In such societies a person who might have become at a later historical stage an innovator or rebel, whose belonging, as such, is marginal and problematic, is drawn instead into roles like those of the shaman or sorcerer. That is, he is drawn into roles that make a socially acceptable contribution, while at the same time they provide the individual with a more or less approved niche. The medieval monastic orders may have served in a similar way to absorb many characterological mutations.

In some of these societies certain individuals are encouraged toward a degree of individuality from childhood, especially if they belong to families of high status. But, since the range of choice, even for high-status people, is minimal, the apparent social need for an individuated type of character is also minimal. It is probably accurate to say that character structure in these societies is very largely "adjusted," in the sense that for most people it appears to be in tune with social institutions. Even the few misfits "fit" to a degree; and only very rarely is one driven out of his social world.

This does not mean, of course, that the people are happy; the society to whose traditions they are adjusted may be a miserable one, ridden with anxiety, sadism, and disease. The point is rather that change, while never completely absent in human affairs, is slowed down as the movement of molecules is slowed down at low temperature; and the social character comes as close as it ever does to looking like the matrix of the social forms themselves.

In western history the Middle Ages can be considered a period in which the majority were tradition-directed. But the term tradition-directed refers to a common element, not only among the people of precapitalist Europe but also among such enormously different types of people as Hindus and Hopi Indians, Zulus and Chinese, North African Arabs and Balinese. There is comfort in relying on the many writers who have found a similiar unity amid diversity, a unity they express in such terms as "folk society" (as against "civilization"), a "status society" (as against a "contract society"), *Gemeinschaft* (as against *"Gesellschaft"*), and so on. Different as the societies envisaged by these terms are, the folk, status, and *Gemeinschaft* societies resemble each other in their relative slowness of change, their dependence on family and kin organization, and—in comparison with later epochs—their tight web of values. And, as is now well recognized by students, the high birth rate of these societies in the stage of high growth potential is not merely the result of a lack of contraceptive knowledge or techniques. A whole way of life—an outlook on chance, on children, on the place of women, on sexuality, on the very meaning of existence—lies between the societies in which human fertility is allowed to take its course and toll and those which prefer to pay other kinds of toll to cut down on fertility by calculation, and, conceivably, as Freud and other observers have suggested, by a decline in sexual energy itself.

TRANSITIONAL GROWTH: INNER-DIRECTED TYPES

The emergence of transitional growth. Except for the west, we know very little about the cumulation of small changes that can eventuate in a breakup of the tradition-directed type of society, leading it to realize its potential for high population growth. As for the west, however, much has been learned about the slow decay of feudalism and the subsequent rise of a type of society in which inner-direction is the dominant mode of insuring conformity. Such a society is likely to be found in the phase of transitional growth of population.

Many writers are apt to view the situation of the tradition-directed peasant as idyllic and to exaggerate by comparison the anomie, the rootlessness, the trapped malaise, of the modern city dweller. There is more than a hint of this in the work of many contemporary social scientists. On the other hand, critical historians, pushing the Renaissance ever back into the Middle Ages, seem sometimes to deny that any decisive change occurred. On the whole, it makes sense to suppose that the greatest social and characterological shift of recent centuries did indeed come when men were driven out of the primary ties that bound them to the western medieval version of tradition-directed society. All later shifts, including the shift from inner-direction to other-direction, seem unimportant by comparison, although of course this latter shift is still under way and we cannot tell what it will look like when complete.

A change in the relatively stable ratio of births to deaths, which characterizes the period of high growth potential, is both the cause and consequence of other profound social changes. In most of the cases known to us a decline takes place in mortality prior to a decline in fertility; hence there is some period in which the population expands rapidly. The drop in death rate occurs as the result of many interacting factors, among them sanitation, improved communications (which permit government to operate over a wider area and also permit easier transport of food to areas of shortage from areas of surplus), the decline, forced or otherwise, of infanticide, cannibalism, and other inbred kinds of violence. Because of improved methods of agriculture the land is able to support more people, and these in turn produce still more people.

As a result population begins increasing nearly in geometric ratio, as it did in Europe between 1650 and 1900 and as it has in recent years been doing in countries like India. Notestein's phrase "transitional growth," is a mild way of putting it. The "transition" is likely to be violent, disrupting the stabilized paths of existence in societies in which tradition-direction has been the principal mode of insuring conformity. The imbalance of births and deaths puts pressure on the society's customary ways. A new slate of character structures is called for or finds its opportunity in coping with the rapid changes—and the need for still more changes—in the social organization.

A definition of inner-direction. In western history the society that emerged with the Renaissance and Reformation and that is only now vanishing serves to illustrate the type of society in which inner-direction is the principal mode of securing conformity. Such a society is characterized by increased personal mobility, by a rapid accumulation of capital (teamed with devastating technological shifts), and by an almost constant *expansion:* intensive expansion in the production of goods and people, and extensive expansion in exploration, colonization, and imperialism. The greater choices this society gives—and the greater initiatives it demands in order to cope with its novel problems —are handled by character types who can manage to live socially without strict and self-evident tradition-direction. These are the inner-directed types.

The concept of inner-direction is intended to cover a very wide range of types. Thus, while it is essential for the study of certain problems to differentiate between Protestant and Catholic countries and their character types, between the effects of the Reformation and the effects of the Renaissance, between the puritan ethic of the European and American north and west and the somewhat more hedonistic ethic of the European east and south, while all these are valid and, for certain purposes, important distinctions, the concentration of this study on the development of modes of conformity permits their neglect. It allows the grouping together of these otherwise distinct developments because they have one thing in common: *the source of direction for the individual is "inner" in the sense that it is implanted early in life by the elders and directed toward generalized but nonetheless inescapably destined goals.*

We can see what this means when we realize that, in societies in which tradition-direction is the dominant mode of insuring conformity, attention is focused on securing external *behavioral* conformity. While behavior is minutely prescribed, individuality of character need not be highly developed to meet prescriptions that are objectified in ritual and etiquette—though to be sure, a social character *capable* of such behavioral attention and obedience is requisite. By contrast, societies in which inner-direction becomes important, though they also are concerned with behavioral conformity, cannot be satisfied with behavioral conformity alone. Too many novel situations are presented, situations which a code cannot encompass in advance. Consequently the problem of personal choice, solved in the earlier period of high growth potential by channeling choice through rigid social organization, in the period of transitional growth is solved by channeling choice through a rigid though highly individualized character.

This rigidity is a complex matter. While any society dependent on inner-direction seems to present people with a wide choice of aims— such as money, possessions, power, knowledge, fame, goodness— these aims are ideologically interrelated, and the selection made by any one individual remains relatively unalterable throughout his life. Moreover, the means to those ends, though not fitted into as tight a social frame of reference as in the society dependent on tradition-direction, are nevertheless limited by the new voluntary associations —for instance, the Quakers, the Masons, the Mechanics' Associations—to which people tie themselves. Indeed, the term "tradition-direction" could be misleading if the reader were to conclude that the force of tradition has no weight for the inner-directed character. On the contrary, he is very considerably bound by traditions: they limit his ends and inhibit his choice of means. The point is rather that a splintering of tradition takes place, connected in part with the increasing division of labor and stratification of society. Even if the individual's choice of tradition is largely determined for him by his family, as it is in most cases, he cannot help becoming aware of the existence of competing traditions—hence of tradition as such. As a result he possesses a somewhat greater degree of flexibility in adapting himself to ever changing requirements and in return requires more from his environment.

As the situational controls of the primary group are loosened— the group that both socializes the young and controls the adult in the earlier era—a new psychological mechanism appropriate to the more open society is "invented": it is a psychological gyroscope.[6] This instrument, once it is set by the parents and other authorities, keeps the inner-directed person, as we shall see, "on course" even when tradition, as responded to by his character, no longer dictates his moves. The inner-directed person becomes capable of maintaining a delicate balance between the demands upon him of his life goal and the buffetings of his external environment.

This metaphor of the gyroscope, like any other, must not be taken literally. It would be a mistake to see the inner-directed man as incapable of learning from experience or as insensitive to public opinion in matters of external conformity. He can receive and utilize certain signals from outside, provided that they can be reconciled

6. Since writing the above I have discovered Gardner Murphy's use of the same metaphor in his volume *Personality*.

with the limited maneuverability that his gyroscope permits him. His pilot is not quite automatic.

Huizinga's *The Waning of the Middle Ages* gives a picture of the anguish and turmoil, the conflict of values, out of which the new forms slowly emerged. As early as the late Middle Ages people were forced to live under new conditions of awareness. As their self-consciousness and their individuality developed, they had to make themselves at home in the world in novel ways. They still have to.

INCIPIENT DECLINE OF POPULATION: OTHER-DIRECTED TYPES

The emergence of the next phase: incipient decline. The problem facing the societies in the stage of transitional growth is that of reaching a point at which resources become plentiful enough or are utilized effectively enough to permit a rapid accumulation of capital. This rapid accumulation has to be achieved even while the social product is being drawn on at an accelerated rate to satisfy the consumer demands that go with the way of life that has already been adopted. For most countries, unless capital and techniques can be imported from other countries in still later phases of the population curve, every effort to increase national resources at a rapid rate must actually be at the expense of current standards of living. We have seen this occur in the U.S.S.R., now in the stage of transitional growth. Only a fantastically large increase in productive capacity will, without a prolonged period of misery, permit an increase in the supply of food and other commodities sufficient to stimulate migration from country to city and at the same time to accommodate the change from large-family to small-family ideational patterns. For Europe this transition was long, drawn out, and painful; and this may be one reason that countries such as France, despite their demographic transformation into the third stage of incipient decline, still retain modes of conformity appropriate to an economy in the second stage or even earlier. For America, Canada, and Australia— at once beneficiaries of European technique and native resources— the transition was rapid and relatively easy.

As has been said, the tradition-directed character hardly thinks of himself as an individual. Still less does it occur to him that he might shape his own destiny in terms of personal, lifelong goals or that the destiny of his children might be separate from that of the family group. He is not sufficiently separated psychologically from himself (or, therefore, sufficiently close to himself), his family, or group to think in these terms. In the phase of transitional growth, however, people of inner-directed character do gain a feeling of control over their own lives and see their children also as individuals with careers to make. At the same time, with the shift out of agriculture and, later, with the banning of child labor in factories (a humanitarian measure both needed and possible because of the altered social relations introduced by industrialization), children no longer become an unequivocal economic asset. And with the growth of habits of scientific thought, religious and magical views of human fertility—views that in an earlier phase of the population curve made sense for the culture if it was to reproduce itself—give way to "rational," individualistic attitudes. Indeed, just as the rapid accumulation of productive capital requires that people be imbued with the "Protestant ethic" (as Max Weber characterized one manifestation of what is here termed inner-direction), so also the decreased number of progeny requires a profound change in values—a change so deep that, in all probability, it has to be rooted in character structure.

As the birth rate begins to follow the death rate downward, societies move toward the epoch of incipient decline of population—the prelude to the time when the birth rate will plunge below the already lowered death rate, so that total population will decline.

This problem of incipient population decline has been much discussed in the western countries, notably in France, Britain, and the Scandinavian countries, where the population is nearing stability or hovering on the verge of actual decrease. Production here has at last outrun even greatly expanded consumption, and the standard of living, which Malthus already realized was a cultural and psychological index, has completed its work by subtle psychological pressures on fertility—though not every social class shares equally in these developments. Fewer and fewer people work on the land or in the extractive industries or even in manufacturing. Hours are short. People may have material abundance and leisure besides. They pay for these changes however—here, as always, the solution of old problems gives rise to new ones—by finding themselves in a centralized and bureaucratized society and a world shrunken and agitated by the contact—accelerated by industrialization—of races, nations, and cultures.

The hard enduringness and enterprise of the inner-directed types are somewhat less necessary under these new conditions. Increasingly, *other people* are the problem, not the material environment. And as people mix more widely and become more sensitive to each other, the surviving traditions from the stage of high growth potential—much disrupted, in any case, during the violent spurt of industrialization— become still further attenuated. Gyroscopic control is no longer sufficiently flexible, and a new psychological mechanism is called for.

Furthermore, the "scarcity psychology" of many inner-directed people, which was socially adaptive during the period of heavy capital accumulation that accompanied transitional growth of population, needs to give way to an "abundance psychology" capable of "wasteful" luxury consumption of leisure and of the surplus product. Unless people want to destroy the surplus product in war, which still does require heavy capital equipment, they must learn to enjoy and engage in those services that are expensive in terms of man power but not of capital—poetry and philosophy, for instance.[7] Indeed, in the period of incipient decline, nonproductive consumers, both the increasing number of old people and the diminishing number of as yet untrained young, form a high proportion of the population, and these need both the economic opportunity to be prodigal and the character structure to allow it.

Has this need for still another slate of character types actually been acknowledged to any degree? My observations lead me to believe that in America it has.

A definition of other-direction. The type of character I shall describe as other-directed seems to be emerging in very recent years in the upper middle class of our larger cities: more prominent in New York than in Boston, in Los Angeles than in Spokane, in Cincinnati than in Chillicothe. Yet in some respects this type is strikingly similar to *the* American, whom Tocqueville and other curious and astonished visitors from Europe, even before the Revolution, thought to be a new kind of man. Indeed, travelers' reports on America impress us with their unanimity. The American is said to be shallower, freer with his money, friendlier, more uncertain of himself and his values, more demanding of approval than the European. It all adds up to a pattern which, without stretching matters too far, resembles the kind of character that a number of social scientists have seen as developing in

7. These examples are given by Allan G. B. Fisher, *The Clash of Progress and Security* (London, Macmillan, 1935).

contemporary, highly industrialized, and bureaucratic America: Fromm's "marketer," Mills's "fixer," Arnold Green's "middle class male child." [8]

This raises several questions which, as I said earlier, I have not been able to answer. It is my impression that the middle-class American of today is decisively different from those Americans of Tocqueville's writings who strike us as so contemporary, and much of this book will be devoted to discussing these differences.[9] It is also my impression that the conditions I believe to be responsible for other-direction are affecting increasing numbers of people in the metropolitan centers of the advanced industrial countries. However, the available comparative studies of European "national character," broken down by social class, are not yet sufficiently inclusive to permit comparison. Given impetus by the late Ruth Benedict, Gorer, Kardiner, Kluckhohn, Margaret Mead, and others, such studies are now under way. Meanwhile, my analysis of the other-directed character is at once an analysis of the American and of contemporary man. Much of the time I find it hard or impossible to say where one ends and the other begins. Tentatively, I am inclined to think that the other-directed type does find itself most at home in America, due to certain constant elements in American society, such as its recruitment from Europe and its lack of any seriously feudal past. As against this, I am also inclined to put more weight on capitalism, industrialism, and urbanization—these being international tendencies—than on any character-forming peculiarities of the American scene.

Bearing these qualifications in mind, it seems appropriate to treat

8. See Erich Fromm, *Man for Himself;* C. Wright Mills, "The Competitive Personality," *Partisan Review,* XIII (1946), 433; Arnold Green, "The Middle Class Male Child and Neurosis," *American Sociological Review,* XI (1946), 31. See also the work of Jurgen Ruesch, Martin B. Loeb, and co-workers on the "infantile personality."

9. I have tried to discover, by reading the eyewitness social observers of the early nineteenth century in America, whether Tocqueville "saw" America or "foresaw" it, to what extent he was influenced—as visiting firemen of today also are—by American snobs who take their image of Europe as the norm in describing their own countrymen. And to what extent, in establishing America's polarity from Europe, he tendentiously noticed those things that were different rather than those that were the same. From conversations with Phillips Bradley and Arthur Schlesinger, Jr., and from G. W. Pierson, *Tocqueville and Beaumont in America* (New York, Oxford University Press, 1938) I get the impression that all these qualifications must be put on Tocqueville's picture of America in the 1830's..On the general problem of whether there is an American character, and if so what are its sources, and how such questions might be investigated, I have profited from the work of Oscar Handlin and from suggestions made by him. Thomas and Znaniecki's *Polish Peasant* may be thought of as a pioneer effort, unfortunately too little followed up, to attack the problem in terms of the experience of a particular ethnic group.

contemporary metropolitan America as our illustration of a society—so far, perhaps, the only illustration—in which other-direction is the dominant mode of insuring conformity. It would be premature, however, to say that it is already the dominant mode in America as a whole. But since the other-directed types are to be found among the young, in the larger cities, and among the upper income groups, we may assume that, unless present trends are reversed, the hegemony of other-direction lies not far off.

If we wanted to cast our social character types into social class molds, we could say that inner-direction is the typical character of the "old" middle class—the banker, the tradesman, the small entrepreneur, the technically oriented engineer, etc.—while other-direction is becoming the typical character of the "new" middle class—the bureaucrat, the salaried employee in business, etc. Many of the economic factors associated with the recent growth of the "new" middle class are well known. They have been discussed by James Burnham, Colin Clark, Peter Drucker, and others. There is a decline in the numbers and in the proportion of the working population engaged in production and extraction—agriculture, heavy industry, heavy transport—and an increase in the numbers and the proportion engaged in white-collar work and the service trades.

Furthermore, societies in the phase of incipient decline (societies, that is, in which we expect other-directed types to come to the fore) are not only highly urbanized but have a high level of capital equipment and technological skill built up during the period of transitional growth. People who are literate, educated, and provided with the necessities of life by machine industry and agriculture, turn increasingly to the "tertiary" economic realm. The service industries prosper among the people as a whole and no longer only in court circles. Education, leisure, services, these go together with an increased consumption of words and images from the mass media of communications in societies that have moved into the incipient decline stage via the route of industrialization. Hence, while societies in the phase of transitional growth begin the process of distributing words from urban centers, the flow becomes a torrent in the societies of incipient population decline. This process, while modulated by profound national and class differences, connected with differences in literacy and loquacity, takes place everywhere in the industrialized lands. Increasingly, relations with the outer world and with oneself are mediated by the flow of mass communication. For the other-directed types political events are likewise experienced through a screen of words by which the events are habitually atomized and personalized—or pseudopersonalized. For the inner-directed person who remains still extant in this period the tendency is rather to systematize and moralize this flow of words.

These developments lead, for large numbers of people, to changes in paths to success and to the requirement of more "socialized" behavior both for success and for marital and personal adaptation. Connected with such changes are changes in the family and in child-rearing practices. In the smaller families of urban life, and with the spread of "permissive" child care to ever wider strata of the population, there is a relaxation of older patterns of discipline. Under these newer patterns the peer-group (the age- and class-graded group in a child's school and neighborhood) becomes much more important to the child, while the parents make him feel guilty not so much about violation of inner standards as about failure to be popular or otherwise to manage his relations with these other children. Moreover, the pressures of the school and the peer-group are reinforced and continued—in a manner whose inner paradoxes I shall discuss later—by the mass media: movies, radio, comics, and popular culture media generally. Under these conditions types of character emerge that we shall here term other-directed. To them much of the discussion in the ensuing chapters is devoted. *What is common to all other-directeds is that their contemporaries are the source of direction for the individual —either those known to him or those with whom he is indirectly acquainted, through friends and through the mass media. This source is of course "internalized" in the sense that dependence on it for guidance in life is implanted early. The goals toward which the other-directed person strives shift with that guidance: it is only the process of striving itself and the process of paying close attention to the signals from others that remain unaltered throughout life.* This mode of keeping in touch with others permits a close behavioral conformity, not through drill in behavior itself, as in the tradition-directed character, but rather through an exceptional sensitivity to the actions and wishes of others.

Of course, it matters very much who these "others" are: whether they are the individual's immediate circle or a "higher" circle or the anonymous voices of the mass media; whether the individual fears the hostility of chance acquaintances or only of those who "count." But his need for approval and direction from others—and contemporary others rather than ancestors—goes beyond the reasons that lead most people in any era to care very much what others think of them. While all people want and need to be liked by some of the people some of the time, it is only the modern other-directed types who make this their chief source of direction and chief area of sensitivity.[10]

It is perhaps the insatiable force of this psychological need for approval that differentiates people of the metropolitan, American upper middle class, whom we regard as other-directed, from very similar types that have appeared in capital cities and among other classes in previous historical periods, whether in Imperial Canton, in eighteenth- and nineteenth-century Europe, or in ancient Athens, Alexandria, or Rome. In all these groups fashion not only ruled as a substitute for morals and customs, but it was a rapidly changing fashion that held sway. It could do so because, although the mass media were in their infancy, the group corresponding to the American upper middle class was comparably small and the elite structure was extremely reverberant. It can be argued, for example, that a copy of *The Spectator* covered its potential readership about as thoroughly in the late eighteenth century as *The New Yorker* covers its readership today. In eighteenth- and nineteenth-century English and French writing as well as in Tolstoy we find portraits of the sort of people who operated in the upper reaches of bureaucracy and had to be prepared for rapid changes of signals. Stepan Arkadyevitch Oblonsky in *Anna Karenina* is one of the more likeable and less opportunistic examples, especially striking because of the way Tolstoy contrasts him with Levin, a moralizing, inner-directed person. At any dinner party Stepan manifests exceptional social skills; his political skills as described in the following quotation are also highly social:

Stepan Arkadyevitch took in and read a liberal newspaper, not an extreme one, but one advocating the views held by the majority. And in spite of the fact that science, art, and politics had no special interest for him, he firmly held those views on all subjects which were held by the majority and by his

10. This picture of the other-directed person has been stimulated by, and developed from, Erich Fromm's discussion of the "marketing orientation" in *Man for Himself*, pp. 67–82. I have also drawn on my portrait of "The Cash Customer," *Common Sense*, XI (1942), 183.

paper, and he only changed them when the majority changed them—or, more strictly speaking, he did not change them, but they imperceptively changed of themselves within him.

Stepan Arkadyevitch had not chosen his political opinions or his views; these political opinions and views had come to him of themselves, just as he did not choose the shapes of his hats or coats, but simply took those that were being worn. And for him, living in a certain society—owing to the need, ordinarily developed at years of discretion, for some degree of mental activity—to have views was just as indispensable as to have a hat. If there was a reason for his preferring liberal to conservative views, which were held also by many of his circle, it arose not from his considering liberalism more rational, but from its being in closer accord with his manner of life . . . And so liberalism had become a habit of Stepan Arkadyevitch's, and he liked his newspaper, as he did his cigar after dinner, for the slight fog it diffused in his brain.

It would, of course, be better if there were space for more than one such description to reinforce my point that Stepan, while his good-natured gregariousness makes him seem like a modern middle-class American, is not fully other-directed. This gregariousness alone, without a certain sensitivity to others as individuals and as a source of direction, is not the identifying trait. Just so, we must differentiate the nineteenth-century American, gregarious and subservient to public opinion though he was found to be by Tocqueville, Bryce, and others, from the other-directed American as he emerges today, an American who in his character is more capable of and more interested in maintaining responsive contact with others both at work and at play. This point needs to be emphasized, since the distinction is easily misunderstood. The inner-directed person, though he often sought and sometimes achieved a relative independence of public opinion and of what the neighbors thought of him, was in most cases very much concerned with his good repute and, at least in America, with "keeping up with the Joneses." These conformities, however, were primarily external, typified in such details as clothes, curtains, and bank credit. For, indeed, the conformities were to a standard, evidence of which was provided by the "best people" in one's milieu. In contrast with this pattern, the other-directed person, though he has his eye very much on the Joneses, aims to keep up with them not so much in external details as in the quality of his inner experience. That is, his great sensitivity keeps him in touch with others on many more levels than the externals of appearance and propriety. Nor does any ideal of independence or of reliance on God alone modify his desire to look to the others—and the "good guys" as well as the best people—for guidance in what experiences to seek and in how to interpret them.

The three types compared. While for analytic purposes it is sound to visualize all these differences sharply, it would be a mistake to expect to find such a sharp separation in the world of living people. In one respect all human behavior is inner-directed, in the sense that it is motivated, and all human behavior is other-directed, in the sense that it results from the process of socialization by others. And, of course, neither the tradition-directed nor the inner-directed person is immune to the impact of the opinions and directions of others. Nevertheless, one way to see the structural differences between the three types is to see the differences—again, as a matter of degree only—in the emotional sanction, control, or "tuning" in each type.

The tradition-directed person feels the impact of his culture as a unit, but it is nevertheless mediated through the specific, small number of individuals with whom he is in daily contact. These expect of him not so much that he be a certain type of person but that he behave in the approved way. Consequently the sanction for behavior tends to be the fear of being *shamed*.

The inner-directed person has early incorporated a psychic gyroscope which is set going by his parents and can receive signals later on from other authorities who resemble his parents. He goes through life less independent than he seems, obeying this internal piloting. Getting off course, whether in response to inner impulses or to the fluctuating voices of contemporaries, may lead to the feeling of *guilt*.

Since the direction to be taken in life has been learned in the privacy of the home from a small number of guides and since principles, rather than details of behavior, are internalized, the inner-directed person is capable of great stability. Especially so when it turns out that his fellows have gyroscopes too, spinning at the same speed and set in the same direction. But many inner-directed individuals can remain stable even when the reinforcement of social approval is not available—as in the upright life of the stock Englishman in the tropics.

Contrasted with such a type as this, the other-directed person learns

OUTER DIRECTED

to respond to signals from a far wider circle than is constituted by his parents. The family is no longer a closely knit unit to which he belongs but merely part of a wider social environment to which he early becomes attentive. In these respects the other-directed person resembles the tradition-directed person: both live in a group milieu and lack the inner-directed person's capacity to go it alone. The nature of this group milieu, however, differs radically in the two cases. The other-directed person is cosmopolitan. For him the border between the familiar and the strange—a border clearly marked in the societies depending on tradition-direction—has broken down. As the family continuously absorbs the strange and so reshapes itself, so the strange becomes familiar. While the inner-directed person could be "at home abroad" by virtue of his relative insensitivity to others, the other-directed person is, in a sense, at home everywhere and nowhere, capable of a superficial intimacy with and response to everyone.

The tradition-directed person takes his signals from others, but they come in a cultural monotone; he needs no complex receiving equipment to pick them up. The other-directed person must be able to receive signals from far and near; the sources are many, the changes rapid. What can be internalized, then, is not a code of behavior but the elaborate equipment needed to attend to such messages and occasionally to participate in their circulation. As against guilt-and-shame controls, though of course these survive, one prime psychological lever of the other-directed person is a diffuse *anxiety*. This control equipment, instead of being like a gyroscope, is like a radar.[11]

A caveat. Population analysis is, I believe, a useful approach to the study of society and character, for it enables us to isolate certain important questions. But I should like to anticipate the entirely reasonable criticism that an inference drawn from only one observation—in this case, from the suggested correlation between character type and population phase in modern western history—is unwarranted. Unless we are to stop with mere description of a way of life—a description bound to be somewhat biased by our very closeness to this way of life —we must further test our concepts in the laboratory of history. With this in mind, studies have been initiated with the view of determining insofar as possible whether the hypothetical correlation is to be rejected or accepted on the basis of information available for other

11. The "radar" metaphor was suggested by Karl Wittfogel.

societies. Such research is of course handicapped both by the lack of reliable population statistics for ancient civilizations and primitive communities, and by the inevitable sifting of data by history—for much of that which is produced by an earlier generation is discarded by the later as it passes through the phase of transitional growth, and only civilizations of fairly high technological development keep many records capable of interpretation.

Living today, we of course do not know whether population decline is the last phase of the S-curve or merely a kink in some other curve. In all likelihood the tremendous growth of world population since about 1650 is unique in the history of mankind and the consequence of an altogether new (industrialized) type of technological, economic, and social organization. Nonetheless, the fact that every society has some form of organization and some "technology," be it the most unscientific ritual, constitutes proof of an effort, more or less successful, to bring down the death rate and improve the standard of living over that of mere animal existence.

Therefore we must not and need not be content with an inference concerning the relationship between character and population drawn solely from observations of extant cultures. Could other civilizations, such as the ancient Hebrew, Greek, and Roman, also be characterized at successive stages in their population-subsistence development as tradition-directed, inner-directed, and other-directed? Exploratory efforts stimulated by these concepts of character and population have been rewarding. By way of illustration, we might briefly examine the history of the Athenian empire.[12]

What scant evidence we have of the long-term trend of population growth in the empire must be derived from the patient studies of present-day demographers and from the remarks of ancient Greek authors. The Homeric epics depict a volatile society in which the institution of private property had already disrupted the tradition-directed communal organization of tribe, phratry, and clan. Revolutionary improvements in cultivation of the soil, made possible by continued settlement in one place, increased the standard of living and, as a corollary, initiated a phase of population growth that was to continue for several centuries. Private ownership, the development of an exchange economy, and the patrilineal inheritance of property

12. The following discussion draws on an unpublished monograph by Sheila Spaulding, "Prolegomena to the Study of Athenian Democracy" (Yale Law School Library, 1949).

encouraged the concentration of wealth and produced economic and social inequality. A new, three-fold social stratification interpenetrated the traditional organization and not only loosened the hold of the clan upon its members but also encouraged the coalescence of individuals with like economic status from different tribes and phratries. As the result of developments poorly recorded and only dimly understood, a rudimentary state was organized, whose citizens acquired rights and obligations independent of the tribe. The existence of this state, designed to protect and further the interests of the property-holding nobles, bespeaks an inherent mobility and suggests that it was possible for individuals or families to acquire property and so move from one class to another. The reform measures taken by Solon and others in succeeding generations also clearly imply that some individuals and families were far more successful than others in achieving the new economic goals of leisure and material wealth.

During the five hundred years after the founding of the Athenian state there seems to have existed an expanding "frontier" economy, based in part upon the exploitation of internal resources, made possible by technological improvement and the institution of slavery, and in greater part upon the conquest of other peoples and the incorporation of their wealth into the domestic economy. One might well adduce as indications of inner-direction during this period the changing attitudes toward the family and the upbringing of children; the laws which enhanced the freedom of the individual, for example, the significant reforms which permitted the free alienation of property and the initiation of a criminal prosecution by a "third party"; the multiplication of opportunities for profitable employment in commerce, agriculture, and industry; the drift from country to city; the enthusiasm for exploration and conquest; and the increasing interest in philosophic speculation and science.

By the turn of the fifth century the Athenian empire had reached the zenith of its power; and the Greeks of this period were familiar with the idea of an expanding population. Both Plato and Aristotle advocated a stationary population. Polybius, writing in the second century, declared that the population of Greece was dying out because of the practice of infanticide. This is undoubtedly an overstatement; infanticide was confined, as contraception tends to be today, largely to the upper and upper middle classes. Nevertheless, it indicates the trend toward artificial limitation of the size of the family and suggests that the population had reached the period not only of incipient but of actual decline. It is precisely at the same period in Athenian history that we see the rise of social forms that seem to indicate the presence of the other-directed mode of conformity.

For example, the institution of ostracism, introduced as a means of preventing tyranny, became in the fifth century a formidable weapon of public opinion, wielded capriciously as a means of insuring conformity of taste and "cutting down to size" those statesmen, playwrights, and orators of markedly superior ability. In addition, the common people produced a numerous brood of informers "who were constantly accusing the better and most influential men in the State, with a view to subjecting them to the envy of the multitude." In *The Jealousy of the Gods and Criminal Law in Athens* Svend Ranulf has meticulously traced the incidence and development of the "disinterested tendency to inflict punishment" which, based upon a diffuse characterological anxiety, could perhaps be described as the ascendancy of an omnipotent "peer-group."

All this was accompanied by a decline in inner-directed dutifulness toward the political sphere. In spite of the deference shown by many authors to Athenian "democracy" of the fifth century, one is struck by the apathy of the voting population. What had earlier been a hard-won privilege of the lower classes—attendance at the ecclesia or popular assembly—became during the rule of the demos an obligation. Various punitive measures were introduced to insure a quorum; and when these failed the "right to vote" became a paid service to the state.

Here in the history of the Athenian empire we have an area in which more detailed research and analysis might very profitably be undertaken; obviously, no more has been done in these remarks than to suggest certain problems that would be relevant for such research. Similarly, the problems of Rome during the reign of Augustus suggest the emergence and ascendancy of the other-directed character type as the population reached the phase of incipient decline. The importation of a new poetic language legitimating the importance of subtle states of personal feeling, in the Alexandrian-influenced work of such poets as Catullus, and probably Gallus, may evidence shifts toward other-direction in the dominant classes.

To return to the question of whether or not the American character is something novel and unique, one is immediately curious as to why, though the incipient decline of population has not gone so far in America as it has in certain parts of Europe (such as France), only American society seems to present a picture of a society increasingly dominated by other-direction. In part, this may be because America had almost no experience with the epoch of high growth potential and its tradition-bound patterns. It may also be because of the rapid and—despite the Civil War and the enormous amount of hard work that went into settling and building up the country—relatively peaceful and prosperous passage through the mill race of transitional population growth. Yet we realize that New Zealand, Australia, and Canada have had roughly similar fates without developing to anything like the same degree a predominantly other-directed character. To deal with such matters we obviously have to go outside a population theory; and it is, in my view, the population theory which provides the starting point that enables us to go systematically beyond it. We want to ask, for instance, what the future will show as other countries not only move into the stage of incipient population decline but also develop the economic abundance and leisure orientation that this stage can foster. We say "can foster" rather than "must," since these consequences need not follow if the surplus product is consumed in armament and destroyed in war or is simply left unproduced through the introduction of featherbedding from the top to the bottom of society.

A further caveat needs to be entered. The limitations of language may make it appear that we see societies as always managing to produce the social organization and character types they need in order to survive. Such an assumption would introduce an unwarranted teleology into social change.

The manner of speaking employed so far raises the image of a separate body, "society," making certain demands on people and testing out various processes. What seems to happen is that by sheer "accident" any of a number of ways of insuring characterological conformity may exist in a given society. Those which have been successful in preserving a coherent society are transmitted as unconsciously as they arose; but, since by their historical success, they present themselves for study and investigation, it appears as if some teleological force, serving the interest of society, has introduced the successful—or fairly successful—mode of insuring conformity. Yet we must recognize that societies do disintegrate and die out despite what may appear to be successful methods of insuring character perpetuation. Correspondingly, we must not deny the probability that societies can tolerate, even without disintegration, much more disorganization and even ruin than many people recognize.

II. THE CHARACTEROLOGICAL STRUGGLE

We can picture for ourselves the last few hundred years of western history in terms of a gradual succession to dominance of each of these three types. The tradition-directed type gives way to the inner-directed, and the inner-directed gives way to the other-directed. Shifts in type of society and type of character do not, of course, occur all at once. Rather, there is an overlapping, so that within a given culture one may find groups representing all phases of the population curve and demonstrating, with more or less lag, a variety of characterological adaptations to their particular phase. This mixture is made even more various by the migration of peoples, by imperialism, and by forces that constantly throw together people of different character structures, people who "date," metaphorically, from different points on the population curve.

The struggle of classes and societies may therefore be viewed, to some extent, as a struggle among different characterological adaptations to the situation created by the dominance of a given mode of insuring conformity. These character types, like geological or archaeological strata, pile one on top of the other. A cross section of society at any given time reveals the earlier as well as the later character types, the earlier changed through the pressure of being submerged by the later. One notices the dominance of tradition-directed types in Latin America, agricultural southern Europe, in Asia and Africa. One notices the dominance of inner-directed types in rural and small-town United States and Canada, in northwestern Europe, and to a degree in Central Europe. One notices an energetic campaign to introduce the inner-directed pattern in eastern Europe, in Turkey, and in parts of Asia. And one notices the beginnings of dominance by other-directed types in the metropolitan centers of the United States and, more doubtfully, their emergence in the big cities of northwestern Europe. This last and newest type is spreading outward into areas where inner-direction still prevails, just as the latter is spreading into unconquered areas where tradition-directed types still hang on.

Such a view may help us to understand American character structures. In America it is still possible to find southern rural groups, Negro and poor white, in the phase of high growth potential—and it is here that we look for the remnants of tradition-directed types. Similarly, immigrants to America who came from rural and small-town areas in Europe carried their fertility rates and character patterns with them to our major cities as well as to the countryside. In some cases these people were and are forced to make, in one lifetime, the jump from a society in which tradition-direction was the dominant mode of insuring conformity to one in which other-direction is the dominant mode. More frequently the jump is made in two generations: the peasant first moves to a neighboring town, and generally becomes converted to inner-directed ways; then his children make the jump to the American metropolis and other-direction.

The mixing of people of different character types, as of different races and religions, as a result of industrialization and colonization, is to be found everywhere in the world. Character types that would have been well adapted to their situation find themselves under pressure from newer, better-adapted types. They may resign themselves to a subordinate position. Or they may be tempted by the new goals which enter their view with the decline of their own mode of conformity. They may even seek these goals without reference to the culturally prescribed means of attaining them.

Inner-directed types, for instance, in the urban American environment may be forced into resentment or rebellion. They may be unable to adapt because they lack the proper receiving equipment for the radar signals that increasingly direct attitude and behavior in the phase of incipient population decline. They may refuse to adapt because of moral disapproval of what the signals convey. Or they may be discouraged by the fact that the signals, though inviting enough, do not seem meant for them. This is true, for instance, of minority groups whose facial type or coloring is not approved of for managerial or professional positions, or in the value hierarchy portrayed in the mass media of communication. The same thing holds for those whose ancestry is adequate but whose "personality" in subtle ways lacks the pliability and sensitivity to others that is required.

Studies of American Indians provide analogies for some of the things that may happen when an older character type is under pressure from a newer one. Among Sioux reservation children, as described by Erik H. Erikson, there seem to be two reactions to white culture: one is resentful resistance, the other is what might be termed "compliant resistance." The practitioner of the former seems, to the white educator, incorrigible; of the latter, almost too ingratiating, too angelic. In both cases, because he has at least the tacit approval of his parents and other Sioux adults, the child preserves something of the Sioux character and tradition whether or not he yields overtly to the whites. The conflict, however, drains the child of emotional energy; often he appears to be lazy. Both the resistant and the seemingly compliant are apathetic toward the white culture and white politics.

I think that there are millions of inner-directed Americans who reject in similar fashion the values that emanate from the growing dominance of other-directed types. American political moralizers as described in later chapters are often what might be termed "residual inner-directeds"—and also "marginal other-directeds"—who have not acquired the animated mask for apathy of the fully other-directed. Their resentment is conscious and vocal. As with the Sioux, this resentment is culturally supported both by the old-timers and by the long historical past which is present to all in rural and small-town areas. This past is carried in the tales of the old men and the editorials of the rural press, not yet blotted out by urban sights and sounds. Hence, the resentment can express itself and win local victories over the representatives of other-directed types. Nevertheless, the moralizers do not feel secure—the weight of the urban world outside is against them—and their resentment hardens until the residual inner-directed is scarcely more than a caricature of his characterological ancestor in the days of his dominance.

A second locus of resistance and resentment is among the vanishing tradition-directed migrants to America—migrants both from America's colonies: Puerto Rico, the deep South, and previously the Philippines, and from Mexico, Italy, and the Orient. Here it is more difficult for the parents to give cultural support to the child's resistance to the enforced change of signals called "Americanization." For one thing, the comforts of history, with their support for "un-American" attitudes, have been geographically and linguistically left behind; urban ghettos are a poor substitute. The southern poor white or the poor Negro who moves North does not have to learn a new language, but he is usually about as deracinated as are the migrants from abroad. The costume and manners of the zoot-suiter were a pathetic example of the effort to combine smooth urban ways with a resentful refusal to be completely overwhelmed by the inner-directed norms that are still the official culture of the city public schools.

A similar resentment style is to be found among miners, lumber-jacks, ranch hands, and some urban factory workers. As in many other societies, the active dislike of these workers for the dominant culture is coupled with a feeling of manly contempt for smooth or soft city ways. These men have their own cocky legends as the Sioux have stories of the cowboy as well as of their own belligerent past. We must ask to what extent all these groups may be dying out, like their Sioux counterparts, as other-direction spreads down the class ladder and beyond the metropolitan areas. In the absence of a home base, a reservation, these people have their choice, if indeed there be a choice, between homelessness and rapid acculturation to other-directed values.[13]

The characterological struggle has been discussed so far as though it were something that goes on only within a single country and among the groups within that country who stand at different points on the curve of character and population. However, as we know, the countries in the phase of incipient decline feel threatened by the pressure of population and expansion on the part of countries in the phase of transitional growth. At the same time both these groups feel menaced by the huge oriental countries still in the phase of high growth potential. These international tensions, acting in a vicious circle, help to preserve, in countries of incipient decline, the inner-directed char-

13. In describing these aspects of the "characterological struggle" there is no intent to deny the existence of other kinds of social struggle. The class struggle and the characterological struggle overlap. We can study where one begins and the other leaves off only by meticulous examination of individuals who, while they belong to the same social strata, are of different character type. It seems possible that the open class struggle is characteristic of societies in the stage of transitional growth—this is the period that Marx lived in and observed in western Europe—while in these same societies in the stage of incipient decline the social struggle goes on primarily among people of nominally identical class and status positions, that is, among the vastly increased and differentiated middle classes. Here in America it seems to take the form of a silent struggle between those who have adapted themselves in the approved other-directed ways and those who either cannot adapt and give up or attempt to change the society and its characterological demands.

acter types and their scarcity psychology, appropriate in the earlier era of transitional growth. Thus the slate of character types befitting a society of abundance—a society of which men have dreamed for centuries—is held in historical abeyance, and the gap between character structure and the potentialities of the economic structure remains.

One can take various attitudes toward this gap. One would be that, because another world war—this time between the two highly polarized world powers—is possible or even probable, it makes little sense to talk about the age of abundance, its character types, and its anticipated problems. Or, one may come to the same conclusion by a different route, arguing that in effect it is immoral, if not politically impractical, to discuss abundance *in America* when famine and misery remain the lot of most of the world's agriculturists and many of its city dwellers. These are real issues. But I would like to point out as to the first—the imminence and immanence of war—that to a slight degree nations, like neurotics, bring on themselves the dangers by which they are obsessed, the dangers that, in place of true vitality and growth, help structure their lives; though obviously the decision, war or not, does not rest with the United States or even, if the world is fortunate, with the United States and Russia jointly. As to the second issue, it seems to me that to use world misery as an argument against speculation about possible abundance is actually to help prolong the very scarcity psychology that, originating in misery, perpetuates it. Pushed to its absurd extreme, the argument would prevent leadership in human affairs except by those who are worst off. On the other hand, those who are best off may fail as models not only out of surfeit but out of despair. Contrary to the situation prevailing in the nineteenth century, pessimism has become an opiate, and the small chance that the dangers so obviously menacing the world can be avoided is rendered even smaller by our use of these menaces in order to rationalize our resignation and asceticism.

Fundamentally, I think the "unrealistic" Godwin was correct who, in contrast to his great opponent Malthus, thought that we would someday be able to grow food for the world in a flowerpot. Technologically, we virtually have the flowerpots.

II

From Morality to Morale: Changes in the Agents of Character Formation

Q. Do you think the teachers should punish the children for using make-up?

A. Yes, I think they should punish them, but understand, I'm a modern mother and while I'm strict with my daughters, I am still modern. You know you can't punish your children too much or they begin to think you are mean and other children tell them you are mean.

From an interview.

BEFORE exploring the linkage between character and political style, we must examine at close range the way in which the three types are formed. We must scrutinize particularly the human agents of production who influence the lives of children: the parents, the teachers, the members of the peer-group, and the story-tellers. For children live at the wave front of the successive population phases and are the partially plastic receivers of the social character of the future. In this chapter we consider the changing role of parents and teachers in socializing the young in each of the three population phases. Chapter III considers the socializing function of the peer-group. Chapter IV treats of the changes in the role of the storytellers, or, as they are now called, the mass media of communication.

Very little is known about socialization. In an unrehearsed radio program on ABC recently a group of children were discussing comic strips. The youngsters showed a clever knowledge not only of the comics themselves but of arguments about them. "They are good for our morale," said the children. "They relax us. They teach us that crime does not pay. Terry teaches us about China. Everybody reads them." But the children's wit serves to raise questions that even the brightest children probably could not answer.

Is it the purpose of comic strips to be good for morale, to be relaxing, to teach that crime does not pay? Do comic strips possess a character-forming purpose? Does *any* socializing agency have a character-forming purpose? If it does, who is to say that the character it helps to form is what the society wants or needs? We are caught in a circle when thus analyzing the formative agencies. We impute a purpose to society's formation of character types—and then see the results of that process as verifying the existence of the purpose.

We do know, in fact, that parents and other adult authorities try to train children in the way society says they should be trained. We must recognize this purposefulness and take it into account. We also know that the important steps taken in the formation of children's character are often taken unconsciously; and this is as true of the makers and purveyors of comic strips as it is of the parents and other adult authorities. Just as it is often more important what parents *are* than what they intend to do, so it is often more important what the comic strip *is* as an art object than what it *seems to say* as a message.

Yet, while analysis of the social role of any particular agent becomes exceedingly difficult, we can be sure of several general propositions. What the parents or parental surrogates *are* at any given time depends on *their* parents and also on their contemporary life conditions. Moreover, it is largely as the socializing agents are affected by these life conditions that there is a break in the genealogical succession of more or less identical character types. Furthermore, we can be sure that changes in general social conditions can alter the competitive position, and therefore the influence, of competing agencies of socialization. As we shall see in the next chapter, the peer-group and school now take over some of the functions previously performed by the family alone. The fact is that changes in the character of the agents of socialization never occur in isolation from changes in the distribution of function among various competing and cooperating agents. The character-forming processes of a given time and place are affected by both types of change.

There are many difficulties in the way of understanding these shifting relations among the agencies. The influences that mold character are impalpable and cumulative; and they are mediated through the prodigious variety of significant persons in the environment of each child. The child's own awareness of having been influenced is limited—even apart from the emotional blockages to recollection that the process of influence itself imposes. It is particularly difficult to study the effects of nonverbal communication: the way babies are held, for instance, or perhaps even the way they are influenced by living in rooms of a particular size and color. While these questions may, in principle, be answerable—anthropologists and followers of Freud and Piaget have made a good start—it will be some time before we know enough to come very close to answering them.

We shall concentrate here on the shift from inner-direction to other-direction as the principal mode of insuring conformity in the urban American middle class. Perspective, however, requires a glance at societies in which tradition-direction is the principal mode of insuring conformity; and since the tradition-directed types have played a very minor role in America, we will take examples from primitive and medieval society. As we compare methods of socialization we shall see what is new about the newer types—and particularly what is new about other-direction.

To speak of changes from one type of society or character to another type as if these changes occurred only in historical sequence is of course a simplification; and it may be misleading if it is taken for more than an expositional method. In any period certain societies, certain people, and certain characters are far from "up to date"; the three types of society and character can therefore be found existing simultaneously. Furthermore, we associate the historical shifts from type to type with the phenomenon of certain classes replacing others in social dominance. Thus, one cause and effect of the shift toward inner-direction was the decline of the feudal class and the ascendance of the bourgeois class.

I. CHANGES IN THE ROLE OF THE PARENTS

There has been a tendency in current social research, influenced as it is by psychoanalysis, to overemphasize and overgeneralize the importance of very early childhood in character formation. Even within this early period an almost technological attention has sometimes been focused on what might be called the tricks of the child-rearing trade: feeding and toilet-training schedules. The view implicit in this emphasis happens to be, at the same time, a counsel of optimism and of despair. It is an optimistic view because it makes it appear as though facile mechanical changes in what the parent does would profoundly alter the character of the progeny. It is pessimistic because it assumes that once the child has reached, say, the weaning stage its character structure is so formed that barring intensive psychiatric intervention not much that happens afterward will do more than bring out tendencies already set.

It is increasingly recognized, however, that character may change greatly after this early period and that cultural agents other than the parents may play important roles. Cultures differ widely not only in their timing of the various steps in character formation but also in the agents they rely on at each step. Each historical phase on the curve of population is marked by an increase in the length of life and in the period of socialization—that is, the period before full entry into one's adult social and economic role. At the same time there is an increase in the responsibility placed on character-forming agents outside the home, the clan, or the village.

PARENTAL ROLE IN THE STAGE OF TRADITION-DIRECTION

In societies depending on tradition-direction children can be "finished off" at an early point to assume an adult role. Adult roles are almost unchanging from generation to generation, and apart from training toward technical and manual skill, which may often be intensive, grown-up life demands little in the way of complex and literate instruction. Children begin very early to learn how to act like adults simply by watching adults around them. In the population phase of high growth potential there are many children to imitate a comparatively small number of adult models. The children live, ordinarily, in a large family setting. What the adults do is simple enough for children to grasp, so simple that children can often understand and imitate it before they have the physical skills to take a full part. Social maturity waits on biological maturity. Yet the biological roles of adult life are not themselves remote, even in those primitive societies (such as the Manus described by Margaret Mead) where an age-graded separation between child and adult culture is made. Since there is little inhibition of childhood play and curiosity, children know what there is to know about sex and other adult functions—

even though certain ceremonial mysteries may remain to testify to adult power and child helplessness.

Physical living patterns are an important factor in this setting. Houses consist typically of one room, without walls to separate the age groups and their varied functions. The households are often also economic units; the man does not go off to office or factory—or he does not go far. People are not yet so worried about saving time that they feel children are a nuisance; indeed, they may not feel themselves to be so very different from children anyway.

Furthermore, societies in the phase of high growth potential are characterized by a very low degree of social mobility. The parents train the child to succeed *them,* rather than to "succeed" by rising in the social system. Within any given social class society is age ranked, so that a person rises as a cork does in water: it is simply a matter of time, and little *in him* needs to change.

The upper social groups in such a society mature almost as quickly as the lower ones; while children in both ranks of society must learn a role, the roles differ only slightly in complexity. Even so, it is likely that a greater degree of individualization occurs at an earlier historical point in the upper strata than in the lower—as seems to have been the case in the Middle Ages when nobles, wandering artists, and priests were often closer to inner-direction than to the peasant's type of tradition-direction. Yet while the training of the leaders is of course somewhat more prolonged and their characters are more individuated, the young at all social levels take their places quickly in work, ceremony, and sexual role.

In summary: the major agency of character formation in societies dependent on tradition-direction is the extended family and its environing clan or group. Models for imitation are apt to be generalized in terms of the adult group as a whole rather than confined to the parents. What is imitated is behavior and specific traits such as bravery or cunning. The growing child does not confront problems of choice very different from those he watched his elders face; and his growth is conceived as a process of becoming an older, and therefore wiser, interpreter of tradition.

PARENTAL ROLE IN THE STAGE OF INNER-DIRECTION

Character and social mobility. With the onset of the transitional-growth phase of population, opportunities open for a good deal of social and geographical mobility. People begin to pioneer on new frontiers: frontiers of production, of colonization, of intellectual discovery. Although this affects only a few directly, society as mediated by the primary group no longer proclaims unequivocally what one must do in order to conform. Rather, the growing child soon becomes aware of competing sets of customs—competing paths of life—from among which he is, in principle, free to choose. And while parentage and social origins are still all but determinative for most people, the wider horizon of possibilities and of wants requires, if conformity is to be maintained, a character which can adhere to rather generalized and more abstractly defined goals. Such a character must produce under its own motive power the appropriate specific means to gain these general ends.

To be sure, the goals and ideals that are held up to children and exemplified for them by their parents' own goals and ideals differ very much as between the confident, secular man of the Renaissance, glorying in his individuality and freedom from old restraints, and the God-fearing puritan, driven by conscience and anxious about his salvation.[1] Yet both types *are* very much individuals, both are internally driven, and both are capable of pioneering. Finally, a society in which many people are internally driven—and are driven toward values, such as wealth and power, which are by their nature limited—contains in itself a dynamic of change by the very competitive forces it sets up. Even those who do not care to compete for higher places must do so in order not to descend in the social system, which has become a more open and less age-graded and birth-graded one.

All these tendencies are reinforced when roles become more complicated as the division of labor progresses. The acceleration of the division of labor means that increasing numbers of children can no longer take their parents' roles as models. This is especially true on the male side; characterological change in the west seems to occur first with men. Mothers and grandmothers could until very recent times train daughters for the feminine role on the basis of tradition

1. Margaret Mead, whose contribution to this whole field has been tremendously stimulating, has pointed out how the Protestant parent passed on to the child the legacy of his own unfulfilled strivings to live up to an ideal and how this drive spurred progress and change even though the statement of the ideal as such did not change. See, e.g., "Social Change and Cultural Surrogates," *Journal of Educational Sociology*, 14 (1940), 92; reprinted in *Personality in Nature, Society, and Culture*, ed. Kluckhohn and Murray, p. 511, and especially pp. 520–521.

alone. Thus in the recent movie, *House of Strangers,* the Italian-born banker who, like Giannini or Ponzi, rises out of an immigrant setting and departs from his own father's pattern, sets for himself ambitious goals of power and money such as he believes to be characteristic of a true-born American, while his wife is a stereotype of the woman who clings to the tradition-directed ways of her early background.

Yet, while parents in the stage of transitional growth of population cannot be sure of what the adult working role and mode of life of their children will be, neither can conformity to that role be left to chance and behavioral opportunism. To possess the drive that is required to fulfill demanding and ever more demanding roles calls for greater attention to formal character training. Especially in the Protestant countries character training becomes an important part of education, though of course this does not mean that most parents consciously undertake to produce children to meet new social specifications.

The new situation created by increased social mobility implies that children must frequently be socialized in such a way as to be unfitted for their parents' roles, while being fitted for roles not as yet fully determined. Homing pigeons can be taught to fly home, but the inner-directed child must be taught to fly a straight course away from home, with destination unknown; naturally many meet the fate of Icarus. Nevertheless, the drive instilled in the child is to *live up to ideals* and to test his ability to be on his own by continuous experiments in self-mastery—instead of by following tradition.

Character training as a conscious parental task. In a society depending on tradition-direction to insure conformity, much of the parent's effort is directed toward keeping the child from being a nuisance to the adult world; and this task is regularly delegated to older brothers or sisters or to other adults. The child soon learns that behavioral conformity is the price of peace, and he learns to propitiate—or at least not to annoy—those around him. The inner-directed parent, on the other hand, asks more of his child, just as he asks more of himself. He can do this because, with the passing of the extended kinship family, the parent has his children much more under his own undivided and intensive scrutiny and control. Not satisfied with mere behavioral conformity, such a parent demands conformity of a more subtle sort, conformity as evidence of characterological fitness and self-discipline. The Puritan, especially, relentlessly scrutinizes his children as well as himself for the signs of election, that is, of salvation by the predestining God. And with secularization these signs are translated into signs favoring social mobility—signs that facilitate "passing," not from hell to heaven, or in skin-color ranks, but in the status hierarchy. On the one hand the parent looks for signs of potential failure—this search arises in part from guilty and anxious preoccupation about himself. On the other hand he looks for signs of talent—this must not be wasted.

In this way begins the process we see in extravagant form in the forced-draft childhood of John Stuart Mill, who studied the classics and wrote long essays under the zealous eye of his father before he was ten. Even when parents are less self-consciously pedagogical than James Mill, they may unconsciously impose their demands on children merely by being forceful, tense, and highly charged themselves. Indeed, the inner-directed man is frequently quite incapable of casual relationships. For one thing, he is preoccupied with his own concerns and therefore worried about wasting time; conversely, by not wasting time he avoids anxious self-preoccupation. For another thing, his relation to people, his children included, is mediated by his continuing, character-conditioned need to test and discipline himself.

This process, in the Renaissance-Reformation character which we term inner-directed, is less tense in the Latin countries than in the Protestant or Jansenist north, and in the north less tense in Lutheran or Anglican communicants than in the Calvinistic and Pietistic sects. Wherever inner-direction has attained relatively undisputed sway in a significantly large middle class, however, the production of the character structures of the coming generation becomes increasingly rationalized, just as is production in the nondomestic economy. In both cases the task of production is no longer left to an external group sanction or situational pressure but is installed as a drive in the individual, and tremendous energies are unleashed toward the alteration of the material, social, and intellectual environment and toward the alteration of the self.

The social and spatial arrangements of middle-class life make it hard for the child to see through, let alone evade, the pressures put upon him to become inner-directed. As compared with the one-room house of the peasant or the long house of many primitive tribes, he grows up within walls that are physical symbols of the privacy of parental dominance. Walls separate parents from children, office from home, and make it hard if not impossible for the children to criticize the parents' injunctions by an "undress" view of the parents or of other parents. What the parents say becomes more real in many cases than what they do—significant training for a society in which words become increasingly important as a means of exchange, direction, and control. The conversation between parent and child, interrupted by the social distance that separates them, is continued by the child with himself in private.

The very pressure applied to the process of socialization by strict child rearing prolongs, as compared with the earlier era, the period in which socialization takes place. Freud has described this situation wonderfully in his concept of the watchful superego as a socializing agency incorporated into the child and accompanying him throughout life with ever renewed injunctions. This concept, while less fruitful in application to other societies, does seem to fit the middle class during the heyday of inner-direction in the west. One might even say that the character structure of the inner-directed person consists of the tension between superego, ego, and id. In a current cliché children are "brought up" rather than, as some would have it, "loved up"; and even when they have left home they continue to bring themselves up. They tend to feel throughout life that their characters are something to be worked on. The diary keeping that is so significant a symptom of the new type of character may be viewed as a kind of inner time-and-motion study by which the individual records and judges his output day by day. It is evidence of the separation between the behaving and the scrutinizing self.

Passage from home. As the growing child takes over from his parents the duty of self-observation and character training, he becomes prepared to face and meet situations that are novel. Indeed, if he rises in the occupational hierarchy that becomes increasingly elaborated in the phase of transitional growth or if he moves toward the various opening frontiers, he finds that he can flexibly adapt his behavior precisely because he need not change his character. He can separate the two by virtue of the fact that he is an *individual* with a historically new level of self-awareness.

This awareness of the self is cause and consequence of the fact that choice is no longer automatically provided—or, rather, excluded—by the social setting of the primary group. Under the new conditions the individual must decide what to do—and therefore what to do with himself. This feeling of personal responsibility, this feeling that he matters as an individual, apart from his family or clan, makes him sensitive to the signals emanating from his internalized ideal. If the ideal, as in the puritan, is to be "good" or, as in the child of the Renaissance, to be "great," what must he do to fulfill the injunction? And how does he know that he has fulfilled these difficult self-demands? As Max Weber and R. H. Tawney saw very clearly in their portraits of the puritan, little rest is available to those who ask themselves such questions.

The relative uncomfortableness of the more powerfully inner-directed homes—the lack of indulgence and casualness in dealing with children—prepares the child for the loneliness and psychic uncomfortableness of such questions and of the social situations that he may confront. Or, more exactly, the child's character is such that he feels comfortable in an environment which, like his home, is demanding and which he struggles to master.

We may say, then, that parents who are themselves inner-directed install a psychological gyroscope in their child and set it going; it is built to their own and other authoritative specifications; if the child has good luck the governor will spin neither too fast, with the danger of hysteric outcomes, nor too slow, with the danger of social failure.

PARENTAL ROLE IN THE STAGE OF OTHER-DIRECTION

Obviously, if parents always succeeded in reproducing themselves in their children, history would not present a panorama of changing character types. I suspect that even in the societies I label as dependent on tradition-direction a close look would show considerable change over the generations, for I doubt whether the process of cultural transmission is ever completely free of upsets and misses. It is plain that new social forces, impinging both on the domestic "factory" and on its "product," alter, to a degree, what parents do in transmitting the social heritage; alter their success, if not their intention; and alter the other influences, outside the home, that impinge on children. Even children brought up in an environment unequivocally inner-directed may still have some flexibility to move toward other-direction if, on reaching adulthood, the social cues which stimulate other-direction are in the air. In the course of time, therefore, sons may no longer "know" their own fathers, and especially their grandfathers, as changes in social structure and character structure draw visible and invisible lines between the generations.

I turn now to some of the social changes which have helped to bring out latent other-direction in people and to alter, indirectly, parental tactics in handling their children.

Character and social mobility. In the phase of incipient population decline, as the number of elders in proportion to the young grows, social mobility slows or appears to slow down—those who hold the top places refuse to die off—and with the spread of education there is more competition for the openings, though these also expand. More important, in my opinion, the conditions for advancement alter.

The inner-directed person is able to see industrial and commercial possibilities and to work with the zeal and ruthlessness required by expanding frontiers in the phase of transitional growth of population. Societies in the phase of incipient population decline, on the other hand, need neither such zeal nor such independence. Business, government, the professions, become heavily bureaucratized, as we see most strikingly, for instance, in France. Such societies increasingly turn to the remaining refractory components of the industrial process: the men who run the machines. Social mobility under these conditions continues to exist. But it depends less on what one is and what one does than on what others think of one—and how competent one is in manipulating others and being oneself manipulated. To look at it from another point of view, when the basic physical plant of a society is felt to be built, or rather when the building can be routinized by management planning, there begins to be room at the top for the other-directed person who can see the subtle opportunities given in the human setting.[2] Though material abundance becomes technologically possible, people continue to work—and make work—at a pace more in keeping with the earlier era of transitional growth: mobility drives are still imbedded in their character. *But the product now in demand is neither a staple nor a machine; it is a personality.*

To bring the other-directed personality type and his typical eco-

2. Of course there is no law that societies in the stage of incipient population decline have to become top-heavy and bureaucratic. It is conceivable that even more mobility could be opened up by shifting population and other resources rapidly into tertiary services, by greatly expanding leisure and the industries catering to leisure. We shall return to these matters in Part III.

nomic framework together it might be observed that there exists in the production of personality the same sort of "marginal differentiation" that is characteristic of monopolistic competition generally. The economists apply the term "product differentiation" to a firm's effort to distinguish products not by price but by small differences, sufficient, however, in connection with advertising, to take the product out of direct price competition with otherwise similar competing products. Thus one cigarette is made slightly longer, another nearly oval, while still another is given a cork tip or a green box. *Time* and *Newsweek* engage in marginal differentiation. So do the makers of automobiles, streamliners, and toothpastes, and the operators of hotels and universities. So, too, people who are competing for jobs in the hierarchies of business, government, and professional life try to differentiate their personalities (as contrasted with their actual technical skills) —without getting as far out of line, let us say, as a 1934 prematurely streamlined Chrysler. In this study, the social aspect of this competitive procedure, since it will be extended to cover persons and services as well as commodities, will be termed "marginal differentiation," and thus distinguished from the related concept used by the economists.

Freud coined the phrase "narcissism with respect to minor differences" for the pride which individuals, groups, and nations manifest about small insignia which distinguish them from other individuals, groups, and nations. Marginal differentiation sometimes does have this quality of pride or of what Veblen called "invidious distinction." But the phenomenon I have in mind is one of anxiety rather than pride, of veiled competition rather than openly rivalrous display; the narcissism is muted or, as we shall see, alloyed with other, stronger elements.

Here again the new developments are most marked in the United States even though the rise of the new middle class is a phenomenon of other western countries as well. In 1947 C. Wright Mills of Columbia University obtained a number of intensive interviews with white-collar employees in and near New York: shopgirls, insurance salesmen, receptionists, and so on. Reading the reports of these interviews, I was struck by the extent to which these people, often coming from backgrounds where inner-direction prevailed, manifested other-directed patterns of behavior. Their work meant to them primarily getting along with people. They saw advancement—and, beyond that, happiness—in terms of improving their social skills. And they looked to their contemporaries for guidance not only as to how to do things but as to what things were worth doing. While we speak in this book primarily of the upper ranks of the middle class in the larger cities, both Mills's interviews and our own (in which we used some of the same questions developed by Mills) seemed to us to indicate that the other-directed character is widely distributed, at least in certain white-collar occupations of the lower middle class—where, indeed, other-direction is often more helpless, more overt, more submissive. Nor are such tendencies absent among young people from farm and factory families.

Under the new conditions of social and economic life parents who try, in inner-directed fashion, to compel the internalization of disciplined pursuit of clear goals run the risk of having their children styled clear out of the personality market. Gyroscopic direction is just not flexible enough for the rapid adaptations of personality that are required, precisely because there will be other competitors who do not have gyroscopes. Inhibited from presenting their children with sharply silhouetted images of self and society, parents in our era can only equip the child to do his best, whatever that may turn out to be. What is best is not in their control but in the hands of the school and peer-group that will help locate the child eventually in the hierarchy. But even these authorities speak vaguely; the clear principles of selection that once guided people of inner-directed character no longer apply. For example, social climbing itself may be called into public question at the same time that it is no longer so unequivocally desirable in terms of private wish. As recent *Fortune* surveys indicate, a safe and secure job may be preferred to a risky one involving high stakes. What is more, it is no longer clear which way *is* up even if one wants to rise, for with the growth of the new middle class the older, hierarchical patterns disintegrate, and it is not easy to compare ranks among the several sets of hierarchies that do exist. Does an army colonel "rank" the head of an international union? A physics professor, a bank vice-president? A commentator, the head of an oil company?

Increasingly in doubt as to how to bring up their children, parents turn to other contemporaries for advice; they also look to the mass media; and like the mother quoted at the outset of this chapter they turn, in effect, to the children themselves. They may, nevertheless, fasten on some inflexible scheme of child rearing and follow that. Yet they cannot help show their children, by their own anxiety, how little they depend on themselves and how much on others. Whatever they may seem to be teaching the child in terms of content, they are passing on to him their own contagious, highly diffuse anxiety. They reinforce this teaching by giving the child approval—and approving themselves because of the child—when he makes good.

To be sure, inner-directed parents also often were able to "love" only those children who made good in the outer world. But at least the canons of success were reasonably clear. The other-directed child, however, faces not only the requirement that he make good but also the problem of defining what making good means. He finds that both the definition and the evaluation of himself depend on the company he keeps: first, on his schoolmates and teachers; later, on peers and superiors. But perhaps the company one keeps is itself at fault? One can then shop for other preferred companies in the mass circulation media.

Approval itself, irrespective of content, becomes almost the only unequivocal good in this situation: one makes good when one is approved of. Thus all power, not merely some power, is in the hands of the actual or imaginary approving group, and the child learns from his parents' reactions to him that nothing in his character, no possession he owns, no inheritance of name or talent, no work he has done is valued for itself but only for its effect on others. Making good becomes almost equivalent to making friends, or at any rate the right kind of friends. "To him that hath approval, shall be given more approval."

From bringing up children to "Bringing up Father." The typical other-directed child grows up in a small family, in close urban quarters, or in a suburb. Even more than in the earlier epoch the father leaves home to go to work, and he goes too far to return for lunch. Home, moreover, is no longer an area of solid privacy. As the size and living space of the family diminish and as the pattern of living with older relatives declines, the child even more directly faces the emotional tensions of his parents. There is a heightening of awareness of the self in relation to others under these conditions, especially since the parents, too, are increasingly self-conscious.

The parents lack not only the self-assurance that successful inner-direction brings but also the strategy of withdrawal available to many unsuccessful inner-directed types. The loss of old certainties in the spheres of work and social relations is accompanied by doubt as to how to bring up children. Moreover, the parents no longer feel themselves superior to the children. While children no longer have immediate economic value, they are less numerous, "scarcer" in relation to the number of adults: the effort is made, and it is objectively possible to want all children who are conceived and to raise very nearly all children who are born. More is staked on every single child than in the earlier epoch when many children were not raised to maturity. In addition, apart from the fact that the children may be better Americans than the parents, in ethnic or social terms—as Jiggs's daughter is more up to date than he—there are undoubtedly other solid reasons for the general emphasis on youth which runs through all forms of popular culture.[3]

Historical changes in the lives of adolescents can be seen most clearly, perhaps, if one looks back to those *Bildungsromane* of the nineteenth century that described the misunderstood youth who struggled against the harsh or hypocritical tyranny of his parents, particularly if one compares one of the best of such novels, Samuel Butler's *The Way of All Flesh,* with one of the best of our contemporary examples, for instance Lionel Trilling's short story, "The Other Margaret."[4] In Trilling's story we have a picture of a precocious young girl in the intellectual, urban, upper middle class. Margaret, who goes to a progressive school, believes that Negroes are exploited, and she resents the inferior position in the home of "the other Margaret," a Negro domestic. It is the daughter Margaret who is self-righteous, not the parents.

In the face of her criticism, buttressed as it is by the authority of the school, the parents, themselves progressive, are on the defensive. They are tense and very much concerned with what their daughter thinks —and thinks of them. Eventually, all three adults manage to destroy Margaret's illusion of the virtues of the other Margaret—the parents by reasoning; the other Margaret by bad behavior. But in the end the parents are anxious about their victory, lest it harm their sensitive child. They possess little of the certainty and security of Theobald's parents in *The Way of All Flesh.*

---

3. This, too, is a development whose importance Margaret Mead has stressed. See *And Keep Your Powder Dry* (New York, William Morrow, 1942).

4. *Partisan Review,* XII (1945), 381.

In this change of parental attitude the mass media of communication play a dual role. From the mass media—radio, movies, comics—as well as from their own peers children can easily learn what the norm of parental behavior is, and hold it over their parents' heads. Thus a kind of realism is restored to the child which was his property much more simply in the societies depending on tradition-direction: the other-directed child is often more knowing than his parents—like the proverbial Harvard man, there is little they can tell *him*.[5]

As already noted, the parents also have their sources of direction in the mass media. For in their uneasiness as to how to bring up children they turn increasingly to books, magazines, government pamphlets, and radio programs. These tell the already anxious mother to accept her children. She learns that there are no problem children, only problem parents; and she learns to look into her own psyche whenever she is moved to deny the children anything, including an uninterrupted flow of affection. If the children are cross then the mother must be withholding something. And while these tutors also tell the mother to "relax" and to "enjoy her children," even this becomes an additional injunction to be anxiously followed.

It may be that children today do not gain the strength that adults—no longer inner-directed—have lost. To be sure, this was often a factitious strength, as Samuel Butler saw; but it was usually sufficient both to crush the child's spontaneity and anesthetize his diffuse anxiety. "Shades of the prison-house begin to close upon the growing boy" —and the prisoner might feel oppressed, even guilty, but not too anxious behind his bars. In contrast, what the other-directed child

5. Yet the knowingness, particularly in the middle class, has limits that were less important in the tradition-directed family. There the child, knowledgeable for example about sex, could see reflections of it in the daily adult life around him. He would know that if his uncle was particularly gay or particularly cross at work this was connected with what happened in the village the night before. As against this, the other-directed child knows about sex only, so to speak, in the abstract. He cannot reasonably connect the night life he knows exists with the seriousness of the adult world that faces him at school, at the store, or at home. While he has doffed the myths of sex that Freud found among the young of his day, he still finds passion playing a greater role in the comics and the movies than in the life he is able to observe—the latter being a life in which people are trained to hide their passions and to act generally in a disembodied way. Perhaps this is one reason why sex often remains an exciting mystery for the other-directed adult—as we shall see in Chap. VII—despite all his learning, all his disenchantment, and even all his experience of it. And, in general, the other-directed child's realism about the adult world is hampered not so much by Victorian inhibitions as by the far subtler partitions of adult life itself, such as the shadowy partitions between work and play to be discussed later.

does "learn" from his parents is anxiety—the emotional tuning appropriate to his other-directed adjustment.

The rule of "reason." Despite the diminution of their authority, the parents still try to control matters; but with the loss of self-assurance their techniques change. They can neither hold themselves up as exemplars—when both they and the child know better—nor resort, in good conscience, to severe corporal punishment and deprivations. At most there are token spankings, with open physical warfare confined to the lower classes.

The parents' recourse, especially in the upper middle class, is to "personnel" methods—to manipulation in the form of reasoning, or, more accurately, of rationalizing. The child responds in the same manner. One might summarize the historical sequence by saying that the tradition-directed child propitiates his parents; the inner-directed child fights or succumbs to them; the other-directed child manipulates them and is in turn manipulated.

A movie of several years ago, *The Curse of the Cat People,* while it testified to American preoccupation with certain child-rearing themes which do not directly concern us here, also provides an interesting example of these manipulative relations between parent and child. A little girl lives in a suburban, middle middle-class home with its typical neatness, garden, and Negro servant. As in "The Other Margaret," there is a terrific pressure of adult emotion focused around this one child from the parents and servant. The child is supposed to invite the other children in the neighborhood for her birthday party; but believing her father's joke that the big tree in the yard is a mailbox, she puts the invitations there and they never go out. When her birthday arrives, the other children whom she had said she would invite tease her and refuse to play with her. Her father scolds her for taking him seriously, and she is also in difficulties for not getting along better with the other children. But the parents (plus servant) decide to go ahead with the party anyway, "as if." There follows a "party" which tries to persuade the child that there has been no tragedy, that this party is just as good as the one which failed.

The parents insist that the child somehow know, without a formal etiquette, when things are supposed to be "real" and when "pretend." The tree as the mailbox is pretend; the party real. Feeling misunderstood and alone, the little girl discovers a real friend in a strange woman who lives almost as a recluse in a great house. The parents frown upon this "friend" and her gift of a ring to the child. The little girl then discovers an imaginary friend at the bottom of the yard, a beautiful older woman with whom she talks. The father cannot see, that is to say "see," this latter friend and punishes the child for lying.

Notice this fictional family's lack of privacy for the child. The discovery of the gift of the ring seems to be typical of the fact that few of her excitements escape parental scrutiny. Moreover, the very fact that the father suggests to the daughter the secret about the make-believe "mailbox tree" is symbolic of the intrusion of his knowledge: the daughter is not allowed her own make-believe but must share it with him, subject to his determination of when it applies. That the daughter and father finally come into open conflict over the little girl's fantasy friend is only to be expected; the girl cannot put a lock on the door of her room or the door of her mind. (In a lower-class home there would be, spatially at least, even less privacy; but there might be more psychic privacy because the parents would often be less interested in the child.)

Notice, in the second place, the "reasonable" but subtly manipulative tone of parent-child relations. This is evidenced by the parental planning of the party for the daughter and her peers and by the parental irritation when the plan miscarries. Still more significant is the way in which the family meets the crisis of blocked peer-group communication symbolized by the nonoperative mailbox—a failure that is itself occasioned by a blockage of understanding about the real and the unreal between daughter and parents.

The fiasco is, obviously enough, a matter that requires immediate corrective action; parents in this pass, it seems, should *do* something. The parents of the child in this movie do nothing; they prefer to talk away the situation, to manipulate the child into the acceptance of a formal illusion of party making. The result is to produce a sort of exaggeration and burlesque of the way in which other-directed persons, in parent-child as in all other relations, constantly resort to manipulation and countermanipulation.

As contrasted with all this, the inner-directed parent is not particularly worried by his child's resentment or hostility. Nor is he as apt to be aware of them. He and the child are both protected by the gap that separates them. The other-directed parent, however, has to win not only his child's good behavior but also his child's good will.

Therefore, he is tempted to use his superior dialectic skill to "reason" with the child. And when the child learns—this is part of his sensitive radar equipment—how to argue too, the parent is torn between giving in and falling uneasily back on the sterner methods of *his* inner-directed parents. The father in *The Curse of the Cat People,* after trying to reason away the little girl's belief in her fantasy friend, finally spanks her. But such scenes are always succeeded by parental efforts at reconciliation, turning the spanking itself into a step in the manipulative chain.

Finally, we must observe the change in the content of the issues at stake between parent and child. The more driving and tense inner-directed parents compel their children to work, to save, to clean house, sometimes to study, and sometimes to pray. Other less puritanical types of inner-directed parent want their boys to be manly, their girls to be feminine and chaste. Such demands make either economic or ideological sense in the population phase of transitional growth. The large home could absorb enormous amounts of labor; even today those who putter in small house and small garden can still find lots to do. The parents themselves often set the example, in which they are supported by the school, of work and study: these are believed to be the paths of upward mobility both in this world and in the next.

In the other-directed home, on the other hand, the issues between parent and child concern the nonwork side of life. For in the phase of incipient population decline—most markedly, of course, in America but elsewhere too—there is no work for children to do inside the urban home, and little outside. They need not brush and clean (except themselves)—they are less efficient than a vacuum cleaner. Nor is there an array of younger brothers and sisters to be taken care of. The American mother, educated, healthy, and efficient, has high standards for care of the apartment or small home and would, where she is not working, often feel quite out of a job if the children took over the housework. Fortunately released from the quandary of the old woman who lived in a shoe, she faces—just, as we shall see, as her husband does—the problem of leisure; care for the house and children is frequently her self-justification and escape.

So parents and children debate over eating and sleeping time as later they will debate over use of the family car. And they argue tensely, as in *The Curse of the Cat People,* about the contacts of the child with the "others" and about the emotional hue of the argument itself. But by the nature of these discussions the parents have a less easy victory. In the population phase of transitional growth they can point to self-evident tasks that need doing—self-evident at least according to accepted standards that have survived from the still earlier epoch. In the phase of incipient decline, however, the consumption or leisure issues are no longer self-evident; to decide them, if they are to be decided, one has to resort to models outside the particular home—in search of the ever changing norms of the group in which the parents happen to live. And indeed the radio and print bring the models into the home, like a trial record from which the child and parent legalists prepare briefs.[6]

To sum up: parents in the groups depending on other-direction install in their children something like a psychological radar set—a device not tuned to control movement in any particular direction while guiding and steadying the person from within but rather tuned to detect the action, and especially the symbolic action, of others. Thereafter, the parents influence the children's character only insofar as (a) their own signals mingle with others over the radar, (b) they can locate children in a certain social environment in order to alter to a very limited degree what signals they will receive, (c) they take the risks of a very partial and precarious censorship of incoming messages. Thus the parental role diminishes in importance as compared with the same role among the inner-directed.

II. CHANGES IN THE ROLE OF THE TEACHER

Much could be said about the changing configuration of adult authorities, other than the parents, as society moves from dependence on inner-direction to dependence on other-direction. Largely for economic reasons the governess, mammy, or hired tutor, for instance, virtually disappears from middle- and upper middle-class homes. One significant consequence is that children are no longer raised by people who hold up to them the standard of a family or class. Such a stand-

---

6. As Morris Janowitz has suggested, if one wanted to get a very rough index of homes in which other-direction was being transmitted, as against those in which inner-direction prevailed, one might separate the homes which took only such magazines as *Life, Look,* the comics, or movie journals from those which took such periodicals as the *Saturday Evening Post* or *Collier's*. The former group is for the whole family, interpreted as easily or more easily by children than by adults. The latter group is mainly for the grownups and not shared with the children.

ard is good training in inner-direction—in the acquisition of generalized goals; it is at the same time a partial buffer against the indiscrim-
inate influence of the peer-group. But there is another more subtle
consequence. The child who has been raised by a governess and educated by a tutor gains a very keen sense for the disparities of power
in the home and in the society. When he goes off to boarding school
or college he is likely to remain unimpressed by his teachers—like the
upper-class mother who told the school headmaster: "I don't see why
the masters can't get along with Johnny; all the other servants do."
Such a child is not going to be interested in allowing his teachers to
counsel him in his peer-group relations or emotional life.

Furthermore, the presence of these adults in the home—somewhat
like the extended family in earlier eras—helps reduce the emotional
intensity of parent-child relations. Though the child knows who is
boss in the home, he can still play these other "officials" off against
parental authority. And, indeed, the inner-directed parents, frequently not overeager for warmth from the child, are quite willing
to have the child's experience of affection associated with persons of
lower status. The inner-directed young man raised under these conditions learns to find emotional release with prostitutes and others
of low status. He becomes capable of impersonal relations with people and sometimes incapable of any other kind. This is one of the
prices he pays for his relative impermeability to the needs and wishes
of his peers, and helps account for his ability, when in pursuit of some
end he values, to steel himself against their indifference or hostility.

Grandmothers as authorities are almost as obsolete as governesses.
There is no room for them in the modern apartment, nor can they,
any more than the children themselves, find a useful economic role.
Nevertheless they endure, concomitant with the increased longevity
of the later population phases. The increased personalization of relationships that other-direction brings means that "strangers" in the
home are less and less endurable: the in-law problem, a standard
joke in many cultures over many centuries, takes on new meaning
where sensitive, highly individuated people live without characterological defenses against others.

The elimination of the grandmother from a central role in the
home is, moreover, symbolic of the rapidity of the changes we are
discussing. She is two generations removed from current practices

on the "frontier of consumption." While the parents try to keep up with their children, both as a means of staying young and as a means of staying influential, this is seldom possible for the grandparents. Hence their role in the formation of the other-directed character is negligible. Far from presenting the child with a relatively consistent "family portrait," standing in back of the parents and strengthening them, grandparents stand as emblems of how little one can learn from one's elders about the things that matter.

A parallel development removes another set of parent surrogates who played an important role in earlier periods: the older brothers or sisters who, like sophomores, hazed the younger in subjecting them to the family pattern of discipline. Today the older children—if any there are—are frequently more willing to earn cash as baby sitters than to supervise the training of their own younger brothers and sisters. The lure of a job may get children to work outside their homes; that still makes sense to them. But within their own home they are the privileged guests in a rather second-rate hotel, a hotel whose harassed but smiling managers they put under constant pressure for renovation.

THE TEACHER'S ROLE IN THE STAGE OF INNER-DIRECTION

One important authority, however, remains: a proxy parent whose power has probably increased as a consequence of the shift to other-direction. This is the schoolteacher, and we turn now to a fuller exploration of the change in her role.

In the period when inner-direction insures middle-class conformity, school starts relatively late—there are few nursery schools. The teacher's task is largely to train the children in decorum and in intellectual matters. The decorum may be the minimum of discipline needed to keep order in the classroom or the maximum of polish needed to decorate girls of the upper social strata. As schools become more plentiful and more readily accessible and "democratic," the obligation to train the child in middle-class speech and manners—that he may be aided in his rise above his parents' rank—falls upon the teacher. But the teacher does not work close to the child's emotional level. And the teacher regards her job as a limited one, sharply demarcated from the equally rigorous task of the home.

The physical arrangements of the school, both in this period and the next, symbolize its psychological impact and play a part in that impact. Seating in the preprogressive era is arranged formally—all face front—and often alphabetically. The walls are decorated with the ruins of Pompeii and the bust of Caesar. For all but the few exceptional children who can transcend the dead forms of their classical education and make the ancient world come alive, these etchings and statues signify the irrelevance of the school to the emotional problems of the child.

The teacher herself has neither understanding of nor time for these emotional problems, and the child's relation to other children enters her purview only in disciplinary cases. Often she has simply no authority: she is a common scold with too large a brood. Or she manages to maintain discipline by strictures and punishments. But these absorb the emotional attention of the children, often uniting them, at least within social class lines, in opposition to authority.

In the recent Swedish movie *Torment* we see this pattern still at work in the near-contemporary scene. Teachers and parents share the task of instilling inner-directed values. The villain is a harsh and overbearing, neurotic prep-school teacher. All the boys hate him; some fear him; no self-respecting boy would dream—despite the teacher's groping efforts—of being his friend. The hero is a boy who rebels, not so much because he wants to as because he is forced to by his teacher. He and his friends suffer, but their parents and teachers do not invade their lives, and they have privacy with each other and with girls, so long as no serious breach of decorum is evident. This rebellion itself—its success is not the issue—is part of the process of developing an inner-directed character.

An equally moving portrait is Antonia White's novel of a girl's convent school, *Frost in May*. Though the nuns at the school go quite far in "molding character" and viciously cut down signs of spontaneity and open-mindedness in the gifted heroine, they have back of them only the old-fashioned sanctions of penance and salvation. Their charges break or bend or run away or join the church—they do not open up to the nuns as friends. The very existence of uniforms, as in a military school, symbolizes the walls that separate the authorities from the children.

We may sum all this up by saying that the school of this period is concerned largely with impersonal matters. The sexes are segregated from each other. The focus is on an intellectual content that for most children has little emotional bite. Elocution, like female accomplishment, is impersonal, too; the child is not asked to "be himself"—nor does the school aim to be like "real life." Teachers, whether spinsterly or motherly types, do not know enough, even if they had the time and energy, to take an active hand in the socialization of tastes or of peer-group relations. While parents may permit the teachers to enforce certain rules of morality directly related to school, such as modesty of dress and honesty in examinations, and to inculcate certain rules of manners directly related to social ascent, they hardly allow interference with play groups, even in the interests of enforcing ethnic or economic democracy. The teacher is supposed to see that the children learn a curriculum, not that they enjoy it or learn group cooperation. The present practice of progressive grammar schools which decide whether or not to take a child by putting him in his putative group and seeing how he fits in would hardly have been conceivable.

Nevertheless, despite the social distance between teacher and child, the school's unquestioning emphasis on intellectual ability is profoundly important in shaping the inner-directed character. It affirms to the child that what matters is what he can *accomplish,* not how nice is his smile or how cooperative his attitude. And while the objectivity of the criteria for judging these skills and competences is rightfully called into question today—when we can see very clearly, for instance, the class bias in intelligence tests and paper examinations —the inner-directed school is not aware of such biases, and hence its standards can appear unequivocal and unalterable. For this reason these standards can be internalized both by those who succeed and by those who fail. They are felt as real and given, not as somebody's whim. Thus the school reinforces the home in setting for the child goals that are clear to all and that give direction and meaning to life thereafter.

Whatever the security that children gain from knowing where they stand—a security they no longer have in the other-directed progressive school—we must not forget how harshly this system bears on those who cannot make the grade: they are often broken; there is little mercy for them on psychological grounds. Brains, status, perhaps also docility, win the teacher, rather than "personality" or "problems." Some of the failures rebel. But these, too, are hammered into shape by the school—bad shape. Occasionally the frontier and other opportunities for mobility provide an exit for the academically outclassed;

and, still more occasionally, the rebel returns, like a mythical hero, having lived his troubles down, to alleviate the guilt of other misfits and give them hope for their own future. By and large, however, the very unequivocality of the school's standards that gives the children a certain security also means that the standards will be internalized even by those who fail. They will carry with them the aftereffects of emotional shock whose violence lies beyond criticism—sometimes even beyond recall.

THE TEACHER'S ROLE IN THE STAGE OF OTHER-DIRECTION

Progressive education began as a movement to liberate children from the crushing of talent and breaking of will that was the fate of many, even of those whose inner-direction might have seemed to them and to the observer stable and sound enough. Its aim, and to a very considerable degree, its achievement, was to develop the individuality of the child; and its method was to focus the teacher's attention on more facets of the child than his intellectual abilities. Today, however, progressive education is often no longer progressive; as people have become more other-directed, educational methods that were once liberating may even tend to thwart individuality rather than advance and protect it. The story can be quickly told.

Progressive schools have helped lower the age of school entry; the two- to five-year-old groups learn to associate school not with forbidding adults and dreary subjects but with play and understanding adults. The latter are, increasingly, young college graduates who have been taught to be more concerned with the child's social and psychological adjustment than with his academic progress—indeed, to scan the intellectual performance for signs of social maladjustment. These new teachers are more specialized. They don't claim to "understand children" but to have studied under Gesell on the "fives" or the "nines"; and this greater knowledge not only prevents the children from uniting in a wall of distrust or conspiracy against the school but also permits the teacher to take a greater hand in the socialization of spheres—consumption, friendship, fantasy—which the older-type teacher, whatever her personal desires, could not touch. Our wealthier society can afford this amount of individuation and "unnecessary" schooling.

Here also physical arrangements—in seating, age grading, decoration—symbolize the changes in the teacher's function. The sexes are mixed. Seating is arranged "informally." That is, *alphabetic* forms disappear, often to be replaced by *sociometric* forms that bring together compeers. This often means that where to sit becomes problematical—a clue to one's location on the friendship chart. Gesell grading is as severe as intellectual grading was in the earlier era; whatever their intellectual gifts, children stay with their presumed social peers.[7] The desks change their form, too; they are more apt to be movable tables with open shelves than places where one may hide things. The teacher no longer sits on a dais or struts before a blackboard but joins the family circle.

Above all, the walls change their look. The walls of the modern grade school are decorated with the paintings of the children or their montages from the class in social studies. Thus the competitive and contemporary problems of the children look down on them from walls which, like the teacher herself, are no longer impersonal. This looks progressive, looks like a salute to creativeness and individuality; but again we meet paradox. While the school de-emphasizes grades and report cards, the displays seem almost to ask the children: "Mirror, mirror on the wall, who is fairest of us all?"[8]

7. Howard C. Becker, a graduate student at the University of Chicago now engaged in a study of schoolteachers under the direction of Everett C. Hughes, has been observing the classroom consequences of the decline of the practice both of skipping grades and of holding children back who must repeat the grade. The teachers, faced with a group of identical age but vastly different capacities and willingnesses, meet the situation by dividing the class into two or three like-minded groups. Mobility between groups is discouraged, and children are encouraged to imitate their groupmates. The teacher herself, in the public schools, is probably inner-directed, but she is forced by her situation to promote other-direction among her charges.

Though in interview material it is always difficult to distinguish ideology from character, it is possible that the following quotation from one of Mr. Becker's interviews is a poignant example of the unwilling promotion of other-direction, as a result of this teacher's practice of using "telling time" and group shame as pressure on the child to have more interesting week ends: "Every class I have I start out the year by making a survey. I have each child get up and tell what he did over the week end. These last few years I've noticed that more and more children get up and say, 'Saturday I went to the show, Sunday I went to the show' . . . I've been teaching twenty-five years, and it never used to be like that. Children used to do more interesting things, they would go places instead of 'Saturday I went to the show, Sunday I went to the show' . . . What I do is to give a talk on all the interesting things that could be done—like going to museums and things like that. And also things like playing baseball and going on bike rides. By the end of the term a child is ashamed if he has to get up and say, 'Saturday I went to the show, Sunday I went to the show.' All the rest of the children laugh at him. So they really try to do some interesting things."

8. Still more paradoxically, it often happens that those schools that insist most strongly that the child be original and creative by this very demand make it difficult for him to be so. He dare not imitate an established master nor, in some cases, even imitate his own earlier work. Though the introduction of the arts into the school opens up the whole art world to many children, who would have no time or stimulation outside, other children are forced to socialize performances that would earlier have gone unnoticed by peers and adults.

What is perhaps most important, while the children's paintings and montages show considerable imaginative gift in the preadolescent period, the school itself is still one of the agencies for the destruction of fantasy, as it was in the preceding era. Imagination withers in most of the children by adolescence. What survives is neither artistic craft nor artistic fantasy but the socialization of taste and interest that can already be seen in process in the stylization of perception in the children's paintings and stories. The stories of the later progressive grades are apt to be characterized by "realism." This realism is subtly influenced by the ideals of the progressive movement. Caesar and Pompeii are replaced by visits to stores and dairies, by maps from *Life,* and by *The Weekly Reader;* and fairy tales are replaced by stories about trains, telephones, and grocery stores, and, later, by material on race relations or the United Nations or "our Latin American neighbors."

These changes in arrangement and topic assist the breakdown of walls between teacher and pupil; and this in turn helps to break down walls between student and student, permitting that rapid circulation of tastes which is a prelude to other-directed socialization. Whereas the inner-directed school child might well have hidden his stories and paintings under his bed—like the adult who, as we saw, often kept a diary—the other-directed child reads his stories to the group and puts his paintings on the wall. Play, which in the earlier epoch is often an extracurricular and private hobby, shared at most with a small group, now becomes part of the school enterprise itself, serving a "realistic" purpose.

The teacher's role in this situation is often that of opinion leader. She is the spreader of the messages concerning taste that come from the progressive urban centers. She conveys to the children that what matters is not their industry or learning as such but their adjustment in the group, their cooperation, their (carefully stylized and limited) initiative and leadership.

Especially important is the fact that the cooperation and leadership that are inculcated in and expected of the children are frequently contentless. In nursery school it is not important whether Johnny plays with a truck or in the sandbox, but it matters very much whether he involves himself with Bill—via any object at all. To be sure, there are a few, a very few, truly progressive schools where the children operating on the Dalton plan and similar plans exercise genuine choice of their program, move at their own pace, and use the teacher as a friendly reference library; here cooperation is necessary and meaningful in actual work on serious projects. Far more frequently, however, the teacher continues to hold the reins of authority in her hands, hiding her authority, like her compeer, the other-directed parent, under the cloak of "reasoning" and manipulation. She determines the program and its pace—indeed, often holding the children back because she fails to realize that children, left to themselves, are capable of curiosity about highly abstract matters. She may delay them by making arithmetic "realistic" and languages fun—as well as by substituting social studies for history. In extreme forms of this situation there is nothing on which the children have to cooperate in order to get it done. The teacher will do it for them anyway. Hence when she asks that they be cooperative she is really asking simply that they be nice.

Not too progressive

However, though the request seems simple, it is not casually made: the teacher is very tense about it. Deprived of older methods of discipline, she is, if anything, even more helpless than the parents who can always fall back on those methods in a pinch, though guiltily and rather ineffectively. The teacher neither dares to nor cares to; she has been taught that bad behavior on the children's part implies poor management on her part. Moreover, she herself is not interested in the intellectual content of what is taught, nor is this content apt to come up in a staff meeting or PTA discussion. These adult groups are often concerned with teaching tolerance, both ethnic and economic; and the emphasis on social studies that results means that intellectual content and skill become still more attenuated. Consequently, the teacher's emotional energies are channeled into the area of group relations. Her social skills develop; she may be sensitive to cliques based on "mere friendship" and seek to break them up lest any be left out. Correspondingly, her love for certain specific children may be trained out of her. All the more, she needs the general cooperation of all the children to assure herself that she is doing her job. Her surface amiability and friendliness, coupled with this underlying anxiety concerning the children's response, must be very confusing to the children who will probably conclude that to be uncooperative is about the worst thing one can be.

Of course the teacher will see to it that the children practice cooperation in small matters: in deciding whether to study the Peruvians or the Colombians, in nominating class officers for early practice in the great contemporary rituals of electioneering and parliamenteering, and in organizing contributions for the Red Cross or a Tag Day. Thus the children are supposed to learn democracy by underplaying the skills of intellect and overplaying the skills of gregariousness and amiability—skill democracy, in fact, based on respect for ability to *do* something, tends to survive only in athletics.

There is, therefore, a curious resemblance between the role of the teacher in the small-class modern school—a role that has spread from the progressive private schools to some of the public schools—and the role of the industrial relations department in a modern factory. The latter is also increasingly concerned with cooperation between men and men and between men and management, as technical skill becomes less and less of a major concern. In a few of the more advanced plants there is even a pattern of democratic decision on moot matters —occasionally important because it affects piecework rates and seniority rules, but usually as trivial as the similar decisions of grammar-school government. Thus the other-directed child is taught at school to take his place in a society where the concern of the group is less with what it produces than with its internal group relations, its morale.

III

A Jury of Their Peers: Changes in the Agents of Character Formation (*Continued*)

Individualism is a stage of transition between two types of social organization.

W. I. Thomas, The Unadjusted Girl

I. THE PEER-GROUP IN THE STAGE OF INNER-DIRECTION

WITH THE decline of the extended kinship family (the type of tradition-directed family that may include uncles, aunts, cousins, and other relatives), the child is often confronted in the inner-directed home with the close oppressiveness of idealized parents. He may compete with his brothers and sisters for the parents' favors, or to ward off their disapprobation. In theory the children in a family can unite against tyrannical parents, but, judging from the novels, it is more likely that parents divide and rule. Children in a family cannot react as a peer-group because of the age differentials among them. Consequently any given child at any single moment faces obviously unique problems and is alone with them—barring the luck of a sympathetic maid or aunt.

This is the price the inner-directed child pays for a situation in which his maturity is not delayed by having to wait for his age-graded peer-group. His parents do not hold him down because, according to "authorities," he is not ready for something. In Lord Chesterfield's letters to his son we find the assumption that pervades much literature of the earliest industrial period, that the child is simply a young, somewhat inexperienced adult. Lord Chesterfield writes as though his fifteen-year-old son had gained full sexual and intellectual maturity and needed only to ripen in wisdom and to acquire influence in his commerce with adults. The problems of training children to play with other children outside the home or to cooperate amicably with them do not present themselves to the inner-directed adult as part of his parental responsibility.

As a result the child, surrounded by inner-directed adults, often faces demands that are quite unreasonable. He is not held back but neither is he given a break. The growing child may respond to these demands by guilt and desperate effort to live up to the model or to rebel in solitude against it; he does not respond, as in the other-directed environment, by using the peer-group as a club to bring anxious adults into line if they have unreasonable or even unusual expectations of him. Indeed, in this era, it is sometimes possible to bring up the child in relative isolation from the peer-group, even though he has formal contact with other children at school. The images of the poor little rich boy and poor little rich girl are creations of this epoch, when children are often the social prisoners of parents and governesses.

In fact, the location of the home tends to have entirely different meanings in each of the three phases of the population curve. In the phase of high growth potential the home, except among the hunting and nomadic peoples, is fixed. As the locus of most activities in the socialization process, it symbolizes the extended family's overwhelming importance in that process. In the phase of transitional growth the young adult must navigate the passage from home and found a new home somewhere else. He goes to an undeveloped frontier or an undeveloped city; there he marries and settles down. This new home plays a part of decisive significance in the socialization of his children, though the school and other specialized agencies outside the home also play an increasing part.

In the phase of incipient population decline people still move around, but in search of frontiers of consumption as well as of production. That is, they look for nice neighborhoods in which their children will meet nice people. Although much of the moving about in America today, within and between cities, is in search of better jobs, it is also increasingly in search of better neighborhoods and the better schools that go with them. Since many others, too, will also be shopping for better neighborhoods, this pressure, combined with the rapid shift of residential values and fashions characteristic of American cities, means that no one can ever settle down assuredly for the rest of life. And when the children have grown up and made homes of their own, the parents will feel inclined to move again, perhaps in search of such consumption values as sunlight for themselves. Thus by their very location the other-directed parents show how much store they put on their children's contacts. And, of course, living in a small space with one child or two, the urban and suburban family needs to use space—physical and emotional space—outside the confined home for the activities of the growing children. (During the same period the working-class family has obtained access to much greater living space than during the earlier stages of industrialization; but it is the history of the middle-class family only that we are discussing here.)

Returning now to the situation of the inner-directed child, we see that he finds his playmates either among his own brothers and sisters or in an equally wide age range outside the home. This pattern still exists in country districts, where the gang at the swimming hole or ball field will be widely ranged in age; there are no partitioned playgrounds. However, after an age of "social discretion" is reached, the inner-directed child is expected to confine his friendships to those of approximately his own social class. Class has to be a conscious barrier because neighborhoods are somewhat less carefully restricted along class and ethnic lines than many suburbs are today—just as the southern whites and Negroes still frequently live in close physical proximity. Between five and fifteen, sex is also a barrier for the inner-directed child, since coeducation is infrequent and even where it formally exists little more effort is made to mix the sexes than to mix the social classes: proms for sixth and seventh graders are not yet de rigueur. The inner-directed child, limited in his friendship choices and limiting himself by a clear recognition of his status and the status to which he aspires, would seem "choosy" to many other-directed children of today.

Within the limits permitted by geography and taboo, then, the inner-directed child approaching his teens seeks out a chum or two. He may find in an older relative or friend someone to imitate and admire. But in many cases he will choose a chum on the basis of an interest in similar games and hobbies—hobbies that tend to be highly idiosyncratic and that are often continued into adult life. One can still observe this pattern at an English boys' school, where almost everyone has a hobby. Some hobbyists are quite satisfied to be by themselves—their hobby is company enough. Or one will find fast friendships among bird lovers, motorcycle fans, mineral collectors, poetry fanciers.

As we shall see in Chapter XVII, a hobby or craft is not of itself a clear sign of inner-direction: hobbies may be pursued also by children who are other-directed. Even, to a degree, the hobbies of both types may nominally coincide. But the meaning and social context of the hobbies are quite different for the two types of children. The inner-directed child will seldom share his hobby with a large peer-group—though stamp collecting may be an exception—and when hobbyists of this sort meet it is to swap technical details and enthusiasms, as two dairy farmers might swap accounts of their respective favorite breeds. There is nothing anxious about such a meeting: no problem of maintaining marginal differentiation (difference, that is, but not too much) in taste such as we find in other-directed hobbyists. The child is not shaken in his own hobby by the fact that others have a different hobby; rather, he is confirmed in the idiosyncrasy which, within wide limits, is respected.

Let me warn the reader, however, not to view all this too nostalgically with, say *Penrod* or *Huckleberry Finn* or even perhaps his own idealized childhood, in mind. In sports and studies the peer-group can become fiercely competitive, aided and abetted by coaches, teachers, and other adults. Many boys and girls who win honors in grade school are crushed when they do not surmount the tougher competition of high school. Much is at stake—and still more *seems* to be at stake—in such contests; and the inner-directed child cannot easily, sour-grapes fashion, change the instilled goals when they loom unattainable. Moreover, parents and teachers in their psychological naïveté may hold up as models the detestable young who work hard, dress neatly, and are polite.

Beyond all that, the fate of many inner-directed children is loneliness in and outside the home. Both may be places for hazing, persecution, misunderstanding. No adult intervenes on behalf of the lonely or hazed child to proffer sympathy, ask questions, or give advice. Adults do not think children's play is very important anyway; they will criticize children who seem too much concerned with play and too little with work. No sociometrically inclined teacher will try to break up friendship cliques in school to see that no one is left out. How savagely snobbish boys and girls can be is typified by the story, in the Lynds' *Middletown*, of the daughter who quit high school because her mother could not afford to give her silk stockings. Often the children, unaware that they have rights to friendship, under- standing, or agreeable play—unaware, indeed, that the adults could be greatly interested in such matters—suffer in silence and submit to the intolerable.

Only with the perspective of today can we see the advantages of these disadvantages. We can see that in a society which values inner- direction loneliness and even persecution are not thought of as the worst of fates. The parents, sometimes even the teachers, may have crushing moral authority, but the peer-group has less moral weight, glamorous or menacing though it may be. While adults seldom inter- vene to guide and help the lonely child, neither do they tell him that he should be part of a crowd and *must* have fun.

II. THE PEER-GROUP IN THE STAGE OF OTHER-DIRECTION

The parents in the era dominated by other-direction lose their once undisputed role; the old man is no longer "the governor"—and the installer of governors. Other adult authorities such as the governess and grandmother either almost disappear or, like the teacher, take on the new role of peer-group facilitator and mediator—a role not too different perhaps from that of many clergymen who, in the adult congregation, move from morality to morale.

As already indicated, moreover, the city in which the other-directed child grows up is large enough and stratified enough—taking into account its ring of suburbs—to create an age- and class-graded group for him. It will be possible to put him into school and playground, and camp in the summer, with other children of virtually the same age and social position. If the adults are the judge, these peers are the jury. And, as in America the judge is hemmed in by rules which give the jury a power it has in no other common-law land, so the Ameri- can peer-group, too, cannot be matched for power throughout the middle-class world.

THE TRIAL

While the inner-directed parent frequently forced the pace of the child in its home setting, as, for example, in cleanliness and toilet-training habits, the other-directed parent, more apt to be permissive in such matters, forces the pace, with like impatience, in the child's social life, though often hardly aware of doing so. Parents today are the stage managers for the meetings of three- and four-year-olds, just as, in earlier eras, the adults managed marriages. Hence, while "self-demand" feeding schedules are gaining ground for infants, self-demand is not observed when it comes to socialization outside the home. The daily schedule is an effort, with mother as chauffeur and booking agent, to cultivate all the currently essential talents, especially the gregarious ones. It is inconceivable to some supervising adults that a child might prefer his own company or that of just one other child.

The child is thus confronted by what we have termed his socio-metric peers and is not surrounded by those who are his peers in less visible matters, such as temperament and taste. Yet since there are no *visible* differences he is hard put to it to justify, even to be aware of, these *invisible* differences. On the overt level the situation is highly standardized: any given child faces the culture of the fives or the sixes at a particular moment of the fashion cycle in child-training and child-amusement practices. Indeed it is this very standardization which, as we saw, weakens the power of the parents, whose difference from the standards is felt by them and by the child to demonstrate their inexperience and inadequacy. In this setting the adults are anxious that the child succeed in the peer-group and therefore are concerned with his "adjustment." They, too, tend to ignore and even suppress invisible differences between their child and the children of others. Such differences might cast doubt on their own adjustment, their own correct tuning to the signals concerning child rearing.

The majority of children learn very fast under these conditions; the same adult authorities who patronize children's intellects and therefore slow them down are perhaps not sufficiently impressed with how poised in many social situations modern other-directed children are. These children are not shy, either with adults or with the opposite sex whom they have accompanied to proms and parties and seen daily in and out of school. This adaptability, moreover, prepares the child for a type of social mobility somewhat different from the social-climbing experiences of the parvenu in an inner-directed environment. The latter only rarely acquired the intellectual and social graces of his new associates—or he ridiculously overacquired them. He either kept his rough and lowly manners or painfully tried to learn new ones as he moved up; in either case the standard, limited code of conduct expected of him was unequivocal. In contrast with this the other-directed child is able to move among new associates with an almost automatic adjustment to the subtlest insignia of status.

Bearing in mind these positive achievements of other-directed sociability, let us turn our attention from what the peer-group teaches and evokes to what it represses. Today six-year-olds and up have a phrase—"he [or she] thinks he's *big*" (or "he thinks he's *something*")—which symbolizes the role of the peer-group in the creation of other-directed types. The effort is to cut everyone down to size who stands up or stands out in any direction. Beginning with the very young and going on from there, overt vanity is treated as one of the worst offenses, as perhaps dishonesty would have been earlier. Being high-hat is forbidden.

Temper, manifest jealousy, moodiness—these, too, are offenses in the code of the peer-group. All "knobby" or idiosyncratic qualities and vices are more or less eliminated or repressed. And judgments of others by peer-group members are so clearly matters of taste that their expression has to resort to the vaguest phrases, constantly changed: cute, lousy, square, darling, good guy, honey, swell, bitch (without precise meaning), etc. Sociometry reflects this situation when it asks children about such things as whom they like to sit next to or not to sit next to, to have for a friend, a leader, and so on. The judgments can be meaningfully scaled because, and only because, they are all based on uncomplicated continua of *taste,* on which the children are constantly ranking each other.

But to say that judgments of peer-groupers are matters of taste, not of morality or even opportunism, is not to say that any particular child can afford to ignore these judgments. On the contrary he is, as never before, at their mercy. If the peer-group were—and we continue to deal here with the urban middle classes only—a wild, torturing, obviously vicious group, the individual child might still feel moral indignation as a defense against its commands. But like adult authorities in the other-directed socialization process, the peer-group is friendly and tolerant. It stresses fair play. Its conditions for entry seem reasonable and well meaning. But even where this is not so, moral indignation is out of fashion. The child is therefore exposed to trial by jury without any defenses either from the side of its own morality or from the adults. All the morality is the group's. Indeed, even the fact that it is a morality is concealed by the confusing notion that the function of the group is to have fun, to play; the deadly seriousness of the business, which might justify the child in making an issue of it, is therefore hidden.

MANEUVERS OF DEFENSE AND THE POPULARITY KIT

In the eyes of the jury of peers one may be a good guy one day, a stinker the next. Toleration, let alone leadership, depends on having a highly sensitive response to swings of fashion. This ability is sought in several ways. One way is to surrender any claim to independence of judgment and taste—a kind of plea of nolo contendere. Another is to build a plea for special consideration by acquiring unusual facility in one's duties as a consumer—in performance, that is, of the leisure arts. With good luck one may even become a taste and opinion leader, with great influence over the jury.

Each particular peer-group has its group fandoms and lingoes. Safety consists not in mastering a difficult craft but in mastering a battery of taste preferences and the mode of their expression. The preferences are for articles or "heroes" of consumption and for members of the group itself. The proper mode of expression requires feeling out with skill and sensitivity the probable tastes of the others and then swapping mutual likes and dislikes to maneuver intimacy.

Now some of this is familiar even in the period depending on inner-direction; it is important, therefore, to realize the degree to which training in consumer taste has replaced training in etiquette. Formal etiquette may be thought of as a means of handling relations with people with whom one does not seek intimacy. It is particularly useful when adults and young, men and women, upper classes and lower classes, are sharply separated and when a code is necessary to mediate exchanges across these lines. Thus etiquette can be at the same time a means of approaching people and of staying clear of them. For some, etiquette may be a matter of little emotional weight —an easy behavioral cloak; for others the ordering of human relations through etiquette can become highly charged emotionally—an evidence of characterological compulsiveness. But in either case etiquette is concerned not with encounters between individuals but with encounters between them as representatives of their carefully graded social roles.

In comparison with this, training in consumer taste, which tends to replace etiquette among other-directeds, is useful not so much across age and social class lines as within the jury room of one's age and class peers. As in some groups—children as well as adults—discussion turns to the marginal differentiation between Cadillacs and Lincolns, so in other groups discussion centers on Fords and Chevrolets. What matters in either case is an ability at continual sniffing out of others' tastes, often a far more intrusive process than the exchange of courtesies and pleasantries required by etiquette. Not, of course, that the child really gets close to the "others" with whom he is exchanging consumption preferences—these exchanges are often mere gossip about goods. Yet a certain emotional energy, even excitement, permeates the transaction. For one thing, the other-directed person acquires an intense interest in the ephemeral tastes of the "others"— an interest inconceivable to the tradition-directed or inner-directed child whose tastes have undergone a less differentiated socialization. For another thing, the other-directed child is concerned with learning from these interchanges whether his radar equipment is in proper order.

It has always been true in social classes dominated by fashion that to escape being left behind by a swing of fashion requires the ability to adopt new fashions rapidly; to escape the danger of a conviction for being different from the "others" requires that one can be different—in look and talk and manner—from *oneself* as one was yesterday. Here, also, it is necessary to see precisely what has changed. In general the processes of fashion are expanded in class terms and speeded in time terms. In the leisure economy of incipient population decline the distributive machinery of society improves, in terms of both income distribution and goods distribution. It becomes possible to accelerate swings of fashion as well as to differentiate goods by very minute gradients. For, in its late stages, mass production and mass distribution permit and require a vast increase not only in quantity but in qualitative differences among products—not only as a consequence of monopolistic efforts at marginal differentiation but also because the machinery and organization are present for rapidly designing, producing, and distributing a wide variety of goods.

This means that the consumer trainee has a lot more to learn than in the early days of industrialization. To take one example, the foreigner who visits America is likely to think that salesgirls, society ladies, and movie actresses all dress alike, as compared with the clear status differences of Europe. But the American knows—has to know if he is to get along in life and love—that this is simply an error: that one must look for small qualitative differences that signify style and status, to observe for instance the strained casualness sometimes found in upper-class dress as against the strained formality of working-class dress. In the days of etiquette the differences were far more sharp, like the great differences of voice and accent that bespoke one's birth and breeding.

One must listen to quite young children discussing television models, automobile styling, or the merits of various streamliners to see how gifted they are as consumers long before they have a decisive say themselves—though their influence in family councils must not be underestimated. Children join in this exchange of verdicts even if their parents cannot afford the gadgets under discussion; indeed, the economy would slow down if only those were trained as consumers who at any given moment had the wherewithal.

The wider ambit of taste socialization today is shown in still another decisive change from the era depending on inner-direction. Then, by the rules of etiquette and class, certain spheres of life were regarded as private: it was a breach of etiquette to intrude or permit intrusion on them. Today, however, one must be prepared to open up on cross-examination almost any sphere in which the peer-group may become interested. It may become fashionable, as recent articles in the "Profile of Youth" series in the *Ladies' Home Journal* have shown, for young girls to discuss their rivals' necking techniques with their particular partner.[1] While the game of post office is old, the breakdown of privacy for reasonably serious love-making is new. Dating at twelve and thirteen, the child is early made aware of the fact that his taste in emotions as well as in consumer goods must be

1. A student who read this passage in an earlier draft wrote me as follows: "In male bu[l] sessions one can no longer play the gentleman and keep quiet about sexual adventures. H[e] has to furnish names, dates, and all the exact details of the conquest. Where fellows get int[o] trouble is when they have a sincere feeling for a girl and yet are forced to tell. The measur[e] of the peer-group's strength and their other-directedness is that they *can* be forced to tell.

socialized and available for small talk. Whereas etiquette built barriers between people, socialized exchange of consumer taste requires that privacy either be given up, or be kept, like a liberal theologian's God, in some interstices of one's nature. Before the peer-group jury there is no privilege against self-incrimination.

True, we have not yet been able to measure with much refinement how widespread these newer patterns are. I have assumed that the more privately pursued craft hobbies are declining in relative importance among the children who have money and leisure for them. The only evidence I have for this assumption so far is the report that "reading, hobbies and pets," occupying 24 per cent of American leisure spending in 1900, occupied 18 per cent in 1929.[2] It is true that the same progressive schools that foster "groupiness" also encourage arts and crafts that were neglected by schools in the earlier era. Some, in an effort to break down friendship cliques, seek to build up interest cliques. Children build model planes and boats, become amateur photographers, and still collect stamps. The *Hot Rod,* trade journal for the hot-rod (stripped-down, souped-up car) enthusiasts, is said to have a circulation of one hundred and fifty thousand. It may be that one appeal of the hot rod, and of similar activities of which adults are ignorant or disapproving, is that it permits escape from the school's efforts to socialize tastes. No teacher of crafts is likely, for instance, to censor, control, or encourage the ingenuity of the hot rodder—though as adults become aware of the hazards they may try to cope with them by infiltrating the movement with sage counsel and supervision. Of course, as the school embraces more activities, these escapes become more difficult to find; and when they are found, it too often turns out, as with jazz and hot rods, that their pursuit is already partially commercialized and standardized. It is along just such lines that we need many more studies of young people, what they do, and what it means to them, before we can make more accurate judgments of their activities and tastes.

The same forces that consolidate the socialization of tastes also make for more socialized standards of performance. The other-directed child, learning to play the piano, is in daily competition

2. F. Frederick Dewhurst *et al., America's Needs and Resources* (The Twentieth-Century Fund, 1947), p. 279.

with studio stars. He cannot remember a period when either his peers or their adult guides were not engaged in comparing his performance with these models. Whatever he attempts—an artistic accomplishment, a manner of speaking, a sleight-of-hand trick—the peer-group is on hand to identify it in some way and to pass judgment on it with the connoisseurship typical of the mass-media audience. Soon enough this process becomes internalized, and the child feels himself in competition with Eddie Duchin or Horowitz even if no one else is around. Hence it is difficult for the other-directed child to cultivate a highly personalized gift: the standards are too high, and there is little private time for maturation.

The newer pattern of popularity depends less on ability to play an instrument than on ability to express the proper musical preferences. In the fall of 1947 I conducted some interviews among teenagers in Chicago concerning their tastes in popular music and also consulted professional musicians, juke-box listings, and other sources to round out my impressions. My interest was principally in seeing how these young people used their musical interests in the process of peer-group adjustment. Like the "trading cards" which symbolize competitive consumption for the eight- to eleven-year-olds, the collection of records seemed to be one way of establishing one's relatedness to the group, just as the ability to hum current tunes was part of the popularity kit. The requirements were stiffer among girls than boys, though the latter were not exempt. Tunes meant people: roads to people, remembrances of them. At the same time the teen-agers showed great anxiety about having the "right" preferences. When I had the occasion to interview a group its individual members looked around to see what the others thought before committing themselves —at least as to specific songs or records, if not as to a general type of music, such as symphonic or hillbilly, where they might be certain as to their group's reactions. Readers who have not themselves observed the extent of this fear of nonconformity may be inclined to dismiss it by remarking that young people have always been conformists in their groups. True; yet it seems to me that the point is one of degree and that the need for musical conformity is today much more specialized and demanding than it was in an earlier era, when some children could be, or were forced by their parents to be, musical, and others could leave music alone.

Even among those interviewed who took piano lessons musical interest as such seemed virtually nonexistent. One boy of fourteen did appear to have genuine musical interests, playing "classics" on the piano. His mother told the interviewer, however, that she was not letting him practice too much lest he get out of step with the other boys, and was insisting that he excel in sports. "I hope to keep him a normal boy," she said. These research experiences seem to hint that preferences in the consumption field are not viewed as a development of the human ability to relate oneself discriminatingly to cultural objects. For the objects are hardly given meaning in private and personal values when they are so heavily used as counters in a preferential method of relating oneself to the peers. The cultural objects, whatever their nature, are mementos that somehow remain unhumanized by the force of a genuinely fetishistic attachment.

Moving somewhere beyond mere taste exchanging are those opinion leaders [3] who try to influence verdicts as well as to repeat them— a dangerous game indeed. The risks are minimized, however, by playing within the limits imposed by marginal differentiation. Thus my interviews showed that each age group within a limited region and class had its own musical taste; the younger ones, for instance, liked "sweet" stuff that was "corn" to those slightly older. Within this general trend a girl might decide that she could not *stand* Vaughn Monroe or that Perry Como was tops. If she expressed herself so forcibly in detail, the chances were that she was, or wanted to be, an opinion leader. For many of the young people did not express any strong likes or specific dislikes—though they might share a strong revulsion against a whole taste range, like hot jazz or hillbilly. These latter were the opinion followers, scarcely capable even of marginal differentiation.

3. The concept of the opinion leader and empirical methods for spotting him in a community have been developed particularly by Paul Lazarsfeld, Robert K. Merton, C. Wright Mills of the Bureau of Applied Social Research of Columbia University, and Bernard Berelson of the University of Chicago. The concept is an important one for our purposes, since the spread of other-directed patterns beyond the metropolitan centers is often due to the influence of opinion leaders who have learned these patterns while away at high school, at college, or on a job and who continue to keep in touch with the newer values through the mass media, which in turn support their efforts with their local "constituency." The Columbia group has observed this process in the spread of attitudes and preferences; to see how these in turn shape character is a more complex and as yet unaccomplished task. Walter Bagehot has some interesting speculations on the problem. *Physics and Politics*, ed. Barzun (New York, Alfred A. Knopf, 1948), pp. 91 *et seq.*

III. FASHIONS IN VERDICTS

The peer-group is not an American invention. In many societies dependent on tradition-direction the peer-group can be about as powerful as it is in the contemporary American scene—and even more inescapable. In order to see more precisely just what it is that has changed, I turn now to two problems. What is the role of the peer-group in training its members to take their places on the economic scene in the role that now matters most, that of the consumer? And how does the group become its own consumption product, engaged in an "antagonistic cooperation" which is mediated by exchange of linguistic signals?

"THE TALK OF THE TOWN": THE SOCIALIZATION OF CONSUMPTION PREFERENCES

In the societies depending on inner-direction that developed in the west, all values were translatable, at least in principle, into the impersonal standard of money. This was the possession that gave value to all other possessions. True, money itself fluctuated in value, depending not only on directly technological factors but also on sociopsychological ones.[4] Nevertheless, money felt substantial to parents, was made to feel so to children, and served in countless subtle ways as the goal and norm of both society and socialization.

"Money talks," people said, meaning that it also smiles on those who have it and frowns on those who do not. Money, little as we like to recognize the fact today in our ascetic or self-righteous attitudes about it, permitted the cash customer to pursue his private purposes—good or bad—with no other justification than his pocketbook. Today the currency into which all values tend to be translated is no longer money but appraisal by the peer-group. And this value, much more patently than money, is subject to booms and busts on manifest sociopsychological grounds; it does not feel substantial either to parents or to children. The appraisal of the peer-group is always stated, in the final analysis, in terms of a consumption preference. Whereas the simple cost of a commodity was the most important fact about it in the days of inner-direction, today in other-directed circles, though

---

4. It is interesting to see the struggle of Adam Smith and later economists with the whole problem of "value" as a search for a solid standard.

money still makes a difference, it is the peer-group that does most of the "talking." Price influences the group's verdict—but only up to a point. Children and adolescents, far more sophisticated than the old people, form a consumers' union; indeed each child in the middle class is automatically a consumer trainee before he can walk; and his practice in consumer's research begins long before he can count change. To a degree he will be judged on his ability as a trainee as, in earlier eras, he might have been sized up as a potential recruit for the army or for the production economy.

Such changes constitute our most dramatic evidence that, in the phase of incipient population decline, there is a great advance in the standard of living and in the position of children. Children are not subjected to a period of deprivation and hardship which leads to compensatory dreams of a life of ease and pleasure. Girls are not, as they were in some earlier societies, drudges at home until, at puberty, they were suddenly given the only "capital" they were ever likely to find—that of their bodies—to live on as income, or exhaust as principal. Even boys from comfortable homes were expected until recently to hit the sunrise trail with paper routes or other economically profitable and "character-building" chores. Other-directed children who have not faced such deprivations and dreamed compensatory dreams of wild purchasing power find it easier than these dream-driven children to become sophisticated consumers, more preoccupied with their sophistication—the verdict on consumption—than with consumption itself.

While the other-directed person's tremendous outpouring of energy is channeled into the ever expanding frontiers of consumption, the inner-directed person's energy was channeled relentlessly into production—production that underwent fantastic expansion in the phase of transitional growth of population. Inner-directed patterns often discouraged consumption for adults as well as children. But at other times, and especially in the higher social strata less affected by Puritan asceticism, the inner-directed person consumed—with time out, so to speak, for saving and for good behavior—as relentlessly as he (or his progenitors) produced. Most clearly in the case of upper-class conspicuous consumption he lusted for possessions and display, once the old tradition-directed restraints had worn away. He pursued clear acquisition and consumption goals with a fierce individualism. To be sure, his goals were socially determined, but less by a contemporary union of consumers than by inherited patterns of desire, hardly less stable than the desire for money itself. Goals such as fine houses, fine horses, fine women, fine objets d'art—these could be investments because their value scarcely changed in the scale of consumption preference.

These relatively stable and individualistic pursuits are today being replaced by the fluctuating tastes which the other-directed person accepts from his peer-group. (Women, as we shall see in Chapter VII, are still desired objects of consumption, but judgments as to what is desirable in a woman change with the same rapidity as women's styles in dress—indeed, these styles symbolize the degrees and kinds of fashionableness and femininity that men will want or accept.) Moreover, many of the desires that drove men to work and to madness in societies depending on inner-direction are now satisfied relatively easily; they are incorporated into the standard of living taken for granted by millions. But the craving remains. It is a craving for the satisfactions others seem to have, an *objectless craving*. The consumer today has most of his potential individuality trained out of him bv his membership in the consumers' union. He is kept within his consumption limits not by goal-directed but by other-directed guidance, kept from splurging too much by fear of others' envy, and from consuming too little by fear of his own envy of the others.

These observations would amount to a digression from the child's world into the adult's were it not for the fact that today there is no fast line that separates the consumption patterns of the adult world from those of the child, except the consumption objects themselves. The child may consume comics or toys while the adult consumes editorials and cars; more and more both consume in the same way. Some of the reasons for the increasing over-all conformity of consumption are analyzed in later chapters which deal specifically with the adult world of consumption. It is sufficient to remark here that we can think of the child as one among the many kinds of consumer trainees we find in our economy.

In the consumers' union of the peer-group the child's discipline as a consumer begins today very early in life—and lasts late. It is true that in the era of inner-direction it was difficult enough for children to understand the work roles of their parents. It was perhaps as difficult then, especially for boys, as it is today. But this did not mean that the inner-directed child displaced his energies for judging work into judging consumption; he was supposed to be "job-minded" even if the job itself was not clear in his mind. Today the future occupation of all moppets is to be skilled consumers.

This is visible early in children's play-at-consumption. In this area there is a noticeable increase in the range of children's toys. Added to boys' toys, for example production-imitating equipment like trucks and steam shovels or toy soldiers and miniature war material, is a whole new range of objects modeled after the service trades: laundry trucks, toy telephones, service stations, and so forth. Added to girls' toys, the doll and her wardrobe, are juvenile make-up outfits and voice recorders.

These props of the child's playtime hours, however, are not so striking as the increasing rationalization of children's preferences in everything they consume. In the period of inner-direction children accepted trade-marked cereals largely because that was what was set for them at table. Today they eat Wheaties, or other cereal, influenced by some specific reason that all can talk about: "Wheaties makes champions." And comics, children will say if pressed, "relax champions." In this way the other-directed child rapidly learns that there always is and always must be a reason for consuming anything. One "reason" is that the commodity he is consuming is the "best" in its line. As the child develops as a consumer trainee, advertising no longer is given all the credit for answering the question of what is the best in its line. The product approved by most of the others, or by a suitable testimonial from a peer consumer, becomes the "best." The most popular products, by this formula, are the products that happen to be used by the most popular peer or group of peers. And to be sure, these pace setters themselves have a "reason," often enough picked out from the mass media, if not from the advertising pages; thus the hunt for the reason goes on in an endless regress.

These patterns place extra burdens on girls, partly because women are the accepted consumption leaders in our society, partly because women, much more than men, feel pressure to play any role they are accepted in by the men. At every social level boys are permitted a greater amount of aggression than girls; they are also permitted a wider range of preferences and can get by with a good deal of aggressive resistance to the taste-exchanging process. The media may exaggerate, but do not greatly exaggerate, the role of young girls in the pattern which requires that what is learned in the peer-group must be marketed at home, rather than vice versa.

Finally, the child consumer trainee becomes a consumer tutor in the home circle, "bringing up" mother as well as father. *Life* magazine recently ran a leading article on "Teen-age Fun," showing the etiquettes and pastimes prevailing in certain American cities; these pastimes were news even to some recent high-school graduates. Teenagers must initiate adults rather than vice versa; typical is the case, also cited in *Life,* where teachers at a Denver high school imitated the idiomatic greeting style of the "most popular" boy.

THE ANTAGONISTIC COOPERATORS OF THE PEER-GROUP

It is, possibly, no accident that it was his *greeting style* on which this boy exercised his gifts for opinion leadership and marginal differentiation. The point is that, over and beyond the socialization of consumption preferences and the exchange of consumption shoptalk by the consumers' union, the membership is engaged in *consuming itself.* That is, people themselves, friendships, are viewed as the greatest of all consumables; the peer-group is itself a main object of consumption, its own main competition in taste. The "sociometric" exchange of peer-group ratings is ceaseless and is carried on, as a conversation with the self, in "private" also; who is my best friend, my next best, and so on, down to the most disliked. The more thoroughly other-directed the individual is, the more unhesitatingly able he is to classify his preferences and to compare them with those of others. In fact, as compared with their inner-directed predecessors, other-directed children are extraordinarily knowledgeable about popularity ratings. Physical prowess probably remains a chief road, though declining, to status among working-class boys. However, popularity among upper middle-class boys and girls seems to hinge on much vaguer criteria, frequently impenetrable to the adult observer but, while they last, crystal clear to the peer-group itself.

It appears that the tremendous competitive energies which the inner-directed person had available for the sphere of production and, secondarily, for consumption, now flow into competition for the much more amorphous security of the peer-group's approval. But just because it is approval for which one competes one must repress one's overt competitiveness. Here the phrase "antagonistic cooperation," borrowed from other contexts, is apt.

This transformation is so important that we devote several sections to it in Chapter VI, but now we need only note a few reference points. The parents, harking back as they do in their character structures to an earlier era, are themselves competitive—more overtly so than the children. Much of our ideology—free enterprise, individualism, and all the rest—remains competitive and is handed down by parents, teachers, and the mass media. At the same time there has been an enormous ideological shift favoring submission to the group, a shift whose decisiveness is concealed by the persistence of the older ideological patterns. The peer-group becomes the measure of all things; the individual has no defenses the group cannot batter down. In this situation the competitive drives for achievement sponsored in children by the remnants of inner-direction in their parents come into conflict with the cooperative demands sponsored by the peer-group. The child therefore is forced to rechannel the competitive drive for achievement, as demanded by the parent, into his drive for approval from the peers. Neither parent, child, nor the peer-group itself is particularly conscious of this process. As a result all three participants in the process may remain unaware of the degree to which the force of an older individualistic ideology provides the energies for filling out the forms of a newer, group-oriented characterology.

IV

Storytellers as Tutors in Technique: Changes in the Agents of Character Formation (*Continued*)

A. I like Superman better than the others because they can't do everything Superman can do. Batman can't fly and that is very important.

Q. Would you like to be able to fly?

A. I would like to be able to fly if everybody else did, but otherwise it would be kind of conspicuous.

From an interview with a twelve-year-old girl.[1]

LANGUAGE, as we noted in the previous chapter, becomes a refined and powerful aspect of the organization of the peer-group engaged in consuming its own taste preferences and in marching up its own taste gradients. For the insiders language becomes a chief key to the taste socializations and mood currents that are prevalent in this group at any moment. For the outsiders, including adult observers, language becomes a mysterious opacity, constantly carrying peer-group messages which are full of precisions that remain untranslatable.

When we look more closely at the use of language in the young peer-groups we see how various its aspects are. Language itself becomes a sort of consumption product. It is used neither to direct the work economy, nor to relate the self to others in any really intimate

---

1. Katherine M. Wolfe and Marjorie Fiske, "The Children Talk About Comics," *Communications Research 1948–1949*, ed. Paul F. Lazarsfeld and Frank Stanton (New York, Harper, 1949), pp. 26–27.

way, nor to recall the past, nor yet as sheer word play. Rather it is used in the peer-groups today much as popular tunes seem to be used: as a set of counters by which one establishes that one is "in" and by which one participates in the peer-group's arduously self-socializing "work." And the peer-groups, while they exercise power more than ever before through the use of words, are more than ever before the victims of words. While they learn to cling desperately to words— most signals are given in words—at the same time they learn to distrust them. As we have seen, verdicts in the peer-group are often quite ambiguous. Some of the older words, such as bastard and skunk, remain, but their meaning is vaguer—they may even be said with a smile! Whole new glossaries crop up every few years.

Mass literacy of course plays a complex part in this process. The peer-group accepts a substantial responsibility in the flow of modern communications. It stands midway between the individuals of whom each group is composed and the messages which flow to the group's opinion leaders from the mass media. The mass media are the wholesalers; the peer-groups, the retailers of the communications industry. But the flow is not all one way. Not only do the peers decide, to a large extent, which tastes, skills, and words, appearing for the first time within their circle, shall be given approval, but they also select some for wider publicity through contiguous groups and eventually back to the mass media for still wider distribution. If we look at this process we see that the individual who develops, say, a particular style of expression, is either ignored by the peers or accepted by them. If he and his style are accepted, his style is taken over by the group, and in at least this sense it is no longer *his*. But the same thing can happen to a given peer-group in its turn. To understand the way in which individual and personal style is siphoned up through these stages of impersonalization we have to understand the work of the main machine in the process—the mass media.

Our interest in this chapter will not be in the commercial purveyors of language and imagery or the storytellers themselves but in the effects on the child audience. And of course these effects cannot be considered in isolation from the constellation of parents, teachers, and peer-groupers who operate on the assembly line of character. If we find, for instance, a child who seems more affected by print than by people, it may be because people are so overwhelming for him that he must take refuge in print. Furthermore, cultures differ very

much in the perceptions they stress in teaching the child to differentiate among images and to differentiate among people. But in general it seems fair to say that the storytellers (or more technically the
mass media of communication) are indispensable agents of socialization. They picture the world for the child and thus give both form
and limits to his memory and imagination.[2]

In exploring this topic we must not confuse the genres of literature
with the problem of social-psychological effects. We are going to
use "story" broadly in this chapter to include not only poetry and
fiction but any fabulous and embroidered account: a "true" newsreel
might by this definition be a story. Nor, considering the prestige of
the pictorial, shall we confine ourselves to the imagery of language
alone.

Societies in the phase of incipient population decline can afford,
can technically provide, and have both the time and the need to receive a bounteous flow of imagery from urban centers of distribution.
Industrialism and mass literacy seem to go together. These same societies, moreover, rely more heavily than their predecessors on character-forming agencies outside the home. Hence, as we would expect, the storytellers of the mass media play a great role among other-
directed children. We can see what has changed in recent generations
only by comparing today's experience with that of children in societies
depending on tradition-direction and inner-direction.

I. SONG AND STORY IN THE STAGE OF

TRADITION-DIRECTION

The society which depends for conformity on tradition-direction
uses as part of its stock in trade its oral traditions, its myths, legends,
and songs. These are transmitted by the same family members who
play an active part in all the other phases of socializing the young.

CHIMNEY-CORNER MEDIA

When we find a society in which stories are transmitted by word
of mouth, we put our finger on one of the very indexes by which we
know it as a society depending on tradition-direction. In terms of

2. See the remarkable discussion by Ernest Schachtel, "On Memory and Childhood Amnesia,"
Psychiatry, X (1947), 1; see also Evelyn T. Riesman, "Childhood Memory in the Painting of
Joan Miró," *ETC*, VI (1949), 160.

the technique of transmission, the important thing is that the story or fable is told orally, not in print. In terms of the storytelling situaion, the important thing is that the story is told, ordinarily, by a family member or by a professional or semiprofessional closely connected with the extended family group. In both cases the result is that the story is modulated for, and built into, the web of values that the storyteller also controls and relates himself to in active ways. One way of expressing this is to say that storytelling is like a handicraft industry: each telling is different from the other, and each is tailored to the taste and disposition of the audience.

These factors are all-important in their effect on audiences. Since the physical and social distance between the teller and listener is slight, the listener is to some extent a participant in the telling. A child can correct the teller or criticize the theme or elaborate the narrative—though more often he is probably confined to asking questions. This means that the listener, even as a child, is in a position to find and develop his own likings. What is more, the unity of the web of social values and personal relations in which the story is transmitted is such that both the story and the vehicle have a resolute meaning. This does not mean that fairy tales and traditional myths lack ambiguity—indeed they possess it to a rich extent and at many levels—but rather that the ambiguity could often be resolved in a slightly different manner for different audiences. For the act of telling, as we have seen, occurs within a context whose physical and psychological dimensions are largely grasped by tellers and hearers.

It is not surprising that songs and stories rendered in face-to-face performance among relatives and friends are often baldly cautionary tales; they tell what happens to those who disobey the community or the supernatural authorities. Or they illustrate by reference to the illustrious what kind of person one ought to be in the culture in terms of such traits as bravery and endurance. A surprising number of tales, however, in many cultures depending on tradition-direction are not cautionary in this direct sense. As in the Bible, some tales recount rebellions, successful or tragic, against the powers that be—though in many cases the theme of rebellion is disguised.

TALES OF NORM AND "ABNORM"

As we move over to the consideration of content, we can take the rebellious note struck in these tales to indicate that even in a society depending on tradition-direction there still remain strivings which are not completely socialized. By and large, people accept the harness of their culture, and it is hard for them to conceive of another make of harness. But they are not unaware of constraint, and their stories, as frequently their dreams, are the refuge and succor of this awareness and help to make it possible to go on with ordinary life. The communal load of shame or anxiety is reduced by the common "confession," the common release which the myth permits. There is in these myths, then, a good deal of "realism" about stubborn, unsocialized human nature—this is precisely why they can appeal to us across the centuries and across the cultural boundaries. They show people to be more fierce, more jealous, more rebellious than appears on the surface.

Why is this so? It appears that if people were only "adjusted"—if they never had even a thought which transcended the cultural prohibitions—life would have so little savor as to endanger the culture itself. Cultures depending upon tradition-direction usually manage to institutionalize a degree of rebellion not only for their deviants but for everybody. Sometimes this is done on a life-cycle basis. Thus some cultures permit, even encourage, sauciness from children only to clamp down on the adult; others allow the older women a bawdiness denied the younger ones. Sometimes there are special days —feast days—when bars are down.

Now when the aperture for rebellion lies in the realm of culturally approved fantasy, the socializing function of the tales and stories which are the predecessors of the mass media is clearly a dual one. The elders use the stories to tell the young: you must be like so-and-so if you are to be admired and to live up to the noble traditions of the group. But the young are also told—sometimes in the very same message—that there have been people like so-and-so who broke the rules, who did many worse things than you ever did, and perhaps ever dreamed of, and whether he lived to tell the tale or not, he *did live* and we speak of him.

This very ambivalence of the stories helps the young to integrate their forbidden impulses by recognizing them as part of their legacy as human beings. Stories make it possible for the face-to-face group which is charged with socialization of the young to draw on a cultural warehouse that provides models for behavior not to be found completely in any given face-to-face group. In this tradition-directed form of "popular culture" stories make it possible to form an underground connection, via myth, between repressed sectors of the adults and sectors of the young. Finally, they make it possible to hold the young to both more and less than what they see around them, either of approved behavior or of behavior which, while disapproved, is still done.

And yet it is more complicated than that. Indeed, we may suppose that the change to inner-direction occurs first in circles which, through literacy or otherwise, acquire access to many multiplying ambiguities of direction. As in the mathematical theory of communications all channels mix what is technically called noise with what is technically called information and thus limit the freedom of the sender, so also messages intended or believed to socialize the young cannot help but contain noises which may have diverse effects, effects which may oversocialize or undersocialize them.

II. THE SOCIALIZING FUNCTIONS OF PRINT IN THE
STAGE OF INNER-DIRECTION

When societies enter the phase of transitional growth of population, formal schooling increases, in part to train people for the new, more specialized tasks of industry and agriculture, in part to absorb the young who are no longer needed on farms and whose schooling can be supported by the greater productivity of the society. Of course, these young people learn to read. But the excitement and novelty of literacy in this period affect old as well as young. There is a hunger for the press and for books—a hunger that the technology and distributive facilities of the phase arouse but do not entirely satisfy. This excitement, this hunger, is a sign of the characterological revolution which is accompanying the industrial one.

In the United States, as in other countries of incipient population decline, this hunger has abated; indeed, it has been succeeded for many by a kind of satiety with serious print, coupled with insatiability for the amusements and agenda of popular culture. To remind ourselves of the older pattern we need only look at countries such as Mexico and Russia, now undergoing industrialization, where the old are avid for print and the young admired for learning. Some of this we can still see among the largely self-educated Negroes of the deep South who live among our surviving stratum of white and black illiterates.

How this development aided the shift from tradition-direction to inner-direction can be vividly traced in Thomas and Znaniecki's *Polish Peasant*.[3] These writers describe the way in which the Polish rural press helped to restructure attitudes and values among the peasantry at the turn of the last century. They show that an individual peasant who learned to read at that time did not merely acquire a skill with little impact on his character; rather he made a decisive break with the primary group, with tradition-direction. The press picked him up at this turning point and supported his uncertain steps away from the primary group by criticizing the values of that group and by giving him a sense of having allies, albeit anonymous ones, in this move.

In this way the press helped link the newly individuated person to the newly forming society. The Polish press also supported very specific "character-building" measures, such as temperance and thrift, and fostered scientific farming as the American agricultural extension services have done; science was viewed as a kind of inner-directed morality as against the superstition of the remaining, tradition-directed peasantry. These attitudes, expounded in newspaper nonfiction, were reinforced in newspaper and periodical "edifying" fiction.

In these ways the local reader could escape into print from the criticisms of his neighbors and could test his inner-direction against the models given in the press. And by writing for the press himself, as he occasionally might do as local correspondent, he could bring his performance up for approval before an audience which believed in the magic attached to print itself—much like the Americans who, in the last century, contributed local poetry to their local press. By this public performance, no longer for a face-to-face audience, he confirmed himself on his inner-directed course.

THE WHIP OF THE WORD

These themes from the *Polish Peasant* might make it appear that literacy and the mass media are the tools of a well-understood shift toward well-understood changes in goal. But the conditions under

---

3. W. I. Thomas and Florian Znaniecki, *The Polish Peasant in Europe and America* (New York, Knopf, 1927), II, 1367–1396.

which print is added to word of mouth and picture as a means of transmitting and mass-transmitting a message are seldom simple. The very existence of print opens up the writer-reader relation to a wider range of goals, even of exploitations. Literacy is indeed a somewhat ambiguous blessing in the early capitalistic period of western history. The tradition-directed person has not only a traditional standard of living but a traditional standard of how hard and long he works; and print serves, along with other agencies of socialization, to destroy both of these standards. The inner-directed man, open to "reason" via print, often develops a character structure which drives him to work longer hours and to live on lower budgets of leisure and laxity than would have been deemed possible before. He can be driven because he is ready to drive himself.

The skeptic may ask how can words, especially printed words, mold character? We might ask him in turn whether he has ever been frightened reading a detective story or excited reading a love story. Words not only affect us temporarily; they change us, they socialize or unsocialize us. Doubtless the printing press alone cannot completely assure any particular form of social coercion—and of course not all children, even in the inner-directed middle class, were readers. But print can powerfully rationalize the models which tell people what they ought to be like. Reaching children directly as well as through their parents and teachers, it can take the process of socialization out of the communal chimney corner of the era depending on tradition-direction and penetrate into the private bedrooms and libraries of the rising middle class: the child is allowed to gird himself for the battle of life in the small circle of light cast by his reading lamp or candle.

To understand this more fully we must realize that the rise of literacy affects not only the content and style of the literary and journalistic genres but also their audience reception. The increased quantitative flow of content brings about an enormous increase in the selectivity of each child, as compared with the era of tradition-direction. With widely increased literacy and extensive print distribution, more and more people begin to read messages not meant for them. And they read them in situations no longer controlled and structured by the teller—or by their own participation. This increase in the number, variety, and "scatter" of the messages, along with the general impersonalization in print which induces these specific effects, becomes one of the powerful factors in social change. The classic instance in western history, of course, is the translation of the Vulgate Bible into the spoken languages, a translation which allowed the people to read a book which only the priests could read before. This shift, repeated in secular form since the days of Erasmus, marks a decisive change in the sociology of audiences.

Some of the genuine difficulties of discussing the shift from the era depending on tradition-direction to that of inner-direction arise from the teleological drift of the language we are likely to use. For example, we are prone to overlook the unintended audience because it is always easier to assume that a given medium was deliberately aimed at the audience it actually succeeded in reaching—and vice versa. Yet there is no proof that the media have ever been so accurate in aim. Indeed, there are reasons for thinking that, in a period dependent on inner-direction, wide misses are possible. The very impersonality of the situation in which print is absorbed helps to increase the chances of underreception or overreception in many of its listeners. Thus the aristocrats were often displeased by what they considered the overreception of mobility strivings in many they would have liked to keep "in their place."

The receptive overeffects I have most in mind, however, are those in individuals whose characterological guilts and tensions were increased by the pressure of print. Their character structure simply could not handle the demand put upon it in a society depending on inner-direction. Their gyroscopes spun wildly and erratically. Not finding justification in print—not finding, as many modern readers do, a "union of sinners," the "One Big Union" of mankind extending back through the past—they experienced print simply as an intensified proof of their maladjustment. The printed sermons of a Colonial divine could cast his readers into hell-fire through print alone—as if every day were Sunday.

Thus, while the myths and symbolism of the societies depending on tradition-direction support the tradition by integrating the rebellious tendencies of the listener into a pattern of the culture, the word-in-print may disorient as well as orient its audience. This is evident in the cry for censorship which goes up as soon as literacy becomes widespread. And not only formal censorship. In America the increasing piety of print, if we compare, for instance, today's press with that of the early republic, may be in part explained by the sheer weight of the informal pressure put on "responsible" editors by near-universal literacy. As the editor of a metropolitan paper used to say if his staff verged on bawdry: "Don't forget, gentlemen, that this paper goes into the *homes*." Or as the *New York Times* puts it: "All the news that's fit to print."

While it is beyond our ability to measure precisely to what degree the media of the early capitalist period might have been "dysfunctional," [4] by reaching unintended audiences in unintended ways, we can be sure that print simply contains more noise along its channels than does oral, face-to-face transmission.

This general relation between teller and reader becomes a special case in situations in which the child is the reader. By teaching children to read, a gain is made in the efficiency of the socialization process. The supervising adult cannot be present all the time; but when he is not there, or is unimpressive, the written words and their accompanying illustration speak for him. The child, no longer a listener at the adult's knee, begins to take a more active part in the process of forming his own character by his selection among possible readings and possible interpretations of what is read. In his choice among socializing agencies in the mass communications field, he is soon engaged in inner-directed activity. While in one respect he is socialized from outside, in another he calculates his social possibilities himself as he reads. He begins to make more use of the increase in the number of possible relationships between himself and the storytellers following the change from word of mouth to print.

MODELS IN PRINT

With this image of the print-influenced child in mind, we can turn to examine the homiletic themes which, in the period dependent on inner-direction, unite the otherwise disparate media of the Protestant and Catholic lands. One main purpose of print is to teach the child something about the variety of adult roles he may enter upon and to permit him to "try on" these roles in fantasy. Life during the period of transitional population growth differs from earlier epochs in that the adult engages in activities which the growing child no longer sees

---

4. The term is that of Lazarsfeld and Merton, "Mass Communication, Popular Taste and Organized Social Action," *The Communication of Ideas*, ed. Lyman Bryson (New York, Harper, 1948), p. 95, and especially pp. 105 *et seq.*

nor understands. This is why he needs not only the rich vicariousness of print but also a mode of internal direction other than tradition to guide him in unaccustomed places and situations. Both the printed media and other forms of popular culture meet this need by adding their own spurs to the parents' admonitions on behalf of ambition as well as by offering more specific guidance about the variety of new paths to success.

These new paths, in both northern and southern lands after the Renaissance, are conceived and described in adult terms. For in the earlier stages of population growth adult life is not long, on the average; the age difference—and perhaps the difference in maturity—between the literate child and the full-grown adult is less than in the period of incipient decline of population. Moreover, while the distribution of imagery and print becomes wider and cheaper than ever before, there are still many people excluded by poverty from the storyteller's market; some of these are also the overworked young. In such a society the adult stories and adult styles of narrative are often made to do for children. Even when the trick, later so prevalent, of using the child's own language, gets started, the storyteller works on the notion that he can more successfully instill *adult* ideas if he uses the language of children.

Among the earliest signposts erected on the printed path to success, aside from the indirect guides of catechism and religious teaching, were the great authorities on etiquette. A volume like Castiglione's *The Courtier,* for example, was meant for adults; but there was nothing else on the subject for the near-adult to read. At the same time people were willing to assume, as Lord Chesterfield did, that the young man was ready in his teens to operate successfully in situations requiring etiquette. In the Protestant lands and classes however, after 1600 or so, the purpose of print is concerned more and more directly with how to succeed not in love or war but in business. Then follows the commercial inspirational literature that reached a sort of climax in Victorian England with the success biographies written by Samuel Smiles—and in the United States with the Horatio Alger books, which come closer to being slanted for the teen-age market.

The variety of such books is great, but it is not unfair to refer their pattern to such an exemplar as Franklin's *Poor Richard's Almanack.* It is the more useful to us because it happens to be the text selected by Max Weber as a typical self-inspirational document of the period of the Protestant ethic. The same themes appear in earlier works, such as *Pilgrim's Progress* or *Robinson Crusoe,* which on the surface do not seem to be concerned with proper conduct for would-be enterprisers. Yet in the first we can trace the motive of social election and salvation which can so easily become secularized, while in the second the motive of economic self-sufficiency is expressed in its classical paradigm. Both works aim to fire the ambition and élan, spiritual and adventurous, of inner-directed youth.

Parallel tasks are undertaken, somewhat less openly, by all fictional literature and much art for the expanding bourgeois market. It would seem that great changes have occurred in the style of myth, as contrasted with the preindustrial era dependent on tradition-direction. In the Middle Ages—to take our example of an era dependent on tradition-direction—the individual learns about human nature from accounts no less realistic because couched in symbolic language—whether Christian, classical, or folk. Often, as is well known, they are not in verbal form at all, like the superabundance of messages in the glass and stone of a cathedral. The child is trained to understand—or, better, he is not trained away from understanding—symbolic meanings. As against this, the rising middle class dependent on inner-direction establishes for itself a new style of realism from which any direct use of symbolism is rigorously excluded.

This documentary style is the literary index of an era increasingly dependent on inner-direction. There is leisure in such an era for fiction—but little for fantasy. Defoe may be taken as archetypical. He used a variety of techniques, such as first person narration, elaborate descriptions of food, clothing, and shelter, diary-like accounts of money transactions, and collaborative witnesses, to provide a realistic setting for his wildly adventurous tales. In this respect he is certainly the ancestor of the comic book, which excels in exploiting realism of detail as a distraction to hide improbability of situation. Such handling of literary material is connected in subtle ways with the handling of life experiences generally for the inner-directed middle-class Protestant. For him life is lived in its detailed externals; its symbolic meaning seeks richness of expression in the strenuously concrete.

Gradually, the early naturalism of Defoe gives way, both in England and on the continent, to a specifically psychological handling of the complex interpersonal relations of town life that arise in the era of transitional growth of population when people are pouring into the cities. With the growth of social classes in the modern sense, the novel begins to concern itself with subtle class differences between individuals: rises, falls, and collisions of status are perhaps its prime preoccupation. The child is instructed in an ambiguous social world, into which he will later move, by learning to recognize the subtly individualizing traits that bespeak class position and class morality.[5] Thus fiction as well as almanac and manual provide vocational (and status-oriented avocational) guidance.

To us today many of the individuals in the early Victorian novels, or in American Victorian melodrama like *East Lynne* or *Intolerance* —or even in some of Balzac's novels—appear as stereotypes. To their earliest audiences, however, these studies of personality and class in a society of shifting possibilities—a society of more people, and more people moving around—were perhaps not clichés which hindered understanding but explorations of a confusing world, helping to make sense of that world for the young. One can still attend a modern rural high school production of *Aaron Slick of Punkin Crick* and see to what extent an unsophisticated inner-directed audience will respond to the characterological "realism" of the play in terms of the older stereotypes of class, ambition, and virtue.

Biography also allows children, in a society dependent on inner-direction, to move away from family and into a rationalized world— cooperating in this way with the parental installation of internal, self-piloting processes. Consider, for instance, the George Washington myth. Not only are little boys told in the era of inner-direction that they may grow up to be president but they are given scales by which to measure and discipline themselves for the job during boyhood. If they do not tell lies, if they work hard, and so on—if, that is, they act in their boyhoods as the legendary Washington acted in his—then they may succeed to his adult role. The role, moreover, by its very nature, is a continuing one; somebody is always president; thus its heroes do not have the once-for-all quality of those in the myths and legends of the earlier era. In fantasy the little boy not only identifies with young Washington in the French and Indian wars but also with the adult role of president—either role will take him far from home, socially and geographically.

5. Compare the brilliant discussion by Lionel Trilling in "Art and Fortune," *Partisan Review*, XV (1948), 1271.

What the story of George Washington was for the white child the story of Booker Washington was for the black. The latter's whole effort was to turn the Negro away from dependence on tradition-direction toward dependence on inner-direction. With the role of the freedman as yet undetermined, he placed enormous emphasis on character building to enable the Negro to assume any role once he was established as a middle-class, respectable American. One of his books addressed to Negroes was called *Character Building;* and *The Negro Worker,* a journal published at Tuskegee, with its strong emphasis on thrift, diligence, and manners, is one of the laggard remnants (of course, under violent attack from northern urban Negroes) of a vast literature concerned not with improving "personality" but with improving "character."

THE OVERSTEERED CHILD

There is, however, a danger for the child in such pious biographical portraits of exemplary persons and roles because of the very fact that he can read in isolation, without the intervention either of adults or peers; he can be "oversteered." This is not so much the danger of being driven by one's character so that one is easily exploited by industrialism, but rather the danger of being set on a course one cannot realistically follow. The inner-directed child, trying to shape his character according to the ideals presented in print, does not see these models, any more than he sees his parents, in a state of undress. There is none of the familiarity with the hero, even the gods in the guise of heroes, to be found in the orally mediated myths of the society depending on tradition-direction. Thus, Washington or Cromwell, Garibaldi or Bismarck, Edison or Ford, take on some of the awesomeness of the Calvinist God. The result for many is a dreadful insecurity as to whether they live up to their exalted models. This insecurity not even the parents (when they do not themselves make matters worse by trying to be such models) can easily assuage.

Nevertheless, this unmitigated pressure for inner-directed activity in pursuit of goodness and fame succeeded, as we know, in producing in many cases an "adjusted" person because social conditions rewarded inhibitions and solaced insecurities. In other cases, however, the gap between the demand for inner-direction and the capacity for it became too great and the individual broke down—the revival meeting represents, at one class level, the emotional pressures of such a conflict. While the parents alone, with their demands on all the children, were often responsible for children's emotional collapse, the storytellers tended to reinforce the social pressures even where the adults might have been more lenient.

The discussion has emphasized but cannot, indeed, emphasize too much the significance of putting some of the task of socializing the child onto other than the face-to-face adults. Just as the whipping Kachinas of the Hopi Indians can tailor their punishing or initiatory blows to a particularly sensitive child, so the adults in the era of tradition-direction can see to it that the bite of the story is not too grim for any in the audience. The child in the inner-directed era, however, leaves home both to go to school and to go to books and other mass-media products; and here such mediation is no longer possible.

Moreover, the child in a period of rising literacy is much more likely than his parents to be able to read. Thus, while some children learn from books and plays how to act in a career which will be different from that of their parents—or indeed that it is possible to have such a career—other children, less able to conform in the characterologically prescribed ways, less self-disciplined and systematic, for instance, learn from precisely the same media how lost they are. Perhaps they learn this especially if their parents are lacking in the proper ethos and have not been able to give them the proper early training in inner-direction. But in other cases they may find that print reinforces their feelings of inadequacy vis-à-vis their parents if they are characterological black sheep who are not able to live up to steep demands of the home.

Yet it is my impression that the stream of print is seldom without alleviating tendencies, even in the theocratic regimes. Almost always there is an underground of a more picaresque sort in which the growing boy at least can take some refuge. To be sure, the power of the parents in an era dependent on inner-direction may keep out such literature, as the pastors in puritan countries might also keep it out of the community. But they can hardly destroy, even in the worst case, the refuge of print itself—and we must not forget that the great reading-hour storehouse of the era depending on inner-direction is the Bible and that the Bible is not one book but many, with an inexhaustible variety of messages.

On the whole, therefore, the influence of the storytellers in the era of inner-direction is probably a liberating one. Print encourages and permits the child to free himself from his family and primary group; and he learns to criticize what he leaves behind, as did the self-emancipating readers of the Polish peasant press. It opens up to him a whole range of models—the "five-foot wardrobe" from which he can try on new roles. The Renaissance is itself testimony to this potency of the written word. Individualistic strivings find support as well as oversupport in the variety of paths of life described in print and drama. To be alone with a book is to be alone in a new way.

III. THE MASS MEDIA IN THE STAGE OF OTHER-DIRECTION

I have assumed that the mass media today—radio, movies, records, comics, books, and magazines for children—play a greater role in shaping character than was the case in previous epochs. Certainly these agencies are more centralized and reach more people more of the time than ever before. Yet with the exception of a few careful and imaginative audience studies, especially by Herta Herzog, T. W. Adorno, Fiske and Wolfe, Lazarsfeld, Merton, and Berelson at the Institute of Social Research and Columbia's Bureau of Applied Social Research, and by Lloyd Warner and William E. Henry at the University of Chicago, we know very little about the audience. It is particularly difficult to study the effects of nonverbal communication such as popular music or the drawings in the comics perhaps because we researchers have lost the easy sense for symbolic meanings with which I credit tradition-directed folk. Moreover, the sheer mass of the mass media is depressing to a student. Indeed, this would seem to be a field in which the techniques of Mass-Observation, an English organization of nonprofessional social scientists who observe and report on the social and cultural life of their vicinity, might promise results. Meanwhile I set forth armed with what sample soundings I have been able to gather from among isolated Mass-Observers like myself.[6] As in the earlier sections of this chapter, the problem is to see how the situation in which the transmission of the story takes place affects the listener (or reader) and how this situation in turn alters the content of the media. And here, also, the very structure of the critical language

6. Including the work of such critics of popular culture as Otis Ferguson, Dwight Macdonald, James Agee, Clement Greenberg, Carl Withers, Bernard Wolfe, David Bazelon, George Orwell, Robert Gorham Davis, Irving Howe, Charles A. Siepmann, and Daniel Bell.

employed forces on the discussion certain overcrude distinctions between situation and content, form and content, response and significance.

THE CHILD MARKET

As we have already seen, in the era of incipient decline of population children begin their training as consumers at an increasingly
young age. In America middle-class children have allowances of their
own at four or five; they have, as opinion leaders in the home, some
say in the family budget. The allowances are expected to be spent,
whereas in the earlier era they were often used as cudgels of thrift.
Moreover, the monopolistic competition characteristic of this era can
afford, and is interested in, building up in the child habits of consumption he will employ as an adult. For he will live long, and so
will the monopoly. Monopoly is, in fact, distinguished by this very
ability to plan ahead, by providing both specialists who do the planning and resources saved from profits which can pay for the planning
and its later implementation. When I was in college we sold a full-
page ad in a crew-race program to the American Tobacco Company.
I figured that only if almost everyone who saw the program smoked
Luckies for the rest of their lives could the company recoup the cost
of the ad. But of course the company was interested in opinion leadership among the young or near-young, and so was willing to pay for
its message in so fugitive and specialized a medium.

For all these reasons, then, it has become worth while for professional storytellers to concentrate on the child market; and by the same
token the controllers of the mass media can afford specialists and
market research on the particular age cultures and class cultures involved. The children are more heavily cultivated in their own terms
than ever before. But while the educator in earlier eras might use the
child's language to put across an adult message, today the child's language may be used to put across the advertiser's and storyteller's idea
of what children are like. No longer is it thought to be the child's job
to learn the adult world as the adult sees it; for one thing, the world
as the adult sees it today is perhaps a more complicated one.[7] Instead,
the mass media ask the child to see the world as "the" child—that is,

7. Certainly the adult literature is more complicated and/or more salacious on its top
levels, as compared with the earlier era when both child and adult could read Mark Twain

the *other* child—sees it. This is partly, but only partly, the result of the technical advances that make it possible for the movies to create the child world of Margaret O'Brien and her compeers, for the radio to have its array of Hardys, Aldriches, and other juveniles, and for advertising and cover art to make use of professional child models. The media have created a picture of what boyhood and girlhood are like (as during the war they created the picture of the GI, again using the considerably edited language of the soldier) and they force children either to accept or aggressively to resist this picture of themselves.

The child begins to be bombarded by radio and comics from the moment he can listen and just barely read. The bombardment—with of course inevitable over- and undershots—hits specifically at very narrow age grades. For example, there seems to be for many children a regular gradation of comic-reading stages: from the animal stories like *Bugs Bunny* to invincible heroes like *Superman,* and from there to heroes like *Batman* who, human in make-up, are vulnerable, though of course they always win. The authors of "The Children Talk About Comics" find that the children themselves are aware of the progression, aware of those laggards who still read romper media when they should have graduated to blue jeans. Correspondingly, self-manipulation begins early, as we saw when we spoke earlier about the children's radio program on which the youngsters showed awareness of the dialogue on the comics carried on among parents and in the press.

To be sure, the change from the preceding era of inner-direction in America is not abrupt; such changes never are. Formerly the mass media catered to the child market in at least three fields: school texts or homilies, magazines designed for children, and penny dreadfuls. But their appraisal of the market was amateurish in comparison with market research today. Moreover, they aimed generally to spur work drives and role experiments in the mobile, rather than to effect any socialization of taste. The English boys' weeklies, as Orwell describes them,[8] usually opposed liquor and tobacco—as did the clergyman authors of school and church readers. Such admonitions remind us of the "crime doesn't pay" lesson of the comics, a façade for messages of

---

even at his most bitter, Dickens even at his most crude, H. G. Wells even at his most involved.

8. George Orwell, *Dickens, Dali & Others* (New York, Reynal & Hitchcock, 1946), p. 76.

more importance. The boys' weeklies and their American counterparts were involved with training the young for the frontiers of production (including warfare), and as an incident of that training the
embryo athlete might eschew smoke and drink. The comparable
media today train the young for the frontiers of consumption—to tell
the difference between Pepsi-Cola and Coca-Cola, as later between
Old Golds and Chesterfields.

We may mark the change by citing an old nursery rhyme:

> "This little pig went to market;
> This little pig stayed at home.
> This little pig had roast beef;
> This little pig had none.
> This little pig went wee-wee-wee
> All the way home."

The rhyme may be taken as a paradigm of individuation and unsocialized behavior among children of an earlier era. Today, however,
all little pigs go to market; none stay home; all have roast beef, if any
do; and all say "we-we."

WINNER TAKE ALL?

Yet perhaps the most important change is the shift in the situation
in which listening and reading occur. In contrast with the lone
reader of the era of inner-direction, we have the group of kids today,
lying on the bed or floor, reading and trading comics and preferences
among comics, or listening jointly to "The Lone Ranger." When
reading and listening are not communal in fact, they are apt to be so
in feeling: one is always conscious of the brooding omnipresence of
the peer-group. Thus the Superman fan quoted at the head of the
chapter cannot allow herself to identify with Superman—the others
would think her foolish—while they would not think her foolish for
believing that flying is very important.

In a society dependent on tradition-direction children are, as we
have seen, introduced to stories by adult storytellers. The latter do not
feel themselves to be in critical competition with the young. Hence
they can encourage, or at least patronize, children's unsophisticated
reactions of alarm or excitement at the tales they are told—and, later
on, encourage the youngster's own tall talk and tale embroidery. But

the peer-groupers who read or listen together without the protective presence of adults are in no such cozy relation of "listen my children and you shall hear . . ." They cannot afford to let go—to fly.

One correlate is that the comic book differs from the fairy tale in several important respects. In the fairy tale the protagonist is frequently an underdog figure, a younger child, an ugly duckling, a commoner, while the villain is frequently an authority figure, a king, a giant, a stepmother. In the comics the protagonist is apt to be an invulnerable or near-invulnerable adult who is equipped, if not with supernatural powers, at least with two guns and a tall, terrific physique. Magical aid comes to the underdog—who remains a peripheral character—only through the mediation of this figure. Thus, whereas Jack of *Jack and the Beanstalk* gains magical assistance chiefly through his own daring, curiosity, and luck, a comic-book Jack would gain magical assistance chiefly through an all-powerful helper. While vaguely similar themes may be found in the stories of Robin Hood and Sir Galahad, the comics show a quantitative increase in the role of the more or less invulnerable authority-hero.

The relative change in this pattern [9] is not the "fault" of the comics. These merely play into a style of reception that is fitted to peer-group reading. Indeed—and this is both the conclusion of "The Children Talk About Comics" and of my own observations—if other-directed child comic fans read or hear stories that are not comics they will read them as if they were comics. They will tend to focus on who won and to miss the internal complexities of the tale, of a moral sort or otherwise. If one asks them, then, how they distinguish the "good guys" from the "bad guys" in the mass media, it usually boils down to the fact that the former always win; they are good guys by definition.

But of course the child wants to anticipate the result and so looks for external clues which will help him pick the winner. In the comics this is no problem: the good guys *look it,* being square-jawed, clear-eyed, tall men; the bad guys also look it, being, for reasons of piety, of no recognizable ethnic group but rather of a generally messy southern European frame—oafish and unshaven or cadaverous and over-

9. Here, too, the abruptness of the change from inner-direction should not be exaggerated. Eliot Freidson, a graduate student in sociology at the University of Chicago, studying the ability of young children to remember stories, found them much more apt to recall a few traditional fairy tales like *Goldilocks* or *The Three Little Pigs* than either Golden Books or comics or movies. "Myth and the Child: an Aspect of Socialization" (Master's thesis, University of Chicago, 1949).

smooth. But in movies (and in some comics with slinky beauties in them) this identification is not easy: the very types that are good guys in most comics may turn out to be villains after all. A striking example I have observed is the bafflement of several comic fans at the movie portrayal of the Countess de Winter (Lana Turner) in *The Three Musketeers*. If she looked so nice, how could she be so mean?

Thus we come to a paradox. The other-directed child is trained to be sensitive to interpersonal relations, and often he understands these with a sophistication few adults had in the era of inner-direction. Yet he is strikingly insensitive to problems of character as presented by his favorite storytellers; he tends to race through the story for its ending, or to read the ending first, and to miss just those problems of personal development that are not telltale clues to the outcome. It looks as though the situation of group reading, of having to sit on the jury that passes out Hooper ratings, forces the pace for the other-directed child. He cannot afford to linger on "irrelevant" detail or to daydream about the heroes. To trade preferences in reading and listening he need know no more about the heroes than the stamp trader needs to know about the countries the stamps come from.

It is not, therefore, the storytellers per se who teach children an emphasis on who wins—an emphasis also found in fairy tales and the Frank Merriwell books. The dime novels and melodramas of the period dependent on inner-direction also emphasized winning; hence it is important to see the precise differences introduced by the contemporary media as well as by the changed focus of the readers.

At the outset it seems helpful to distinguish between the inculcation of ambition and of antagonistic cooperation. "Ambition" I define as an indoctrination of goals in the period of inner-direction; it is a striving for fame or for goodness but always for clear goals: to get the job, to win the battle, to build the bridge. Competition in the era depending on inner-direction is frequently ruthless, but at the same time people are in no doubt as to their place in the race—and that there is a race. If they feel guilt it is when they fail, not when they succeed. By contrast, "antagonistic cooperation" may be defined as an inculcated striving among the groups affected by other-direction. Here the important thing is not the goal but the relationship to the "others"; not one's own victory but the others' failure. In this new-style competition people are often in doubt whether there is a race at all, and if so, what its goals are. Since they are supposed to be cooperative rather than rivalrous, they may well feel guilt about success.[10]

The heroes of boys' literature of the older period were ambitious. They had goals. And the reader identified with them and tried to emulate them, at least in fantasy. Though these heroes might fight Indians or swim icy rivers or detect crime, they were not so remote from the reader as to make identification difficult. These heroes, like the modern ones, always won; but the reader was encouraged to be concerned not only with the final victorious outcome but with the inner struggles that preceded it and made it possible. The virtue which brought victory was frequently an ability to control the self, for instance, to be brave.

While it is often assumed that the comic strip simply continues this older pattern, this is not generally true. For many reasons the child reader does not identify himself with the comic-strip hero so frequently. For one thing, many children prefer the comics where the hero is not man but Superman or Plastic Man—possessing powers that are obviously unique. No correspondence course with Lionel Strongfort will turn one, even in the wildest flight of fantasy, into Superman. What is more important, the realism of petty detail which has reached a fine art in the comics, the radio, and the movies inhibits identification. This realism, with its color effects and sound effects, exceeds by far what Defoe and his direct successors could accomplish. The characters in much fiction of the era dependent on inner-direction are props—stereotypes of the sort indicated in the preceding section. In Jules Verne, for instance, it is the adventures, the mechanical details, not the characters, that are sharply delineated; the latter are loose-fitting uniforms into which many boys could fit themselves. The imaginative, tenebrous illustrations of an artist like Howard Pyle also left openings for identification by the reader who wanted to picture himself as the hero.

Little of this looseness of fit remains for the imagination of the modern reader or listener to fill in. Though comic-strip and comic-book characterization is, if anything, less sharp, externals are pinned down conclusively: every detail of costuming and speech is given. This is the more necessary because, with so many mass-media heroes competing for attention, their portrayers must engage in marginal

10. Cf. Karen Horney, *The Neurotic Personality of Our Time* (New York, W. W. Norton, 1937), pp. 192–193.

differentiation in search of their trade-mark. Bodies by Milton Caniff must be as instantly recognizable as bodies by Fisher.

There is paradox in the reception of this realism. On the one hand, every additional brush stroke of the comic-strip artist rules out identifications for millions; the small-breasted girl, for example, may find only disapproval for herself in the comics. On the other hand, the same realism is one source of the fear of being conspicuous in our little Supergirl cited at the chapter head. If she were Superman, she would be instantly recognizable. She would lack the privacy of narcissism permitted the reader of an earlier day who could gloat over the fact that he was M. Vidocq or Sherlock Holmes—only nobody knew it.[11]

These generalizations need not be pushed too far. There are children—at least one has heard of them—who identify with Superman, or, more easily, with Terry or the Saint. Nor is it out of the question to identify, at the same time, on one level of consciousness with the hero and on another level with the person he rescues. And while the heroes of the comics are ageless, having discovered the secret of eternal youth, the growing child can move from one hero to another who better fits his own changing needs and aspirations. These countertendencies are encouraged by the gadgetry—Superman cloaks, box-top items, and so on—that relates children to their radio, movie, and comic-book heroes. But it would be a mistake to assume that each wearer of a Superman cloak identifies with Superman; he may only be a fan, wearing his hero's colors.

Perhaps it is also significant that the comic book compresses into a few minutes' reading time a sequence which, in the earlier era, was dragged out in many pages of print. Think of the Count of Monte Cristo's years in jail, his suffering, his incredible patience, and the industry and study of the abbé's teaching; both his gain and his vengeance are moralized by these prolongations, and he is an old man

11. One additional dimension here is that the child literature of today, though written by specialists on the child market, often reaches, as in the case of the comics, millions or more or less childish adults. There are no magazines left, such as *The American Boy* or *St. Nicholas,* which the young boy can read without sharing his readership with adults—for which he can even write, occasionally, as we are reminded by Henry Steele Commager's fine *St. Nicholas Anthology.* (A similar lack of sharp cleavage between child and adult life may be seen in the fact that it is no longer a decisive step for a boy to put on long pants or for a girl to put up her hair. With clothes as with books, when and in what doses to "put away childish things" becomes a matter for the peer-group to decide, within the limits of marginal differentiation.)

when, after many chapters, he wins. By contrast, the comic-book or radio-drama hero wins almost effortlessly; the very curtailment of the telling time itself makes this more apparent. To be sure, like his movie counterpart, this hero does frequently get beaten up, but this adds to excitement, not to morality or inner change, and helps justify an even worse beating administered to the "crooks."

Still another aspect of this change is worth looking at. If one does not identify with the winner but is at the very same time preoccupied with the process of winning itself, as the very handle by which one grasps a story, one is prepared for the role of consumer of others' winnings. One is prepared, that is, for the adult role of betting on the right horse, with no interest in the jockey or horse or knowledge of what it takes to be either. The content of the identification is impoverished to the point where virtually the only bond between reader and hero is the fact of the hero's winning. The spectator—the same holds for a quiz game, a sport contest, and, as we shall see, a political contest—wants to become involved with the winner simply in order to make the contest meaningful: this hope of victory makes the event exciting, while the game or contest or story is not appreciated for its own sake.

The victory of the hero, then, is only ostensibly a moral one. To be sure, vestiges of older moralities hang on, often as conventions enforced by censorship or the fear of it. But morality in the sense of a literary character's development, rather than morality in the sense of being on the "right" side, is not depicted. Consequently, morality is an inference from winning. Just as in a whodunit all appear guilty until they are retroactively cleared by finding the real killer, so the victory of the hero retroactively justifies his deeds and misdeeds. "Winner take all" becomes a tautology.

TOOTLE: A MODERN CAUTIONARY TALE

I have spoken as if the comic books, the cheapest and most widespread media, are the chief evidences of the pattern I am describing. It could be easily assumed that, in a home barricaded against the comic books, these patterns of readership would obtain no entrance. On the contrary, however, at least some of the important elements in the pattern are refined, disguised, and introduced into the socializing and informative books of the noncomic variety which are customarily purchased for their children by the middle and upper middle class.

Furthermore, a whole range of these media teaches children the lesson given parents and teachers in many recent works on child development. The slant of that lesson is suggested by a passage from a book in use by teachers and PTA groups:

The usual and desirable developmental picture is one of increasing self-control on the part of the individual children, of increasingly smooth social or play technics, and of an emergence at adolescence or early adulthood of higher forms of cooperation. The adolescent should have learned better "to take it" in group activity, should have developed an improved, though not yet perfect, self-control, and should have real insight into the needs and wishes of others.[12]

Tootle the Engine (text by Gertrude Crampton, pictures by Tibor Gergely) is a popular and in many ways charming volume in the "Little Golden Books" series—a series for children with a circulation of well over two million, an audience which includes, it seems, all classes of children. It is a cautionary tale even though it appears to be simply one of the many books about anthropomorphic vehicles— trucks, fire engines, taxicabs, tugboats, and so on—that are supposed to give a child a picture of real life. Tootle is a young engine who goes to engine school, where two main lessons are taught: stop at a red flag and "always stay on the track no matter what." Diligence in the lessons will result in the young engine's growing up to be a big streamliner. Tootle is obedient for a while and then one day discovers the delight of going off the tracks and finding flowers in the field. This violation of the rules cannot, however, be kept secret; there are telltale traces in the cowcatcher. Nevertheless, Tootle's play becomes more and more of a craving, and despite warnings he continues to go off the tracks and wander in the field. Finally the engine schoolmaster is desperate. He consults the mayor of the little town of Engineville, in which the school is located, the mayor calls a town meeting, and Tootle's failings are discussed—of course Tootle knows nothing of this. The meeting decides on a course of action, and the next time Tootle goes out for a spin alone and goes off the track he runs right into a red flag and halts. He turns in another direction only to encounter another red flag; still another—the result is the same. He turns and twists but can find no spot of grass in which a red flag does

---

12. M. E. Breckenridge and E. L. Vincent, *Child Development* (Philadelphia, W. B Saunders, 1943), p. 456.

not spring up, for all the citizens of the town have cooperated in this lesson.

Chastened and bewildered he looks toward the track, where the inviting green flag of his teacher gives him the signal to return. Confused by conditioned reflexes to stop signs, he is only too glad to use the track and tears happily up and down. He promises that he will never leave the track again, and he returns to the roundhouse to be rewarded by the cheers of the teachers and the citizenry and the assurance that he will indeed grow up to be a streamliner.

The story is an appropriate one for bringing up children in an other-directed mode of conformity. They learn it is bad to go off the tracks and play with flowers and that, in the long run, there is not only success and approval but even freedom to be found in following the green lights. The moral is a very different one from that of *Little Red Riding Hood*. She, too, gets off the track on her trip to the grandmother; she is taught by a wolf about the beauties of nature—a hardly veiled symbol for sex. Then, to be sure, she is eaten—a terrifying fate —but the tables are eventually turned, and she and grandmother both are taken from the wolf's belly by the handsome woodchopper. The story, though it may be read as a cautionary tale, deals with real human passions, sexual and aggressive; it certainly does not present the rewards of virtue in any unambiguous form or show the adult world in any wholly benevolent light. It is, therefore, essentially realistic, underneath the cover of fantasy, or, more accurately, owing to the *quality* of the fantasy.

There is, perhaps, a streak of similar realism in *Tootle*. There the adults play the role we have described earlier: they manipulate the child into conformity with the peer-group and then reward him for the behavior for which they have already set the stage. Moreover, the citizens of Engineville are tolerant of Tootle: they understand and do not get indignant. And while they gang up on him with red flags they do so for his benefit, and they reward him for his obedience as if they had played no hand in bringing it about. The whole story, in fact, might have been written by a student of learning theory, so palpably does it deal in terms of conditioned responses.

Yet with all that, there is something overvarnished in this tale. The adult world (the teachers) is *not* that benevolent, the citizenry (the peer-group) *not* that participative and cooperative, the signals are *not* that clear, nor the rewards of being a streamliner that great or that certain. Nevertheless, the child may be impressed because it is all so nice—there is none of the grimness of Red Riding Hood. There is, therefore, a swindle about the whole thing—a fake like that the citizens put on for Tootle's benefit. At the end Tootle has forgotten that he ever did like flowers anyway—how childish they are in comparison with the great big grown-up world of engines, signals, tracks, and meetings!

While the antagonistic and rebellious elements may be veiled in a folk tale, the children who read *Tootle* or have it read to them are manipulated away from rebellion and taught the lesson of obedience to signals. Strikingly enough, moreover, the story also bears on the presumptive topic of peer-group cooperation: the exercise of consumption preferences. Those middle-class children who read the tale are not going to grow up to be railroad engineers; that is a craft followed by more inner-directed types from the working class. But while neither *Tootle* nor its readers are concerned about what it really means to be an engineer, the book does confirm one of the consumption preferences of the other-directed: big streamliners—if one cannot go by plane—are better than old coal-burning engines.[13] To be sure, *Tootle* has something to teach about train lore. It indicates that there are tracks, signals, roundhouses, just as fairy tales indicate that there are forests, woodchoppers, wolves. On the whole, however, children are attuned to the magic of travel, of communications, not in an adventurous way but in what educators are pleased to call a "realistic" one.

More impalpably, the humanized grimacing engines in *Tootle* symbolize the effort characteristic of the society depending on otherdirection to cover over the impersonal mechanisms of production and transport with a personalized veneer—what we shall later discuss under the heading of false personalization. For in the phase of incipient population decline there is sufficient abundance not only for the luxuriant growth of service trades per se but for allowing even the nonservice trades to deliver "service with a smile." Today the conductors (like engineers, inner-directed types in origin) on Vanderbilt'

13. This preference is so strong that it influences directorates of railroads in coal-mining territory, concerned not only with public relations but with their own feeling for their roa A fine study could be made of railroad management's belated conversion to glamour, an the influence on this of the development of a new generation of consumers—more eag to be told that their conveyance is up to date than to be comfortable—or, more accuratel eager to be *told* they are comfortable.

old railroad are trained on the Twentieth Century Limited and other major runs to remember faces and give service "especially for you." The very books such as *Tootle,* or *Scuffy the Tugboat,* by the same writer and illustrator, that are intended to acquaint children with the objects and forces of the industrial society turn out to condition them to their role in the consumers' union.

We return, finally, to the theme of winning dealt with in the preceding section. Tootle does, after all, win; with his winning ways he will grow up to be a big streamliner. The reader's identification with the consumption of others' winnings is, therefore, not betrayed. But it is not made clear in the story what happens to Tootle's schoolmates in engine school: do they *all* grow up to be streamliners, too? The peer-group relations of Tootle, either to the other engines or the other citizens of Engineville, are entirely amiable, and Tootle's winning does not mean that others fail. It is akin to the "benevolent conspiracy" of progressive parents and teachers who see to it that every child is a leader and that no one is left out, or conspicuous, thus reinforcing the tendencies toward antagonistic cooperation of the peer-group itself. Who can be sure that Tootle would want to be a streamliner if others were not to be streamliners too?

AREAS OF FREEDOM

We have discussed the social situation in which the mass media of today are absorbed by their child readers. We have seen the effects of this situation on the process by which the reader identifies with the protagonists and their roles. We have stressed especially the ambiguously competitive nature of these identifications which on the one hand emphasize winning and on the other hand stringently limit all emotional identifications by the code of the peer-group.

If this were all, we would have to conclude that the peer-group, as one of the mediating agencies in child readership and listening, is simply open to manipulation by the professional storytellers. But I want to raise very briefly the alternative possibility: namely, that the peer-group may have a relatively independent set of criteria which helps it maintain not only marginal differentiation but even a certain leeway in relation to the media. Put the question this way: while the self-confirming process of the peer-group pushes preference exchange to the point of parody, has the peer-group any way of reminding its captives that they are, also, individuals? It is conceivable that, in those peer-groups which succeed in feeding back styles and values to the mass media, there is some feeling of achievement, of having one's contribution recognized. To be sure, the feeling of having been invaded and chased by popularity or unpopularity off one's island of individuation will also be present, and the total outcome may depend on whether the peer-group feels the mass media to be in pursuit of it or whether the group enjoys playing follow the leader, when it is the leader.

In all probability it is rare enough that a youthful peer-group forces the mass media—and hence other peer-groups—to follow its lead. Far more frequent will be the peer-group's opportunity to establish its own standards of media criticism. Groups of young hot-jazz fans, for instance, have highly elaborate standards for evaluating popular music, standards of almost pedantic precision. We must go further, then, and ask whether there may be areas of privacy which children learn to find inside a superficial adjustment to the peer-group and under the cover of a superficial permeability to the mass media. In other words, we must re-explore the assumption made so far that the other-directed child is almost never alone, that by six or seven he no longer talks to himself, invents songs, or dreams unsupervised dreams.

We are aware that children who have been brought up on the radio can shut out its noise like those automatic devices that can be installed to silence commercials. Perhaps such children can also shut out the noise of the peer-group, even while they are contributing to it. Moreover, the comics themselves may be not only a part of peer-group consumption patterns but on occasion a refuge from the peer-group and a defiance against that official adult world which abhors the comics. We shall return in Part III to the question whether the mass media can foster autonomy as well as adjustment, independence from the peer-group as well as conformity to it. But before we can tackle these more complex problems of the relation between the peers and the media, we need the groundwork of another perspective on changing character types in America. We have just scrutinized some aspects of the way in which types of character are formed at the child wave front of population by such typical agents as parents and teachers, the peer-groups, and the media. In the next few chapters let us jump ahead twenty-odd years or more in the life span and approach the structure of character in terms of the spheres of adult life. We can make use of archetypical portraits of the inner-directed and the other-directed man, his work, his play, and his politics.

V

The Inner-directed Round of Life

In
Memory of
Thomas Darling, Esq.
who died Nov. 30, 1789 ———
A Gentleman of strong mental powers,
well improved with science and literature,
——— to the study of philosophy,
habituated to contemplation and reading
——— in moral reasoning.
of deep penetration and sound judgment,
respected for modesty and candor,
benignity and self command
in his intercourse with mankind
honest and benevolent,
amiable in all the relations of social life
and filled a variety of public offices
with fidelity and dignity
eminent abilities as statesman and judge
an early professor of Christianity
its steady friend, ornament, and defender
with a rational and firm faith in his God
and Savior: he knew no other master.

A gravestone inscription in a New Haven cemetery.

THE OLDEST historical types in America, a few still partially
tradition-directed people such as some of the French Canadians of the northeast, the delta Negroes, and the Mexican
"wetbacks" of Texas, survive from societies and social classes whose
modes of conformity were established in a phase of high population

growth potential. The next oldest type, the inner-directeds, survive from the period of transitional population growth in America and abroad. They are still dominant in many regions and many occupations, even in the cities. They are also probably the most numerous type, if we include among them not only those whose inner-direction is clear and unequivocal but also many working-class people who aspire to be inner-directed but are actually unable to adjust either to inner-directed or to other-directed modes of conformity. Finally, the newest type, the other-directeds, are the product of the changes in the agents of character formation discussed in the three preceding chapters—changes most pronounced in the big cities and among the upper income groups.

In this and the following two chapters we shall explore in more detail the way in which the shift of the American population curve into the phase of incipient decline corresponds to a change in the texture of adult work and play. Other-directed character types are produced not only by influences affecting the parents and other early character-forming agents but also by institutions that shape or reshape the character of adults who grew up in an environment more undilutedly inner-directed. While children are the pioneers of the characterological frontiers of population, it is the adults who, even in a child-centered culture, run the engines, rig the signals, write the books and comics, and play politics and other grown-up games.

An inscription such as the one at the head of this chapter reminds us of one of the ideal types of men who flourished in an era depending on inner-direction. Not all of them, of course, were as good as Mr. Darling is said to have been; we must not equate inner-direction with conscience direction. A scoundrel who knows what he aims for can be as unequivocally inner-directed as a God-fearing puritan. Yet as we turn now to recapture the flavor of an era that is near enough to be thought familiar and not far enough away to be fully understood, it is well to think of a man who knew no other master than his God.

In the first part of this chapter we look at the meaning of work for the inner-directed man of the nineteenth century in America; in the second, we look at the uses he made of leisure. The division is arbitrary because the paths of work and paths of pleasure are not truly separate but deeply intertwined. Moreover, the argument in this and the next two chapters advances in a somewhat dialectic fashion: the inner-directed and other-directed patterns are occasionally stated in their most extreme forms, in order to bring out sharply the contrast between them. Since, however, the problems of the inner-directeds are no longer problems many of us face, the reader as well as the writer must be on guard against a tendency to overidealize inner-direction and to be overcritical of other-direction.

I. MEN AT WORK

THE ECONOMIC PROBLEM: THE HARDNESS OF THE MATERIAL

Our task in this and the following chapter is to compare the meaning of work in the epochs depending on inner-direction and other-direction respectively. The change is one of degree, like most changes. The inner-directed man tends to think of work in terms of non-human objects, including an objectified social organization, while the other-directed man tends to think of work in terms of people— people seen as something more than the sum of their workmanlike skills and qualities. Thus for the inner-directed man production is seen and experienced in terms of technological and intellectual processes rather than in terms of human cooperation. Human relations in industry, as well as relations among industries and between industry and society as a whole, seem to the inner-directed man to be managed by the anonymous cooperation brought about through the "invisible hand"—Adam Smith's wonderful phrase for economic planning through the free market.

Men were of course aware, in the period most heavily dependent on inner-direction, that the achievement of cooperation in the organization of work was not simply automatic. There was much talk of the need for discipline, sobriety, and integrity. Yet it is fair to say that the human mood of the work force was not yet felt to be a major problem. For one thing, labor was still too numerous—it spilled over into the factory from the prolific farms and from countries in the phase of high growth potential. For another thing, labor's work force was disciplined by new values and some kept from tradition-direction; in addition, by evangelistic religion in the advanced industrial countries. The managerial work force, on the other hand, was not felt as a problem either, because the size of the administrative staff was small and because inner-directed types could cooperate with each other on physically and intellectually evident tasks whether or not they liked or approved of each other. Their inner-directed code, rather than their cooperative mood, kept them from constant sabotage.

As a result, even in large and bureaucratized organizations people's attention was focused more on products (whether these were goods, decisions, reports, or discoveries makes little difference) and less on the human element. It was the product itself, moreover, not the use made of it by the consumer, that commanded attention. Despite what Marx called "the fetishism of commodities," the inner-directed man could concern himself with the product without himself being a good consumer: he did not need to look at himself through the customer's eyes. The problem of marketing the product, perhaps even its meaning, receded into the psychological background before the *hardness of the material*—the obduracy of the technical tasks themselves.

The opening frontiers called people to a seeming oversupply of material tasks in industry and trade, geography, and scientific discovery. This is especially clear if we look at the geographical frontier. While the frontiersman cooperated with his sparse neighbors in mutual self-help activities, such as housebuilding or politics, his main preoccupation was with physical, not with human, nature. The American frontiersman, as Tocqueville encountered him in Michigan, was, though hospitable, uninterested in people. He found physical nature problematical enough: to alter and adapt it required that he become hard and self-reliant.

The same thing was true in other fields of enterprise and pioneering. Missionary zeal, with its determination to carry the gospel to such far distant lands as India, China, and the Pacific isles, reflected the nineteenth-century pioneering spirit fully as much or more than it did any religious impulse of "brotherhood." And, too, the missionary and his family frequently—as, for example, in Hawaii—became the nucleus of an American element which was finally to gain economic and financial control. So also were the numerous communistic experiments the product of imaginative individualistic thinking. Likewise, entrepreneurs staked out fields of knowledge and threw themselves with passionate curiosity into discovering the secrets of nature. Though they might be as jealous and competitive as Newton, their contacts with co-workers remained on the whole impersonal; they were in communication with one another through very simple channels of papers and congresses and without much formal organization. Here, too, the invisible hand seemed to rule, and work was felt as a mode of relating oneself to physical objects and to ideas, and only indirectly to people.

It is apparent to us today that, in the economic field at least, the invisible hand was partly a fact, though its historically temporary nature escaped people, and partly a myth.[1] Government did a good deal of planning even after mercantilism waned—planning none the less forceful for being relatively unbureaucratized and none the less systematic for being operated through such time-honored levers as the tariff, the judiciary, and canal and railroad subsidies. Moreover, the impersonality of economic life against which moralists and socialists complained in steady chorus from Sir Thomas More to R. H. Tawney was never quite so great as it seemed. Business was often paternal; as we can see in such a novel as Thomas Mann's *Buddenbrooks,* it relied heavily on values that survived from feudalism. Tradition-directed tones of personalization survived in many situations, despite the ideology and, to some degree, the existence of free competition. These personalizations undoubtedly ameliorated some of the severities and abuses of inner-directed individualism.

Nevertheless, as compared with today, the economy was quite loose jointed and impersonal and perhaps seemed even more impersonal than it actually was. This encouraged the ambitious labors of men who could attend to society's expanding capital plant, to the bottle-necks in the technology of agriculture, extractive industry, and manu-facturing. The capital goods industries were of decisive importance; internally, they were needed to bridge the gap between population and subsistence; externally, they were needed to support war-making and colonization. Indeed, the oversteered men of the period, espe-cially in the regions touched by Puritanism or Jansenism, went far beyond the specifically economic requirements and rewards held out to them. They cut themselves off from family and friends, often from humanity in general, by their assiduity and diligence.

Work, one might add, provided a strategic protection for those who could not live up to all the requirements of the prevailing character ideal. For we have no right to assume that even the successful men of the period were in complete adjustment with the social character im-

1. See Karl Polanyi's excellent discussion in *The Great Transformation* (New York, Farrar & Rinehart, 1944).

posed on them. Many apparently well-adjusted men of an older time in American life must have been aware that their acceptance of inner-direction involved their own efforts to conform—that their conformity was far from automatic.

The linkage between work and property in an era of private competitive capitalism (as compared with the later capitalism described by Berle and Means in *The Modern Corporation and Private Property*) reinforced the possibilities of isolation from people. Property, for the inner-directed man, became freely transferable; the individual was not attached to it as in the earlier era by sentimental and traditional ties, but he attached it to himself by his choices, by his energetic actions. No longer an affair of the extended family, property became an extended part, a kind of exoskeleton, for the individual self.[2]

Yet private property of this sort, though useful as a safeguard and testing ground for the inner-directed man, was probably not alone a sufficient condition for his rise. On the frontiers of the expanding Russian economy of the early five-year plans, there were entrepreneurs very much like European and American types of many decades earlier: ambitious, energetic, self-reliant men engaged in transforming physical nature, instituting large-scale formal organization, and revolutionizing technology. The inner-directed man—sometimes models of him were imported from America and Germany—made his appearance at Dneprostroi, Magnitogorsk, and the Turk-Sib railroad.

Even today we can watch similar types emerging in India among the leaders of industry and government. It looks as if, in any large and differentiated population, reservoirs of potential inner-direction exist, only awaiting the onset of a western-oriented type of industrialization in order to come to the fore.

AD ASTRA PER ASPERA

The ambitious note in the inner-directed person's attitude toward work in the phase of transitional growth of population was expressed in the schoolbook proverb: *ad astra per aspera*. The stars were far away, but still he aimed for them, in terms of a lifetime of effort. He could afford such a long-term commitment because of the generality of the aim: he wanted money or power or fame or some lasting achievement in the arts or the professions. He wanted to leave a repu-

[2] Cf. William James's definition of the Self in *Principles of Psychology* (New York, Henry Holt, 1896), I, 291–292; and discussion in Erich Fromm, *Man for Himself*, pp. 135–136.

tation, a memorial, something as tangible as Mr. Darling's tombstone inscription, still fairly legible after one hundred and fifty years of New England weather.

But there was another, a social, reason why long-term ambition of this sort could be afforded. The beckoning frontier of colonization and industrialization, the beckoning frontier of intellectual discovery, too, required long-term investment. To build a railroad or an Indian civil service or the intellectual system of a Comte, a Clerk Maxwell, or a Marx was not an affair of a few months. Competition was keen. Still, the number of competitors in any single field was small, and if a man was bright and energetic, he could hope that his invention, capital investment, or organizational plan would not be rendered rapidly obsolete by others. For, although the invisible hand of technological and intellectual change moved immeasurably faster than it had done in the still earlier population phase of high growth potential, it moved slowly nonetheless in comparison with today. Change was on the scale of a working lifetime; that is, an individual could hope to keep up with the others, even without paying special notice to them: they were not likely to repeal or revise overnight what he knew or did on his own.

As recently as 1920 an American boy of the middle class was not too worried about the problem of committing himself to a career. If he came of good family he could count on connections; if not, he could count on the credit of his social—that is, his visibly inner-directed—character. He could dream of long-term goals because the mere problem of career entry and survival was not acute; that he might for long be out of a job did not occur to him. He could orient himself, if he chose a profession, by his daydreaming identification with the stars in his field. A young doctor might think of Osler, a young lawyer of Choate or Elihu Root or Theodore Roosevelt, a young scientist of Agassiz or Pasteur, a young painter or writer of Renoir or Tolstoy. To be sure, such identifications were often the sheerest sentimentality.

With the idea that attitudes toward ambition help to differentiate inner-directed and other-directed types in contemporary America, our interviews contain a series of questions on the subject of ambition. There is some evidence that the person who on other counts would be judged inner-directed tends to have one of two attitudes toward ambition. Either he admires it, wants it himself, and drives himself to be noted; or he fears it: he has concluded that it makes him unhappy and he feels guilty about his failure to live up to his high aims.

In general the ambition of the inner-directed person is directed to a long-range goal. Among young men it may take the form of wanting to build a bridge, to run a railroad, to write a great novel, to leave some kind of memorial. When we asked a group of some sixty young people whether they most wanted money, fame, or the respect of their community, the overwhelming majority chose the last. One of the only two who chose fame was a southern boy of eighteen at an eastern prep school who planned to become an architect. Strikingly enough, when he was asked another key question, whether he would like to have been born in some other age, he said he would have preferred the late eighteenth or early nineteenth century. Our impression is, from other data also, that the South selectively exports to the North many of its socially mobile and drivingly ambitious youth.

One of our interviewees remarked on his fear, after stating his ambition, that he "might not be able to make it." There is often tragedy in store for the inner-directed person who may fail to live up to grandiose dreams and who may have to struggle in vain against both the intractability of the material and the limitations of his own powers. He will be held, and hold himself, to his commitment. Satirists from Cervantes on have commented on this disparity between pursuing the stars and stumbling over the mere earthiness of earth.

II. THE SIDE SHOW OF PLEASURE

The sphere of pleasure and consumption is only a side show for inner-directeds. This is truer for men than for women. Some men diminish attention to pleasure to the vanishing point, delegating consumption problems to their wives; these are the good providers. Others turn consumption into work: the work of acquisition. Still others, perhaps the majority, are able to use the sphere of pleasure as an escape from the sphere of work.

This divergence is characteristic of the shift from tradition-direction to inner-direction. The tradition-directed man does not make a choice whether to work or to play or whether to create a private blend of his own; matters are decided for him by tradition. To some degree play is marked off from work, linguistically and by special costuming and ceremonial. To some degree work and play are blended, for instance in handicraft art applied to articles of daily use or in ceremonials that accompany a socially or economically useful activity. The inner-directed man, however, is freed from the direction of tradition and he is consciously and sharply aware of the difference between work and play. At least where theocratic controls are relaxed, he must decide on his own how much time to allot to play. To be sure, not much room is left for leisure in terms of time: hours are long and work is arduous: the tired businessman is invented. Nevertheless, the width of choice is sufficient to create two polar types: those who work at consumption with the passion of acquisition and those who consume as a more or less licit and occasional escape.

THE ACQUISITIVE CONSUMER

In an era depending on inner-direction men who are adequately socialized in the sphere of work—as shown by their productivity—can afford a good deal of independence in their moments spared for consumption. The end result, in the America of the last century, is the crazy millionaire who, having established his status, save in the most exalted circles, by satisfying society's requirements on the productive front, can do as he pleases on the pleasure front. He can hang the "do not disturb" sign over his play as well as over his work. Once risen, he can resist or accept as he chooses the ministrations of wives and daughters and even more specialized advisers on consumption, taste, and connoisseurship.

A period when such men live is, therefore, the heyday of conspicuous consumption, when energies identical with those deployed at work are channeled by the rich into their leisure budget. While the producer dynamically creates new networks of transportation in order to exploit resources and distribute the finished and semifinished product, the consumer of this period begins to act with equal dynamism on the market. The producer pushes; the consumer pulls. The first stage in his consumership is a passionate desire to make things *his*.

Perhaps he lavishes money and energy on a house, to the point where it comes to resemble a department store—recall the wonderful sets and furnishings in the films *Citizen Kane* and *The Ghost Goes West*. Perhaps he gathers the treasures of Europe, including titled sons-in-law. Perhaps he goes in for steam yachts or diamonds or libraries or, united with rich cronies in a civic spirit, for theaters, planetariums, and zoos. In most cases the activity is as self-justifying as the search for the North Pole, pursued with hardly more hesitation or boredom than the tasks of the production frontier.

This process of prolonged acquisition is possible because in the period we are describing by the phrase transitional population growth, consumption products, like work commitments, do not become rapidly obsolete but are good for a lifetime. Moreover, mass production, though it has got under way, is not yet sufficiently luxuriant to provide as staples what were once luxuries for the few. Thus sharp gradients separate steps in the ladder of acquisition of consumption products, just as sharp gradients are the rule in the economic hierarchy of production. These gradients of income and class—connected with a social order more dependent on the sharp steps of etiquette than on the marginalia of taste—are sufficiently decisive to protect the acquisitive consumer from the anxiety that what he buys may become obsolete too rapidly or, worse, change its status significance. Indeed, the conspicuous antiquity, or disregard for obsolescence, of the goods he owns may even be a mark of fashion.

The type of acquisitive consumer who is less concerned with building up a private hoard or hobby and more concerned with showing his possessions off with fashion seems, at first glance, other-directed in his attention. Yet, if we go back to Veblen's classic work, we can see, I think, that the consumers he describes are other-directed in appearance only. The Veblenese conspicuous consumer is seeking to fit into a role demanded of him by his station, or hoped-for station, in life; whereas the other-directed consumer seeks experiences rather than things and yearns to be guided by others rather than to dazzle them with display. The conspicuous consumer possesses a standard allowing him readily to measure what others have, namely cash. This standard can penetrate the opacity of objects, even objects unique in their nature, such as a geographical site (so much a front foot) or a beautiful woman (the best money can buy). This gives the consumption of the inner-directed man its relatively impersonal quality—it is as impersonal as his production, of which it is a residue. Similarly, if he collects old masters, he is taking a standardized step on the consumption gradient for his social class at the same time that he is buying a good investment or at least a good gamble. Moreover, he is, in a way, a "master" himself, a technical man, and he can admire the technique of the Renaissance artist as few other-directed consumers of today, even though they may know a good deal more about art, dare admire the esoteric technique, or seeming lack of it, of a non-representational artist.

The conspicuous consumer is engaged, therefore, in an externalized kind of rivalry, as indicated by Veblen's use of such terms as "ostensible," "emulative," "conspicuous," and the rest of his beautifully ironic thesaurus. The other-directed consumer *may* compete in what looks like the same way, but only to the degree that the peers impel him to. His desire to outshine, as we should expect from his mode of peer-group socialization, is very much muted and is allowed expression only to the degree that popularity depends on success in marginal innovation and differentiation in consumption.

To be sure, all these changes are changes in degree, and Veblen's emphases on leisure and consumption—like, in a very different way, Keynes' emphasis on what we might call relentless spending—are indexes of the social changes paving the way for and accompanying the characterological ones.

AWAY FROM IT ALL

The *acquisitive* consumer brings to the sphere of consumption motivations and ideals similar to those he manifests in the sphere of production. The *escaping* consumer, whom we now consider, seeks, on the contrary, to dramatize an emotional polarity between work and play.

Because the whole concept of escape is a very slippery one, we must always ask: escape from what and to what? The inner-directed individual can afford a certain kind of escape since his character and situation give him a core of sufficient self-reliance to permit dreaming without disintegration. He learns this as a boy when he escapes with himself a good deal of the time—playing hooky from the dreary and demanding tasks of home and school. Unlike Tootle the engine, he is seldom worried by the fear that, if he gathers primroses by the river's brim, he will not make the grade—though he may be punished, since the right to play has not yet been granted school children. Perhaps he will feel guilt when he escapes, but the guilt will lend savor to the adventure, turning escape into escapade. Like the Victorian father, the stability of whose family life often depended on an occasional visit to a prostitute, the inner-directed person can let himself go in "unsocialized" ways because in the ways that count, the ways of work, he has a definitely socialized self to return to.

To be sure, he may often be too inhibited for that. He may be unable to stop timetabling himself by the internalized pocket watch that he has substituted for the chimes of the Middle Ages. He may be unable to shift his one-price, one-role policy even in dealing with status inferiors, though this, in the explicit class structure of the era, is unusual. Above all, he may feel that, with the reining in and observing of the self on all fronts, he cannot afford to undertake unsanctioned experiments in spontaneity. He may feel his character, covert as well as overt, as a kind of capital that might be dissipated in a catastrophic gamble—all the more dangerous in view of the lifetime goals to which he is committed. We see this complex process rationalized by the puritan in terms of "saving himself." The puritan treats himself as if he were a firm and, at the same time, the firm's auditor.

But we speak in this section of those who, despite internal and external inhibitions, are able to "escape" in some fashion. Escape as we use it here means a shift of pace and attitude from the nearly all-embracing domain of work. Thus, as we shall see below, it may be escape onto a "higher" level than that of business or professional life, or onto a "lower" level.

Onward and upward with the arts. The great events of leisure time "escape upward" are intermittent: Chautauqua, the traveling theater, the Sunday service complete with one antibusiness preacher per year or per city, the itinerant book peddler. To come into contact with them requires some effort, and making the effort is itself a sign of virtue. There is even a change of dress—Sunday-go-to-meeting dress or top hats—to signify the change of role.

There is, moreover, a good deal of amateur performance. Consider, for example, the enormously widespread distribution of pianos. Even more perhaps than plumbing, amateur musical skills mark the boundary of middle-class aspirations to respectability. At the same time, for the mobile youth from the working class there are the mechanics institutes and the many traveling lecturers, from prison reformers to single taxers, who analyze the workings of the system for their eager audiences. We need only recall the tremendous mushrooming of discussion clubs that greeted Bellamy's *Looking Backward*.

Obviously the motives of such participants are not purely escapist

There is the desire, often thinly disguised, to move onward and upward in the social hierarchy by becoming cultivated. Through religious revivalism and Bible reading the individual may seek to escape not from this world but from the dangers of the next. Daily life is hard and drab; leisure is an occasional essay at refinement.

Aspirations for culture make people want to escape into an image of some past heroic period, as inherited from the prenineteenth-century upper class. Thus, the cultivated bourgeois of the nineteenth century looks back in his leisure to an earlier and more heroic quasi-bourgeois epoch, in Periclean Athens or Renaissance Italy. Work driven, chained to routines, he pictures for himself the swagger and versatility of a Benvenuto Cellini or a Leonardo. As the Chautauqua circuit spreads accounts of contemporary travel and discovery, so there exists a semipopular culture about the achievements of the ancient world—note the popularity of *Ben Hur*—and of the Renaissance. Very often the occupational hardness of the era has its obverse side in leisure sentimentality.

Though fashion, of course, plays a role in the vogue of ancient history, of European travel, and of these other escapist pursuits, it is important, I think, for the security of the inner-directed people that these spheres of interest are remote not only from their work but also from their immediate social concerns. Reading about Greece—even visiting Florence—they are not forced to think about their own epoch or themselves in any realistic sense; such identifications with ancient heroes as there are can be fantastic. We must qualify this only when we arrive at the late Victorian or Edwardian stories of Henry James or E. M. Forster, stories in which travel in Italy may turn out to be much more emotionally problematic than mere escape upward for Anglo-Saxon ladies and gentlemen. These fictional tourists, concerned with whether they are experiencing to the full the cultural contrasts and sensitivities they seek, find foreshadowed the ambiguities of escape that are typical for other-direction.

FEET ON THE RAIL

The inner-directed person, when he escapes at all, may escape down as well as up. He finds in dime novels, in cock fighting, in trotting races, in barbershop song, a variant from his working role. While some visit Chartres, others visit the hootchy-kootch on the midway.

Despite the efforts of the puritans and women folk to drive out of life these recreations that are reminiscent of medieval pastimes, the middle-class men of the nineteenth century make a firm effort to hang on to them.

Sherwood Anderson's work is an epic of men coming into the house after midnight on stocking feet. How much of this lore survives was recently made plain by Allen Funt, on the "Candid Microphone" program of ABC. Funt, next to Paul Lazarsfeld the most ingenious sociologist in America, stood on a street corner at three in the morning and pretended he was afraid to go home. He buttonholed passing men and asked them to come home with him, to explain to the wife why he was overfilled and overdue. All the men were sympathetic. Though none wanted the role of go-between, each suggested the dodge that he himself had found workable in the same spot. One wanted him to telephone first. Another would help him get bandaged up. Still another thought that a present might fix matters. Some suggested stories, others courage. Most of the men, judging from their voices, seemed to be of middle age. Perhaps the major point of all this is that in earlier generations the strictness of the American proper-female regime gave a glamour to sin that obscured its inevitable limitations.

How much this is changed today we can see by recalling the bad woman of the earlier period. She did not have to be very original at being bad to symbolize an effort to keep open the traditional escapes. An analysis of movie bad girls by Wolfenstein and Leites in their book, *Movies,* shows how rapidly the shift has occurred. Even ten years ago the bad girl was a vamp, the good girl a prig. Today the good girl knows all the bad girl ever did, and more; she has all her tricks, which she can use to *seem* bad, that is, highly promiscuous, while being only moderately so. The bad girl of today's movies is a pathetic creature (the movie *Body and Soul* provides a good example) running after men who spurn her; her badness is indicated not so much in her sexual role as in her linkage to the underworld or the national enemy. Thus the sharp discontinuity that once existed between respectability and sin—like that between wealth and poverty, Marmon and Ford, Chippendale and Grand Rapids—has now become a problematic gradient where one must look for marginal differentiation. One cannot escape down if there is no deep end off which to jump.

In thinking of the meaning of escape for the inner-directed man we must not, however, put too much emphasis on the merely convention-breaking patterns of Victorian amusement, vice, and sinful fantasy. Even where the conventions were absent or fragile, another issue was involved. This was the issue of competence in the enjoyment and judgment of recreation.

On the one hand, the American inner-directed man was committed in every generation to face increasingly the demand that his escape be upward with the arts. Sometimes he sought out this escape on his own. More usually, perhaps, mobility strivings and feminine influence put pressure on the man to go beyond the sphere where he felt competent: the sleepy businessman dragged to an opera in a language he could not understand. But on the other hand, he combated becoming merely a passive consumer by protecting, as a rebel in shirt sleeves, his escape downward to the lower arts of drink mixing and drink holding, poker, fancy women, and fancy mummery. Thus he protected in his minor sphere of play, as in his major sphere of work, his feeling of competence in the living of life. The separateness of the play sphere was dramatized precisely because the personal competence involved in these downward escapes could contribute little, or negatively, to his social status in the world of work and family. Because play competence could not be directly geared to the production economy, the inner-directed man was somewhat less likely than other-directed men today to exploit his recreation by telling himself that he owed it to himself to have fun. If he went to baseball games (one of the few sports where the other-directed man's competence, too, rests considerably on having once played the game), it was not part of an act designed to prove himself "one of the boys."

However, we must not exaggerate these distinctions between inner-directed and other-directed escapes. Many inner-directed men worked painfully hard to maintain their showing of recreational competence. The Reverend Endicott Peabody, later founder of Groton, established himself as the hero of a western frontier town in which he held a pastorate by getting up a baseball team. A similiar strategy, with its roots in an era depending on tradition-direction, appears in the modern movie characterization of the Catholic priest, brother, or nun who is a good sport—as in Bing Crosby's *Going My Way*. Moreover, many inner-directed American business and professional men exploited, and still exploit, their leisure to make contacts. Their golf game was anything but an escape, and their wives' gardening was often harnessed to the same mobility drives. Such men had a great deal at stake economically, even if they had less at stake psychologically than the other-directed.

But there were often psychological stakes, too. The oversteered men of the period, unable to either throw off or accept their inhibitions, were not always able to guard them by withdrawal into privacy. Where there was pressure to prove oneself a good fellow in tavern or brothel, their bodies sometimes betrayed them into nausea or impotence—in the effort to be competent weakness of the flesh gave away unwillingness of the spirit. On the whole, however, the inner-directed man was much less susceptible than men are today to the requirement that he be liked for his recreations and loved for his vices.

III. THE STRUGGLE FOR SELF-APPROVAL

We may sum up much that is significant about inner-direction by saying that, in a society where it is dominant, its tendency is to protect the individual against the others at the price of leaving him vulnerable to himself.

One bit of evidence for this is in the widespread fear of and attack upon apathy which seems to date from the era of inner-direction. The monastic orders had faced the problem of sloth or *accidie* as psychological dangers to their regimen—dangers of which St. Augustine was acutely aware in his own struggle with himself. When puritanism, as Max Weber put it, turned the world into a monastery, the fear of this inner danger began to plague whole social classes and not merely a few select monks. The puritan inner-directed man was made to feel as if he had constantly to hold on to himself; that without ceaseless vigilance he would let go and drift—on the assumption that one *can* let go if one wills or, rather, if one stops willing. It is as if his character, despite its seeming stability, did not feel stable and, indeed, the puritan, in a theological projection of this inner feeling, had constantly to fight against doubts concerning his state of grace or election.

Out of his continuing battle against the Demon of Sloth that sometimes turned into a hypochondria about apathy he built up a myth, still very much with us, that the tradition-directed person is completely easy going, lacking "get up and go." This attack against others as apathetic—as today, for instance, in the constant complaints over political and civic apathy—sometimes served as a way of fighting against apathy in oneself. In fact, the inner-directed person testifies to his unconscious awareness that his gyroscope is not *his* but is installed by others through his chronic panic that it will stop spinning, that he is really not a self-starter, that life itself is not a process and renewal but an effortful staving off of psychic death.

Moreover, for easier bookkeeping in the control of apathy, the inner-directed person frequently divides his life into sectors, in each of which he can test his psychic defenses against it. Within himself he remains the child, committed early to goals and ideals that may transcend his powers. If these drives are demanding, no amount of contemporary acclaim can drown the feeling of inadequacy: the acclaim of others may in fact be the by-product of efforts to satisfy the self. Within himself he must find justification not only in what he does but in what he is—not by works but by faith is he saved. And while clever bookkeeping can transmute works into faith, self-criticism is seldom completely silenced. *Mere behavioral conformity cannot meet the characterological ideal.*

These internalized standards of the inner-directed man allow him, on the other hand, a certain freedom to fail in the eyes of the others without being convinced *by them* of his own inadequacy. Like Edison he will try and try again, sustained by his internal judgment of his worth. For while the others cannot protect him against self-criticism, self-criticism can protect him against the others. The inner-directed man can justify his existence not only by what he has done but what he will do. But this holds only up to a point. If repeated failures destroy his hope of future accomplishment, then it is likely that his internal strengths can no longer hold the fort against the external evidence. Overwhelmed with guilt, he will despise himself for his failures and inadequacies. The judgment, though set off by external happenings, is all the more severe for being internalized. Durkheim was right to see comparatively high suicide rates in the advanced industrial countries as symptoms of a psychological malaise uncontrolled by any cultural tradition.

VI

The Other-directed Round of Life: from Invisible Hand to Glad Hand

Since sociability in its pure form has no ulterior end, no content and no result outside itself, it is oriented completely about personalities. . . . But precisely because all is oriented about them, the personalities must not emphasize themselves too individually.

Georg Simmel, *The Sociology of Sociability*

THE INNER-DIRECTED person is not only chained to the endless demands of the production sphere; he must also spend his entire life in the internal production of his own character. The discomforts of this internal frontier are as inexhaustible as the discomforts of the frontier of work itself. Like the fear of being retired or unemployed in the economic realm, apathy in many sectors of his inner or outer life is felt as underemployment of characterological resources. The inner-directed man has a generalized need to master resource exploitation on all the fronts of which he is conscious. He is job-minded.

The frontiers for the other-directed man are people; he is people-minded. Hence both work and pleasure are felt as activities involving people. Many of the job titles that exist today existed in the earlier era; many recreations likewise. My effort is to see how change of character is connected with change of meaning in the same pursuits as well as with development of new pursuits. The description in this and the following chapter of the spheres of work and pleasure is, in very large measure, an exploration of the patterns of sociability that lead to the overlapping of these spheres.

I. THE ECONOMIC PROBLEM: THE HUMAN ELEMENT

Doubtless, we are inclined today to overestimate the freedom of free trade under the regimen of the invisible hand and to underestimate trade freedom under the present regimen of the glad hand. Nevertheless, there can be no doubt that the aims of business and professional life have gradually changed, although the changes are concealed beneath the traditional ideology of free enterprise. These aims are changed both by institutional alterations in the phase of incipient population decline and by new motivations brought to business by other-directed folk.

As the phase of transitional growth drew to an end in America, the "no help wanted" sign was posted on the frontier in 1890, in imagination if not in actual land-grant practice, and the same sign was hung out on our borders in 1924 with the virtual cutting off of immigration from Europe. With these valedictories a great symbol of hope and movement in the western world was destroyed, with repercussions perhaps more immediate in such countries as Italy than in America itself. Yet in America the combination of curtailed immigration and a falling birth rate (brought about by a high, urbanized standard of living) eventually altered the population profile of the country; and, in the ways already hinted at, its characterological profile as well. Today it is the "softness" of men rather than the "hardness" of material that calls on talent and opens new channels of social mobility.

Whereas the production frontier, and even the land frontier, may actually be roomy even in the phase of incipient population decline, it nevertheless feels crowded; and certainly the society is no longer felt as a wilderness or jungle as it often was earlier.

This is particularly true in industry and the professions. Take, for example, the position of the foreman. He no longer stands alone, a straw boss in a clear hierarchy, but is surrounded with people. He is a two-way communication channel between the men under him and a host of experts above and around him: personnel men, safety directors, production engineers, comptroller's representatives, and all the rest of the indirect managerial work force. The plant manager is hardly better off for emotional elbowroom: he is confronted not only with the elaborate intraplant hierarchy but with the public outside: the trade association group, the unions, consumers, suppliers, the government, and public opinion. Likewise, the professional man feels surrounded by a swarm of competitors, turned out by the vastly expanded educational system of a society whose capital plant is in such good shape that it can afford to devote—in fact, can hardly help devoting—a large share of the national income to the service trades and professions and to education for their proper use.

People, therefore, become the central problem of industry. This does not mean that modern developments of the older revolutions in tooling, the machine process, and factory organization come to a halt. Rather, advances here are increasingly routinized; the continuing increment in productivity becomes a by-product of institutional forms. However, the newer industrial revolution which has reached its greatest force in America (and hits elsewhere, as in England) is concerned with techniques of communication and control, not of tooling or factory layout. It is symbolized by the telephone, the servo-mechanism, the IBM machine, the electronic calculator, and modern statistical methods of controlling the quality of products; by the Hawthorne counseling experiment and the general preoccupation with industrial morale. The era of economic abundance and incipient population decline calls for the work of men whose tool is symbolism and whose aim is some observable response from people. These manipulators, of course, are not necessarily other-directed in character. Many inner-directed people are successful manipulators of people; often, their very inner-direction makes them unaware of how much they do manipulate and exploit others. Nevertheless, for manipulating others, there is a somewhat greater compatibility between characterological other-direction and sensitivity to others' subtler wants.

This can be explained more clearly by reference to one of our interviews. The man interviewed is the vice-president for sales and advertising of a large west coast machine-tool company, and he is also head of one of the leading trade associations for his industry. In origin he is the son of a Congregationalist preacher in a small midwestern town. His background, his mobility drive, his initial technical orientation are typical for the inner-directed; but his situation calls for the negotiating skill and interpersonal sensitivity more characteristic of the other-directed. This conflict produces strain. Asked about political issues on which he has recently changed his mind, he says:

. . . I don't think this fits the category you're working on now, but I've become a great deal more tolerant of labor leaders and organizers [then catching himself]—not agitators, necessarily. I've come to appreciate what they're doing. They don't have much choice in taking the particular methods and means sometimes. I need a psychoanalyst.

He also told the interviewer that his principal worry is that he does not get along too well with another top executive of his company. He was troubled when a suggestion of his that was rejected later turned out to be right—and the other chap knew it was right. In such a situation he felt exposed. He cannot eat before going into a board meeting, and wondered to the interviewer whether he might not be better off running his own small company rather than as an official of a large one. For recreation he plays golf, though he does not seem to care for it and, in good inner-directed style, or perhaps simply good American style, does "a little fooling around with tools in the basement."

Material from interviews is, of course, open to a variety of possible interpretations. It would be erroneous to conclude that a more unequivocally other-directed person than this executive (and most people are blends of inner-direction and other-direction just as he seems to be) would feel no strain in his contacts with others. The point is rather that the modern executive is put under constant social pressure in and out of the office.

FROM CRAFT SKILL TO MANIPULATIVE SKILL

The pressure toward social competence, with its concurrent disregard for technical competence, suggests another aspect of this executive's history which is typical for the emergence of a new pattern in American business and professional life: *if one is successful in one's craft, one is forced to leave it.* The machine-tool man began in the shop; as V.P. for sales and advertising he has become an uneasy manipulator of people and of himself. Likewise, the newspaperman who rises becomes a columnist or deskman, the doctor becomes the head of a clinic or hospital, the professor becomes a dean, president, or foundation official, the factory superintendent becomes a holding company executive. All these men must bury their craft routines and desert their craft companions. They must work less with things and more with people.

To be sure, business was always work with people. But when the size of enterprises was small, the head could remain a colleague among other colleagues; he did not cut connections entirely and enter a new milieu. William Allen White's *Autobiography* shows that he was able to maintain all his life the amiable fiction that he was only a working newspaper man. Similarly, the older generation of college presidents was composed largely of men who continued to think of themselves as scholars. So, too, the older generation of business executives kept their hats on in the office, chewed tobacco, and otherwise tried to retain their connections with the shop. Today; however, the familiar organizational concepts of "staff and line" symbolize the cutting off of direct contact between the executive and the working stiffs of both staff and line. To sit at his new big desk—or to get there—he has to learn a new personality-oriented specialty and unlearn or at least soft-pedal his old skill orientation.

To the point is a story of an engineer who is offered the far more lucrative job of sales manager.[1] He loves engineering, but his wife won't let him turn down the promotion. His sponsor in the organization tells him it is now or never: does he want to be wearing a green eyeshade all his life? He reluctantly accepts. That night he has a dream. He has a slide rule in his hands, and he suddenly realizes that he does not know how to use it. He wakes in panic. The dream symbolizes his feeling of impotence in a new job where he is alienated from his craft.

The executive who has moved up from a professional position can hardly help feeling that his work is air conditioned: fine only so long as the machinery below runs smoothly. Those colleagues whom he has left behind will not be slow, in their envy, to remind him that he can no longer consider himself a competent craftsman among his fellow craftsmen, that he does not fool them if, as an editor or by-line columnist, he occasionally attends a presidential press conference; or, as a college administrator, an occasional scholarly convention; or, as a sales manager, occasionally makes a mark on a drawing board.

Indeed, a society increasingly dependent on manipulation of people is almost as destructive of the craft-oriented professional and businessman as a society in the earlier stages of industrialization is destructive of the handicraft-oriented peasant and artisan. The professional of the more recent period is pushed upstairs into the managerial class while the artisan of the earlier period was pushed into the proletariat; and this testifies to a profound difference in the two historic situa-

1. Professor Everett Hughes of the University of Chicago, who has guided me in the analysis of changing career lines in business and the professions, tells this story.

tions. Yet in both cases the industrial process advances by building into machines and into smooth-flowing organizations the skills that were once built, by a long characterological process, into men.

To be sure, these men who do the building, who, in Karl Mannheim's terms, do the "functional rationalizing," have to become more skilled than before. They must combine enough technological knowledge to talk to the technical men, with enough social skills to sense the wants of the variety of publics that may affect or be affected by their decisions. For men of imagination business offers as many challenges and frontiers as it ever did; and while the number of skilled men in hourly rated jobs in the factory has doubtless declined, the number of jobs in salaried staff positions has vastly increased. Nevertheless, while the objective skills of the inner-directed man cloaked him about with privacy to some degree and made him something more than a salesman of himself or his product, the other-directed man in the modern industrial and professional world cannot as easily take refuge in his skills. Even if he is an engineer with no desire to climb out of the craft, he must be a good teamworker; he must be able to get along with the other engineers and to "sell" the foreman and others down the line. Up-to-date personnel directors today are weeding out of commerce and industry the lone wolf who is not cooperative, no matter what his gifts. "Rate-busters" are no more welcome in the office than they are in the shop.

In this situation the changing style of nepotism is an important factor. Old-style nepotism was a nepotism largely of kith and kin, found today in industry and the professions mostly among ethnic groups such as Italians and eastern European Jews, that have not severed all ties to a culture dependent on tradition-direction. In contrast with this, new-style nepotism seems to be a kind of non-kin patronage system in which promising young men are brought along by elders who take a shine to them, are proud of their finds, and may even seek a kind of immortality through them. Sometimes the patron is consciously building a power pyramid in this way; at other times, he is quite disinterested, and even unaware of his role, consciously assuming that all his judgments are based on merit. In either case the vagueness and fluidity of the system favor the radar-sensitive types who are tuned to subtle and unspoken expectations.

Despite all one might say, however, about the duality of the hierarchy that requires one to leave one's craft in order to rise (or in order to be above doing dirty work) and about the patronage network of medicine or law, these older professions and the other free professions still offer many comfortable places to inner-directed types. The ideology of free enterprise is strong in these circles. The attempt to apply objective criteria in selecting personnel persists, and is strengthened by the otherwise odious emphasis on grades in the educational and licensing system. In a hospital, a law firm, a university, there is room not only for those who can bring people together but for those who can bring together chemicals, citations, or ideas. There are many niches for the work-minded craftsman who does not care to learn, or cannot learn, to move with the crowd.

Thus we see that some sectors of the economy lag behind others and provide in this way protected reservations where pressure for adjustment to other-direction is minimized. And these reservations are not restricted to the professions. Even in big industry some such areas can continue to exist because not all technological problems—problems of the hardness of the material—have been solved or put on a routine problem-solving basis. Moreover, there are certain key spots in big business and big government where at times it is precisely an inner-directed rate-buster who is needed—for instance, a man who can say no without going through an elaborate song and dance. A mobile, ambitious boy who would never have made the grade within the bureaucracy—for many a V.P. never gets to be P.—may be able to become head of U. S. Steel or T.V.A. via the law or occasionally via accounting or other professional work or even via small business.

Moreover, just as modern business puts pressure on many people to become other-directed, the resistance of our many inner-directed people delays the complete capture of the economy by the glad handers: the inner-directeds won't do business that way. Yet despite this, the values characteristic of other-direction may be spread at such a rate as to hit certain sectors of the economy before these sectors have solved their technological problems. In the United States the lure of other-directed work and leisure styles cannot be everywhere modulated to the uneven front of economic advance.

FROM FREE TRADE TO FAIR TRADE

In the days of free trade the inner-directed businessman was insulated from too close a preoccupation with people in a number of ways, especially by the notion of the invisible hand. Tradition mediated his relation to his work force. Bankers mediated his relation with the source of financial supply—often, indeed, bankers were his major antennae to the wider world. Lawyers mediated his relation to government either by litigation or lucre. And he needed no one to tell him what he was in business for. Though his motives might be complex, the push of the invisible hand was on his back and drove him if he wanted to stay in or get to the top.

Today these habits are visibly changing. Relations that were once handled by the price mechanism or fiat are now handled by negotiation. Very soon after the Federal Trade Commission Act of 1914 outlawed unfair competition it became clear that what was unfair was to lower the price of goods, though this view was concealed under attacks against cheating or mislabeling of goods. But in the NRA period this covert attitude received government and public sanction, and it became libelous to call someone a price cutter. With the passage of the Robinson-Patman Act and state fair-trade laws, free trade and fair trade became antithetical terms. Thus prices must be set by administration and negotiation or, where this is too likely to bring in the Antitrust Division, by "price leadership."

Price leadership often looks to the economist simply as the manipulator of devices to avoid price wars and divide the field. But price leadership has other aspects as well. It is a means by which the burden of decision is put onto the "others." The so-called price leaders themselves look to the government for clues, since cost—that mythical will-of-the-wisp—is no longer, if it ever really was, an unequivocal guide. Follow-the-leader is also played in arriving at the price and working conditions of labor; and unions have profited from their ability to play on the wishes of top management to be in stride with the industry leaders, and to be good fellows to boot. As we shall see later, the other-directed pattern of politics tends to resemble the other-directed pattern of business: leadership is in the same amorphous state. Moreover, both in business and in politics, the other-directed executive prefers to stabilize his situation at a level that does not make too heavy demands on him for performance. Hence, at various points in the decision-making process he will vote for an easier life as against the risks of expansion and free-for-all competition.

Such a business life does not turn out to be the "easy" one. For one thing, the other-directeds do not have things all their own way in business any more than they do in politics. Free trade is still a powerful force, despite the incursions of the fair traders. Many observers, judging the degree of monopoly by looking at the percentage of assets controlled by the large, administered-price corporations, overlook the fact that even a small percentage of companies outside the range of the glad hand can have a leverage quite disproportionate to their assets. Rubber may be a monopoly, but will we always need rubber? Movies may be monopolistic, but what about television or facsimile? In the small and marginal industries, the monopolies not of today but of tomorrow, there is often no need to be a good fellow. What is more, the dynamics of technological change remain challenging; whole departments within industries, as well as whole industries themselves, can become obsolete, despite their ability to negotiate repeated stays of technological death sentence. Even within the great monopolistic industries there are still many technologically oriented folk as well as many technologically oriented departments; no management planning in any one company can completely smooth out and routinize the pressure resulting from their innovations.

For another thing, to the extent that the businessman is freed by his character and situation from cost considerations, he must face the problem of finding new motives for his entrepreneurship. He must tune in to the others to see what they are saying about what a proper business ought to be. Thus, a psychological sensitivity that begins with fear of being called a price cutter spreads to fear of being unfashionable in other ways. The businessman is as afraid of pursuing goals that may be obsolete as of living a style of life that may not be stylish. Oriented as he is to others, and to the consumption sphere, *he views his own business as a consumer.*

We can see the shift in many corporate histories. A business that begins as a small family enterprise, whose founders have their eye on the main chance—with a focus on costs and a "show me" attitude about good will and public relations—often alters its aims in the second generation. *Fortune* is put on the table, a trade association is joined, and the aim becomes not so much dollars as the possession of those appurtenances which an up-to-date company is supposed to have. We see a succession of demi-intellectuals added to the staff industrial relations directors, training directors, safety directors. A house organ is published; consultants are called in on market research, standard operating procedures, and so on; shop and store front have their faces lifted; and in general status is sought, with profits becoming useful as one among many symbols of status and as the reserve for further moves toward a status-dictated expansion.

In many cases this shift is accompanied by a conflict of the older, more inner-directed with the younger, more other-directed generation. The older men have come up through the shop or through a technical school with no pretensions in the field of human relations. The younger ones are imbued with the new ethic. They *seem* still to be concerned about making money, and to some extent they are, but they are also concerned with turning their company into the model which they learned at business school. Businessmen recognize this new orientation when they speak of themselves, as they frequently do, as "trustees" for a variety of publics. And while they try to manipulate these publics and to balance between them, they, like the political leaders, are manipulated by the expectations the public has, or is thought to have, of them.

If one had to set a date for the change, one might say that the old epoch ended with the death of Henry Ford. After his death the firm, a last stronghold of older ways, completed the installation of new labor, accounting, and other management techniques and orientations.

The word *fair* in part reflects a carry-over of peer-group values into business life. The peer-grouper is imbued with the idea of fair play; the businessman, of fair trade. Often this means that he must be willing to negotiate matters on which he might stand on his rights. The negotiator, moreover, is expected to bring home not only a specific victory but also friendly feelings toward him and toward his company. Hence, to a degree, the less he knows about the underlying facts, the easier it will be to trade concessions. He is like the street-corner salesman who, reproached for selling for four cents apples that cost him five, said "But think of the turnover!" Here again craft skill, if not an actual drawback, becomes less important than manipulative skill.

Obviously, much of what has been said applies to the "democratic" trade union bureaucracy, the professions, and to academic life as well as to the business world. The lawyer, for instance, who moves into top positions inside and outside his profession is no longer necessarily a craftsman who has mastered the intricacies of, say, corporate finance, but may be one who has shown himself to be a good contact man.

Since contacts need to be made and remade in every generation and cannot be inherited, this creates lucrative opportunities for the mobile other-directed types whose chief ability is smooth negotiation.

The medical profession is even more clearly a field in which success has come to depend almost entirely (unless one cares to be "unethical") on the esteem of colleagues. To be sure, doctors have always been customer oriented, but the bedside manner is a much easier mask to maintain than the need to propitiate a small number of colleagues who decisively control one's fate. For the bedside manner is a relatively formalized mask of cheerfulness and imperturbability, worn in front of people ready to be impressed by one's status and mystique. But obviously this will not work with colleagues who know one too well and who share the mystique. Before them one must have a mask that pretends to be everything but a mask: a dissimulation that pretends to sincerity, a caution that pretends to casualness, an antagonism that pretends to cooperation. Similarly, we can contrast the small grocer who must please his individual patrons, perhaps by a "counter-side manner," with the chain-store employee who must please both the patrons and his co-workers in the shop; indeed, in pleasing the patrons he cannot antagonize the co-workers, any more than a nurse in a hospital can afford, lest the other nurses ruin her, to become too friendly with the sick. The colleague, like the peer-grouper, is the very person with whom one engages in competition for the scarce commodity of approval and the very person to whom one looks for guidance as to what is desirable.

There is also a change in the same direction in the services provided by the professional and in the way these services are shopped for. Today the housewife is no longer trained to argue with the butcher about all cuts of meat because so many of them are increasingly offered in standard cuts and grades. Just so, the shopper for professional services learns not to trust his layman's judgment but to look for the label. Moreover, shopping is itself a major leisure-time pursuit in a society where the frontiers of consumption seem more exciting than those of production. This is true not only of the housewife but also for business corporations that employ professional consultants. Where interlocking directorates do not dictate the choice, the business may often shop for more up-to-date legal advice or run through a sequence of management consultant firms, each more flamboyant than the last, each engaged in adding to overhead one or more additional sets of semiprofessional specialists.

By and large, business firms until World War I needed only three kinds of professional advice: legal, auditing, and engineering. These were relatively impersonal services, even when, in the case of the lawyers, the services included buying—for cash on the barrelhead—a few legislators or judges. Since the number of available specialists was fairly small in comparison with demand, they could be absorbed into either or both of the two types of prevailing nexus: one, the family-status-connection nexus which persisted from earlier times in the smaller communities and does so even today in these communities and in the South; the other, the cash nexus based on performance, or on "character" in the older sense. Today the buyer is, first of all, not sure which of many services to buy: shall he get a lawyer *or* a public relations man *or* a market research agency *or* call in a management consulting firm to decide; second, he is not sure of his choice among the many potential suppliers of each of these services—none of whom must he accept either for family-status-connection reasons or for obviously superior character and performance. Thus choice will turn on a complex of more or less accidental, whimsical factors: a chance contact or conversation, a story in *Business Week* or a "confidential" newsletter, the luck of a salesman. In this situation the professional man's uneasy relation to his craft resembles that of a husband to a good-looking and flirtatious wife in a roomful of competitive men. The recurrent codes of ethics devised by the various professional associations are symptoms of this malaise; and so is the effort to draw, in the fluid competitive setting, lines of ethnic or social inacceptability aimed at eliminating some of the competitors. The kinds of competition that are to be deemed fair are always subject to the negotiation of the peer-group and its interpretations of the rules of the game.

FROM THE BANK ACCOUNT TO THE EXPENSE ACCOUNT

In this phrase Professor Paul Lazarsfeld once summed up some recent changes in economic attitudes. There was a time when many inner-directed men thought of their bank account as their most solid and reliable friend. In those days of an unequivocal gold standard (unequivocal because it was "understood" only by bankers and economists and held to be too mysterious for politicians to tinker with) property could serve as a protective shell for the inner-directed man. Property in our time has become an uncertain asset for its anxious possessors. Taxes, inflation, panic liquidity have made it factually vaporous; and changed attitudes toward wealth have made it emotionally elusive. The rich man must use his expense account to establish himself as a fine fellow and to protect, in his own eyes as well as the eyes of others, his right to his bank account.

The expense account is tied in with today's emphasis on consumption practices as firmly as the bank account in the old days was tied in with production ideals. The expense account gives the glad hand its grip. In doing so it still further breaks down the wall that in the era depending on inner-direction separated the paths of pleasure and of work. The successful other-directed man brings to business the set of attitudes learned in the consumption sphere not only when he appraises his own firm with a customer's eye but also when he is "in conference."

Business is supposed to be fun. As World War II inflation cooled off, the business pages repeatedly carried speeches at conventions on the theme: "Now selling will be fun again!" The demand to have fun is one that the inner-directed businessman never faced. He could afford to be properly gloomy and grim. The shortening of hours which in any case has affected the working class more than the middle class, has extended the requirements for office sociability largely in the top management of business, government, and academic life. Here people spend long·hours in the company of their office peer group. Their lunches are long; their golf games longer still. Much time in the office itself is also spent in sociability: exchanging office gossip ("conferences"), making good-will tours ("inspection"), talking to salesmen and joshing secretaries ("morale"). In fact, depleting the expense account can serve as an almost limitless occupational therapy for men who, out of a tradition of hard work, a dislike of their wives, a lingering asceticism, and an anxiety about their antagonistic cooperators, still feel that they must put in a good day's work at the office. But, of course, Simmel would not admit, in his brilliant essay from which I quoted at the head of this chapter, that this kind of sociability, carrying so much workaday freight, was either free or sociable.

For the new type of career there must be a new type of education

This is one factor, of course not the only one, behind the increasing vogue of general education and the introduction of the humanities and social studies into technical high school and university programs. The educators who sponsor these programs urge cultivating the "whole man," speak of training citizens for democracy, and denounce narrow specialisms—all valuable themes. Indeed this book grows in part out of the stimulation of teaching in a general social science program. But since the social studies as usually taught are often lacking in humanistic import, it may be doubtful that engineers and businessmen will become either better citizens or better people for having been exposed to them. On the other hand, there is the great probability that they will be more suave. They may be able to demonstrate their edge on the roughnecks from the "tech" schools by trotting out discourse on human relations. Such eloquence may be as necessary for professional and business success today as a knowledge of the classics was to the English politician and high civil servant of the last century.

Meanwhile, I do not wish to exaggerate the extent of "false personalization" and emphasis on human relations even in the bureaucratized sectors of the economy. There is much variety still: some companies, such as Sears Roebuck, are run by glad handers, while others like, let us say, Montgomery Ward, are not; some, like Anaconda, are public relations conscious; others, like Kennecott, are less so. Much current progress in distribution, even in selling, tends to reduce the importance of the human agent as salesman. This is clear enough in the Automat. Moreover, the human agent as salesman is minimized wherever a technician is needed: for instance, salesmen of specialized equipment which requires a reorientation of the customer's work force. Though IBM salesmen have to be go-getters, they also have to know how to wire a tabulating machine and, still more important, how to rationalize the information flow within a company. Hence, although they are facilitators of the communications revolution, they must be no less craft oriented than the salesmen of the less complex equipment of an earlier era. Within most such industries there is a great need for technically minded people who are, to a considerable degree, protected by their indispensable skills from having to be nice to everybody, with or without an expense account.

But as we shall see when we return to these matters in Chapter XV, we are a long way from having the indices that would allow us to quantify the extent of glad-hand personalization in the economy.

II. THE MILKY WAY

In the preceding chapter, I symbolized the ambition of the inner-directed man by referring to a frequent motto of his period: ad astra per aspera. The inner-directed man, socialized with reference to an older model, might choose for emulation a star from the heroes of his field. By contrast, the other-directed person does not so often think of his life in terms of an individualized career. He seeks not fame, which represents limited transcendence of a particular peer-group or a particular culture, but the respect and, more than the respect, the affection, of an amorphous and shifting, though contemporary, jury of peers.

To attain this goal he struggles not with the hardness of the material but with the very antagonistic cooperators who are engaged in the same pursuit and to whom he looks at the same time for values and for judgments of value. In place of referring himself to the great men of the past and matching himself against his stars, the other-directed person moves in the midst of a veritable Milky Way of almost but not quite indistinguishable contemporaries. This is partly a tribute to the size of the educated middle class in the phase of incipient decline of population.

Conceivably, the uncertainty of life in our day also helps explain the refusal of young people to commit themselves to long-term goals. War, depression, military service, are felt today as obstacles to planning a career far more than in the period prior to World War I. But these changes are not the whole story. While the felt uncertainty of the last three decades is one factor in the creation of the type of man who will not commit himself to long-range goals, this type in turn, once created, rationalizes his perspective on the future and his deferral of commitment by pointing to the all too evident uncertainties. We can conceive of people living at a time of equal uncertainty who would, out of ignorance and insensitivity as much as out of strength of character, plow ahead in pursuit of extensive aims.

Doubtless, many other factors are also in the air. Paradoxically as life expectancy has lengthened, timetables for living have been speeded up, have turned into hourly rated jobs and other short-term contractual patterns. Both as economic producers and consumers, moreover, we are faced with the threat of obsolescence of capital equipment and consumer goods, based not on their wearing out (usually, they long outlive their depreciation-allowance periods under the internal revenue code or "sound accounting practice") but on their becoming unfashionable—like steam engines, hand-wound victrolas, and old men in a low death-rate society. Moreover, as we saw in a preceding section, mobility often depends on leaving one's craft skill behind; and this very fork in the road which separates avenues within a craft from those achievable only by leaving the craft, suggests itself at an early stage of occupational life and complicates the career planning of the mobile youth. A responsive sensitivity to the duality of the paths and a proper self-guidance in two divergent directions are knacks most easily achieved by the other-directed person who takes his cues from the expectations of others at each stage of ascent rather than from a goal internalized in childhood and adolescence. In gauging this situation we cannot always be sure that ambition as a character trait has become less frequent; it may simply hide itself because it needs to be so strenuously repressed. Our urban upper middle-class youth, when asked about ambition, often tell the interviewer that ambition should be moderate; they do not avow ambitious aims. This may be only the expression of an ideology of cooperation and modesty they have superficially accepted; they may be in the position of the fifteen-year-old boy who told us, when asked what he considered to be his worst trait, that it was "always trying to be the best." Yet I think we deal here not only with a profound change in verbalized values among middle-class youth but also with a change in character that is tied, both as cause and consequence, to the change in values.

Admittedly, there are certain positive sides to this development. The seemingly easy commitment of many inner-directed youths was based on an unquestioning acceptance of parental orders and parental ranking of occupations. The other-directed youth of today often asks more of a job than that it satisfy conventional status and pecuniary requirements; he is not content with the authoritative rankings of earlier generations. While the increasing bureaucratization of life tends to force career choice on the young at an ever earlier time—so that one has to decide on a medical career often even before choosing a college—the young fight this pressure by occasionally delaying decision up to and beyond the "points of no return" of the various professions. This delay allows time for radar scanning to see what professional pastures may look greener at the moment—and some of these may actually be greener for the individual. Thus other-direction opens up the possibilities of more individuated and satisfying career choice, once society's pressure for an early decision, and the person's feeling of panic if he can make no decision, can be relaxed.

It follows from all this that the heavens of achievement look quite different to the other-directed youth than to his inner-directed predecessor. The latter found security in moving to the periphery of the various frontiers and establishing an isolated and recognizable claim on a new piece of territory—often with quite grandiose and imperialistic trappings. If he founded a firm, this was his lengthened shadow. Today the man is the shadow of the firm. Such long-term aims as exist are built into the firm, the institution; this is also the repository of the imperialist drives that sometimes take shape as the firm harnesses the mild and tractable wills of many other-directed people who are competing for places of marginal differentiation on the Milky Way.

To outdistance these competitors, to shine alone, seems hopeless, and also dangerous. To be sure, one may try to steal a march—to work harder, for instance, than the propaganda about working would permit—but these are petty thefts, not major stick-ups. They do, however, keep the competition for a position on the major streamlined runs of occupational life from being entirely cooperative. Yet even such behavior that may marginally flout the prevailing concepts of fairness looks to the peer-group for its norms of what is to be desired. And since each projects his own tendencies to unfair play onto the others, this, too, requires living in a state of constant alert as to what the others may be up to.

Certainly the Milky Way is not an easy way, though its hardships differ from those of the earlier era. Obliged to conciliate or manipulate a variety of people, the other-directed person handles all men as customers who are always right; but he must do this with the uneasy realization that, as Everett Hughes has put it, some are more right than others. This diversity of roles to be taken with a diversity of customers is not institutionalized or clear cut, and the other-directed

person tends to become merely his succession of roles and encounters
and hence to doubt who he is or where he is going. Just as the firm
gives up the one-price policy for an administered price that is set in
secrecy and differs with each class of customer depending on the latter's apparent power and "good will" requirements, so the other-
directed person gives up the one-face policy of the inner-directed man
for a multiface policy that he sets in secrecy and varies with each class
of encounters.

In the economic field the insecurity of this monopolistic procedure
is obvious. In brand-name competition the seller never knows when
he may lose a market utterly as a result of one of those sudden obso-
lescences that occur frequently in a luxury-oriented society. In less
specialized free-market days, by contrast, he might lose profits but
could never be completely frozen out; his staple goods remained
salable at some point on the demand curve. Businessmen have combated this insecurity by cooperation, by instituting long-term political
and economic measures of protection: the research department and
the lobby are such measures. However, while the specialized corporate enterprise can do this planning quite effectively, the individual
can do it only less effectively. Unable to figure on a lifelong market
for his personality as it is, he defends himself by amateurish market
research, using his radar to adjust himself as a commodity.

United with others, however, he can seek a modicum of social, economic, and political protection. The peer-group can decide that there
are certain outcasts, in class or ethnic terms, to whom the glad hand
need not be extended, or who can (like the Negro in the South) be
forced to personalize without the privilege of demanding a reciprocal
response. A class of customers can be politically created who are by
definition wrong. Yet no amount of exclusiveness, though it may
make life a bit easier for the insiders, can completely guarantee continuance in a place of visibility and approval in the Milky Way.

VII

The Other-directed Round of Life (*Continued*): the Night Shift

But it must not be supposed that in the midst of all their toils the people who live in democracies think themselves to be pitied; the contrary is noticed to be the case. No men are fonder of their own condition. Life would have no relish for them if they were delivered from the anxieties which harass them, and they show more attachment to their cares than aristocratic nations to their pleasures.

Tocqueville, *Democracy in America*

THE ONLY thing that has changed since Tocqueville wrote (no small change, it is true) is that the sphere of pleasures has itself become a sphere of cares.

I. CHANGES IN THE SYMBOLIC MEANING OF FOOD AND SEX

American society in the phase of incipient decline of population becomes consumption oriented. Leisure time is greatly expanded as the result of urbanization and industrialization. The high level of income that affected first the death rate and then the birth rate needs to be spent. As I have implied, American variants of Keynesian economics are the reflexive economic theories for such a phase, since they emphasize the dangers of oversaving and the virtues of a fiscal policy that distributes income to those who are the spenders, not the savers.

One of the consumables on which much money is spent is education, which in turn provides the peer-group with its opportunity to train people for their role in the consumers' union. People must be taught to spend. For industry to be able to pull people from the farms into the cities, people usually must learn to want some of the consumables for which the city stands. When unions first tried to organize the South in recent years, it was discovered that for many ex-sharecroppers—as with most preindustrial people all over the world —a bigger pay check was not especially significant; they would not know what to do with the money, except to take more time off, since they were already earning more than they ever had. Some of the unions instituted courses in homemaking designed to open up a wider area of consumer wants, in order to indirectly create pressure for unionization through pressure for higher wages.

It is, in fact, now widely accepted that the American economy depends on opening up internal frontiers of consumption as the frontiers of production and land use begin to close down. The difficulty is, however, that many of the physical hardships of the older frontier have survived in altered, psychological form on the newer one. Just as we saw in the previous chapter that the day shift of work-mindedness is invaded by glad-hand attitudes and values that stem in part from the sphere of leisure, so the night shift of leisure-mindedness is haunted by the others with whom one works at having a good time.

First of all, however, with the rise of other-direction, we see the passing both of the acquisitive consumers and of the escapists of the earlier era. The passion for acquisition diminishes when property no longer has its old stability and objective validity; escape diminishes by the very fact that work and pleasure are interlaced. We can see these new tendencies in what is perhaps their most extreme form: the attitudes toward food and sexual experience prevailing among some upper middle-class groups.

THREE SQUARES A DAY

Among inner-directed types there is of course great variation as to interest in food. In America—the story is different among the food-loving peoples of the rest of the world—puritans and nonpuritans of the recent past might use food for display, with relatively standardized menus for company and for dining out; what was put on display was a choice cut of meat, an elegant table, and good solid cooking. All this was an affair largely of the women, and in many circles food was not a proper topic for dinner conversation. Having the proper food was something one owed to one's status, one's claim to respectability, and more recently to one's hygiene of calories and vitamins. (This last pattern did not spread to the South, where an older, more gastronomically rugged tradition of ceremonial fondness for food prevailed.) The earlier editions of the *Boston Cooking School Cookbook* breathe this air of solidity, conservatism, and nutrition-mindedness.

The other-directed person of the midtwentieth century in America, on the contrary, puts on display his *taste* and not directly his wealth, respectability, cubic capacity, or caloric soundness. Indeed we saw in Chapter IV how the radio begins the other-directed person's training in food taste even before the child goes to school and how seriously he takes his lessons. While well-educated upper middle-class parents are becoming hesitant to tell children to eat something because it is good for them—lest they create oral complexes—they join the radio in discussion of what is "good" as a matter of taste. Often, in fact, this merely disguises the emotion focused on the child's eating habits, almost as much emotion as *their* parents concentrated on the regimen of no-nonsense plate cleaning. The other-directed person is thus prepared for the search for marginal differentiation not only in what he sets before his guests but in how it is talked about with them.

Earlier there existed a small coterie of gourmets; fastidious enjoyment of food was one hobby, among others, that inner-directed people might choose. Today, in wide circles, many people are and many more feel that they must be gourmets. The abundance of America in the phase of incipient population decline is perhaps the most important factor in this development; it has made the good foods available to nearly everybody. The seasonal and geographic limitations that in the earlier period narrowed food variations for all but the very rich have now been largely done away with by the network of distribution and the techniques of food preservation—both being legacies from the phase of transitional population growth. The consumer's choice among foods can therefore no longer be made on the basis either of tradition or of Malthusian limits.

As a result, both the setting of the meal and its content are affected. Informality breaks down the puritan inhibition against talking about food and drink, just as Mexican casseroles and copper kettles replace the white napery and classic decor of the nineteenth-century middle-class table. More important still, the housewife can no longer blame the preferential and limited cuisine offered by a kitchen servant for her failure to personalize her own tastes in food. In the period of incipient population decline servants disappear from the middle-class home, and where they do not, they lack any traditional pattern of prerogatives that allows them, rather than the host and hostess, to control the menu and its stylized serving. No walls of privacy, status, or asceticism remain to protect or prevent one from displaying personalized taste in food and decor as an element in one's competition with others. The diner has the power, unlike Jiggs, to decide that corned beef and cabbage is an amusing dish; he can ransack immigrant cookeries or follow the lead of food columnist Clementine Paddleford toward exoticism. Only at conventional conventions can one still find the uniform menu of steak or chicken, potatoes, and marbled peas. And at home, in place of the staple menu, the hostess today must substitute her own specialty, such as lasagna or rüstoffel. Men are involved, as Jacques Barzun has observed, almost as much as women, and in the kitchen as well as at the back-yard grill.

The most popular cookbook today is said to be *The Joy of Cooking,* and the number of specialized cookbooks—ethnic, chatty, and atmospheric—constantly increases to meet the demand for marginal differentiation. The older books are, of course, still published and still very popular, among them the *Better Homes and Gardens* and *Woman's Home Companion* cookbooks, the *Settlement Cookbook,* and the *Boston Cooking School Cookbook.* While undergoing constant revision, these books nevertheless remain staid, sedate, and matter of fact in their presentation; they are basic and extensive and do include recipes for fairly "fancy" dishes prepared with wines, sauces, and the like. These cookbooks, however, are a heritage from the era depending on inner-direction, when the hostess could be satisfied that if she spent enough money and care she could have presentable meals fitting her station in life. And although there are few homes today without one or more of these "standard" volumes, hostesses constantly add to their collections the new cookbooks of the chatty and informal variety. The very change in titles—from the *Boston Cooking School Cookbook* to *How to Cook a Wolf* or *Food is a Four Letter Word*—reveals the changing attitude. For the other-directed person cannot lean on such objective standards of success as those which guided the inner-directed person: he may be haunted by a feeling that he misses the joy in food or drink which he is supposed to feel. Mealtime must now be "pleasurable"; the new *Fireside Cookbook* is offered to "people who are not content to regard food just as something one transfers periodically from plate to mouth." And if one still fails to get much joy out of the recipes given there, he may search in books like *Specialité de la Maison* to see what "others" are eating— to get the "favorite recipes" of such people as Noel Coward, Lucius Beebe, and others. Fred MacMurray and Claudette Colbert testify to the delights of new concoctions such as "The Egg and I Julep"; and "There is nothing," writes MacMurray in a little collection of his favorite egg recipes, "so appealing as a pair of fried eggs with their limpid golden eyes gazing fondly at you from the center of a breakfast plate, festooned with strips of crisp bacon or little-pig sausage. Or poached, gaily riding a raft of toast." The most popular translation of an old French cookbook, *Tante Marie,* is also extremely chatty, and *The Joy of Cooking* explains its chattiness by saying that originally the recipes were collected and written down for the author's daughter, who in turn thought "other daughters" might like them. (As there is today less teaching of daughters by mothers, the daughter must rely on the instruction of an outsider, if she is to cook at all.) In short, the other-directed person in his approach to food, as in his sexual encounters, is constantly looking for a qualitative element that may elude him. He suffers from what Martha Wolfenstein and Nathan Leites call "fun-morality." [1]

Of course, putting matters this way exaggerates the disadvantages of the shift: undeniably, many more people today really enjoy food and enjoy talk about food than was the case when the monotony of the American diet was notorious.

In the business world the steep absolute rise in overhead and especially in general and administrative expense might be a rough index of the spread of other-directed patterns of entrepreneurship. Correspondingly, in the world of consumption, we might demarcate the geographical and social boundaries of explicit other-direction by an analysis of menus and of talk about cookery. As tossed salads and garlic, elaborate sauces, dishes en casserole, *Gourmet* magazine, wine and liqueurs, spread west from New York and east from San Francisco, as men take two-hour lunch periods and exhibit their taste in food and wine, as the personalized cookbook tends to replace the

1. In *Movies* (Glencoe, Illinois, The Free Press, 1950).

Boston Cooking School type—in all these signs of the times we see indications of the new type of character.

Recently, Russell Lynes, in his article "Highbrow, Lowbrow, Middlebrow," [2] acutely delineated the contemporary urban American social system in terms of similar consumption indexes. Thus, the tossed salad is the sign of the high-brow, who may also be tagged by his taste in cars, clothes, and posture. What we really see emerging is an embryonic social system whose criteria of status are inconsistent with the criteria of the more traditional class system. This has been seen by Lloyd Warner, who actually defines class less in terms of wealth or power and more in terms of sociability habits and consumption styles.

Most people are able to live in both social systems, the older one based on wealth and the emerging one based on taste, without experiencing the contradiction of criteria as much of a personal dilemma. But there are groups where the contradiction can be seen in pathological form—those intellectuals, for instance, who wish that all of society recognized the Russell Lynes hierarchy, with them at the top of it, and are unaware (as we shall see in later chapters) how much of this recognition is already here. Jazz musicians face the conflict in the very texture of their work: are they to play music that offends high-brow (and their own) taste and climb in the economic hierarchy while sinking in the "brow" hierarchy? The issue often drives them, and other commercial artists, to drink and an early death. But we must ask whether similar, though less acute, anxieties about which hierarchy matters most are not becoming increasingly widespread. The other-directed character would be the first to feel the tension, and by his presence he testifies to the duality.

SEX: THE LAST FRONTIER

In the era depending on inner-direction sex might be inhibited, as in classes and areas affected strongly by the Reformation and Counter Reformation. Or its gratification might be taken for granted among men and within given limits, as in Italy, Spain, and the non-respectable elements, such as the "riverbottom people," in every population. In both cases there was a certain simplification of sex, in the one instance by taboos, in the other by tradition. Economic or power

2. *Harper's, 198* (1949), 19.

problems, problems of mere existence or of "amounting to something," were uppermost; and sex was relegated to its "proper" time and place: night, the wife or whore, occasional rough speech, and daydreams. Only in the upper classes, precursors of modern other-directed types, did the making of love take precedence over the making of goods (allegedly so in France) and reach the status of a daytime agenda. In these circles sex was almost totally separated from reproduction.

This separation, when it goes beyond the upper class and spreads over almost the whole society, is a sign that a society, through birth control and all that it implies, has entered the population phase of incipient decline by the route of industrialization. In this phase there is not only a growth of leisure, but work itself becomes both less interesting and less demanding for many; increased supervision and subdivision of tasks routinize the industrial process even beyond what was accomplished in the phase of transitional growth of population. More than before, as job-mindedness declines, sex permeates the daytime as well as the playtime consciousness. It is viewed as a consumption good not only by the old leisure classes but by the modern leisure masses.

The other-directed person, who suffers from low responsiveness, may pursue what looks like a "cult of effortlessness" in many spheres of life. He may welcome the routinization of his economic role and of his domestic life; the auto companies may tempt him by self-opening windows and self-shifting gears; he may withdraw all emotion from politics. Yet he cannot handle his sex life in this way. Though there is tremendous insecurity about *how* the game of sex should be played, there is little doubt as to *whether* it should be played or not. Even when we are consciously bored with sex, we must still obey its drive. Sex, therefore, provides a kind of defense against the threat of total apathy. This is one of the reasons why so much excitement is channeled into sex by the other-directed person. He looks to it for reassurance that he is alive. The inner-directed person, driven by his internal gyroscope and oriented toward the production problems of the outer world, did not need this evidence. Moreover, his relatively unemancipated wife and socially inferior mistresses could not seriously challenge the quality of his sexual performance.

While the inner-directed acquisitive consumer could pursue the ever receding frontiers of material acquisition, these frontiers have lost much of their lure for the other-directed person. As we saw in Chapter III, the latter begins as a very young child to know his way around among available consumption goods. He travels widely, to camp or with his family. He knows that the rich man's car is only marginally, if at all, different from his own—a matter at best of a few additional horsepower. He knows anyway that next year's model will be better than this year's. Even if he has not been there, he knows what the night clubs are like; and he has seen television. Whereas the deprived inner-directed person often lusted for possessions as a goal whose glamour a wealthy adulthood could not dim, the other-directed person can scarcely conceive of a consumption good that can maintain for any length of time undisputed dominance over his imagination. Except perhaps sex.

For the making and consumption of love, despite all the efforts of the mass media, do remain hidden from public view. If someone else has a new Cadillac, the other-directed person knows what that is, and that he can duplicate the experience, more or less. But if someone else has a new lover, he cannot know what that means. Cadillacs have been democratized. So has sexual glamour, to a degree: without the mass production of good-looking, well-groomed youth, the American pattern of sexual competition could not exist. But there is a difference between Cadillacs and sexual partners in the degree of mystery. And with the loss or submergence of moral shame and inhibitions, but not completely of a certain unconscious innocence, the other-directed person has no defenses against his own envy. He is not ambitious to break the quantitative records of the acquisitive sex consumers like Don Juan, but he does not want to miss, day in day out, the qualities of experience he tells himself the others are having.

In a way this development is paradoxical. For while cookbooks have become more glamorous with the era of other-direction, sex books have become less so. The older marriage manuals, such as that of Van der Velde (still popular, however), breathe an ecstatic tone; they are travelogues of the joy of love. The newer ones, including some high school sex manuals, are matter of fact, toneless, and hygienic—Boston Cooking School style. Nevertheless, much as young people may appear to take sex in stride along with their vitamins, it remains an area of competition and a locus of the search, never completely suppressed, for meaning and emotional response in life. The other-directed person looks to sex not for display but for a test of his or her ability to attract, his or her place in the "rating-dating" scale—and beyond that, in order to experience life and love.

One reason for the change is that women are no longer objects for the acquisitive consumer but are peer-groupers themselves. Freed by technology from many household tasks, given by technology many "aids to romance," millions of women have become pioneers, with men, on the frontier of sex. As they become knowing consumers, the anxiety of men lest they fail to satisfy the women also grows—but at the same time this is another test that attracts men who, in their character, want to be judged by others. The very ability of women to respond in a way that only courtesans were supposed to in an earlier age means, moreover, that qualitative differences of sex experience—the impenetrable mystery—can be sought for night after night, and not only in periodic visits to a mistress or brothel. Whereas the pattern of an earlier era was often to make fun of sex, whether on the level of the music hall or of Balzac's *Droll Stories,* sex today carries too much psychic freight to be really funny for the other-directed person. By a disguised asceticism it becomes at the same time too anxious a business and too sacred an illusion. Popular culture, as Everett Hughes has pointed out, increasingly plays sex for excitement, not for a laugh.

The work of Kinsey, valuable as it is, does not provide us with data concerning qualitative shifts of the sort described—shifts confined in any case to a minority of the population. But it makes sense to suppose that the inner-directed person, for whom sex is a variation from his workaday role—a variation modified no doubt by sublimations, repressions, and displacements—will regard sex differently from the other-directed person, for whom life generally is geared to interpersonal relations in both work and leisure and for whom meaning and excitement is found in "taking the role of the other."

This anxious competitiveness in the realm of sex has very little in common with older patterns of social climbing. To be sure, women still use sex as a means to status in spheres controlled by men. But they can do this chiefly in industries that are still competitive in the premonopolistic patterns. Thus until recently the theater and the movies were controlled by *novi homines* who remind us of those early nineteenth-century British mill owners who, before the Factory Acts, relied on their mills as a harem.[3] And Warner, Havighurst, and Loeb in *Who Shall be Educated?* [4] describe how women schoolteachers may still cabin-date their way in the relatively unbureaucratized hierarchies of local school systems. These, however, are exceptional cases; consumption habits in food and sex have, for most consumers, only the most peripheral connections with social mobility.

A particularly striking illustration of the use of leisure by the other-directed person for whom means have become ends is the cult of sun tanning. Marginal differentiation by means of bodily adornment (of which sun tanning is of course but one style) we know to be characteristic of all cultures. Yet there is a difference between contemporary American concern for body image and the patterns to be found elsewhere. For one thing, competition in dress, war paint, or tattooing is definitely related in most cultures to other "external" conventions such as one's status in the social hierarchy or one's role in the economy. But competition in body shape and color as it appears so intensely in America is not related to economic or social advance and only marginally even to sexual conquest. Color competition is an end in itself, not a means to any other end nor an insignia of one's achievements. In summer and even in winter both men and women enter a beauty contest in which they can appraise their personalities and compare nuances in shade and hue of epiderm. Their taste buds, tastes, body image and skin, their "pep," "vitality," and intellectual and sensuous qualities, are not exploited as avenues of ascent in a well-defined hierarchy. Instead, they are opened to inspection and introspection by a desire to share in the leisure agendas of the adult self-exploiting peer-group.[5]

3. See G. M. Young, *Portrait of an Age* (London, Oxford University Press, 1936), p. 16, n. 1.

4. W. Lloyd Warner, Robert J. Havighurst, and Martin Loeb, *Who Shall Be Educated?* (New York, Harper, 1944), e.g., p. 103.

5. The extreme case of self-exploitation for reasons not necessarily associated with economic or social advance is plastic surgery of the sort which, unlike straightening children's teeth or removing a mole, actually alters the person's Gestalt, so that he is no longer visually the *same person.* As the beggar exaggerates his deformity to excite pity, and by that very fact shows how hard the world bears on him, so the person who "normalizes" his looks to the point of change of Gestalt shows the degree of pressure put on the physiologically and psychologically underprivileged by the personality market of leisure and work. American race relations should be viewed in this among other contexts.

II. CHANGES IN THE MODE OF CONSUMPTION OF
POPULAR CULTURE

Mass production, in its constant search for novelty, encroaches on nonpopular avant-garde culture which, to escape these embraces, is continually in flight. The commercialization of jazz, for instance, has forced many serious devotees into the world of bebop. But, to the horror of the boppers, the most edgeless and sweet name bands today have bop arrangers, so that technically bop has been taken over by such men as Guy Lombardo and David Rose.[6] The standards of virtuosity in the mass media have been elevated to a very high degree by this chase of the avant-garde, a chase that is also connected with the need of the now centralized producers of popular culture to distinguish themselves by marginal differentiation.

As a result, the consumer, in his leisure pursuits, meets vastly increased standards of technical competence. These increase his anxiety about his ability as a consumer. He can no longer evaluate the work, the artistry of the performer, by reference back to the working sphere of his own life. He tends to respond to the performer as he responds to his business associates and politicians: in terms of personality, not performance. Unlike the square dancer of an earlier era who could participate in the caller's innovations, the consumer of modern popular culture has virtually no opportunities for participation. He is, in Marxian terms, alienated both from the means of production and from the (participative) means of consumption. The so-called audience-participation show is made intentionally so poor that the audience can patronize it. The popularity of these shows, with their faked unslickness, may be an evidence of the thwarted desire for participation and for criteria of performer judgment.

In Chapter XVII we shall return to this problem of audience competence and participation and explore some of the new kinds of critical competence the other-directed man seems to be developing. Here, however, my purpose is simply to set the stage, in broad outline, for an analysis of the changed uses of leisure by other-directed people. While it would be an exaggeration to say that people no longer find in their resort to popular culture the escape downward or uplift up-

6. Lasswell would call the process "restriction [of innovation or revolution] by partial incorporation." See Harold D. Lasswell, *World Politics and Personal Insecurity* (New York, McGraw-Hill, 1935), p. 6.

ward that they found in the era dependent on inner-direction (these old aims survive), their escapes are no longer clear cut, no longer so clearly differentiated from the drives of work. Entertainment today, far more than in a period dependent on inner-direction, operates in a context where energy is channeled toward problems of consumption rather than production. Entertainment, therefore, for the adult continues his training in consumer orientation; and the audience tends to become a group working at its role as consumer.

This situation is far different from that of the inner-directed man who, because he was escaping from his role as producer when he looked for entertainment, effectively left behind his daily life. Today's seeker of entertainment finds that the themes of the mass media take up the roles of his everyday life of consumership. If he reads *Life* magazine, for example, he will find himself confronted with making judgments of taste in art, home furnishings, and architecture —judgments that move him always to discard earlier affections and affectations for later, more high-brow, and more sophisticated ones. He is not dragged once a season to opera or ballet, like the inner-directed "upward escapist," but is confronted weekly with a critique of his surroundings, a critique, moreover, that moves in a constantly ascending gradient.[7] The reader is passive, in the sense that he does not participate appreciably in forming the taste standards he sees portrayed in the mass media. Yet, while perhaps most readers of *Life* are not bothered by a need to conform to its taste signals, some readers, including many readers of the more high-brow books and journals, are not passive, but active, in the sense that they feel driven to work at themselves to have the proper reactions. It is this that marks the shift from the slower-moving, more external conformity of the inner-directed devotee of fashion.

This overlapping of the adult education of consumers with the consumption or leisure sphere itself results in a general confusion of

---

7. Charles Livermore, formerly a CIO official, recently called my attention to the extremely rapid disavowal by Detroit auto workers of overstuffed, Grand Rapids furniture. Many in the last several years have gone in for modern design.

My point here, of course, is not to patronize *Life,* or self-improving auto workers, but rather to illustrate the rapidity with which high fashion circulates, forcing people to abandon, if not betray, earlier aesthetic commitments, while readying themselves for still further abandonments. Obviously there are many positive things one might say about the great improvements in American taste, and concern for taste, that are the concomitants of this development. (An interesting study might be made of the relation between installment-buying practices and taste commitment.)

entertainment with consumer orientation. Later chapters have more to say about this. Here I shall concentrate on another type of orientation, namely, the use of entertainment to counsel people in problems of personal relations. This is an instructively typical overlapping of the work sphere and the social sphere. Entertainment today, far more than in an era of inner-directed modes of conformity, takes up the task of telling members of large groups of mobile people what they can expect of each other and what they should expect of themselves. The inner-directed man learned what he needed to know of these matters in a primary group, or by a purposeful internalization of his schooling and reading. The mass media today are expected to perform ten-minute miracles of social introduction between people from a variety of ways of life and background. The entertainment fields serve the audience today less and less as an escape from daily life, more and more as a continuous sugar-coated lecture on how to get along with the "others."

ENTERTAINMENT AS GROUP ADJUSTMENT

In Chapter IV we saw how the inner-directed youth was made ready to leave home and go far both by directly didactic literature and by novels and biographies that gave him a sense of possible roles on the frontiers of production. In contrast to this, the other-directed person has recourse to a large literature that is intended to orient him in the noneconomic side of life. This orientation is needed because, with the virtually complete disappearance of tradition-direction, no possibility remains of learning the art of life in the primary group— a possibility that persisted even in the mobile families of the era dependent on inner-direction. The child must look early to his mass-media tutors for instruction in the techniques of getting life directions as well as for specific tricks of the trade.

We can trace an edifying sequence that runs from the success biography (Samuel Smiles or the Horatio Alger series) to the contemporary books and periodicals that deal with peace of mind. The earlier books are directly concerned with social and economic advance, dealt with as achievable by the virtues of thrift, hard work, and so on. Then we find in the first years of this century the development in America of the now almost forgotten "New Thought" movement. As described by A. Whitney Griswold, the movement's motto was: "Think

Your Way to Wealth." [8] That is, wealth was to be achieved no longer
by activity in the real world but by self-manipulation, a kind of economic Couéism. But wealth itself as a goal was unquestioned.

From then on, inspirational literature becomes less and less exclusively concerned with social and economic mobility. Dale Carnegie's
How to Win Friends and Influence People, written in 1937, recom-
mends self-manipulative exercises for the sake of not only business
success but of such vaguer, leisure goals as popularity. Perhaps it is
not only the change from depression to full employment that led
Carnegie to write *How to Stop Worrying and Start Living* in 1948,
in which self-manipulation is no longer oriented toward some social
achievement but is used in a solipsistic way to adjust one to one's fate
and social state. The same tendencies can be found in a large group
of periodicals, with an interlocking directorate of authors and with
titles such as *Journal of Living, Your Personality, Your Life,* which
testify to the alteration of mobility paths and hopes and the increase
of anxiety as a spur to social control. The *New York Times Book
Review* of April 24, 1949, advertises *Calm Yourself* and *How to be
Happy While Single;* the latter deals according to the advertisement
with such problems as "how to handle the men in your life (heavy
dates, office companions, friends, drunks) . . . making conversation
. . . liquor, boredom—just about every problem you'll encounter on
your own."

Obviously the tremendous growth in counseling services, including psychotherapy, also testifies to people's need for group adjustment. Certainly, there are many positive sides to a development that
substitutes for the older, external, and often pointless goals such as
wealth and power, the newer, internal goals of happiness and peace
of mind, though of course, one must always ask whether, in changing
oneself, one hopes eventually to change the world or whether one is
simply adapting to the world as it is without protest or criticism.
These problems will concern us again in Part III. Here, however, I
am concerned with showing how popular culture is exploited for
group-adjustment purposes not only in the form of manifestly didactic literature and services but also in fictional guise.

There is nothing new in the observation that people who would

8. "The American Cult of Success" (Doctor's thesis, Yale University, 1933); abstracted in
American Journal of Sociology, XL (1934), 309–318.

rather not admit their need for help, or who prefer to spice it with fun, look to the movies and other popular media as the sources of enlightenment. In the studies of the movies made under the Payne Fund twenty years ago, much evidence was gathered concerning use of the movies by young people who wanted to learn how to look, dress, and make love.[9] The combination of learning and excitement was clear in these cases, many of them being children of lower-class origin suddenly brought face to face with sex and splendor. Today, however, as audiences have become more sophisticated, the mixture of messages has become more subtle.

From a sample of a group of women's magazines, *Ladies' Home Journal, American, Good Housekeeping,* and *Mademoiselle* for October, 1948, I concluded that on the whole stories and features and, of course, far less subtly, many ads, dealt largely with modes of manipulating the self in order to manipulate others, primarily for the attainment of intangible assets such as affection. Two stories will illustrate: "The Rebellion of Willy Kepper" by Willard Temple in *Ladies' Home Journal* and "Let's Go Out Tonight" by Lorna Slocombe in the *American* magazine.

Handling the office. "The Rebellion of Willy Kepper" is unusual in that it deals with a work situation rather than a domestic and leisure one. It is the story of a paint salesman, Willy, a shy young man who has worked himself up through the factory. There is a pretty file clerk whom Willy wants to know better but does not know how to approach. At this point the stockholder's son enters the business, gets the promotion Willy hoped for, and makes time with the file clerk. Willy, previously so mild, loses his temper and becomes gruff and rasping with people in the office and shop. This is his "rebellion." His change of mood is of course noticed at once.

Willy, however, has built up an enormous capital of good will by his previous good temper, so that plant people, instead of turning on him, try to find out what the trouble is; it cannot be Willy's fault. They discover that the stockholder's son is to blame, and they set out to hex him—he trips into paint, gets orders mixed up, and rapidly learns how dependent he is on others' liking him if he is to do his job. Willy, in fact, saves him from his worst jam with a customer, and

9. See, for example, Herbert Blumer and Philip Hauser, *Movies, Delinquency, and Crime* (New York, Macmillan, 1933), pp. 102 *et seq.*

after a few knocks of this sort the son decides to start at the bottom in the factory, in order to earn his capital of good will. Thus the road to Willy's promotion is reopened. At the end Willy asks the stockholder's son what techniques he used with the file clerk. He is told to compliment her on her eyes; he does so and succeeds in making a date.

There are some fairly obvious things to be said about this story. In the first place, though it is set in the sphere of production, it deals not only with selling but also with a factory which is a net of interpersonal relations that will deliver paint to the customer only against a bill of lading marked "good will." The work situation is seen in terms of its human element and its noneconomic incentives. There are no problems about paint, but only about people. In the second place, the stockholder's son was able to date the girl not because of his wealth and position but because of his line, his skill in the leisure arts of language. Language is presented as a free consumers' good; one, moreover, of which the consumer is also a producer; there is no patent or monopoly on lines. Finally, we have a picture of the "antagonistic cooperators" of the same sex—Willy and the son—whose rivalry for job and girl is so muted that they can exchange advice on how to win both; in a way, they are more interested in each other's approval than in victory. In the end Willy has regained his lost good temper and his rival has given up his early arrogance.

Handling the home. "Let's Go Out Tonight" pictures the consumption frontier of a young, college-bred suburban matron. Her husband is a good provider and faithful; her two children are healthy; she has everything—except enough attention from her tired businessman spouse. The latter comes home, reads a paper, goes to bed, and his wife complains to her friend in their morning telephone chat that they never go places and do things any more. She looks back nostalgically on her college days when he was courting her and when life seemed glamorous. Suddenly she decides to go back to her college to see just what the magic was in those days.

When she gets to her old room she realizes that only in retrospect was her college dating effortless. Actually, she recalls, she slaved to arrange parties for her future husband, to manipulate him into kissing her and finally into proposing. She concludes that she just has been loafing on her job as a housewife, and returns full of tolerant understanding for her husband and enthusiasm for new and improved manipulation. By buying a new dress, arranging with a sitter to have the children taken care of, and similar measures, she inveigles her husband into a theater date and is able to report success to her friend on the telephone.

What is striking here, as in "Willy Kepper" and most of the stories—as indeed, in most popular culture for the middle- and upper middle-class urban listener and reader—is the realistic surface. These stories are close to home both in dealing with domestic-type problems and in dealing with them in an orientational way. In "Let's Go Out Tonight" the housewife reader finds a story about a housewife who has a tired businessman husband, and a solution that tells her: there is no perfect bliss and she had best resign herself to working hard for lesser and, indeed, symbolic gains. In both stories the ends are given by the social system—for Willy, the job and the pretty girl; for the housewife, being taken out—and the latter end is patently lacking in substantive content: it is itself a means. Assuming the ends, the stories concentrate on the means: the technique, the smooth achievement of interpersonal response for its own sake.

By this type of "realism," however, the reader is permitted to "escape" neither into uplifting thoughts or into distant ones. There is no uplift because of the refusal, especially clear in "Let's Go Out Tonight," to admit that there can be decisively better marriages than this one, with its continuous petty deception. The reader is not encouraged to make great demands on life or on himself. Rather, both stories assume that there is a solution that involves neither risk nor hardship but only the commodities—interpersonal effort and tolerance—that the other-directed person has in surplus stock anyway.

Handling "reality." The other-directed person would hardly know how to respond to some of the older themes of literature. Observe, for example, audience reactions to such a play as the recent Robinson Jeffers' version of *Medea*. A number of people who saw this play agreed with me that the play's themes of fiery vengeance and jealousy struck many in the audience as funny or remote. Some critics, judging by their reviews, saw the play primarily as "a fine vehicle for Judith Anderson"; some in the audience, judging by their comments, also reacted as connoisseurs of Miss Anderson's virtuosity; this consumer preference was the only thing that could strike home to them. Yet the play has been a box-office success; possibly, portrayals of passion fascinate people who have themselves lost their ability for emotional response.[10]

Stories such as "Willy Kepper" and "Let's Go Out Tonight" provide neither escape nor orientation. It is an understatement to say that they fail to probe the abyss of rage and anxiety that underlies the actions they portray. Taking their people, and their people's tricks, at face value, they do not really understand them, nor criticize the ends they seek. They are *Tootle the Engine* all over again, this time for adults. Does this mean that they are calculated steps in a manipulative chain?

"Conspiracy" theories of popular culture are quite old, summed up as they are in the concept of "bread and circuses." In "The Breadline and the Movies" Thorstein Veblen presented a more sophisticated concept, namely, that the modern American masses paid the ruling class for the privilege of the very entertainments that helped to keep them under laughing gas. Such views assume the culture to be more of a piece than it is; and we shall return in Part II to the question whether America really has a ruling class today. In any case, group adjustment and orientational influence in contemporary popular culture are not necessarily in the interest of any particular class. As a matter of fact, pressures for other-directed conformity appear strongest in the upper middle classes, although to the extent that the class line grows increasingly indistinct these influences permeate, with varying consequences for character, the middle and lower classes as well. The form these pressures take may best be illustrated by a few examples.

Heavy harmony. The head of a progressive boarding school in the East recently addressed the parents of its children as follows:

The music department at X School wishes to provide for every child, as rich a musical experience as possible.

---

10. Paradoxically, much criticism of popular culture is aimed just at those elements of apparent fantasy which, in a broader perspective, are most real. Hortense Powdermaker, for instance, criticizes such movies as *Smash-up* and *Unfaithful* as unreal because they show women driven to drink or murder by love. ("An Anthropologist Looks at the Movies," *The Annals,* 254 [1947], 80.) Yet such movies, by admitting the possibility of no adequate solution and by revealing passionate jealousy, may actually present a truer picture of alternatives than the more statistically correct "Let's Go Out Tonight." If the heroine of the latter could recognize her frustration rather than displace it, she might become less adjusted socially but might stand a chance of becoming more integrated psychologically, more autonomous. In that sense there is nothing more distorting than the gloss finish of "realism"— and nothing more true and evocative than seeming extremes of fantasy.

We believe that music is a necessary part of life and its influence is felt in every phase of living. Singing and playing together can bring understanding and good-will and it seems to me that this world needs more of this kind of harmony.

At X, we try to provide some kind of music participation for every child and wish to encourage more musical activity, especially that of playing with a group in an orchestra.

This letter does not betray much interest in music as such. It sees music primarily as a way of bringing people together locally and internationally too. Music as a way of escape into one's individual creative life—a private refuge—would strike many such school authorities today as selfish.

An experience I had when discussing John Stuart Mill's *On Liberty* with a class of college students is a further illustration. Mill expresses in the essay his prescient awareness, shared by his friend Tocqueville, of the growing pressure of other-directed conformity. The students were quite hostile to Mill, and to sharpen the issue I asked them how they would feel about a fellow student who took no part in politics or group activity of any sort, did no harm to anyone else, refused to concern himself with social science, and devoted himself passionately to his music. The students found the very notion of such a student shocking. They felt such a person would not be justified, as one of them put it, to care only about music in the age of the Bomb. Some would have allowed an exception to be made if he were a genius!

A similar theme appears in more refined form in Helen Howe's novel of Harvard academic life, *We Happy Few*.[11] The heroine Dorothea is viewed by Miss Howe as a selfish woman who, during the war, escapes from her social duties by having a love affair and by playing Bach and Mozart to herself on the piano. She is taken in the novel through a series of group-adjustment experiences that deflate what Miss Howe regards as her intellectual snobbery. Becoming a nurse's aid, she meets other nurses's aids socially; they are fine and dull. Traveling to Coeur d'Alene to be near her son in training, she "sees" America: in the stench of the ladies' room, the sadness of platform partings, the goodheartedness of midwesterners. The townsfolk of Coeur d'Alene are another group-adjusting experience; they, too, are fine and dull. At the end Dorothea returns to Cambridge a sadder and wiser woman: her pride is gone, and she has learned humbly to admire the

11. I have dealt with the implications of this book in more detail in "The Ethics of We Happy Few," *University Observer*, I (1947), 19; I draw on this article in what follows.

great open spaces and the open sentiments usually associated with them in song and story.

As a symbol of the learning process, Miss Howe writes that Dorothea, while a nurse's aid staggering through agonizing days at the hospital, learns in her few off hours to enjoy Schumann as well as her beloved Bach and Mozart: "Her aesthetic as well as her human taste was stretching, too—cruder, possibly, but warmer and more inclusive."

This quotation hardly needs comment. Instead of permitting the heroine to escape either up or down from the exasperating human contacts of a nurse's work day, Dorothea must move sideways. She must acquire warmer, group-adjusted musical tastes—she would be forgiven even more, doubtless, if she learned to like Ethelbert Nevin.

The reference to warmth is especially significant in the analysis of peer-group consumption preferences for people. In a very interesting set of experiments, the psychologist Solomon Asch has shown that the warm-cold axis is for his student subjects the controlling dimension of personality: people who are said to be warm are positively valued no matter what other traits they have, while people who are cold are distrusted no matter how honorable and brave they may be.[12] A kind of generalized "more inclusive" warmth is the oil by which the other-directed person adjusts the friction bearings of his human contacts—it is the warmth of the glad handers whom Dorothea learns to admire.

Yet granting that Dorothea should learn this interpersonal art as a benefit to her work as a nurse's aid—perhaps the sick are a special case and do need warmth of this sort—it is striking that she must bring the identical attitude into her leisure time: no change of roles is permitted. Leisure and work must, like Dorothea herself, be stretched (assuming, falsely, that Schumann's sentimentality is "warmer") until they completely overlap. The theme of both is group adjustment.

What I have said is not to be understood as a polemic for coldness as against warmth or as a criticism of the genuine elements in the other-directed person's concern for warmth, in himself and in others. Certainly it is an advance to get away from the compulsory emotional constriction, the frightening coldness, of many inner-directed Americans—an advance to open up group sociability to a wider and more outgoing type of responsiveness.

12. See Solomon E. Asch, "A Test for Personality," *Journal of Abnormal and Social Psychology, 41* (1946), 258–290.

Lonely successes. In our discussion of the comics and of *Tootle* we saw how modern popular culture teaches the dangers of aloneness and, by contrast, the virtues of group-mindedness. In a thoughtful article, "The Gangster as Tragic Hero," Robert Warshow deals with a number of recent gangster films from this perspective.[13] He notes that, inevitably, the gangster's success spells his undoing. For it cuts him off from the group—not only the law-abiding community but also his own gang. At the peak of success he is therefore miserable and frightened, waiting to be cut down from the heights.

We can interpret this legend as a cautionary tale as to what happens if one goes off on one's own pursuits. Success is fatal. According to the code of the movies one is not permitted to identify with the lonely escapist; his lot is pictured, like that of Dorothea in the novel, as a set of miseries and penances. The movie *Body and Soul* points a similar moral. The hero (John Garfield) is a Jewish boy from the East Side who gets to be boxing champion and proceeds to alienate all surrounding groups: his family circle and faithful girl; his unambitious, devoted retinue; the East Side Jews who see him as a hero. He agrees for a large sum to throw his last fight and bets against himself, which would have brought him wealth—and utter alienation from these groups. En route to the fight he is told that the Jews see him as a hero, a champion in the fight against Hitler. Recalled to "himself," he double-crosses his gangster backers by winning the fight; and, poor again, he is restored to the primary group of family, girl, and Jews. There was no way for this winner to take all; had he thrown the fight, he would by the movie code have had to meet disaster, but he is saved by his financial reversal.

A movie or book occasionally comes along that departs from this formula. *The Fountainhead,* by Ayn Rand, a popular book and movie, pictures its architect hero as standing out, in violent integrity, against the pressure for group adjustment and, in the end, successfully bringing the jury of his peers along with him. He *does* take all: the heights of fame, his rival's wife, the death of his rival. What is most striking in all this, however, is the unintended caricature, both of group adjustment and of group resistance. The group is made out not as tolerant but as mean, inartistic, and corrupt. And group resistance is seen in terms of nobility on the part of the sadistic hero, who wants to deny any ties to humanity, any dependency. This superman

13. *Partisan Review,* XV (1948), 240.

for adults is the very apotheosis of the lonely success, to be admired perhaps by the reader but too stagey to be imitated.

In all likelihood, moreover, the Ayn Rand audience that applauds fiery denunciations of group-mindedness and submission to others, is quite unaware of its own tendencies to submission in the small, undramatic situations of daily life. In that sense *The Fountainhead* is escapist.

GOOD-BYE TO ESCAPE?

So far, in these illustrations, we have seen little that would correspond to the unambiguous escapes of the inner-directed. Rather, we have seen popular culture used, often quite desperately, for training in consumer orientation and group adjustment. Despite appearances the other-directed person seems often unable to get away from himself or to waste time with any gestures of abundance or abandon. (Of course, if we compared patterns of alcoholic escape, we might come up with somewhat different results.)

The inner-directed person, if influenced by Protestantism, is of course also unable to waste time. The mobile youth from the lower classes shows his commitment to inner-direction by cutting himself off from hard-drinking, horse-play-indulging pals: he continues the production of an inner-directed character through practicing a kind of mental bookkeeping by which the demons of Waste and Sloth are ruthlessly driven out. Such a person has little leisure, unless he can justify it as self-improving, and a life that has never an idle moment must have many a tense one. On the face of it the other-directed person is no puritan; he seems much less preoccupied with waste. But an attenuated puritanism survives in his exploitation of his leisure. He may say, when he takes a vacation or stretches a weekend, "I owe it to myself"—but the self in question is viewed like a car or house whose upkeep must be carefully maintained for resale purposes. The other-directed person has no clear core of self to escape from; no clear line between production and consumption; between adjusting to the group and serving private interests; between work and play.

One interesting index of this is the decline of evening dress, especially among men, and conversely, the invasion of the office by sport clothes. This looks like an offshoot of the cult of effortlessness, and of course men say "it's too much trouble" in explaining why they don't change for dinner or the evening. But the answer lies rather in the fact that men today simply do not know how to change roles, let alone mark the change by proper costuming. Another reason may be the fear of being thought high-hat; one can wear gaudy shirts but not stiff ones. Thus the sport shirt and casual dress show that one is a good fellow not only on the golf course or on vacation but in the office and at dinner too.

Women are still permitted-required to dress for the evening, a sign, perhaps, of their laggard response to changing modes. (Similarly, one would expect to find tuxedos more frequently worn among the Negro than among the white middle classes.) Women are more involved than men in the dying patterns of conspicuous consumption. However, they probably make more of an actual shift from housework and babies to dinner party than many men do, who exchange office gossip both at work and play: moreover, they really like the shift, dragging the men, who would just as soon be in the office, along with them. I have observed that women's shop talk of children and domestic matters is often—though certainly not always!—conducted with more skill, interest, and realism than that of men since the change of role refreshes both work and play.

What is it that drives men who have been surrounded with people and their problems on the day shift to seek often exactly the same company (or its reflection in popular culture) on the night shift? Perhaps in part it is the terror of loneliness that the gangster movies symbolize. But certainly it makes for strain. Though popular culture on one level "fills in" between people so as to avoid any demand for conversational or sexual gambits, on another level the popular-culture performance is not simply a way of killing time: in the peer-group situation, it makes a demand that it be appraised. The other-directed girl who goes in company to the movies need not talk to the others during the picture but is sometimes faced with the problem: should she cry at the sad places or not? What is the proper reaction, the sophisticated line about what is going on? Observing movie audiences coming out of a "little" or "art" theater, it is sometimes apparent that people feel they ought to react, but how?

As against this, the inner-directed person, reading a book alone, is less aware of the others looking on; moreover, he has time to return at his own pace from being transported by his reading—to return and put on whatever mask he cares to. The poker game in the back room, with its praise of masks, fits his habituation to social distance, even loneliness. His successor, dreading loneliness, tries to assuage it not only in his crowd but in a song like "Night and Day."

Popular culture, then, is used as an indirect recourse to people. When I asked young people in interviews how they would feel if for some reason the radio should be shut off, quite a few were frightened at the prospect. They asked, "Is the government planning to do that to us?" One veteran of the Pacific campaign, who had spent two years in Korea, said he had once been at a summer place in Wisconsin where for two weeks there had been no radio. He said he couldn't stand it; nothing in the army, where he had the Armed Forces Network, was so bad. Without the noise of the radio, it seems, people feel as if their own receptors are dead. And indeed they have used the noise of the others to deaden the noise of the self.

It should not surprise us that the topics dealt with in popular fiction, are, as in the illustrations I have chosen, increasingly drawn from interpersonal problems in the consumption sphere. This marks a change from an earlier day, not so much in the content of fiction as in its implications. In a sense, popular literature has always been concerned with heroes and problems of consumption. The heroes of the classics were often aristocrats without visible means of support. The heroes of picaresque novels were not especially interested in work. The point is not so much that there has been a change in the topics of fantasy, but that what was once fantasy is now only one jump from being real. The inner-directed reader had much less chance of waking up as Robinson Crusoe or Cinderella than the other-directed reader has of driving the same make of car and of drinking the same kind of cocktail as Frank Sinatra or Joan Crawford. Certainly, he can have the same problems as Willy Kepper or the heroine of "Let's Go Out Tonight." Even when he tries to escape into fantasy, the other-directed person cannot get away from the "others" and his relationships with them.

To put this another way, the child enjoys reading stories about personalized animals or personalized engines and tugboats because the world of people is still new and strange, even somewhat terrifying. By reading Aesop or *Bugs Bunny* or *Peter Rabbit* he can play with his problem of understanding people and their motives. If he is inner-directed he may grow up to read historical novels (of the older, pre-*Forever Amber* variety) or science fiction such as the *War of the*

Worlds and its current interplanetary successors, stories not involving contemporary problems of interpersonal relations. But the other-directed child moves from stories about personalized animals to comics about personalized figures of the underworld, and from them to movies, radio, and fiction that, unlike the slowly disappearing B-thrillers and westerns, are aimed at the audience's problems of orientation. But what is play for the child is work for the adult, and there is no escape from leisure.

III. A CAVEAT

As remarked in the Preface, my terminology favors a tendency, that I have noticed in discussing my character types with people, to think of inner-direction as preferable to other-direction, despite my insistence that direction in *both* cases comes from outside and is simply internalized at an early point in the life cycle of the inner-directeds. Moreover, certain overemphases result from taking an ideal-typical other-directed person and seeing him through the round of work and play as if, in all spheres, he is in fact as other-directed as it is possible to be. Real people, however, are not to be mistaken for social science constructions: within any schema of character types they cannot be fitted whole. Some men, for instance, may be inner-directed in their hobbies; other-directed in their work; autonomous, or indeed directionless, in still other spheres. We must see real people as a whole and through their entire life cycle, if we can, before we presume to pass judgment as to their satisfactions in living.

Furthermore, there are factors outside of terminology that may lead readers to conclude that inner-direction is better. Academic and professional people are frequently only too pleased to be told that those horrid businessmen, those glad-handing advertisers, are manipulative. And, as we all know, the businessmen and advertiser themselves flock to plays and movies that tell them what miserable sinners they are. Of course it is especially gratifying to look down one's nose at Hollywood, soap opera, and other mass-culture phenomena.

The inner-directeds of high status, moreover, are associated with the Anglo-Saxon tradition and with the reverence we pay to those among the aged who are still powerful. Furthermore, since the inner-directeds face problems that are not the problems of the other directed, they seem to be made of sterner and more intrepid stuff. As we already find the Victorians charming, so we can patronize the inner-directeds, especially if we did not personally suffer from their limitations, and view the era depending on inner-direction with understandable nostalgia.

These were, in fact, among the considerations that led me to employ the term "other-directed" in preference to Erich Fromm's term "the marketing orientation," despite the germinal role this latter concept played in the development of our own typology. For, out of context, "the marketer" might seem to refer only to a person actively engaged in marketing, i.e., in business; as we shall see more fully in Chapter XIII, I believe businessmen tend already to be viewed with an excessive contempt.

I do not want to be understood as saying it is wrong to be concerned with the "others," with human relations. That we can afford to be concerned with such problems is one of the important abundances of a high technology society. We must ask anyone who opposes the manipulation of men in modern industry whether he prefers to return to their brutalization, as in the early days of the industrial revolution. In my scheme of values, persuasion, even manipulative persuasion, is to be preferred to force. There is the danger, in fact, when one speaks of the "softness of the personnel," that one will be understood to prefer hardness. On the contrary, one of the main contentions of this book is that the other-directed person, as things are, is already too hard on himself in certain ways and that his anxieties, as child consumer-trainee, as parent, as worker and player, are very great. He is often torn between the illusion that life should be easy, if he could only find his way to the proper group-adjustment practices, and the half-buried feeling that it is not easy for him. Under these conditions it would only complicate his life still further to hold up the opposite illusion of stern inner-direction as an ideal, though this, as we shall see in Part III, is just what many people propose.

To be sure, in the preceding pages I have occasionally been sharp in comment on the other-directed round of life and especially on child-rearing practices conducive to other-direction; but I have not wanted to score verbal victories over tendencies which may not be present in many readers anyway—rather to strike at powerfully supported but still not fully understood developments. Yet it is difficult not to mistake one's emphasis, as should be clear from the discussion in Chapter IV of the ambiguities inevitably present in the reception of print. I know that there is much snobbery and asceticism behind current criticism, including socialist criticism, of mass leisure and of personnel relations. Indeed, a critique of the glad hand can be made from many standpoints, radical or reactionary. But such a critique makes perhaps less sense if it is based on models developed in the era of the invisible hand, or even earlier, than if it rests in part on an at least implicitly new view of society, a view of the potentialities of leisure and abundance to which both the glad hand and the search for self- and group-adjusting lessons in popular culture are themselves often poignant testimonials.

PART II

POLITICS

VIII

Recognizing the Political

It is difficult to say what place is taken up in the life of an inhabitant of the United States by his concern for politics. To take a hand in the regulation of society and to discuss it is his biggest concern, and, so to speak, the only pleasure an American knows. . . .

In some countries, the inhabitants seem unwilling to avail themselves of the political privileges which the law gives them; it would seem that they set too high a value upon their time to spend it on the interests of the community . . . But if an American were condemned to confine his activities to his own affairs, he would be robbed of one half of his existence; he would feel an immense void in the life which he is accustomed to lead, and his wretchedness would be unbearable.

Tocqueville, *Democracy in America*

I TURN IN this part of the book to an introductory effort to apply to American politics the theory of character developed in the preceding part. First, however, the problems and limitations of this sort of approach to politics must be pointed out. My general thesis is that the inner-directed character tended and still tends in politics to express himself in the style of the "moralizer," while the other-directed character tends to express himself politically in the style of an "inside-dopester." These styles are also linked with a shift in political mood from "indignation" to "tolerance," and a shift in political decision from dominance by a ruling class to power dispersal among many marginally competing pressure groups. Some of these shifts are, in fact, among the causative factors for the rise of other-direction; a character structure which, when manifested in a political style, then intensifies the tendencies in political life that encourage still more other-direction.

Having said this, I must immediately make certain qualifications. Indeed, I fear I have all too often called to the reader's attention the limitations of social class and region, and of observational standpoint, which bound the picture of character in America I have presented. Furthermore, as I have also said before, real people are blends, more complicated and various—things of shreds and patches—than any scheme can encompass. They may, for example, be on the whole other-directed, but politics may be a sphere in which they are more inner-directed than otherwise. Or, people may manage to be productive in politics—to have a style that is superior to that of the moralizer and that of the inside-dopester—even though in their life as a whole they appear to be "lost": politics may be their most healthy activity. Conversely, many people who are generally autonomous in character, neither inner-directed nor other-directed, may in politics be indifferents, or moralizers, or inside-dopesters: politics may be a sphere in which, for any number of reasons, they are less adequate than in others.

But these "chameleonings" of character are not the only factors that forbid us to explain or predict specific political behavior on psychological grounds alone. To take only one instance, the crisis mood of much contemporary politics, its often stale atmosphere of unimaginative vicious circling, may be in itself enough, or virtually enough, to explain the failure of people to develop new political styles—to bring, that is, new motivations to politics and new ways of defining what politics is, even though their character may have changed.

My investigation is not directly concerned with the political as defined from the standpoint of the state or from the standpoint of the groups, parties, and classes into which the state is divided for purposes of formal political analysis. While not denying that the formal approach is useful, my emphasis, like that of many people today, is not so much on the political sphere itself as on the process by which people become related to it, and the consequent stylizing of political emotions. Obviously, the line between these two spheres cannot be too neatly drawn; the great tradition of modern political science that runs from Machiavelli and Hobbes to Tocqueville and Marx is concerned with both. This is one reason why, in speaking of the political consequences of character, I use the impressionistic term "style." [1] If poli-

---

[1]. While the term "style" is used here in a different sense from that employed by Lasswell in his "Style in the Language of Politics," in Harold D. Lasswell, Nathan Leites, et al., Language of Politics (New York, George W. Stewart, 1949), pp. 20–39, I am indebted to this essay; and my collaborators and I, in trying to relate politics to character, owe much to Lasswell's great body of work in this field which began with Psychopathology and Politics.

tics is a ballet on a stage set by history, style tells us neither whence the dancers come nor whither they move but only in what manner they play their parts and how the audience responds.

When I proceed, later on, from the problem of style to the problem of power, the connection between character structure and political structure will become even more tenuous than the word "style" implies. It is obvious, on the one hand, that many people today flee from the realities of power into psychological interpretations of social behavior in order either to avoid the challenge of contemporary political faiths or to restore a wished-for malleability to politics by reliance on a new analytical gadget. Nevertheless, it should be equally obvious that a political realism that ignores the dimension of character, that ignores how people interpret power configurations on the basis of their psychic needs, will only be useful in very short-run interpretations and not always even there. Chapters XI, XII, and XIII are an attempt to deal with some contemporary mythologies about power, for the light they may shed both on power itself, which always rests to a degree on mythology anyway, and on the character structure of the people who hold such views. Here, as in the rest of the book, what I have to say is to be taken for the experimental microcosm that it is.

Political history is a hard and perilous area—especially for one who is not a political historian. Let me begin by asking, keeping in mind observations like that of Tocqueville at the chapter head, what has changed in American politics in the last hundred years? How is the question to be answered? By reliance on Tocqueville himself and other gifted observers? He and other Europeans were amazed at the fury with which Americans before the Civil War threw themselves into political activity to the neglect, it seemed, of other aspects of life: culture, family life, love, the arts, and even perhaps statesmanship. Yet by way of contrast with the America that George III or Tocqueville saw, we must be aware of the America that Lord Bryce saw: an America in which the men of greatest ability, of strongest character and most impressive intellectual achievement, avoided politics like the plague; in which the great American cities, whether inhabited by foreign or rural immigrants, accepted corruption on an enormous scale as a matter of course; in which the proportion of voters to the total eligible voters dropped while the franchise was extended to women and the number of foreign-born declined. This was an America in which the people, in order to reform the "shame of the cities," finally resorted to city-manager plans and other schemes that called for the recruiting of experts to handle the vastly increased functions of the federal government. In short, it was an America in which the people divorced themselves from a large number of the functions Tocqueville had seen them exercising so enthusiastically in the 1830's.

Are we confronted here with established fact or illusion? Is it really true that political apathy constitutes a crucial and growing problem for America? Is it true, as many observers suppose, that there has been a great decline in political involvement in the last hundred years? Or is it possible that this concern about apathy among many middle-class people—social scientists, the League of Women Voters, Americans for Democratic Action, and so forth—says more about those who are concerned than about what has changed or is changing in America? It is plain that anxiety exists in the minds of many about the American's participation in his own political life. Yet, while it may be true that the American has given up old styles of political interest, it may also be that he has acquired new ones. Where shall we find, among the vast range of enthusiasms and cynicisms, a standpoint from which to interpret these changing political styles?

The standard test of an American's ability to respond to political signals has been his willingness to go and cast a principled vote. But in recent years we have come to recognize that the ballot is a crude index of individual aptitude for and relatedness to politics, just as the ballot box is a crude tool of political representation. On the one hand, we have seen that the sphere of the political is larger than the activity of being a candidate, helping a candidate, or voting for him. And on the other hand, we have found that political attitudes and opinions often can express themselves and influence policy more effectively through the new tool of public-opinion polling than through the older tool of ballot polling. Not surprisingly, while opinion polling began as a supplement to the classic methods of studying political behavior, the opinion poll itself has gradually become a channel for new types of political responses, in the hands of both pollsters and the polled. This may be one of the reasons why the opinion poll today has become in some senses a more ambiguous analytical instrument than it was when it was new.

For the polls demonstrate in new ways that all political behavior of large groups has a self-concealing capacity and that all methods of measurement create their peculiar ambiguities. In the days when the ballot box decided the issue, an opinion refused or obscured retreated to the periphery of the scene where the ballot box could not force it to a decision. Even the votes that were cast created obscurities. Did "Rum, Romanism, and Rebellion" really decide Blaine's fate? Did Hughes' fluked encounter with Hiram Johnson really give California to Wilson? Ballots decide, but always by creating some final indeterminacy about the way in which they decided. Likewise, the opinion polls answer some questions of meaning but create others. For instance, those interviewees who refuse to answer or register "Don't Know" on the opinion poll are, for one reason or another, refugees from the sphere of decision. To understand why they are refugees is to seek an understanding of some statistically marginal but emotionally determinative forces of American political life.

Let us take, for example, the problems that arise if one accepts the "Don't Know" answer more or less literally. Let us leave aside those "Don't Knows" who could not use and organize political information even if they had it. Let us leave aside those who get information but remain indecisive. The residue must be those who could use information but do not get it. Yet to assume the existence of such a group leads us to the question: how can they miss getting it when the mass media of communication pour it into them from almost every side? What sustains their resistance against receiving information that other Americans are so busily imbibing? How is it possible to live in America, speak and read English, own a radio, without having heard of the Marshall Plan, Henry Wallace, and even—as in one of our interviews with a high school senior—without being sure what party Truman belongs to?

If, on the other hand, we ask why so many people for whom political information has no conceivable relation to their political orientation are nonetheless informed, we are equally baffled. Why do the "Do Knows" know? The question opens one of the most interesting methods for study of American political life: the study of the way in which Americans obtain and exchange their political information. We can study their big talk and small talk about politics, and we can study the mass media as conveyors of political information and shapers of political mood. And since the mass media are massive, it is possible for the mathematically minded investigator to examine their content with a certain quantitative precision. Yet the mass media, too, possess a self-concealing capacity. As we know, there is not only the content of the media to consider but also the situation in which the content is received. The media not only supply information but also, as we might expect from the analysis of their complicated function in Chapters IV and VII, act as tutors in the way in which the information is to be consumed. In this they join the peer-groups of listeners and readers in creating a situation in which information is mixed with noise in the very process of communication, with the result that the media end up, often despite themselves, as creators of political mood and style.

Thus, no matter how refined the tests that are applied to the raw returns of a ballot box, an opinion poll, or a dip into the information-bearing streams of the mass media, the subjectivity of political attitudes tends to elude us. We cannot be sure what the effect has been of the expansion of the franchise, of the polls, and of the media. Consider the ballot. It was once believed by many that, if suffrage were universal, the electoral process would change and general political activity be heightened and improved. Who is certain that this has really happened as a result of total suffrage? In connection with the opinion poll, I am suggesting here that public opinion learns to organize itself in the individual, the peer-group, and the society in response to the expectation of being elicited—not, of course, by the poll taker primarily, but by others who are like him in social position and function. Hence the preorganization of the opinion response conceals some of its meaning from the poll taker.

Finally, when we look at the information stream provided by the mass media, it is even harder to be sure what its political effect has been. Doubtless the radio gives people bigger and better political coverage than they ever had—or if they had it, ever trusted. Yet many thoughtful people suspect that the increase of public information has accompanied a decline in private meaningfulness.

It is not my purpose to criticize these three levels of investigation but to add to them if I can. Any level of investigation makes brittle assumptions. The pollster, given his present techniques, must assume, for example, that his statistical groups, once he has broken them down by social class, region, sex, age, religion, and so on, are composed of individuals whose opinions, verbally similar, are also dynamically similar. However, as Paul Lazarsfeld and his co-workers have shown, it is possible to go far beyond this by the panel method, which requires taking the same individuals and studying the change in their opinions over the period, say, of an election campaign. Here the pollster no longer stands where the state abstractly stands—in the center of a field of group interests—but moves around in the dimension of time like a friend of the family, dropping in to see how things are going. Methods such as this make it possible to assess the political not only from the standpoint of the state, as a system of dynamic relations between one vote and another, one opinion and another, one political news story and another, but also from the standpoint of the individual.

To illustrate: the panel method and similar approaches make it possible to observe how Americans have learned to talk about politics. And how do they talk about it? In somewhat the same terms, with somewhat the same gestures and emotional style generally as they talk about the ball game, the movie, or the symphony. They seem to attach the same psychological meaning to their political attitudes that they attach to their consumption preferences in other spheres.

In a number of interviews, for example, when we asked young people, amid a series of questions on politics, what recent events they had read about, or heard on the radio, that got them indignant or excited, we received such answers as "the revolt of the Southern Democrats and the Dodgers losing," or "the Communists and that story about an ice man (a local street accident)." In such cases the boundaries of political attention seem almost completely amorphous.

Yet how can we be sure of the meanings contained in any overt political style? What, for example, does it mean when we find someone who discusses politics as if it were a ball game? Is this a mere convention, hiding a nonspectatorial attitude? Is it the often imaginative recourse to American metaphors derived from sports, but having an altogether different connotation? Finally, what part does situation play in the determination of political style, what part character, what part other elements of personality? An increasingly searching combination of intensive studies of individuals with less intensive studies of groups is being used, notably in work under way at Berkeley, in an effort to answer such questions; what follows profits from such work. We shall regard politics as one of the spheres in which inner-directed and other-directed people carry out their respective rounds of life and encounter each other in antagonistic or symbiotic fashion—as a sphere, that is, of the characterological struggle.

IX

Tradition-directed, Inner-directed, and Other-directed Political Styles: Indifferents, Moralizers, Inside-Dopesters

Sometimes people call me an idealist. Well, that is the way I know I am an American. America is the only idealist nation in the world.

Woodrow Wilson

I. THE INDIFFERENTS

OLD STYLE

THE NOTION that all adult members of a given community must be involved in its policy-making affairs is recent. In the ancient oriental societies, for instance, it was clear that only the dynasty and a small group of advisers and nobles were called upon to take the attitudes required to deal with affairs of state. Only among these ruling groups could the problem of indifference even arise. The rest of the population was not apathetic, but politically asleep. Likewise, in the Greek city-state we can think of apathy only among the citizens—women, aliens, and slaves were simply excluded from the sphere of political involvement.

The tradition-directeds in America are numbered among political indifferents of this type. Theirs is the classic indifference of the masses of antiquity or the Middle Ages—the people who, throughout history, have accepted, with recurrent cynicism and sporadic revolts, the tyranny of an elite. They have no means of being articulate politically, nor have they any conception of what this would involve. They

lack the elementary political tools of literacy, political education, and
organizational experience.

In the United States today the number of such tradition-directed
indifferents is small. There are few "reservations" where people can
avoid being affected by inner-directed or other-directed values or
both. However, among some immigrant groups and rural Negroes,
the old indifference of tradition-direction remains, at least to a degree.
I will take one example from an interview [1] with a middle-aged cleaning woman from the British West Indies, now living in Harlem.
Though she has been strongly affected by inner-direction, her political attitudes (allowing for guarded response) do seem representative
of certain themes of an indifference resting on tradition-direction.

Q. Do you consider yourself a person who's very interested in
politics, not so interested, or hardly interested at all?

A. Nooooo. My husband yes. He's a talker. He can hold debates.

Q. Do you make up your mind about what's going on? Like do
you know who you want to win the election?

A. No. I believe the best man wins.

Q. You don't think it makes any difference who wins, then?

A. No difference. The best man wins. They're all alike anyway
when they get in. All the same. They do the same things. A Republican gets in, or a Democrat. They're all the same.

Q. Do you ever hear things on the radio about politics that make
you mad?

A. No, I not interested so I no get mad.

Q. Do you hear anything else over the radio that makes you mad—
not politics?

A. No.

Q. Do you hear anything that makes you glad?

A. No.

Q. What kind of people do you think are interested in politics?

A. Oh . . . I believe more rich folks. Poor class would be too, but
they don't have no chance.

Q. Do you think wars can be avoided?

A. No. The Bible says the Romans will fight. (Something like that
—I didn't quite get it.) I believe there will always be wars (said al-

---

1. The interview was one of a number conducted in 1948 by Dr. Genevieve Knupfer
among migrants to Harlem from the deep South, the Caribbean, and Italy.

most with satisfaction, as you'd say "There'll always be an England").
Generation after generation—the Bible tells you that.

Q. Do you think we can do something to avoid depressions?

A. I think you can work and try to have something—but some
times will be hard and some times better. And if you have a little
something it's better but you can get along somehow.

Q. Do you think the people in Washington know better than other
people whether there'll be a war?

A. Only God in Heaven knows. Man don't know. We just hope.

Q. Do you think that on the whole the United States is a democracy?

A. I'll say one thing, she is a blessed country. Out of all the countries of the world, she is blessed.

Characteristic of the tradition-directed indifferent is an attitude
that politics is someone else's job; with the interviewee above, politics
is for her husband, the rich, and very likely the club of the white man.
The depth and tenacity of these proxy conventions are such that the
political indifferent of this type, though excluded from direct political
participation, has no cause to feel at sea. Having no sense of personal
responsibility for the political sphere, such a person seeks no power
over, and therefore seldom feels frustrated or guilty about, politics.
Indeed, beyond the ministrations of the "wise, the good, and the rich"
—to use Fisher Ames's words—responsibility for the political is not
man's, but God's.

NEW STYLE

So much for the increasingly rare indifferents whose political style
is compatible with a tradition-directed character, lowly class position,
poverty, and lack of political education. Much more important are
the indifferents who, no longer tradition-directed, have acquired the
elementary political tools of literacy, a certain amount of organizational competence, and a certain awareness of the uses that may be
made of political activity. To be sure, when we study the efforts to
bring political education and organization to those who live either in
rural or in urban slum areas, it often appears that the conditions of
their life do not train them in the political motivations or techniques
(such simple techniques, for instance, as the easy use of the telephone)
that are taken for granted in some politically conscious and active sec-

tions of the middle class. Yet in the course of the last century the spread of education, the shortening and easing of working hours, the rise of unions, and other more or less formal associations, the increase in experience with government forms and routines, seem to have increased the ability, if not the desire, of the poorer citizens to maneuver in the political sphere.

New style

Nevertheless, these people, in the main, do not participate. They vote, of course, when someone takes the trouble to get them out; perhaps for a price they will do more than vote. But only about two per cent of unionized workers voluntarily takes part in routine union affairs, and as the studies of Mirra Komarovsky and others have shown, only a slightly larger per cent takes part in community affairs of some sort. The Army Information and Education services discovered, as have many other groups, how little interest most people can muster in the more general aspects of politics. But this apathy of the great majority is not the classic, quiescent indifference of the tradition-directed. It is to a large degree the indifference of people who know enough about politics to reject it, enough about political information to refuse it, enough about their political responsibilities as citizens to evade them. Some of these new-style indifferents we may classify as inner-directed or other-directed people who happen not to have adopted a political style more characteristic for their type. Otherwise, they are people who are on the move, characterologically and socially, from one character type and social situation to another: uprooted tradition-directeds not yet acculturated to inner-direction, inner-directeds not yet acculturated to other-direction, and all shades between.

This is speculative, of course. External factors in the present political scene are often sufficient to explain a similar indifference in all classes and all character types. It is clear that an individual may withdraw completely from politics because the scene looks so hopeful that no action seems necessary. One might argue that American life can be sufficiently satisfying, even for many in lower-income ranks, to justify indifference to political efforts at improvement: in this light, as the Americans are rich enough and comfortable enough to afford more food, more telephones, more trips than most people, in their security they can afford more political indifference. Contrariwise, a person may withdraw completely from politics because the scene looks so confused that no action seems adequate or so hopeless that no action looks promising; and these too, are the feelings of many

Americans. A failure to act politically or to inform oneself, motivated in any of these ways, does not mean that the individual's indifference has anything to do with his character. All we can say is that a person's habitual failure over a long period of time to make any overt response to political stimuli may contribute to or in fact constitute what psychologists call a withdrawal of affect. This can spread from politics to other spheres as well as vice versa, with eventual results for character.

We would need many studies of the political consequences of characterological, as well as social, transition before we could make a definitive statement. To illustrate the problem, however, I will draw on a group of interviews conducted in a small county-seat town in Vermont,[2] where the older generation seems to be inner-directed, and the younger generation is becoming other-directed.

The old people in this community express feelings of responsibility for politics. Despite their lack of actual participation, they feel their relatedness to government, though it is often expressed only in grievance and guilt feelings. Thus, they say they ought to take part in politics. In referring to events they use the pronoun "I": "I" think, "I" want, "I" hate, and so on. They talk as if it were up to them to judge what happens in politics and, to the limit of their gifts and available energies, to guide it.

The young people of the town, on the other hand, while they have greater education and the elementary political tools, feel that political doings are no business of theirs. They have less grievance and less guilt. Both kinds of feelings, which might relate them to politics, even though inadequately, have been withdrawn. Instead, they take whatever government gives them, including the draft, with an almost total passivity.[3] Their references to politics are almost devoid of the pronoun "I"; sometimes the reference is to a group "we" and mostly to a group "they." More socialized, more cooperative than their parents, they do not react as individuals to what happens to them. They have passed from the indignation of their elders to indifference. This,

2. These interviews were conducted under the direction of Mr. and Mrs. Martin Meyerson, as part of a general study of the community's political attitudes and political history, in the summer of 1948. Rosalie Hankey assisted in the work of interpretation.

3. I am not saying, of course, that they should resist the draft by becoming conscientious objectors—that requires a rare heroism or fanaticism. It is their subjective attitude of which I speak, not their overt behavior: they have surrendered the privilege to criticize, to respect and express at least their own feelings.

plainly, is not the indifference of the tradition-directed. Perhaps it is the indifference of those caught between inner-direction and other-direction.

Whether their political style—even their character—will change when they in turn are the elder generation, no one can predict. Very likely, there may be a life cycle of political styles for the individual, in which relatedness is gained as well as lost as one grows older. Nevertheless, I am inclined to think that the new-style indifferents, passive and resigned today, will scarcely alter their political stance as they grow older—provided, of course, that general social conditions do not change appreciably. Their life experiences may bring them some degree of competence—if, for instance, they get involved with the Farm Bureau or union political leg work, but even their frustrations will be accepted, not resisted. We see here, if these speculations are correct, evidence of a long-range historical change in political style rather than evidence for the existence of a phase in the life cycle in which anyone might be indifferent.

Indifferents, old style and new style as I define them, probably account for more than a majority of the American population. We have already seen that they are not necessarily equivalent to the nonvoters: these indifferents may perform quite a few political chores, for a price or under pressure. Nor are they devoid of political opinions. Indeed, if we accept the evidence of public opinion polls that only some 10 per cent of the population refuses to be polled at all, while another 10 per cent or so gets into the "Don't Know" column, we might conclude that people in all regions and social classes have a sense of direct and easy influence on the forum of opinion and policy and that their willingness to have and state an opinion is a sign of political health. But closer examination of the attitudes that accompany the interviewing and polling process fails to support that judgment. Actually, these political opinions are connected neither with direct political self-interest nor with clear emotional ties to politics. They resemble, rather, the peer-group exchange of consumption preferences, though unlike the latter, the preferences are seldom taken into the political market and translated into purchases of political commodities. For the indifferents do not believe that, by virtue of anything they do, know, or believe, they can buy a political package that will substantially improve their lives. And so, subject to occasional manipulations, they tend to view politics in most of its large-scale forms as if they were spectators.

Since, however, these new-style indifferents have some education and organizational competence and since they are neither morally committed to political principles nor emotionally related to political events, they are rather easily welded into cadres for political action—much as they are capable of being welded into a modern mechanized and specialized army. The old-style tradition-directed indifferents, on the other hand, have no such potential; at best, they are capable of sporadic and more or less spontaneous action. The new-style indifferents, however, are attached neither to their privacy, which would make politics intrusive, nor to their class groupings, which would make politics limited: rather, like the young Vermonters previously described, they are socialized, passive, and cooperative—not only in politics, of course. Their loyalty is at large, ready to be captured by any movement that can undercut their frequent cynicism or exploit it. In all these ways they place hardly any barriers, even those of their own tastes and feelings, between themselves and the politically organized community. The only barrier is their apathy.

This apathy cuts two ways. It deprives them of the capacity for enthusiasm and for genuine political involvement, but it also helps protect them from falling for many of the fairy tales about politics that have mobilized people in the past for political adventures. And while the tradition-directed person can sometimes be roused, in his inexperience, into indignation and is even sometimes hungry for political indoctrination (as for literacy of any sort) the modern indifferent in this country has built up a fairly high and often fairly useful immunity to politics—though not to cynical attacks on "politics."

II. THE MORALIZERS

The typical style of the inner-directed person in nineteenth-century American politics is that of the moralizer. Since the inner-directed man is work driven and work oriented, his profoundest feelings wrapped up in work and the competence with which work is done, when he turns to politics he sees it as a field of work—and judges it accordingly. Presented with a political message, he sees a task in it, and, far from seeking to demonstrate his knowledge of personalities by explaining its meaning, he responds with emotional directness and often naiveté. While this, however, does not mean that all inner-directed people are responsive to politics and are moralizers, one sees in America of the nineteenth century a powerful tendency to moralize the well-defined interests of the self and hence to respond to political attack by political indignation. Therefore, moralizing becomes a virtually uniform political style for the inner-directed.

One variant of the moralizer projects on the political scene his characterological tendency toward self-improvement: he wants to improve all men and institutions. The fringes of the Granger Movement harbored such types in the last quarter of the nineteenth century, and perhaps the Cross of Gold speech marked a peak of enthusiastic moralizing of the "fisc." But by the time the issue arose of American adherence to the League of Nations Wilson was considered by many to be merely a moralizer, an idealist, unable to get his friends, his enemies, and perhaps himself to understand how aware he was of practical, manipulative problems. Another variant on the type expresses his moralizing capacity less by concern with achieving the possible good than by concern with preventing the perpetual recurrence of evil. This interest in repressing the evil rather than in evoking the good is carried over from his own personal struggle. Evil defines itself for him with ease and clarity: for instance, a lack of seriousness toward work is sloth, a comfortable attitude toward pleasure is debauchery, a skeptical attitude about property is socialism.

The inner-directed man, when he approaches politics, has a tendency to underestimate the values of easygoing looseness of political articulation. He does not look to politics for intellectual orientation in a confusing world, and generally he does not see it as a game to be watched for its human interest. Rather, he turns to politics to protect his vested interests, and whether these are of a "practical" or an "ideal" sort, he feels little ambivalence about them. Thus we might find in the same characterological and even political camp a tariff logroller and a prohibitionist or prison reformer, provided only that the former had some emotional charge behind his political pressure.

As we saw in discussing the characterological struggle in the first chapter, it makes a great deal of difference whether a character type is on the increase or the wane. The moralizer-in-power is representative of a class (the "old" middle class) and of a character type (the inner-directed) dominant in the nineteenth century. We turn first to look at his style, then at the altered style of the moralizer-in-retreat who represents the same class and character in their mid-twentieth-century decline.

THE STYLE OF THE MORALIZER-IN-POWER

Early nineteenth-century Britain presents an example of an inner directed political mood. Clear-cut class leadership was combined with a sense of participation in the history-making process; and history itself seemed goal-directed. Tolerance as a skill was called for primarily on the international scene, where British diplomats continued to practice veto-power (that is, balance of power) politics, until interfered with by the moralizer Gladstone. But the domestic scene seemed manageable and hence attracted the moralizers. Wilberforce and his cohorts succeeded in prohibiting the African slave trade despite the pressure of powerful commercial interests.

Much of what we know of nineteenth-century American politics may be seen in terms of inner-directed self-interest and inner-directed moralizing. While today we tend to think of moralizing and self-interest as contradictory approaches to politics, amalgamated only through hypocrisy, this very outlook says something about our own loss of political simplicities. In the nineteenth century moralizing and self-interested stances were compatible because, as compared with today, there was little conflict between the clear emotions felt and the clear interests recognized by the inner-directeds. The *Federalist Papers* are perhaps the classic example of this. To be sure, with the broadening of the electorate it became increasingly difficult to be as frank as the Founding Fathers—as Nicholas Biddle learned to his sorrow—and one result was an increasing tendency to divorce interest from morality or to cloud their junction in vague, demogogic ideology. Even so, until the Civil War, unconcealed economic interests constantly intruded on the political sphere, shaping up in great arguments over fiscal policy, internal development, taxation, and property interests in slavery or antislavery. Likewise, moralizing interests made themselves felt quite openly in the government of towns, in arguments about manhood suffrage, universal education, and slavery.

Let me give two illustrations of the shift away from these nineteenth-century patterns of political relatedness. If we look, first, at the platforms and programs of the pre-Civil War unions and Mechanics' Associations, we see that the self-educating workmen and their journalist friends were passionately concerned with questions of political, legal, and economic justice and only indirectly interested in wages and working conditions. These workmen were unashamed moralizers, eager to participate in middle-class religious and educational values. Their press and their meetings did not look at everything from the labor angle. Today such an outlook has all but vanished from the labor press and program, save for a few old-time Socialists or ex-ministers in the CIO. It has not been succeeded by a vision of clear labor interest, but rather by a labor line laid down as an ideology by the union officials to an indifferent mass of nominal union members.

Our second example is from a belated sector of American culture, that of the Negro. If we examine the masthead of the Chicago *Defender,* one of the largest and most influential of Negro papers, we see that the program for Negro improvement laid down in 1905 was almost exclusively put in terms of simple political and economic advance: the right to vote, to get jobs on streetcars, and so on. It is clear that today neither the editors nor readers of the *Defender* are so sure as to which way is up for the Negro. Moralizing has perhaps not declined, but it has become more diffuse; unequivocal interests and straightforward moralizing have been replaced by a growth of ideology, a Negro line laid down by the race leaders and applied by them to specific issues on which it is desired to have an audience respond.

In general the press in the era depending on inner-direction fortified its readers in their political role playing—reassured them that they had roles, and that politics was responding to their playing of them. Journalism zealously preserved an individualistic slant, personal rather than personalized—as it could more easily do before the days of the AP, mailed boilerplate, and chain newspapers—and its individualism helped foster the feeling of the reader that his individual political decision always mattered for him and usually mattered for the country. Cynicism toward politics as a whole (as against cynicism about democracy or bossism or other specific political form or usage) was virtually unknown. Indeed, a feeling prevailed in many circles that the millennium was near. The defined political problems of the period were felt to be manageable by their customary devotees: a few professionals (the bosses and a small corps of career officials) and the amateurs who worked part time or full time (the statesmen and good government people). The simplicity of the pattern is evident enough in the way it was reflected in the woman's suffrage conventions. With a brief look at related social issues, such as the labor of working mothers, they asked what any middle-class person would ask of politics in the nineteenth century—a right to vote for a duly selected politician.

Thus, the limits of the political sphere as well as its meaning were self-evident to the inner-directed man of the nineteenth century. Political activity was no more baffling in terms of motivation than work. So many political tasks needed doing and were obviously obligatory on the basis of one's class position, regional location, and morality, that each active person could find satisfying political employment. This employment was satisfying because many problems were indeed finally overcome by the reformer's zeal: not only was the franchise extended and free education spread, but the prisons and asylums were somewhat ameliorated, factory legislation was introduced, and so on. Perhaps it was only because these were, at least when taken singly, relatively limited goals that reformers were so successful; the reformers operated within the changing climate of that capitalist civilization which Professor Joseph Schumpeter has brilliantly described in *Capitalism, Socialism and Democracy*. In any case, however, there was little in England and America to compare with the enormous frustrations of the twentieth century.

In fact, it was characteristic of the moralizers, and perhaps of the inner-directeds generally, not to be aware of the narrow limits they imposed on their relation to the political sphere. Each reform movement of the nineteenth century powerfully channelized the energies of its friends and foes, without necessarily producing in either group a larger, more comprehensive and hence more realistic political awareness. If the aim sought was attained, whether it was emancipation or railroad legislation, the moralizer's grip on politics vanished in success. If the aim sought did not succeed, as the women's movement did not succeed in the nineteenth century, its members remained prisoners of a crusade. Even then, however, they felt the political sphere to be malleable: success would come, as it would to their own mobility strivings, if they worked hard enough and were of good character.

In conclusion, when we think of the inner-directed man's political style, we must always think of the interests he brought to the political sphere. He participated not because he felt obliged to further a highly cooperative group life but because he had something specific at stake: a responsibility to himself or to others or both. In general, and despite its partial compartmentalization, the political sphere served to further the interests of his class position, class aspirations, or class antagonisms. Since politics existed to satisfy needs other than amusement and psychic escape, it was felt to react passively to the pressure of those needs; men were masters of their politics. Conversely, politics could not and did not invade a man's privacy, since it could only touch him so far as he felt that it was responding, or refusing to respond, to the pressure of what he was sure were his interests. And this is perhaps one major reason why the political was a comparatively well-defined and indeed often overdefined and constricted sphere in the nineteenth as compared to the twentieth century.

THE STYLE OF THE MORALIZER-IN-RETREAT

These last remarks must be qualified by the realization that the old struggles, being dead, have bequeathed to history model partisans who from our present perspective seem more integrated now than they must have to themselves. The "good old days" are the days of Patrick Henry as he appears in the post office mural—a man without doubts, leading men who follow without confusion or anxiety. It is easy to forget that the Federalists were not always Federal, that the Know-Nothings knew something, and that Jackson was not a Jacksonian.

We must also recognize that many moralizers in the nineteenth century viewed politics not only in a confused and ethically limited but also in a slightly paranoid and autistic way. These men, precursors of the modern inner-directeds who feel themselves displaced, did not so much steer politics as permit themselves to be oversteered by their fears, which they projected onto politics. How else can we explain the emotion generated by the recurrent antiforeign crusades, the campaigns against mysterious secret orders, Catholic, Masonic, Phi Beta Kappa? It was often difficult for some Americans to see the difference between the mumbo-jumbo voluntary association such as the Masons, for example, and a social and class conspiracy. Likewise, the feeling of political conservatives that the world will come to an end if "that man" is elected does not make its appearance for the first time under the second Roosevelt.

Morbid anxiety of this sort is the fruit of an envy and bewilderment that are rooted in character. While the tradition-directed indifferents feel neither helpless about nor invaded by politics, because of the curtain that separates them from the political, the inner-directed indignants can easily feel helpless and invaded when things do not go well with them. As we saw in Chapter V, the inner-directed man becomes vulnerable to himself when he fails to achieve his internalized goals. Able to forget the invisible hand as long as he is successful, he seeks in his baffled failure to make it visible so that he can smite it. His politics, like his character, becomes *curdled* when lack of success reveals and renders intolerable his lack of understanding.

It is in part the indignant person's baffled incomprehension that makes him see the city slicker as having a great and disagreeable sureness of grasp compared with his own. He envies this, and overrates it. The urban magnates and lawyers of the nineteenth century were, in their character, almost as clearly inner-directed as their rural and small-town enemies. Yet the communications bridge between them, as between regions and classes, was always on the verge of collapse.

Today it is often assumed that, because the gap in education between city and country has narrowed and because such mass media as the radio attract both urban and rural audiences, it follows that the gap in character structure has also narrowed. Perhaps in some parts of the country this has occurred. But I think it more likely that the gap between other-directed city dwellers and inner-directed rural folk has increased and that the well-meant efforts to bridge the gap have frequently served only to make the latter feel still more envious and unsure.

Envy and the feeling of displacement—sources of a political style of curdled indignation—are of course also to be found among those rural immigrants to town who are city dwellers in name only. As long as such people, urban or rural, have political power, their malaise vis-à-vis the other-directeds may be muted; they can shape their world and force it to make sense to them. But when even this avenue toward understanding is cut off, the curdled indignant lashes out in helpless rage or subsides into the sort of passive, frustrated resistance that we commented on in Chapter I in connection with Erikson's studies of American Indians.

Another variety of moralizer, those we might term the "enthusiasts," far from resigning themselves to political frustration, hopefully tackle the most intractable tasks. The changing meaning of the word enthusiast says much about the history of political styles. The enthusiasts in the days of Cromwell and the Long Parliament were the men of spirit and vision, the Quakers or Levellers or Diggers. But in eighteenth-century England the word enthusiast had already begun to lose this religious meaning and to become instead a term of ridicule rather than fear or admiration. It is perhaps part of the same development which has added "do-gooder," "world improver," "reformer," and "Boy Scout" to our colloquial vocabulary as terms of contempt or friendly dismissal: to want to "do good" in politics is obviously to be naïve!

The enthusiast resembles the indignant in that his political emotions frequently outweigh his political intelligence; they lead him into half-thought-out crusades. But he differs from the indignant in the quality of these emotions: these are rosy and cheerful as against the darker emotional hue of the indignant.[4] Though the folklore has it that "still waters run deep" and hence that easily surfaced emotions are not genuine, this is, of course, frequently not the case: we have come to distrust the enthusiast because he violates our tradition of suppressing emotion, or more accurately, because he violates our conventional styles in release of emotion.

The enthusiast is apt not to understand the limits on change in human affairs which politics must recognize: limitations expressed by that disenchanted moralizer Sumner in his famous phrase, "Stateways cannot change folkways." Sometimes the enthusiast fails to realize these limits by focusing on unattainable ends, as the Millerites did; but more frequently by uncritical preoccupation with manageable means. In the nineteenth century the enthusiast was unceasingly active. If challenged, he argued, as he would argue today, that there is always work, and political work, for idle hands to do. Such an argument rests on ascetic feelings of obligation about engaging in or concerning oneself with politics as well as on the American penchant for activity as such—a penchant outlasting the belief in progress which rationalized ceaseless activity for many of the inner-directeds in the nineteenth century.

4. Indignation or hatred of this type is well described in the essay by Svend Ranulf, *Moral Indignation and Middle Class Psychology* (Copenhagen, Levin & Monksgaard, 1938). Though our emphasis throughout is on character, perhaps we cannot avoid here the interjection of temperament factors, such as the ancient distinction between choleric and sanguine types. See, for contemporary discussion of the relationship between temperament and emotion, Ernst Kretschmer, *Physique and Character* (New York, Harcourt, Brace, 1931); and Charles Morris, *Paths of Life* (New York, Harper, 1942).

Wars and technological changes, as well as the shift from inner-direction to other-direction, have brought the moralizing style, in either its indignant or enthusiast versions, into disrepute. The Civil War, itself a complex catharsis of the moral indignation that accompanied the political sphere in the preceding years, initiated a process that has since continued. Probably the few living veterans of the Civil War still retain a fighting faith in the righteousness of their cause. The veterans of World War I are less involved in their cause, though still involved in their experience. The veterans of World War II bring scarcely a trace of moral righteousness into their scant political participation. These men "ain't mad at nobody." It looks as though since the Civil War there has been a decline in the emotionality of political differences, a decline in the histrionic violence of electoral campaigning, and a decline in the reserves of indignation and enthusiasm available to any and all sides of an easily moralized issue.

Certainly, salient examples of the indignant style remain. The sallies of Mencken in the 20's were carefully aimed at the social groups in which most of the extreme moralizing was still to be found: the country people, the midwesterners, the small-town Protestants, the southern APAs, the corn-fed shouting sects, the small lodge-joining businessmen. That such groups have been somewhat more concealed in recent years during which other-direction has spread, does not mean that these older patterns have vanished. But they have been hard hit, and by stronger foes than Mencken.

Today, just as inner-direction in character is partly the result of a moralizing political style, so loss of emotion in politics leads to other-direction in character. In other words, politics itself, as it impinges on the lives of people and shapes their experiences and interpretations of them, becomes one of the agencies of character formation. This complex interplay is one reason why, within our broad scheme of character types linked to the curve of population, we find, and would expect to find, different national variants rooted in different national historical experience. For example, both England and America are countries that have arrived at incipient decline of population as the result of industrialization, urbanization, and the spread of contraceptive substitutes for a Malthusian morality. But both countries encountered these historic crises, as they encountered civil war, at very different periods in their political development. Congreve, living in a postwar reign of tolerance, might have been surprised at the recurrence of moralization in the Victorian Age, when the combination of evangelical revival and the pace and politics of industrialization upset the older political styles. Likewise, in view of the indeterminacies of history, it would be rash to predict that the moralizing style is doomed and that no revival in America is possible. Indeed, if influential others become moralizers, the other-directeds, because they are other-directed, will try to be moralizers, too.

III. THE INSIDE-DOPESTERS

For all the Athenians and strangers which were there spent their time in nothing else, but either to tell, or to hear some new thing.

St. Paul.

The spread of other-direction has brought to the political scene the attitude of the inside-dopester, originating not in the sphere of work but of consumption. This attitude is not entirely new, any more than other-direction is entirely new. Congressional moralizers often retreated before congressional inside-dopesters, and political hard workers often retreated before political glamorizers, even before the Civil War. Here, again, the change is a matter of degree.

The other-directed man possesses a rich store of social skills—skills he needs in order to survive and move about in his social environment; some of these he can deploy in the form of political skills. One of these is his ability to hold his emotional fire, which he must do because of the cooperative pattern of life to which he is committed. This skill is related to his inescapable awareness, lacking in the inner-directed man, that in any situation people are as important as things.

The inside-dopester may be one who has concluded (with good reason) that since he can do nothing to change politics, he can only understand it. Or he may see all political issues in terms of being able to get some insider on the telephone. That is, some inside-dopesters actually crave to *be* on the inside, to join an inner circle or invent one; others aim no higher than to *know* the inside, for whatever peer-group satisfactions this can bring them. I do not try in the ensuing discussion to distinguish sharply between the various types of inside-dopester. I do indicate in a general way what I think are the positive, and what the negative, elements in the several manifestations of this political style.

The inside-dopester of whatever stripe tends to know a great deal about what other people are doing and thinking in the important or "great-issue" spheres of life; he is politically cosmopolitan rather than parochial. If he cannot change the others who dominate his political attention, his characterological drive leads him to manipulate himself in order not to change the others but to resemble them. He will go to great lengths to keep from looking and feeling like the uninformed outsider. As we shall see, not all other-directed people are inside-dopesters, but perhaps, for the lack of a more mature form of their type, many of them aspire to be.

The inside-dopester is competent in the way that the school system and the mass media of communication have taught him to be competent. Ideology demands that, living in a politically saturated milieu, he know the political score as he must know the score in other fields of entertainment, such as sports. But while the lower-class person is apt to know a good deal about "policy," the numbers game, the upper middle-class inside-dopester focuses on "public policy" in terms of the game of politics.

The majority of inside-dopesters take no active part in politics, but there are those who do. Thus, we find many government and party officials who handle the political news in the way encouraged by their jobs, in fragments of office gossip. There are political newsmen and broadcasters who, after long training, have succeeded in eliminating any emotional response to politics and who pride themselves on achieving the inside-dopesters' goal: never to be taken in by any person, cause, or event. Even in radical politics inside-dopesterism is on the increase. For instance, the passionate concern with Marxist fundamentals prevalent among an earlier generation of Communists is avoided, even feared, by the present generation. Hence the young Stalinist of today may know how to get his candidate in a union local elected or how to corral fellow travelers for a front organization, but he lacks the kind of enthusiasm or indignation, fanatical though this frequently was, that sustained the earlier Bolsheviks.

Our interviews show, however, that some urban young people who are on the fringes of the Stalinist movement (mainly, people who were strongly for Henry Wallace in 1948) are numbered among the political indignants. Frequently, they use their inside knowledge simply as a means of getting themselves worked up about American political abuses: they have a positive tropism to evidences of race dis-

crimination, police brutality, corporate skullduggery, etc. At the same
time the interviews give some indication that this political stance becomes de rigueur among some groups of politically-oriented youth;
in these circles group conformity leads not to tolerance and political
consumption but to indignation and political action. Hence, paradoxically enough, successful other-direction may lead to moralizing, just
as we shall see that it does among some controllers of the mass media.

In general, when the other-directed man comes to apply his skills
and motivations to politics, the style he selects will depend on the
situation created for him by the others who set the expectations to
which he responds. This situation itself is not in the first instance the
product of his character; but it is his character that leads him to per-
ceive it only *in terms of the others*—to see not a landscape with figures
but figures with a landscape. His ability to assimilate issues in terms
of people induces him to see issues as others see them and, with seeing,
to pardon rather than to moralize. This virtue of tolerance, however,
turns to a vice when it serves to lower his own emotional tone by the
constant demand he puts on himself to be objective. This demand is
especially severe, perhaps, when he must try to live down his own
residual moralizing tendencies and bend his efforts to discovering the
inside dope. No matter how politically active the inside-dopester may
appear, he is essentially passive—a self-conscious puppet tolerantly
watching and making sure that the strings that move him do not
touch his heart.

THE BALANCE SHEET OF INSIDE DOPE

While the moralizer generally defined politics narrowly as the affair of a single stage called politics, the inside-dopester is quite prepared to see politics as a set of revolving stages. Indeed, politics today
refuses to fit into its nineteenth-century compartment. With the mass
media behind it, it invades the privacy of the citizen with its noise and
claims. This invasion destroys the older, easy transitions from individual to local, local to national, and national to international interests
and plunges the individual directly into the complexities of world
politics, without any clear-cut notion of where his interests lie.

At the same time politics becomes more difficult to understand in a
purely technical sense, partly because it invades previously semi-
independent spheres like economics, partly because of the growing

scope and interdependence of political decisions. For instance, in modern war people must understand that higher taxes are necessary, not to meet government expenditures or even to redistribute income, but because industrial and private consumers must be kept from spending too much and fueling inflation and because the government needs to buy goods and services that would be scarce if people were left with money to buy them.

The incomprehensibility of politics gains momentum not only from the increase in its objective complexity but from what is in some respects a drop in the general level of skills relevant to understanding what goes on in politics. While formal education has increased, the education provided by the effort to run a farm, an independent business, or a shop, has decreased along with the increase in the number of employees; and while there may be little or no decline in the number of independent enterpreneurs, a larger proportion of the factors leading to success or failure is no longer in the hands of those remaining as entrepreneurs. No longer can one judge the work and competence of the politician or government administrator from the confident, often overconfident, base line of one's own work and competence.

To be sure, one can still find many businessmen who think themselves competent to judge the job performance of politicians and administrators—men who believe that they owe their own position purely to their industry and ability. Such observers often deceive themselves (for example, by the formula that what government needs is more businessmen-administrators); and their illusion that they are judging the actual job performance of the politician is easily dispelled. The nineteenth-century businessman who put a ward boss on his payroll had a pretty good idea of where the money went or at least had no doubts he could find out if he cared to. Likewise he had a pretty clear idea of what would advance the interests of the business class. Today, however, the businessman who hires lawyers, fixers, and market researchers to deal with the government feels a good deal more helpless in the hands of the specialists and is doubtful as to just what may be his own interests.

We saw in Chapter VI that the other-directed businessman hires a similar crew to tell him what a proper business should be like; these men tutor him for his trusteeship. Likewise, he hires people to tell him what he should do about politics: what the score is and what it means to business and, incidentally, to him. We can see a shift in the type of man who profits from this particular opportunity to frighten businessmen. He is no longer the lawyer who frightens them about what a tiny but significant public, the judges or legislators, might do to them. He is the public relations man (often enough trained as a lawyer or at least not untrained by his legal craft learning) who frightens businessmen about what a host of amorphous publics, as likely to disappear on inspection as the Cheshire cat, might do to them or for them. This new-type counselor is apt to be an inside-dopester himself, and his businessmen clients are often accessible to him because of their own other-directed tendencies. But sometimes the man who lives by frightening businessmen is an indignant moralizer, goading his clients to crusades against enemies as shadowy as any the Know-Nothings went after; as we shall see later on, the other-directed man is vulnerable to others' indignation where this is not too ridiculous. While the moralizer's gullibility is often the result of the limitations he imposes on the political, the inside-dopester's gullibility is often the result of his belief that there are those who, like Walter Winchell, Kiplinger, *Newsweek's* "Periscope," and RKO News, see all and know all.

In sharp contrast with all these weaknesses, the inside-dopester does bring to politics a certain kind of realism that the moralizer often lacked. The notion of transcending the inevitable never arises for the inside-dopester. Though as we shall see in discussing "Conversation of the Classes," he sometimes has illusions about his own political power, on the whole he accepts politics as given. He has neither the moralizer's conviction about his own interest nor the moralizer's readiness to "go fight city hall."

This "realism" is, in fact, very much the same brand that he buys in his popular culture. D. W. Brogan wittily describes in *The American Character* how American women in the nineteenth century tried to moralize and reform their husbands. As against this, the heroine of "Let's Go Out Tonight" tries neither to get rid of her husband nor to reform him but to settle for small tactical gains achieved primarily by manipulation. The inside-dopester-as-spectator, as well as the inside-dopester-as-operator, has a very good idea of what the limits are; he does not set his sights very high.

Moreover, though the loss of competence and interest in work affects the ability of many people to judge politics, the conditions of modern urban life have created many new occupations where political innocence is fatal. A barkeep, handling cops, union business agents, and licensing authorities; an oil company economist, steeped in Middle East politics and its Washington extensions; an atomic physicist negotiating a Navy research contract and getting clearance for a colleague through the FBI—the knowingness of such people must be weighed against the loss of competence of the older type of entrepreneur. Likewise, the millions who play policy, or otherwise engage in illegal activity, probably gain some political sophistication at what is called the local level.

As against the mythical oversimplifications of many moralizers, the inside-dopesters include a corps of specialists who know much more than the often narrowly partisan indignants and enthusiasts even in the days of their power, let alone in the days of their wane. Many people, not only specialists, have become accustomed to thinking in world-political terms, and cross-cultural terms, such as were hardly to be found amid the ethnocentrisms—or world-brotherhood idealisms —of even a generation ago. Perhaps most important of all, the other-directed man has carried what are essentially political skills into many areas outside of formal political science as defined by the moralizer—for example, in the fields of city planning and labor-management relations.

While the excellent discussions of the press in *The Age of Jackson* [5] remind us that the editorializers of the early nineteenth century included a wider spectrum of opinion with more sophisticated elements than is often assumed, most nineteenth-century press discussions of international politics drew on such parochial slogans as "national honor"—in the case of Mason and Slidell, for instance, or the *Maine* Today, however, the mass media almost invariably discuss world politics in terms of strategic, including propaganda, considerations. The public is often asked to support a policy because such support, in a kind of self-manipulative balancing act, will influence public opinion; such arguments can only be made because of the heightened understanding, in an era increasingly dependent on other-direction, or psychological forces in politics.

Some may find current talk about our "way of life" reminiscent o

---

5. Arthur Schlesinger, Jr., *The Age of Jackson* (Boston, Houghton Mifflin, 1945). I am indebted to Professor Schlesinger for a number of helpful suggestions concerning this chapter

discussions of national honor. But the change is not merely one of phrasing. "National honor" could be a hypocritical phrase to cover such clear-cut class interests as led to our invasion of Haiti, or it could be grouped with the various internal xenophobias of the nineteenth century. Yet however vague the content of the phrase, what it de- manded of the national enemy was quite specific. "Our way of life," on the other hand, has many more psychological connotations; it is fairly specific in domestic content but highly unspecific in foreign policy demand. "National honor" sometimes strait-jacketed our for- eign policy in moralizing beyond our power resources or power readi- ness. As against this, "our way of life" gives almost no moral guidance to foreign policy, which seems, therefore, to be left to *Realpolitik*. Only seems to be, however. For just as the phrase "national honor" calls to mind a Victorian form of hypocrisy, so the phrase "our way of life" reminds us that the other-directed man conceals from himself as well as from others such morality as he possesses by taking refuge in seemingly expediential considerations. A young veteran interviewed in 1947 by the University of Michigan Survey Research Center, when asked whether he thought the United States had given in or had its own way too much in the United Nations, replied:

This will sound funny, but I think we are getting our own way too much. (Why do you say that? he was questioned.) Because we don't want the other nations to feel that we are trying to take over their countries. They know that Russia wants that and I think that's why there is so much argu- ment. But if they feel we are trying to grab, they won't trust us either and then we won't be able to steer this whole program which is what I think we should do. So when we don't get what we want and the headlines say we have been beaten on something, I think that's really good because it makes the other countries feel that we're just like them and that we are having troubles too. That would make them more sympathetic to us and more friendly.[6]

Psychological understanding such as this represents a real advance. The moralizer would not ordinarily have been capable of such sub- tleties, or interested in them. But this advance in understanding is partial only. The power of principle in politics tends to be underesti- mated.

6. Taken from the pamphlet, *Four Americans Discuss Aid to Europe,* Study No. 18 (Ann Arbor, Michigan, University of Michigan Survey Research Center, 1947), p. 13.

THE INSIDE-DOPESTER'S MORALE

In Chapter III I suggested that there were certain analogies between the tradition-directed and the other-directed person, as compared with the inner-directed. There is also a certain similarity in their helpless attitude toward politics. We saw above that the tradition-directed indifferent does feel helpless though not irresponsible vis-à-vis politics. He feels that politics is under the control of people quite unlike himself and that politics is to be dealt with by prayer or propitiation—and by fatalism when disaster strikes. The inner-directed moralizer was likely to feel confident about politics in the days of his power because his personal ignorance of the workings of the invisible hand was irrelevant, by laissez-faire definitions, to the continuance of his social structure. The inside-dopester on the other hand feels helpless vis-à-vis politics because he knows too much to be comforted and too little to be helped.

On the face of it this outlook might be thought to resemble that of nineteenth-century political observers who insisted that man was limited and to some extent rendered impotent to effect far-reaching social changes, by his own nature and by the organic nature of society that followed its own laws of development. Edmund Burke and other conservative critics of the French Revolution at the beginning of the century, and the Social Darwinists at its end, represent two strands in this general line of thought. However, these feelings of limitation were not necessarily accompanied by subjective feelings of powerlessness; and, at least in the case of the Social Darwinists and perhaps also in the case of Burke, a positively optimistic view was taken as to the course of society's organic development. If the world took care of itself—if reformers would only let it alone—one would not need to feel frustrated and helpless: one merely had to acknowledge this limitation and devote oneself to less than apocalyptic changes.

Contemporary forms of social determinism, on the other hand tend to assume that our civilization is running down, a view we find in the nineteenth century only in a few observers, like Brooks Adams who could hardly believe their own prophesies. Even the pessimist of the last century could not envisage how terrible politics might become in the twentieth century. But today men feel politically impotent, and their philosophizing reinforces the mood that befits their character and situation.

Does the inside-dopester withdraw his emotional allegiance from a political scene because it has become too complex, or does it appear too complex and unmanageable to him because his emotional allegiance has been withdrawn? It would seem that both processes occur and that each reinforces the other. Concerned with being "right," fearing to be taken in, hostile above all to "wishful thinking" which he equates with any introduction of his humaneness into his judgments—the inside-dopester deprives himself of the best yardstick he could use to test his experience: namely, his own reactions as a "political animal." In this, as in much else, he resembles the new-style indifferents; he differs from them chiefly in belonging to a peer-group that, reinforced by the mass media, approves and even demands his being up on politics. Yet understanding of historical change and understanding of the as yet unrealized potentialities of the present can almost never come from the highly selective classification of events handed out as the inside story or made even more alluring by being stamped as classified or confidential information. Such sources of information are, rather, the *class* media on which the inside-dopester of the upper middle class feeds, as against the *mass* media which sustain his imitators in the lower middle class.

Furthermore, in order to keep up with the political branch of the consumers' union, the inside-dopester must be prepared for rapid changes of line. In this respect he is like the negotiator whom we discussed in Chapter VI, who is better able to bring home the bacon of good will if he is hazy about and has not pressed his legal rights in the matter; the inside-dopester can make an easier opinion shift if he has lost the moralizer's ability to relate political events to himself and his practical interests. That is perhaps why the portrait of the inside-dopester as an official, in *Anna Karenina* (the image of Stepan Arkadyevitch Oblonsky as quoted in Chapter I), of Bilibin of *War and Peace,* and of Ivan Ilyitch in Tolstoy's short story "The Death of Ivan Ilyitch"—why these nineteenth-century Russians, attuned to the class media of the court, seem under their strange names so very contemporary.

There is evidence that in America rapid fluctuation of opinion is to be found primarily in the better educated groups, the groups in which we also expect to find the inside-dopesters. Thus, the very interesting study made at the Harvard Department of Social Relations of attitudes toward Russia provides evidence that middle-class opinion vis-à-vis Russia has swung much more widely than lower-class opinion, which was always hostile and suspicious. For the middle class, Russia became a wartime ally and, for a time, a postwar friend; this has been succeeded by violent hostility. Other studies show the same thing with respect to isolationism and war. On all these matters the middle classes, being caught up in politics and, on the whole, susceptible to the way the mass media present events, are capable of attending to a much more rapid change of signals than the lower classes.

Politics, as we have said, serves the inside-dopester chiefly as a means for group conformity. He must have acceptable opinions, and where he engages in politics he must do so in acceptable ways. In the upper class, as among radical groups, the influence of the moralizer is still strong, and many people who set the cultural patterns carry on with an ideology of political responsibility; they act as if politics were a meaningful sphere for them. The college student or young professional or businessman of the upper middle class may take up politics as he takes up golf or any other acceptable hobby: it is a fulfillment of social role and in addition it is good fun, good business, and a way to meet interesting people. It happens, of course, that people who enter politics, on one or another level, with inside-dopester motivations, may find themselves becoming emotionally involved, and stay for quite other reasons. More common, probably, are those inside-dopesters who use their political experience to justify their emotional anemia, drawing on their acquaintance with the inside story to look down on those who get excited.

With these inside-dopesters of the upper middle class we must compare those who can be found in small towns and rural areas who are in easy contact with their local and even state officials. In the small towns social distance between the politically influential and the non-influential is small, and very little in the machinery of government is opaque—the telephone party line on which everybody listens may be thought of as symbolizing this. Though ordinarily these people can muster quite a bit of indignation over the local issues, this is not always the case; and we find occasional small-town and rural people who, bringing to politics the cosmopolitan style of the other-directeds, give a good imitation of urban inside-dopesters.[7]

7. Compare the valuable discussion in Robert K. Merton, "Patterns of Influence: a Study

Indeed, the distinction between the inside-dopester and the new-style indifferent is often hard to draw. To qualify as an inside-dopester one has to have some familiarity with the political score. But then the question arises, which score? In the UN, in Washington, the precinct, the union local, the Will Rogers Memorial Committee, or where? And are we, in passing judgment, to set different standards for different regions, ages, sexes, and to make allowances for such subtle factors as intelligence? When we seek for criteria which, in the case of concrete individuals, will permit us to differentiate among political styles, such questions become exceedingly difficult. But when we compare groups rather than single individuals, it is perhaps somewhat easier to assess the social factors at work which separate those groups consisting of new-style indifferents, who imbibe some atomized political information, but not very much, from those consisting of inside-dopesters, who are avid and often discriminating consumers of politics. For ordinarily the inside-dopester, unlike the indifferent, is subordinate to a peer-group in which politics is an important consumable and in which the correct—that is, the unemotional—attitude toward one's consumption is equally important. The new-style indifferent can take politics or leave it alone, while the inside-dopester is tied to it by motivations hardly less compelling than those of the moralizer.

Even so, important questions remain. Why do so many peer-groups in which the other-directeds move continue to put politics on their bill of fare, and why is it that fashion does not, as it has with many intellectuals, substitute something else, for instance, religion? This is hard to say; what should surprise us in America is not the number of the indifferents but why their number is not greater still and why people hang on as moralizers and seek to inform themselves as inside-dopesters. I suggest as a partial explanation that the mass media of communication play a complex part in the training and sustaining of people (of appropriate character) in both these latter styles. The media are at the same time continuous bringers of information and tutors in tolerance for would-be inside-dopesters, and tutors and provocateurs in indignation for would-be moralizers.

---

of Interpersonal Influence and of Communications Behavior in a Local Community," *Communications Research 1948–1949,* ed. Lazarsfeld and Stanton, pp. 180–219.

Political Persuasions:
Indignation and Tolerance

The super market that "offers the shopper the subtle, psychological values" will have a better chance to build a profitable customer following than one which depends solely on low price and good quality merchandise, G. L. Clements, vice-president and general manager of the Jewel Food Stores of Chicago, asserted here today . . .

In determining how to provide "psychological values" attractive to the customer, Mr. Clements said he thought a business should seek to develop "the same traits that we like in our friends." He outlined these traits as being cleanliness, up-to-date appearance, generosity, courtesy, honesty, patience, sincerity, sympathy and good-naturedness. Each store operator, he said, should ask himself whether his store has these traits.

"Price and quality may be given as reasons why your customers shop at your store," Mr. Clements stated, "yet they will be the same reasons given by others why they do not shop at your store, but prefer other stores . . ."

Mr. Clements asserted that in seeking to understand the psychological forces motivating customers "we might start out by asking the question: 'Do people really know what they want?'" The answer to the question indicates that people do not know what they "want," Mr. Clements said. But they do know what they "like or do not like," he asserted, adding that "we must watch their reactions to determine what they do need or would like."

> From the report of the twelfth annual convention of the Super Market Institute, *New York Herald Tribune,* May 10 1949.

THE INNER-DIRECTED moralizer, as we have seen, brings to politics an attitude derived from the sphere of production. Politics is work, and work is good. Political activity is to be criticized in terms of its relation to morality and economics. Politicians are workers—or ought to be. As against this, the other-directed inside-dopester brings to politics an attitude derived from the sphere of consumption. Politics is good (or bad) for morale and is to be appraised in terms of consumption preferences. Politicians are people—and the more glamorous, the better. Moreover, in imitating consumption patterns, politics becomes a place where the manner and mood of doing things is quite as important as what is done. This corresponds with the other-directed man's tendency to put more emphasis on means than the inner-directed man did, and less emphasis on ends.

The mass media of communication are perhaps the most important channels between the other-directed actors on the stage of politics and their audience. The media criticize the actors and the show generally, and both directly and indirectly train the audience in techniques of political consumership. The direct training media are the modern descendants of the *Springfield Republican* or the *New York Tribune* and a very small number of old-time newspapers, with their inner-directed moralizing editorializers. Much larger and more influential are the media of indirect training: they include the whole range of contemporary popular culture from comic books to television. They dominate the use of leisure in all American classes except at the very top and perhaps also the very bottom; and their influence is very great in creating the other-directed style of response.

Although the pattern of this influence is complex it may be summed up in three generalizations.

First, since popular culture is in essence a tutor in consumption, it teaches the other-directed man to consume politics and to regard politics and political information and attitudes as consumption goods. They are products, games, entertainments, recreations; and he is their purchaser, player, spectator, or leisure-time observer.

Second, the media, by their very sensitivity to pressure and their addiction to piety, have a stake in tolerance. But even where they are moralizers in intention, the mood of the audience of peer-groupers will cause the indignant message to be received in an unindignant way. This audience situation, moreover, leads to an emphasis not on what the media say in terms of content but on the "sincerity" of the presentation. This focus on sincerity, both in popular culture and in politics, leads the audience to tolerantly overlook the competence of performance.

Third, while there is a significant residue of inner-directed moralizing in American political news coverage and editorializing, it slows down but does not halt the persuasions exercised by popular culture in favor of other-directed tolerance and passivity.

I. POLITICS AS AN OBJECT OF CONSUMPTION

We saw in Chapter VII that the other-directed man cannot escape from his characteristic life style in the way that the inner-directed man did, because the style of the other-directed is oriented toward consumption, including the consumption of approval. One can escape from work; one cannot escape from consumption. The inner-directed person can put away childish things, and only returns to them surreptitiously as an adult; the other-directed person cannot put away his childhood training in the art of consumption. Nor can the other-directed person escape as an adult from the increasing elaboration and refinement of consumer values and consumer roles—as we saw in the discussion of food and sex as consumables. The child, of course, begins his taste training in food early, while he must postpone his training in sex until adolescence (this postponement is perhaps one of the things that gives sex its frontier-like quality). In politics, however, the child can also begin to consume at an early age, especially in the middle class and in the schools that emphasize current events. Adulthood brings voting but otherwise little new consumer experience in politics. Hence politics is not much of a frontier for him.

The other-directed man's inability to know what he wants, while being preoccupied with what he likes—as observed by the retailer quoted at the head of the chapter—applies to politics as well as to other spheres of life. In contrast, the inner-directed man, in those spheres of life, such as politics, that he identified with work, knew what he wanted but did not really allow himself to know what he liked.

The mass media cater to these confusions of the other-directed man. The radio and the newsreel particularly, but also much of the press, cover politics in the very form and fashion in which they cover sports and entertainment news. It is a commonplace that they announce a world crisis and a new toothpaste with similar breathless voice. These tendencies reach their peak in the quiz program in which information, political and otherwise, is atomized in a context of competition, chitchat, and pursuit of the expert's approach. Those who like these programs feel they learn something from them, but it is not clear what it is. While the cultivated citizen of earlier time was supposed to know many irrelevant things—their irrelevancy being, according to Veblen's *The Theory of the Leisure Class,* the sign of his status and invidious distinction—the quiz fan is not entirely sure that what he knows is irrelevant!

This shapelessness of attention is a corollary of the other-directed audience's ability to shift from one sphere to another without making clear differentiations between the values of one sphere and those of another. In terms of the transfer of moods from the entertainment world to the political world, it is a transfer of the tolerance appropriate for the world of changing tastes, to a world structured in quite a different way, a world that, if it is to be changed, demands that people know not only what they like but what they want.

This tolerant consumership is the sign of a political style quite different from the leisured casualness and coolness of the old-time gentleman amateur in politics. He, at least, gained in competence as he became immersed in politics. Like the languid Sherlock Holmes, he was really not passive; his ennui was cultivated, not characterological. As against this, the other-directed consumer of the political news at most learns how to be a better consumer. And yet no matter how active his intake and output of opinions, there is an atrophy of the political sense and political functioning of the individual.

A striking illustration of these tendencies is to be found in a group of interviews conducted in the newly built suburb of Park Forest near Chicago. Park Forest is a development of a federally aided private concern called American Community Builders; the homes are rented to occupants, and the ACB retains the financial functions of government, in cooperation with a sort of town council of residents. Residents were asked in the interviews how they felt about ACB, and what part, if any, they took in local politics, including griping and gossip. Many had complaints about their living quarters and community arrangements generally. What was noteworthy was that these complaints were frequently put in terms of the allegedly—and, as it appeared, actually—"bad public relations" of ACB. That is, direct criticism, based on the residents' wants and feelings, was muted; rather, "they" were criticized because their public relations were so mishandled as to leave people—presumably, people other than the speaker—critical. In effect, people were complaining not about their direct grievances but because they had not been so manipulated as to "make them like it."

Now it might be thought that this repeated reference to poor public relations was simply a politic evasion by the interview respondents, who feared lest their criticisms become known. Apart from the fact that the interviewer seems on the whole to have won the residents' confidence, more decisive evidence that caution does not explain the public relations formulation appears when the entire interview is read. For then it is plain that many of the respondents fall into the other-directed, inside-dopester category, insofar as their character and political style can be gleaned from an intensive interview of two or three hours or more. Not only toward Park Forest but toward national political issues and popular culture their outlook is that of the consumer, not the producer, of politics, who complains if the show is not such a good one as to hold him in thrall and who seeks tolerantly to understand all political events in terms of personality and publicity.[1]

Under these conditions of passive consumership we would expect people to drop out of the league of inside-dopesters into the great mass of the new-style indifferents. Left to themselves, perhaps many would do so. But they are not left to themselves. The political actors want a political audience. Moreover, the residual moralizing influence of the mass media acts as a kind of barker for the political show. The audience, too, finding "the Mexican situation fraught with interest," looks to politics as one of its range of entertainment likings.

To combat this danger of indifference and apathy in the other-directed there is one sovereign remedy: glamour. And this is increasingly called on by those who want the political show to go on. Just as glamour in sex substitutes for both love and the relatively impersonal family ties of the tradition-directed person and just as glamour in packaging and advertising of products substitutes for price competition, so glamour in politics, whether as charisma—packaging—of the leader or as the hopped-up treatment of events by the mass media, substitutes for the types of self-interest that governed the inner-directed. To put this into a general form we shall have occasion to use later: *wherever we see glamour in the object of attention, we must suspect a basic apathy in the spectator.*

The result of the search for glamour in politics is the effort, not dissimilar to that of the retailer quoted above, "to provide 'psychological

1. The Park Forest study is the work of Herbert Gans, a graduate student in sociology at the University of Chicago.

values' attractive to the customer." And, as Mr. Clements told the Super Market Institute, the values are "the same traits that we like in our friends," namely "cleanliness, up-to-date appearance, generosity, courtesy, honesty, patience, sincerity, sympathy, and good-naturedness." Many of the maneuverings of politics can be interpreted in these terms. Truman was felt to lack the up-to-date appearance; Dewey, the sincerity, sympathy, and good-naturedness. Eisenhower seemed irresistibly attractive on all these scores—he had "everything." People wanted a candidate with both appeals, and the spontaneous elements in the Eisenhower movement were to a large degree a tribute to people's desperate search for glamour. But having said this, it must be added that glamour is not only a veneer for apathy but also a sign that people crave a political leadership that, by dispelling their apathy, would allow them to become excited, committed, and related to politics. That is, glamour has an ambivalent effect: it reinforces apathy by invoking consumership motivations, while at the same time people look to glamour as a way of altering their motivations. As we shall see below, the mass media have a similarly ambivalent influence on political style.

The Eisenhower supporters in the 1948 campaign were saying, in effect, that a candidate who "has everything"—whom one could wholeheartedly *like*—would surely know what one *needed*. At the same time one of the things needed is precisely a candidate with whom one can become emotionally involved—who will help one overcome the felt limitations of new-style indifference and inside-dopesterism.

Even where likable qualities are less evident than in Eisenhower's case, people try hard to find a candidate with charm. To be sure, this was true in earlier eras, but I think it likely that this style of political appeal has been growing steadily in the United States in the radio age. For even the hardheaded political bosses in America have learned, enduring their experience of Franklin Roosevelt, to take these appeals into account; the wider the electorate, of course, the more glamour tends to displace issues or old-fashioned patronage considerations.

A very interesting attitude toward Roosevelt's glamour turns up in some of our interviews with young people. When asked what great men, living or dead, they most admire, they name Roosevelt as one of the stars of the political galaxy, along with older names, such as

Lincoln and Jefferson, whom they have heard about in school. They do not name Roosevelt (or any other politicians) as someone they want to emulate personally; they have no hope of growing up to be president, nor would they want to be that conspicuous.[2] On the contrary, they can afford to admire Roosevelt just because they think of him as very much "out of this world." It seems all but impossible for someone in the lower middle or even upper middle class to imagine himself acting with Roosevelt's appearance of aristocratic jauntiness and dexterity. Thus, F.D.R. can be admired without envy. And, even in lower economic ranges, he is not so much a rescuer of families in distress as a "personality."

THE LIMITS OF PSYCHOLOGY

During the 1948 campaign investigators studied a panel of voters in Elmira, New York, who were repeatedly interviewed from May until after the election.[3] The interviewers found this cross section of the political audience bored with the show, even though they recognized that class interests were at stake in the contest. Mostly Republicans, they disliked Dewey, though they thought him qualified. And though they said they would like Truman for a lodge brother, they could not completely discard their feeling that he was not what the times needed.

To admit that even such elaborate investigations did not make it possible to anticipate the Truman victory is to say that such outcomes cannot be explained in psychological terms alone. For one thing, we do not know how much the upset was based on people voting their likes and how much on labor leaders and farmers voting, or getting others to vote, their needs. In any political analysis it is exceedingly difficult to single out those consequences attributable to the specific qualities of the other-directed character and to separate these from the wider American scene in which that character plays an increasing part. We know, for instance, that many lower-income people view politics as a consumable in much the same way that we have described for the other-directed middle class.

2. One of my students, who was in the army's Information and Education Service during the war, reports that when he was asked to lead a discussion among enrolees as to what they would do "if they were president," he could get no response. The question had no meaning for the men, since they neither wanted to be president nor could imagine themselves in such a post.

3. See the preliminary report of Helen Dinerman, "1948 Votes in the Making," *Public Opinion Quarterly*, XII (1948–49), 585.

Yet we can say that character structure is one factor, though not the only one, which is related to a confusion between politics-as-work and politics-as-leisure, between politics as a shop where one makes what one wants and politics as a show where one sees what one likes. While character does not dictate with finality the uses one makes of politics, we must all be struck by the other-directed person's similar ways of perceiving politics and other events from which he is equally distant in genuine emotional response.

II. THE MEDIA AS TUTORS IN TOLERANCE

Since the chief strategy of the media as tutors of consumption is to introduce and rationalize changes, enrichments, or discontinuities in conventional tastes and styles, the media have a stake in taste tolerance. They cannot afford to have people overcommitted to a taste that they may want to change tomorrow. (And while the advertisers would like to commit people to a label, they do not, fair-trade devotees that they are, attack one another.) This media attitude of tolerance, verging on passivity of judgment, becomes the mode of experiencing and viewing everything, including politics. For it is apparent enough that the guides to attractiveness, living, and success that appear in all the media—the entire content of some—are promoters of other-direction. Their message is one that implies constant need of approval by others; they are read with the idea of taking cues from others; and what is more, their formulas are reinforced by their acceptance and circulation in the peer-groups of America's child, adolescent, and adult life.

The political reporting and editorializing of the more serious magazines and newspapers, however, are another matter. While such publications may decorate their pages with stories about the consumption habits and tastes of senators, proconsuls, and elder statesmen, their general attitude toward the political sphere is a moralizing one. Regardless of their partisan position, the serious political story is written with reverence for the American Way, an air of righteousness about such matters as patronage, and concern for American or local interests. The general tone is that of a message addressed to solid citizens—and it reaches some. A Connecticut commuter train, for example, certainly carries, among its readers of the *Herald Tribune,* a loyal cohort of inner-directeds. In terms of class and influence they may range from the hereditary bankers and insurance men to the young up-and-coming accountants, and the conductors, not all *Tootle* trained, of the New York, New Haven, and Hartford itself.

But these compose a declining characterological group. The commuter train will be well filled with other-directeds who, despite the moralizing character and commendable firmness of the *Herald Tribune's* political intention, take it in an inside-dopester's fashion. They will take it not as a reinforcement of their own clear-cut interests and moralizing habits, since they have none, but as a cue to the trend of ideas in the group with which they associate themselves. Their political reading is, therefore, an exercise in group conformity, and the irony of their case is that the group to which they wish to conform is, or appears to be, inner-directed. But since these readers are tolerant, they can tolerate and even adopt a moralizing style that is not their own.

I have chosen an illustration where content and reader reception might point in different directions. But this ambiguity does not arise in many of the large circulation media, whose content is itself slanted toward tolerance. The most powerful factor making for this slant may be the sheer size of the audience. The press, though less terrorized than the movies, is subject to a variety of pressures brought by groups seeking protection from attack; and these pressures are internalized in the very structure of large media management and distribution.

For one thing, the larger the scope of the medium, the more likely it is to be edited and produced in a large metropolitan center where the pressures toward other-directed tolerance are greatest. While freer from pressure of advertisers and local cranks than small-town editors and broadcasters, and, in general, often considerably more daring, big-city media with a city-wide audience cannot help being aware of those attitudes that may offend their complex constituencies. Whereas the early nineteenth-century editor could gamble on a crusade that might bring him both a libel suit and a circulation, the twentieth-century publisher often cannot afford to let his editor gamble even on an increased circulation. Like the modern corporation generally, he wants a relatively inflexible demand curve for his product; he cannot risk sharp losses of circulation and often not sharp increases either, since his managers have guaranteed his circulation to the advertisers, planned his paper supply, and committed him to

Newspaper Guild contracts and distributive relationships long in advance.

Obviously, moreover, as the one-paper towns and cities grow in number, the owner-monopolist has little to gain by attacking a powerful group. He will prefer the comforts of fair trade, as enshrined in the American Newspaper Publishers' Association or the Broadcasters' Code, to the risks of free trade in punches and ideas.

For another thing, there is the pressure that I have already referred to as the piety of print—or the even greater piety of radio. As the audience becomes less stratified in class or age terms, the writer or broadcaster becomes less able to pitch what he has to say in any tone of obloquy based on intimate knowledge of a specific audience. Since he does not know how, in unexpected readership or listenership situations, the virus of indignation may be received, he must be preoccupied with the antibodies of tolerance. Hence, all other things being equal, the larger the scope of the medium, the more it tends to be produced and consumed in a mood of other-directed tolerance and the less it makes an appeal to the indignants.

On the other hand, the very intolerance of some of the older captains of the press and radio, ambitious men with a message, allows them, and the columnistic commissars they encourage to take a "tough" approach, to find and hold an audience among all those indifferent and maladjusted people who seek not political news but excitement and diversion from their apathy. Hearst, McCormick, Gannett, Shepherd of the Yankee network—such men want power through the press and radio, rather than money or approval. Yet their audiences are made up not of political indignants primarily but of political new-style indifferents—would-be inside-dopesters who are attracted by the impiety of Hearst, the *Chicago Tribune,* and especially the *New York Daily News* because this sort of news-handling seems to promise them the unfaked inside story. Having been trained to associate piety with the official culture of sermon, school, and print, they take whatever appears by contrast to be sophisticated, brutal, illegal, or mysterious as true almost by definition and think the editor sincere for letting them in on it.

TOLERANCE AND THE CULT OF SINCERITY

The exploration of what is meaht by sincerity will take us far toward understanding the ways in which popular culture trains its audience in tolerance. We must remind ourselves that sincerity is one of the qualities by which a retail store may hold a loyal clientele, according to Mr. Clements' remarks quoted above.[4]

A graduate student at the University of Chicago collected interviews on attitudes toward popular music and found cropping up again and again such statements as, "I like Dinah Shore because she's so sincere," or, "that's a very sincere record," or, "You can just feel he [Frank Sinatra] is sincere." While it is clear that people want to personalize their relationships to their heroes of consumption and that their yearning for sincerity is a grim reminder of how little they can trust themselves or others in daily life, it is less clear just what it is that they find "sincere" in a singer or other performer.[5] One element may be the apparent freedom of the entertainer to express emotions that others dare not or cannot express. Again, sincerity means performance in a style which is not aggressive or cynical, which may even be defenseless, as the question-answering or press-conference technique of some politicians appears to be. The performer puts himself at the mercy of both his audience and his emotions. Thus sincerity on the side of the performer evokes the audience's tolerance for him: it would not be fair to be too critical of the person who has left himself wide open and extended the glad hand of friendliness.

But the popular emphasis on sincerity means more than this. It means that the source of criteria for judgment has shifted from the content of the performance and its goodness or badness, aesthetically speaking, to the personality of the performer. He is judged for

4. At the University of Chicago a graduate student studying the movement away from craft preoccupations to selling and customer-relation preoccupations among retail furriers, found the word sincerity being used in a similar way, as in the case of one man who, explaining how he defended himself against competition, observed: "You got to be able to talk to the customers . . . . when a customer comes in you can turn her one way or the other . . . . the customers can tell if you're sincere." Success for this man was defined not in terms of money alone but in terms of "a personal following" and "a better class of people." See Louis Kriesberg, "The Relationship of Business Practices and Business Values among Chicago's Retail Furriers" (Master's thesis, University of Chicago, 1949).

We might also note in this connection the statement by Burr Tillstrom, a television producer of children's shows, that "First among the qualities to be sought after is simple sincerity . . ." To which he adds, "Children love to feel that they are part of the show; and if your audiences are part of you, you are pretty certain of their loyalty." See "Children's Shows," *New York Times*, April 17, 1949.

5. See Howard C. Becker, "The Professional Dance Musician in Chicago" (Master's thesis, University of Chicago, 1949). I am much indebted to Mr. Becker for analysis of these interviews. I have also profited from the penetrating discussion of sincerity as applied to audience reactions to a Kate Smith War Bond Drive in Robert K. Merton, *Mass Persuasion* (New York, Harper, 1946).

his attitude toward the audience, an attitude which is either sincere or insincere. The performer of the nineteenth century appears to have been judged rather by his relation to his craft, that is, his honesty and skill.

By ignoring what the audience believes itself to lack (ability to perform) and emphasizing the qualities that it believes itself secretly to possess (capacity for sincerity), the audience is enabled, to a degree, to patronize the artist just as it patronizes the bumbling participants in a give-away show. This protects the audience against making an error in taste—indeed, the mood of tolerance gains in importance when we see it as insurance against making this error. The fear of the divergence of one's own consumption preferences from those of one's peer-group of listeners is minimized by fastening on a criterion which is as generalized and as subjective as sincerity.

I have remarked that the inner-directed style in cultural judgment was to see a person, an event, a political issue, or a theater performance in terms of good and bad. To a large degree the authority of these concepts was a direct transferral from the world of moral right and wrong, or from surviving customary postulates, or from clear, though often bigoted, notions of interest and self-interest. Today such intensity of response is not welcome either in the sphere of entertainment or of politics.

It may well be that the audience that emphasizes an emotional quality of a performer, such as sincerity, escapes from the need for emotional response to the performance itself. Though the listener likes a star who, as the teen-ager says, can "send me," he does not want to go very far; he has his membership card in the consumers' union to consider. By making sincerity appear as an objective quality, or at least one capable of peer-group discussion, he gets some emotional release while preserving safety in numbers. He can "give the little girl a hand" without committing himself to a judgment on her virtuosity. In this sense the sincere artist is like the artist who tries hard.

Viewing the political scene as a market for comparable emotions, it seems that the appeal of many of our political candidates tends to be of this sort. To be sure, candidates who combine sincerity with a good façade are much preferred. But forced to choose between skill and sincerity, many in the audience prefer the latter. They are tolerant of bumbles and obvious ineptness if the leader tries hard.

Sincerity and cynicism. While it may seem at first glance that the other-directed inside-dopester is simply a cynic, the relations between tolerance and sincerity help to show how complex cynicism can be. Cynicism is a trait compatible with both inner-direction and other-direction, but it has a different bearing in the two constellations. The inner-directed cynic is or can be an opportunist, ruthless in pursuing his goals. Or he may be a disgruntled idealist, still in practice committed to rectitude. In pursuit of his aims, good or bad, he may be quite ready to exploit others, just as the inner-directed moralizer may be quite ready to force others to be moral, too. However, the other-directed person, cynical as he often seems, is generally too dependent on others to be completely cynical about them: he may keep looking for sincerity—that is, for personalities who, if they exploit his emotions, will also involve their own. What appears here as cynicism is frequently the readiness of the other-directed person tolerantly to accept the norms of whatever adult peer-group he is in. But this limp acceptance is rather a source for his cynicism about himself than for his cynicism about others to whom he clings in search of goals. In fact, the other-directed man's cynicism about himself is one of the principal reasons that, while he is willing to say what he likes, he cannot believe in himself enough to know what he wants.

The inner-directed man, when he looks at politics, is likely to be exceedingly cynical about people but not cynical about institutions, constitutions, and, as we saw earlier, the value of politics itself. By contrast, the other-directed man, somewhat sentimental about people, is likely to be quite cynical about legal and political institutions, just as he is about the great game of politics itself. Coupled with this outlook, his concern for sincerity in his political personalities becomes a vice. While the concern for sincerity may imply a refusal to be taken in by any abstract notions of good and bad, along with an insistence that the personal emotional tone of the leader is of decisive importance, there are many situations where this orientation leads one astray.

In the first place, the leader's warmth or sincerity is not always important; that depends on the situation. When presented with a cold or mechanical candidate, the other-directed man may oppose him because he does not seem sincere—quite possibly because the candidate is caught, as a small-town boy such as Thomas Dewey seems to have been, between an inner-directed upbringing and an other-directed milieu. Yet even if the candidate possesses the negative qualities attributed to him, the structure of politics and of the electorate may be sufficiently firm to make it unlikely that such a candidate, if successful, could bring about great evils. Once in office, he may be able to do no more harm than a bookkeeper in a bank with a good bank-examining system and insurance coverage. The other-directed person, focused on people as he is, often overlooks such institutional hardness of the material. Thus, just as the moralizer romanticizes a government of laws and not of men, the inside-dopester romanticizes a government of men and not of laws. Both are unattainable ideals.

In the second place, it is obviously most difficult to judge sincerity. While the audience which uses the term sincerity thinks that it is escaping, in its tolerant mood, from the difficulty of judging skills, it is actually moving into a domain of considerably greater complexity. Just because such a premium is put on sincerity, a premium is put on faking it. And as the child learns to tell the good guys from the bad guys in the comics by telltale clues of appearance and decor, so the adult may fall for formulas for deciding on sincerity that are no more meaningful than those summed up in folk proverbs about looking at a person's hands or eyes.[6] Perhaps he could tell more after a psychiatric interview, though this is not—despite the efforts of Harold Lasswell and others—the kind of interview the politician grants. Moreover, we might conceive of a culture in which people are better trained to judge sincerity than either the inner-directeds or the other-directeds. The tribe in the South Seas whose members report their dreams to each other and are masters of the art of dream interpretation may live in such a culture. In the meantime it looks as if the other-directeds have lost the inner-directeds' easy judgments of competence without gaining an equally solid judgment of the more intangible aspects of personality.

Plainly, it is the other-directed person's psychological need, not his political one, that dictates his emphasis on warmth and sincerity. For

6. There is some rather inconclusive evidence that many people solve the problem by believing that "most people can be trusted." A public opinion poll by the National Opinion Research Center found that 77 per cent of college graduates thought that, as against 52 per cent of those with grammar school education—and 6 per cent of the German people. There are of course many reasons other than character structure why the middle class, more than the lower class, would be likely to think as well as say this. In my own interviews we also found general agreement with the proposition that most people can be trusted and also that "most people mean what they say when they talk with you." The other-directed person, as indicated in the text, can perhaps not face the opposite possibility.

leadership the ability to be disagreeable may often be more important. The man who thinks he is sincere, moreover, may deceive himself and others; the man who knows he is not, may watch himself and be watched.[7]

III. DO THE MEDIA ESCAPE FROM POLITICS?

Hollywood's discovery of the Negro problem had given the studios a new cycle, and distributors a tough problem: How would the South take to films denouncing racial prejudice? . . . Having already played nine profitable weeks in Manhattan, *Home of the Brave* opened in Dallas and Houston . . . In Dallas, the Negro elevator operator tried to sum up overheard opinion: "Well, I'll tell you, 99 per cent of the people say it's educational, the other 1 per cent say it's good."

Time, July 18, 1949

Critics of the mass media seem generally to suppose that the media foster political apathy, that they permit and encourage the audience to escape from the political and other realities of life, that, by a kind of Gresham's Law, they drive out the hard money of politics with the soft money of mass entertainment. How can Washington, it is sometimes asked, compete with Hollywood and Broadway?

Scarcity psychology, hanging on from the period of transitional growth of population, assumes that leisure is so limited that time taken, say, by comic reading, is taken from politics. Except for a dwindling number of occupations, most people have ample time for both. Underneath the media critics' position there may be concealed a puritanical dislike for leisure, a feeling that people ought to occupy their (unfortunately) free time with civic affairs and other serious matters. Or there is the neopuritan hygienic feeling that people ought to be doing something, no matter what—a vitamin-conscious view of life. This outlook represents a failure to realize that in a post-Veblenian economy of abundance people can afford to waste both time and other resources.

Actually, however, the much criticized media—especially the press

7. An excellent example of an inner-directed attitude toward the evaluation of sincerity and skill is to be seen in Lincoln's relationships to his wartime generals. As in the case of Grant's drinking, he wanted to know whether these men could do a job, not whether they were nice, or nice to him. Morris Janowitz has called my attention to Lincoln's letters to Burnside, whom he did not trust, did not like, and watched like a hawk. Today, on the other hand, a work-minded general needs a people-minded general to front for him.

—seem to have maintained a surprisingly inner-directed attitude toward the political. The fact is that they pay more attention to politics than their audience seems to demand. Even tabloids print headlines and, often, news pictures on the front page, not comics. True, this is often "news" of sex, crime, and politically irrelevant or distracting exposé, but a few major political topics figure on occasion. Old Indignant Hearst likes to print "the Chief's" editorials rather than cheesecake on page one. Local radio stations with disk jockeys build their self-esteem (and please the FCC) by broadcasting news every hour, which, like the commercials, people do not bother to switch off; in fact, many people like to listen to commercials who may not like newscasts. Likewise, newsreels usually begin with shots of some poltical personage or event, postponing Lew Lehr or the fashion show to the end of the reel. Thus many of the agencies of mass communications give political news a larger play than might be dictated by strict considerations of market research. In this way they help maintain the prestige of politics as a presumed interest on the part of their audience —even though at the same time, they constantly harp on the disreputability of politicians.

This prestige position given to politics is especially important for the other-directed person since he looks to the mass media for guidance in his life plan and value hierarchy. He is led to assume that other people must rate politics as the mass media themselves do—that they are politically alert moralizers even though he is not. He is also encouraged in this assumption by the polls which the press prints. Save for an "inquiring photographer" here and there, these polls ask many questions and report many answers about public issues and rather few about daily living or sports. The media, far from being a conspiracy to dull the political sense of the people, could be viewed as a conspiracy to disguise the extent of political indifference.

Indeed most people in most walks of life are apologetic if they are not up on politics, men especially so. When in our intensive interviews we ask people if they are interested in politics or don't care about it, they generally say that they are interested or that they should be. People do not often make the discovery that others are quite as bored or apathetic about politics (or about other things on which the media confer respectability) as they know themselves to be. In the city, where people do not know each other, the "unbelievers" could only be aware of how numerous they are through the mass media, but these are the very channels that give politics priority.[8]

One reason for this is the desire of those who work for the mass media to do what is right or considered to be right by those to whom they look for leadership. Just as publishers want to publish prestige books even though they may lose money on them, under various rationalizations of good will, so newspapermen and broadcasters want to raise themselves above "the lowest common denominator" without fully exploring the potential financial profitability of the latter. The movie king who speaks for mere entertainment feels on the defensive with the bold producer of *Home of the Brave* and similar problem-films.

For in fact, those who work in the mass communications industries are, despite the moralizing style with which they approach politics, typically other-directed characters. The hypersensitive radar that is their meal ticket is tuned in spare moments not to the audience to whom they sell but to the intellectual strata around and above them. These strata, though engaged in consumption, are frequently contemptuous of consumption of popular culture—perhaps because tempted by it.

Doubtless, a hierarchy among the different kinds of entertainment has always existed. But whereas the hierarchy in earlier days was based, at least to some extent, on criteria of artistry, the hierarchy to-day seems to be based somewhat more on topic than on mode of treatment. As the audience itself is asked to move on a constantly uptilting gradient of topic and taste, from the comics of childhood to the commentators of adulthood, so the makers of the media, in their own combination of social mobility and ethical uplift, are always impatient to get to the point where in addition to entertaining they are, in terms of topic, educating and improving. As the slicks are more high class than the pulps, so politics is more high class than sex. The sports writer wants to become a political columnist; the night-club broadcaster moves over first into political chitchat, then into political fire; many a newspaper publisher who begins as a "no-nonsense" businessman ends up as a bit of a political moralizer. Just as the new rich are "educated" to philanthropy by their associates, so the new

---

8. Cf. Paul Lazarsfeld and Robert K. Merton, "Mass Communication, Popular Taste and Organized Social Action," *The Communication of Ideas,* ed. Lyman Bryson, p. 95, on the "status-conferral" function of the media.

entrants into the mass media are educated away from the "low" commercial motives to ones of more prestige. To take an example, the older pictorial magazines, such as *Life* and *Look* and even some of the less well-known ones, have moved steadily away from pictures, away from cheesecake toward art, away from Sunday-Supplement sensation toward "serious" reading matter and political exhorting; pictures are only the come-on for social issues.

It seems, therefore, that the mass media, among their highly complex and ambiguous effects, do help prop up the prestige of the political sphere in the United States, and that within this sphere they have the effect of favoring the older, moralizing political styles. But this is a residue effect to be explained by special factors; and it is more true of the press than of the movies and radio, just as within the press it is more true of certain magazines and newspapers than of others. The total impact of the mass media on the political attitudes of Americans is composed of forces that do more to encourage other-directed tolerance than to preserve inner-directed indignation. The sheer emphasis on consumer skills in the mass media, an emphasis that both encourages and caters to the other-directed, has cumulative effects. One of the most basic of these is that the inner-directeds and their interests are driven out of the media *in every sphere except that of politics itself.*

IV. THE RESERVOIR OF INDIGNATION

Outside of politics, indeed, the mass media offer the indignants a rather scanty fare. The moral issues dealt with in the media are posed in increasingly subtle form, and they mainly reflect problems of personal relationship. Moreover, the pace of the media is too fast, too sophisticated, for many of the readers who remain inner-directed. What are they to make, for instance, of a Billy Rose column about Broadway morals and mores? How are they to translate the specialized lingoes of many comic strips? How can they possibly make sense of the elusiveness and allusiveness of the "A"-grade problem-film? The indignants are apt to find that even horse operas have become pastoral settings for sadism and sex, no longer like the old westerns whose chief characters were horses and whose moral problems involved hardly more complicated beings. Soap operas probably seem to casual upper middle-class listeners to be bathed in lachrymose moralizing. But typically their characters are preoccupied with straightening out a complex web of tenuous emotions, often needing the specialized services of the professional or semiprofessional helper. The typical curdled indignant, perhaps especially if male, is simply not interested in such things.

We may note the change in popular-culture fare in another medium altogether, by remarking the transformation of the new *Scientific American*. The old *Scientific American* used to be read by inner-directed hobbyists of science; now it has become a slick-paper periodical, catering with brilliance and sophistication to the consumer of science, including social science and philosophy; one old subscriber complained that it was no longer edited to be read by men with greasy hands at workbenches—virtually the only hobby column remaining is the astronomy section. Likewise, we might note that Street and Smith, publishers of such moralizing tales as Alger and Nick Carter, recently killed all but one of their remaining pulps, including *Detective Story, Western Story,* etc., to concentrate on their three booming slicks: *Mademoiselle, Charm,* and *Mademoiselle's Living.* What is the barnacled moralizer to do with them?

This gnawing deficit of acceptable mass media would perhaps be less troublesome to the moralizer if the world in which he lived still appeared to be inner-directed, to be governed, that is, by an invisible hand. But his own life experience is often disappointing; he is deprived of a feeling of competence and place. Even this would not be so bad if the world made sense, if he could apply to what goes on his internalized standards of judgment, but as it is, neither his character nor his work is rewarded. In that situation he tends to turn both on himself—for he is vulnerable to lack of worldly comprehension even more perhaps than to lack of worldly success—and on the world. In a last desperate effort to turn the country back on its inner-directed course so as to make it habitable for him, he is ready to join a political movement whose basic driving force is indignation. A world that refuses him a place—a world that bombards him with messages that make him feel inadequate—may not appear to him worth saving, though his destructiveness may be rationalized by various ideologies.

The mass media cater to this attitude in politics, even if they no longer cater to it in other fields. We have seen one reason for this: the fact that many media leaders, for prestige and other reasons of their own, espouse a moralizing attitude toward politics rather than an inside-dopesterish one. And we have seen another reason: the fact that the media attract and provide an audience for indignant men with a simple message. While most of their readers are new-style indifferents who are titillated by political excitement, some are indignants who find their responses welcomed on the editorial page and in the commentators' columns if nowhere else.

Moreover, the indignation of the lords of press, comment, and column is not as ineffective with the other-directeds in their audience as one might suppose at first glance. Many of these have adopted the moralizer's style as their own—and many are only marginally other-directed. But even the tolerant other-directed person is often fascinated by the indignant's ire, not because it is compatible with his character structure but precisely because it is not. In commercial sports, for instance, he enjoys a rivalry and temper display—even if he knows in a way that it is cooked up for his benefit—that is vanishing or banished from other spheres of his life. As a result, displays of aggression and indignation in the arena of politics are popular with all types—indignants, inside-dopesters and indifferents. "Pour it on, Harry!" the crowds said to President Truman, who, under his grin, harbors a good deal of aggression and vindictiveness. As Americans, whatever their class or character, can enjoy boxing or a rodeo, so they still look upon a political brawl as very much a part of their American heritage, despite the trend toward tolerance.

This leads us to the important consideration that the nature of the election process encourages the entry of the indignant on his own terms. In campaigning, a tradition of moralizing survives, in competition with the newer search for glamour. The machines, though sensitive to glamour, are also aware, from past defeats, of the political power of the indignants—those who did go fight city hall. Even other-directeds may vote for moralizing inner-directeds because the latter present a more familiar, more dramatized, more seemingly appropriate style of attitude toward politics, thus postponing the characterological struggle between the two types.

For the indignants have hold of one of the great traditions of American politics. This is the tradition of asking the government to govern more than it knows how to govern—as in the case of prohibition—a latter-day survival of the time when a state like Connecticut, to Tocqueville's astonishment, could not justify putting less than the Hebraic law on its statute books but could not justify enforcing its harsh penal provisions either. In line with this tradition, the indignants of today can strive in politics to "get the law" on those movements in culture—in literature, the movies, the universities, the libraries—that symbolize urban sophistication and tolerance. They are resisted in this effort less by tolerant other-directed types than by inner-directeds for whom tolerance is a moral principle, not a character trait. The most fervent defenders of civil liberties in America, men such as Roger Baldwin, Alexander Meiklejohn, Grenville Clark, draw political strength from their principles, not from their knowledge of who's who in politics. In contrast, the tolerant inside-dopester may become "objective" about intolerance: he knows enough about people to doubt the efficacy of reason or to be sure of his own resistance. His vulnerabilities, as well as his abilities, spring from the fact that he has his eye on the others and not on his own principles or wants.

In fact, the other-directeds try to defend themselves against the political onslaughts of the indignants by inside operations rather than by countermoralizing. Disinclined to personal militancy, to "getting out on a limb," they put on pressure through groups and associations that speak in their name. As capable handlers of inside tactics and of the communication process—they are, of course, at home among the mass media, not all of which are controlled by moralizers—they can often put the brakes on what the indignants would like to do. As a clever district attorney can mitigate the fury of a grand jury to whom he has to present an indictment by making a deal with the defendant's lawyer to accept a plea to a lesser offense, so the inside-dopester has often, in national and local politics, been able to hold the indignants off with a concession. He can make concessions, since he does not ask of politics that it straighten out the world for him. Indeed, if the indignant asks too much of politics, the tolerant inside-dopester asks too little.

As we have said, the moralizers and the inside-dopesters taken together are a minority of Americans; the majority are political indifferents. To the indifferents, however, the inside-dopester has little to offer in the way of psychic dividends. His very knowledge leads him to be aware of how little can be accomplished in politics and how fantastic it is to hope for "getting rid of politics." But in rousing the indifferents, indignation has great possibilities. Not only does it make for a better show but it also plays on such grievances as the indifferents have. Sometimes these grievances can be brought into the political sphere by an antipolitical appeal.

Many leading writers and speakers, for example, hate politics, even though they would insist that they hate only bad or corrupt politics. Their indignant style is a far cry from the more traditional and amiable American dislike for politics and politicians which is usually coupled with a genuine liking for business and businesslike administration. They must also be differentiated from the many political scientists and other technicians who, fearing conflict, distrust politics and would like to see it superseded not by business administration but by "administrative" administration. The indignation of these latter groups is held in check by a certain amount of competence, as well as by the very overrationality which makes them hostile to the seeming chaos and controversy of politics. But the hatred for politics of a large group of curdled indignants is bottomless, and their hate-filled promises appeal to many of those whose political indifference rests not on the security of tradition-direction but on a purposeful autism.

From similar sources were rallied many of the early Nazis, a large wing of the de Gaullists, and many other groups in various countries who place themselves "above politics," "above parties," and "above opinions." Such groups attack the more traditionally partisan and politically articulate elements of society and demand freedom from politics—from platforms, principles, and parliaments. In our own limited interviewing and experience we have come across a number of people with just such an attitude toward the American party system and pattern of political discourse.[9]

If at any time the indignants can make a junction with the indifferents, they can be very powerful. In international affairs, for example, the mood of tolerance rests on fragile grounds—it can be so easily ruptured either on the international or the domestic front. Internally, indignation can draw on great lower-class reserves of nationalism and xenophobia. Externally, indignation may meet counterindignation, and the congruence of indignants and temporarily aroused indifferents may present the tolerant with a seeming fait accompli. And the tolerant inside-dopesters, as compared with those who are tolerant

9. See, for a profound discussion of totalitarianism and how it differs from earlier forms of tyranny, Hannah Arendt, *The Origins of Totalitarianism* (New York, Harcourt, Brace, forthcoming). I have profited greatly from her work.

from inner-directed principle, are men trained to recognize a fait accompli, not resist it.

There are still plenty of these older character types, often made angry by the very fact of no longer fitting their times. Among them are ambitious men and destructive men. These men may appeal to the indignants and intimidate the tolerant; indeed the latter, when faced with crisis, may even turn to such men out of a feeling of their own inadequacy. Long before the tolerant are able to organize politics after their style and their mood, a stampede of the indignant may have brought on an explosion and may have pushed the tolerant cause and the tolerant character into abeyance.

V. "IN DREAMS BEGIN RESPONSIBILITIES"

The role of the media in dramatizing, organizing, and promoting American political styles is obviously, from all that has been said in this chapter, filled with ambiguities and paradoxes. It follows from what I have said so far that a reorientation of media policy to play down political moralizing and exhortation and to play up escape—in the sense of richly imaginative fantasy—might be the greatest contribution the media could make to developing a political style that would transcend both indignation and inside-dopesterism.

The present political scene is one of seldom alleviated dullness, to which people attach themselves either because of ideas of proper consumership or because of the impious excitement held out, like an alluring movie ad, by the residual indignants who have rejected the convention of tolerance. An increased diet of political moralizing and dutiful editorializing will scarcely liberate our presently impoverished political fantasy. Nor are we likely to liberate it by increasing the time allotted to Dinah Shore or Mel Torme. Nevertheless, I have the feeling that if the media encouraged, and if its audience could permit itself, more genuine escape, "away from it all," we would become stronger psychically and more ready to undertake an awakening of political imagination and commitment.

By going on with our present course of media performance and media criticism, we make it possible for the media to continue to uphold the prestige of the political even when, as for much of our life at present, the political is devoid of substantial content—for one thing, because this very lack of content could only be glimpsed from a less realistic, more fantasy-oriented outlook. The direct impact of the media on political decision may easily become as thin as the impact of the House of Lords on popular opinion in Britain. The serious press refuses to face this situation, and, far from seeking to explore new emotional currents in American life, it strenuously seeks to present to the Commons of the media—radio, TV, movies, and pulps—a hand-me-down agenda of political debate. Since politics is actually less real than the press lords pretend to themselves and their audience that it is, the consumption of political vituperation may easily become more than ever an escape in the usual invidious sense, rationalized by its high, media-based prestige. Thus, the sources in popular art and culture from which eventual political creation may flow are partially dammed up by false prestige considerations and by the displaced guilts and ethical urges shared by those who control the media and those who, in turn, look to them for a bill of cultural fare.

The probabilities are that the media, in their direct, message-bearing impact, are likely to do less either to help or hurt the audience than the controllers of the media and their critics like to think. This alone should save us—to borrow a fine phrase from Justice Holmes—from looking either for panaceas or for sudden ruin as the result of any messages or group of messages the media may carry. Awareness of this fact may then permit both the controllers and the critics of the media to reorient their attention. They are free, much freer than they realize, to attend to the medium itself, rather than to the message it purveys or is believed to purvey. The movie producer or critic who is concerned mainly with messages, for instance of ethnic tolerance, may actually despise the movies as an art form. The editorializer or social scientist who is concerned only with arousing the electorate may hate the English language because it has become for him a mere tool. The broadcaster who wants to atone for his big salary and sponsors by slipping in a crack against business may have little respect for the aesthetic resources of his medium.

As we have just seen, the men who work in radio, film, and fiction tend to give politics, as the press and its uplifters see it, a prestige denied to art, and especially the popular art of the media themselves. There is pathos in this for their personal lives, since it leads them to unwarranted contempt for their own craft. There is irony in this for American politics, since it seems to me that a country which produced artistically first-class movies, papers, and broadcasts—no matter what the topic and, indeed, subordinating the whole question of topic—would be, politically as well as culturally, a livelier and happier land. Good mass-media artists are quite as important, and perhaps even scarcer, than responsible, antiescapist commentators.

We saw in Chapter II that teachers in schools permeated by other-direction tend to train children to devalue skill and to overvalue a contentless cooperation. Thus they are prepared for their role not only in the economy but also in the political audience. Such morality as they bring to politics becomes attached to morale as an end, or hidden under it. At once trusting and distrusting those with whom they are in antagonistic cooperation, they see in "sincerity" an escape from their dilemma: unless he is as glamorous as FDR, they can be loyal only to the candidate who appears sincere and who, unlike, say, Dean Acheson, is not big and does not think he is. We saw in Chapter III that the childhood peer-group is focused less on accomplishment than on popularity ratings and taste exchange. Here, too, there is a parallel with contemporary politics where the vital decisions (war or peace) are felt to be, and usually are, out of the citizen's hands—who is nevertheless urged to "participate" by peer-groups of moralizers and inside-dopesters and their media guides. (That, as we shall see, he often does participate effectively as a member of a "veto group" is sometimes overlooked.) We saw in Chapter IV that the media have a differential impact on inner-directed and other-directed children: the former may be driven to ambitious action; the latter learn to become apt judges of winning. In this sense many comics and radio and TV dramas for children, despite and indeed because of their pious moralizing, prepare them for roles as inside-dopesters and new-style indifferents, save for an occasional encouragement to fantasy.

Yet it would be patently false to conclude that, because similar tendencies are at work which introduce compatibilities between child-training on the one hand and adult politics on the other, there is a ruling class which intends these consequences or even profits by them. Rather, large-scale historical developments—those we short-hand by reference to the curve of population—are reflected both in child-training and in adult life: their compatibility is a complicated *characterological* one, rather than an affair of "the rulers."

XI

Images of Power

Q. After all, does what happens in politics make any difference to the way you live and work?

A. [Long hesitation] In a way in my work, yes. But as far as me living goes—I don't think it changes me much. I don't follow up on politics.

Q. What do you mean: follow up?

A. I mean I'm not so much interested.

Q. How does it affect how you work?

A. In the gas station politics come in and out—mostly all the talk is about politics. If anything changes in politics, I should think things would change in the gas station too.

> From an interview with an eighteen-year-old-boy, a senior in trade school, who works in a gas station after hours.

WHENEVER WE ask, as we did in the last chapter, whether the media do or do not uphold the prestige of the political sphere, we assume some definition of the political sphere itself. But what is that sphere and how does it look to Americans? As I suggested in Chapter VIII, all the formal methods of analysis we have at our disposal, even when backed by quantitative research, leave much unanswered and much unasked. The purpose of the following three chapters is to explore the matter in terms of certain aspects of the political imagery induced in American political styles by the character structure of the population, and especially the other-directed strata. The principal thesis of this chapter is that there has been in the last fifty years a change in American power configurations, from the power hierarchy of a ruling class to the power dispersal of what we shall call the "veto groups." This change has many complex roots and complex consequences, including the change in political mood from moralizing to tolerance. On the one hand, a clear-cut power structure helps to create the clarity of goals of the inner-directeds; on the other hand, an amorphous power structure helps to create the consumer orientation of the other-directeds. The change in power relations which I posit has not, however, been generally recognized. I hope to show that the images of power that prevail are themselves a factor in the change of styles and that people's misconceptions of their power position both affect that position and are evidence for the waning of inner-direction.

I. THE LEADERS AND THE LED

To be sure, this divergence between the ideology about power and the existing power relations is not new in American history but can be traced back to the late eighteenth and early nineteenth centuries. The Federalist leadership—landed-gentry and mercantilist-money leadership—certainly thought of itself as a ruling group, indentured to politics by its sense of noblesse oblige. But long before this leadership was actually dislodged, its power was disputed and, in decisive instances, overruled in the northern and middle states by yeoman farmers and artisans. These latter, having little time or gift for politics, ordinarily left it to their "betters," but they retained a veto on what was done and occasionally, as with Jackson, moved into a more positive command. After the Civil War, however, these farmer and artisan groups lost their capacity to check what was done, and the new plutocracy—the captains of industry—emerged as a ruling class. During their hegemony the images and the actualities of power in America coincided more closely than I think they do today.

CAPTAINS OF INDUSTRY AS POLITICAL LEADERS

According to this view of the matter, the election of 1896 appear. as an historical watershed: the high point of oligarchic rule. In term. of political style, there were moralizers for Bryan and moralizers for McKinley. And there were groups that, whether or not they saw their interests in moral terms, had a clear picture of themselves and of their interests; they, too, responded to the election in an inner-directed way. Only a few people like Brooks Adams, who supported Bryan out of his hatred for the "goldbugs," were aware of some of the ambiguities in the situation.

Certainly, the victorious leaders—McKinley, Hanna, and Morgan in their several bailiwicks—were not aware of ambiguity. The succes.

of their electoral bid is less important to us than the mood of their undertaking. Their mood was one of conscious leadership, directed by conscious class considerations, implying a conscious and explicit relation to those whom they led. This easy, self-conscious leadership took support from the close connection, in an era dependent on inner-direction, between politics and work. The world of work was the great world; politics was an extension that could either facilitate work or sabotage it. Bankers and Grangers had different notions as to what work politics should do and what leave undone, but they agreed as to the primacy of the production side of life.

Of course, the political sphere was not devoid of entertainment for the inner-directed man. It had its occasional but real uses as a "downward" escape from the dignities of the propertied existence, with its opportunity for cracker-barrel argument, beer drinking, and shirt-sleeved good fellowship by torchlight. Yet it was obvious to the inner-directed business classes that parades and free beer were only the shows that served to advance an essentially economic goal: the conquest of American resources. Moreover, the not so invisible hand of enterprise could buy franchises, tariffs, land grants. That is, free trade, political or economic, did not rule out finagling and corruption, if one could get away with it. A Rockefeller might try to cheapen his wares through railroad rebates, as a Vare or Tweed might lengthen his ring's chances by buying votes or stuffing ballot boxes. But in neither case was the competition a monopolistic one in the modern sense of concern for good will and marginal differentiation: the Rockefeller of *Wealth against Commonwealth* sold oil more by force or cheapness than by brand; and the bosses sold their commodities—votes or judges—in the same way. If moralizing would not drive out the Black Horse Cavalry—the legislators who lived by blackmailing businessmen with others' morality as some policemen live today from pimps—then the only political persuasion that would work was cash.

This situation and these inner-directed motivations gave a clarity to the political and social scene in 1896 that it does not appear to have had in Tocqueville's day and has not had since. The bullet that killed McKinley marked the end of the days of explicit class leadership. Muckraking and savage political cartooning—arts that depend on clarity of line—continued for a time and of course have not quite vanished yet. But as the old-time religion depended on a clear image of heaven and hell and clear judgments of good and evil, so the old-time politics depended on a clear class structure and the clear and easily moralized judgments of good and bad that flow from it. It depended, too, and I cannot emphasize the point too much, on an agreement between leaders and led that the work sphere of life was dominant. And because the goals were clear, the obvious job of the leader was to lead; of the led, to follow. Their political cooperation, like their cooperation in industry and agriculture, was based on mutual interests, whether directly moralized or not, rather than on mutual preferences and likings.

What I have said must be taken as an "ideal-typical" political portrait of the age, useful by way of contrast to our own times. Actually, the changes are, as always, changes in emphasis and degree, and the portrait would be seriously overdrawn if the reader should conclude that no emotional moods, no audience concerns for charisma and glamour, eddied about the relations between leaders and led. These relations were not built entirely out of sober moralizing and clear-cut interests, but occasionally, as Veblen described matters, the Captain of Industry served as the "spokesman and exemplar of the kept classes, and served as the legitimate channel by which the community's surplus product has been drained off and consumed, to the greater spiritual comfort of all parties concerned."

Those whom the Captain led, Veblen described as follows:

Men are moved by many impulses and driven by many instinctive dispositions. Among these abiding dispositions are a strong bent to admire and defer to persons of achievement and distinction, as well as a workmanlike disposition to find merit in any work that serves the common good . . Men like to believe that the personages whom they so admire by force of conventional routine are also of some use, as well as of great distinction,– that they even somehow contribute, or at least conduce, to the material well being at large.[1]

Ruling-class theories, applied to contemporary America, seem to be spectral survivals of this earlier time. Indeed, such remarks as Veblen's have a curiously archaic ring today. The type of the captain of industry no longer runs business, no longer runs politics, and no longer provides legitimate "spiritual comfort." Here and there, it true, there are survivals. In the booming Southwest, Texas still produces men like Glenn McCarthy, and California produced an old

1. Thorstein Veblen, *Absentee Ownership* (New York, Viking, 1914), pp. 114–116.

style lion of the jungle in A. P. Giannini—significantly enough, a man whose family had not gone through long grooming in a society heading toward incipient decline of population. Yet even these types are touched by traits that were not nearly so evident in the earlier captains of industry who fascinated Veblen as Lucifer fascinated Milton. Like Henry Kaiser, they depend much more than did the older magnificoes on public opinion and, as a corollary to public opinion, on the attitude of government. To this end they tend to exploit their personalities, or allow them to be exploited, in a way that makes the elder Rockefeller's Ivy Lee stunt of dime-giving seem as remote as the Fuggers.

Much more than their pre-World War I predecessors, then, these surviving captains stay within the limits as well as the possibilities of the economy of the glad hand. If they enter politics they do so because it is a sport for the rich; or simply because, like Henry Kaiser, they are tied in with government at every step in their ramifying enterprises. These latter-day captains neither see themselves nor are recognized as political leaders who, by their presence and by what they stand for, clarify and thereby moralize politics. The elder Morgan and his friends thought it was up to them to stop Bryan and to stop the depression of 1907. No one has taken their place.

CAPTAINS OF CONSUMPTION AS POLITICAL LEADERS

In the focus of public attention the old Captains of Industry have been replaced by an entirely new type: the Captains of Nonindustry, of Consumption and Leisure. Surveys of content in the mass media show a shift in the kinds of information about business and political leaders that audiences ask for.[2] In an earlier day the audience was given a story of the hero's work-minded rise to success. Today, the ladder climbing is taken for granted or is seen in terms of the breaks, and the hero's tastes in dress, food, women, and recreation are emphasized—these are, as we have seen, the frontiers on which the reader can himself compete, while he cannot imagine himself in the work role of the president of the United States or the head of a big company.

What is more, there is a shift in such biographies from an accent

2. See the excellent article by Leo Lowenthal, "Biographies in Popular Magazines," *Radio Research, 1942–43,* ed. Lazarsfeld and Stanton (New York, Duell, Sloan & Pearce, 1944), p. 507. Dr. Lowenthal, to whom I am indebted for helpful suggestions, links the shift from "heroes of production" to "heroes of consumption" to major social changes in American life.

on business leaders to an accent on consumption leaders. Proportion-
ately, actors, artists, entertainers, get more space than they used to,
and the heroes of the office, hustings, and factory get less. These consumers of the surplus product may, in Veblen's terms, provide "spiritual comfort" by their very skill in consumption. But they need not
be "persons of achievement and distinction," and it may be their conventionally defined uselessness that makes them glamorous.

But of course, these captains of consumption are not leaders. They
are still only personalities, employed to adorn movements, not to lead
them.

For an illustration we can turn to a recent American leader—undoubtedly a leader—who shared many characteristics of the artist and
entertainer: Franklin D. Roosevelt. We are accustomed to thinking
of him as a man of great power. Yet his role in leading the country
into war was very different from that of McKinley or even of Wilson.
Think of McKinley pacing the floor of his study, deciding whether or
not to ask for a declaration of war on Spain—when he already knew
that Spain would capitulate. McKinley felt it was up to him; so did
Wilson. Roosevelt felt he could only maneuver within very narrow
limits, limits which came close to leaving the decision to the enemy.

Again, if we compare his activities during the war years with those
of Churchill, we can see important differences. Churchill led the British in something like the old-time sense of an explicit relation between the leader and the follower. That he led, moreover, as a moralizing leader and not, despite his great personal charm, as a "personality," appeared in the readiness of the electorate to follow him in war
and to dispense with him in peace: they were work-minded rather
than consumption-minded about him. Roosevelt on the other hand remained throughout the war, as before, a powerful though tolerant
persuader, even conniver and stimulator, of changes in public opinion
that he followed with deep concern at all times. Churchill exploited
his indignation, Roosevelt his charm.

The admittedly real differences in the military situation of Britain
and the United States during this period are not sufficient to explain
these differences in the mood and method of leadership. Much more
important than the wartime differences between the two countries are
the differing shifts in political pattern during the last half century.
America in the 90's could be led politically and morally. Since then
we have entered a social and political phase in which power is dis-

persed among veto groups. These groups are too many and diverse to
be led by moralizing; what they want is too various to be moralized
and too intangible to be bought off for cash alone; and what is called
political leadership consists, as we could see in Roosevelt's case, in the
tolerant ability to manipulate coalitions.

If the great actor Roosevelt was not a powerful leader in the old
sense, how much less so are the so-called leaders from the sphere of
nonindustry. Even in their own sphere of consumption pattern leadership they are weighed down by heavier sanctions than the old business
leader in *his* sphere. A brief examination of the forces exerted on the
business and political leader of the old days, and the pressure exerted
on the consumption opinion-leader of today, reveals the contrast. It is
true that the old political bosses and business groups had to contend
with a variety of pressures—the pressure of the Grange against the
railroad leaders, for example. But these lobbies were few; they orig-
inated in a small circle of power-minded people for or against business; and they were, as we have seen, manageable. They could be
handled by counterlobbies making their strength felt on a few individuals; they could be handled by deals. And outside the circle of
the leaders there could always be an easily moralized appeal to the
followers for a vote of confidence in the economy and in those whom
the invisible hand had elevated to the seats of power. Money or morality talked more than love or personality. In conflict with radicals,
guns talked.

Today, however, the personalities from the leisure world, no matter
how much loved, lack the strength and the situation for leadership. If
we take the movie star of today as an example we see that his potentialities for action are constricted by a variety of lobbies. If he tries to
put across a political message, in or out of films, he finds himself vulnerable, though his wealth may be as great and his political contacts
as good as a nineteenth-century tycoon's. All sorts of pressures, from
ridicule to boycott, can send him scampering back to his role of
leader merely in consumption patterns and opinions. Yet even there
he is weak. Though we saw the mass media as among the tutors of
the young in Chapter IV and among the steerers of the old in Chapter
VII, it was not intended to suggest that the owners or the personalities
of the media had much power, by conscious effort, to change things;
indeed, we saw in the last chapter how little they can do, despite their
best efforts, to make Americans more serious about politics.

Every vehicle in which the movie star appears is precriticized by the so-called kings who run his own industry. These men, however, in the main want to be led, not to lead; even in their private lives, the present fashion is for nonconspicuous nonconsumption. Pre-audience surveys tell the movie makers what the audience likes. A variety of veto groups tell them what the audience should or, rather, should not have. The Catholics, the Methodists, the organized morticians, the state department, the southerners, the Jews, the doctors, all put their pressure on the vehicle that is being prepared for mass distribution. Piety or decency protects some minority groups that have no lobbies. The movie maker acts as a broker among these veto groups in a situation much too intricate to encourage his taking a firm, moralizing stance. At best, he or someone in his organization may sneak a moral and political message into the film as Roosevelt or someone in his organization sneaked over an appointment or a new coordinating agency. The message, the appointment, the agency—none of them could get very far in the Alice in Wonderland croquet game of the veto groups.

Even when the movie star uses his "personal appearance" rather than his film as a vehicle, he is subject to the same pressures. The area within which he, as an individual, can start consumption fads is minimal: he has the power of marginal differentiation in consumption that any peer-grouper has, and, like the denizens of café society, his peer-group gets publicity. Beyond these limits he cannot move. While his image exercises a power of enchantment over his audiences, he is at the mercy of the biggest and most active lobby in history.

II. WHO HAS THE POWER?

In terms of class, or elite theory, the first decades of American politics can be described as a period of conscious leadership by a mercantile-aristocratic group subject to occasional check, even displacement, by farmers and artisans who usually left politics alone. We might think of the latter as veto groups, and in that sense we can view the period between the end of the Civil War and 1900 as an exceptional period when the old veto groups were in retreat and the new ones had not yet found themselves. Yet, though the analogy between today and a hundred years ago is helpful, it conceals important differences in the mood and structure of the veto groups. Perhaps the most important change is the numerical elaboration and complexity of the latter and the fact that they not only exercise the residual veto of the farmer and artisan groups in the earlier period but also are constantly pressing their claims on the social and political sphere. These veto groups are lobbies, and also more than lobbies.

The shifting nature of the lobby, moreover, provides us with an important clue as to the difference between the present American political scene and that of the age of McKinley. Then there was conscious opposition to the ruling class on the part of those who at any moment wanted a better cut of the economic pie, and who were willing to follow another middle-class would-be elite to get it. In terms of cycles of participation and withdrawal from politics, the era was one in which the masses were drawn up into politics, but their entry was motivated by the search for opportunities to move up the class ladder. The people did not ask that politics be more fun, or provide more fun, but that it help them in their work and status.

To the participants, of course, it often looked as if there was a strong antibusiness movement. And in fact there were groups of moralizers who, through aristocracy or radicalism, were actually seeking a goal antithetical to that of the business class; the latter's leadership was so clear that these antibusiness groups could polarize their own destination by reference to the business position. But these fringe groups were actually quite weak, though they might find momentary resonance in groups of farmers or small businessmen.

With such exceptions, people arriving on the political scene felt themselves to be moving upward and onward. Where "up" and "on" lay, was clear. "Up" was up to the power and pelf of the business class —the lucid, internalized goal for individual inner-direction. "On" was on to the frontiers of production in a series of wars and skirmishes whose limits were set as clearly by the surrounding oceans as the limits of individual aspiration were set by the example of the business and political models of the day.

If we take a snapshot of the country in 1900, we see the South defeated and forgiven, the West bought off by remedial legislation, the world held at bay by the show of the Spanish War. Not before and not since has the class ladder seemed so straight, politics so crooked, and both so simply moralizable.

The lobby's task under these conditions had the simplicity we noted in Chapter IX, where businessmen could relatively easily (though

perhaps mistakenly) decide where their interests lay and what editors, lawyers, and legislators might be paid to advance them. The
latter, and the judiciary too, might be said to constitute a veto group.
But today the legislative lobby—as Pendleton Herring has seen very
clearly—is only a small aspect of the cumulated veto groups—groups
whose relations to their members and to each other are no longer
mediated in the legal and political forums alone but extend throughout the whole structure of American cultural and political life.

THE VETO GROUPS

The lobby in the old days actually ministered to the clear leadership, privilege, and imperative of the business ruling class. Today
we have substituted for that leadership a series of groups, each of
which has struggled for and finally attained a power to stop things
conceivably inimical to its interests and, within far narrower limits,
to start things. The movie-censoring groups, the farm groups and the
labor and professional groups, the major ethnic groups and major
regional groups, have in many instances succeeded in maneuvering
themselves into a position in which they are able to neutralize those
who might attack them. The very increase in the number of these
groups, and in the kinds of interests "practical" and "fictional" they
are protecting, marks therefore, a decisive change from the lobbies of
an earlier day. There is a change in method, too, in the way the groups
are organized, the way they handle each other, and the way they
handle the public, that is, the unorganized.

These veto groups are neither leader-groups nor led-groups. The
only leaders of national scope left in the United States today are those
who can placate the veto groups. The only followers left in the United
States today are those unorganized and sometimes disorganized un-
fortunates who have not yet invented their group.

Within the veto groups, there is, of course, the same struggle of
antagonistic cooperators for top places that goes on in other bureaucratic setups. *Among* the veto groups competition is monopolistic;
rules of fairness and fellowship dictate how far one can go. Despite
the rules there are, of course, occasional "price wars," like the juris-
dictional disputes of labor unions or Jewish defense groups; these are
ended by negotiation, the division of territory, and the formation of a
roof organization for the previously split constituency. These big
monopolies, taken as a single group, are in devastating competition

with the not yet grouped, much as the fair-trade economy competes against the free-trade economy. These latter scattered followers find what protection they can in the interstices around the group-minded.[3]

Each of the veto groups in this pattern is capable of an aggressive move, but the move is sharply limited in its range by the way in which the various groups have already cut up the sphere of politics and arrayed certain massive expectations behind each cut. Both within the groups and in the situation created by their presence, the political mood tends to become one of other-directed tolerance. The vetos so bind action that it is hard for the moralizers to conceive of a program that might in any large way alter the relations between political and personal life or between political and economic life. In the amorphous power structure created by the veto groups it is hard to distinguish rulers from the ruled, those to be aided from those to be opposed, those on your side from those on the other side. This very pattern encourages the inside-dopester who can unravel the personal linkages, and discourages the enthusiast or indignant who wants to install the good or fend off the bad. Probably, most of all it encourages the new-style indifferent who feels and is often told that his and everyone else's affairs are in the hands of the experts and that laymen, though they should "participate," should not really be too inquisitive or aroused.

By their very nature the veto groups exist as defense groups, not as leadership groups. If it is true that they do "have the power," they have it by virtue of a necessary mutual tolerance in which each of these groups allows all the other groups to dominate its agenda of attention. More and more they mirror each other in their style of political action, including their interest in public relations and their emphasis on internal harmony of feelings. There is a tendency for organizations as differently oriented as, say, the Young Socialists and the 4-H Club, to adopt similar psychological methods of salesmanship to obtain and solidify their recruits.

As suggested in Chapter VIII, character structure by no means de-

3. It should be clear that monopolistic competition, both in business and politics, *is* competition. People are very much aware of their rivals, within and without the organization. They know who they are, but by the very nature of monopolistic competition they are seldom able to eliminate them entirely. While we have been talking of fair trade and tolerance, this should not obscure the fact that for the participants the feeling of being in a rivalrous setup is very strong. Indeed, they face the problem of so many other-directed people: how to combine the appearance of friendly, personalized, "sincere" behavior with the ruthless, sometimes almost paranoid, envies of their occupational life.

termines vote, opinion, or informedness but is, on the contrary, an influence that tends to cut across party and opinion lines. So it is likewise clear that the veto groups are not formed along the lines of character structure either. In a business corporation there is room for both inner-directed and other-directed types—and all mixtures between—and in a veto group there can exist complex "symbiotic" relationships among people of different political styles. Thus a team of lobbyists may include both moralizers and inside-dopesters, sometimes working in harness, sometimes in conflict; and the constituency of the team may be composed mainly of new-style political indifferents who have enough literacy and organizational experience to throw weight around when called upon.

It is, however, very difficult to disentangle such relationships in any concrete case. It is necessary to recall, first, that virtually no one is a pure inside-dopester or a pure moralizer; the struggle, often a very bitter one, goes on within each person. Second, in times of any basic change, the less fashionable type learns to look, in some ways, like the more fashionable type. Third, moralizers and inside-dopesters are the extreme wings of character groups that have developed less clear-cut styles of political relatedness. Fourth, occasionally the moralizing of the inner-directed, while increasingly unpopular among those in the know, can find the other-directed instrumentalities that will dress moralizing in the new and fashionably tolerant style. Despite these complications I think it fair to say that the veto groups, even when they are set up to protect a clear-cut moralizing interest, are generally forced to adopt the political manners of the other-directeds.

In saying this I am talking about the national scene. The smaller the constituency, of course, the smaller the number of veto groups involved and the greater the chance that some one of them will be dominant. Thus, in local politics there is more indignation and less tolerance, just as even the *Chicago Tribune* is a tolerant paper in comparison with the community throwaways in many Chicago neighborhoods.

The same problem may be considered from another perspective. Various groups have discovered that they can go quite far in the amorphous power situation in America without being stopped. Our society is behaviorally open enough to permit a considerable community of gangsters a comfortable living under a variety of partisan political regimes. In their lack of concern for public relations these men are belated businessmen. So are some labor leaders who have discovered their power to hold up the economy, though in most situations what is surprising is the moderation of labor demands—a moderation based on psychological restraints rather than any power that could effectively be interposed. Likewise, it is sometimes possible for an aggressive group, while not belonging to the entrenched veto-power teams, to push a bill through a legislature. Thus, the original Social Security Act went through Congress, so far as I can discover, because it was pushed by a devoted but tiny cohort; the large veto groups including organized labor were neither very much for it nor very much against it.

For similar reasons those veto groups are in many political situations strongest whose own memberships are composed of veto groups, especially veto groups of one. The best example of this is the individual farmer who, after one of the farm lobbies has made a deal for him, can still hold out for more. The farm lobby's concern for the reaction of other veto groups, such as labor unions, cuts little ice with the individual farmer. This fact may strengthen the lobby in a negotiation: it can use its internal public relations problems as a counter in bargaining, very much as does a diplomat who tells a foreign minister that he must consider how Senator McKellar will react. For, no matter what the other-directedness of the lobby's leaders, they cannot bind their membership to carry out a public relations approach. Many labor unions have a similar power because they cannot control their memberships who, if not satisfied with a deal made by the union, can walk off or sabotage a job.

In contrast, those veto groups are often weaker whose other-directed orientation can dominate their memberships. Large corporations are vulnerable to a call from the White House because, save for a residual indignant like Sewell Avery, their officials are themselves other-directed and because, once the word from the chief goes out, the factory superintendents, no matter how boiling mad, have to fall into line with the new policy by the very nature of the centralized organization for which they work: they can sabotage top management on minor matters but not, say, on wage rates or tax accounting. As against this, the American Catholic Church possesses immense veto-group power because it combines a certain amount of centralized command—and a public picture of a still greater amount—with a highly decentralized priesthood and a membership organization of wide-ranging ethnic, social, and political loyalties; this structure permits great flexibility in bargaining.

These qualifications, however, do not change the fact that the veto groups, taken together, con⸗titute a new buffer region between the old, altered, and thinning extremes of those who were once leaders and led. It is both the attenuation of leaders and led, and the other-oriented doings of these buffers, that help to give many moralizers a sense of vacuum in American political life. In the economy the monopolies, with their potential for delaying technological progress, are more than held at bay by the leverage of the remaining free sectors and by the inevitable—and inevitably fierce—competition among groups of monopolies for the consumer-dollar vote. In politics a similar form of monopolistic competition goes on as the veto groups in certain situations compete for the unorganized or try to steal a march on one another.[4] But as is obvious, the dollar vote is a far more sensitive instrument than the ballot-box vote, despite efforts, for example by proportional representation, to make the latter more flexible. And while some of the unorganized sectors in politics might like to prod the veto groups in the way the free-trade economy prods the fair-trade economy, they lack the dynamite of technological invention. Thus, such progress as there is in national politics seems slow in comparison with the urgent needs of the present day and in comparison with the hopes, or the fears, of the remaining moralizers.

The veto groups, by the conditions their presence creates and by the requirements they set for leadership in politics, foster the tolerant mood of other-direction and hasten the retreat of the inner-directed indignants.

IS THERE A RULING CLASS LEFT?

Nevertheless, people go on acting as if there still were a decisive ruling class in contemporary America. Recent investigations show that businessmen think labor leaders and politicians run the country. Labor and the left think that "Wall Street" runs it, or the "sixty families." Wall Street, confused perhaps by its dethronement as a telling

4. The analogy between political and economic competition is made, along somewhat different lines, by Professor Joseph A. Schumpeter, *Capitalism, Socialism and Democracy* (New York, Harper, 1942).

barometer of capital-formation weather, may think that the mid-western industrial barons, cushioned on plant expansion money in the form of heavy depreciation reserves and undivided profits, run the country. They might have some evidence for this in the fact that the New Deal was much tougher with finance capital—e.g., the SEC and the Holding Company Act—than with industrial capital and that when, in the undistributed profits tax, it tried to subject the latter to a stockholder and money-market control, the tax was quickly repealed.

But these barons of Pittsburgh, Weirton, Akron, and Detroit, though certainly a tougher crowd than the Wall Streeters, are, as we saw in Chapter VI, coming more and more to think of themselves as trustees whose moves are largely dictated by the expectations, only marginally manipulated, of their beneficiaries. And whereas, from the point of view of labor and the left, these men ran the War Production Board in the interest of their respective companies, one could argue just as easily that the WPB experience was one of the congeries of factors that have tamed the barons. It put them in a situation where they had to view their company from the standpoint of "the others."

Despite the absence of intensive studies of business power and of what happens in a business negotiation, it is easy to get a sense of the change in business behavior in the last generation. In the pages of *Fortune,* that excellent chronicler of business, one can see that there are few survivals of the kinds of dealings—with other businessmen, with labor, with the government—that were standard operating practice for the pre-World War I tycoons. Moreover, in its twenty-year history, *Fortune* itself has shown, and perhaps it may be considered representative of its audience, a steady decline in interest in business as such and a growth of interest in once peripheral matters, such as international relations, social philosophy, and other accoutrements of the modern executive.

But it is of course more difficult to know whether character has changed as well as behavior—whether, as some contend, businessmen simply rule today in a more subtle, more "managerial" way. In "Manager Meets Union" Joseph M. Goldsen and Lillian Low have depicted the psychological dependence of a contemporary sales manager on the approval of the men under him, his willingness to go to great lengths, in terms of concessions, to maintain interpersonal warmth in his relations with them, and his fierce resentment of the union as a barrier to this emotional exchange.[5] As against this, one must set the attitude of some of the auto-supply companies whose leadership still seems much more craft oriented than people oriented and therefore unwilling to make concessions and none too concerned with the emotional atmosphere of negotiations. Likewise, the General Motors-UAW negotiations of 1946, as reported in print, sound more like a cockfight than a Platonic symposium, although in Peter Drucker's *Concept of the Corporation,* a study of General Motors published in the same year, there is much evidence of management eagerness to build a big, happy family.

The point here is that power is not a commodity to be kept under lock and key but is founded, as is now widely realized, on interpersonal expectations and attitudes. If businessmen *feel* weak and dependent they *are* weak and dependent, no matter what material resources may be ascribed to them. My impression, based mainly on experiences of my own in business and law practice, is that businessmen from large manufacturing companies, though they often talk big, are easily frightened by the threat of others' hostility; they may pound the table, but they look to others for leadership and do not care to get out of line with their peer-groupers. Possibly, attitudes toward such an irascible businessman as Sewell Avery might mark a good dividing line between the older and the newer attitudes. Those businessmen who admire Avery, though they might not dare to imitate him, are becoming increasingly an elderly minority, while the younger men generally are shocked by Avery's "highhandedness," his rebuff of the glad hand.

Furthermore, reading accounts in court records of negotiations between little businessmen and gangsters, I have been struck by the resemblance in the mood of their negotiations to the negotiations, say, of big businessmen and labor leaders. These small businessmen sat around in night clubs and taverns and exchanged small talk with the milk, trucking, or other racketeers to whom they were paying tribute. An air of pleasant sociability hung, like tobacco smoke, over the proceedings. Of course these gangsters not only had the power but showed it by occasionally bombing an uncooperative factory or overturning an uncooperative truck. But the gangsters, being illegal, had to use such methods to establish themselves as a veto group. In the big

5. "Manager Meets Union: a Case Study of Personal Immaturity," *Human Factors in Management,* ed. S. D. Hoslett (Parkville, Missouri, Park College Press, 1946), p. 77.

leagues of the big veto groups the limits of power are seldom tested by combat though this restraint, resting, as I think, on psychological grounds, is easily rationalized in terms of power politics and public relations.

Businessmen, moreover, are not the only people who fail to exploit the power position they are supposed, in the eyes of many observers, to have. Army officers are also astonishingly timid about exercising their leadership. During the war one would have thought that the army would be relatively impervious to criticism. But frequently the generals went to great lengths to refrain from doing something about which a congressman might make an unfriendly speech. They did so even at times when they might have brushed the congressman off like an angry fly. When dealing with businessmen or labor leaders, army officers were, as it seemed to me, astonishingly deferential; and this was as true of the West Pointers as of the reservists. Of course, there were exceptions, but in many of the situations where the armed services made concessions to propitiate some veto group, they rationalized the concessions in terms of morale or of postwar public relations needs or, frequently, simply were not aware of their power position.

To be sure, some came to the same result by the route of a democratic tradition of civilian dominance. Very likely, it was a good thing for the country that the services were so self-restrained. I do not here deal with the matter on the merits but use it as an illustration of changing character and changing social structure.

In some circles the images of power of the inside-dopesters are clearly self-confirming. There is the story of a professor who wrote a book that warns the nation against the new slickness in conservative thinking and publicity. He later met a lawyer who seemed to him to represent perfectly the type of sophisticated manipulators of opinion who he thought had a very good chance of taking over the country. A third person, the acquaintance of both, learned that the lawyer used the professor's book as a warning to sell his corporate clients on the need for still more temperate publicity as a counter to, and propitiation of, the "left."

Obviously, not all intellectuals can make a good living this way, but certainly each time a professor writes a book attacking business, even if almost nobody reads it, he makes many jobs in industry for his students! While the old Black Horse Cavalry held up businessmen by threatening to pass crippling legislation desired by antibusiness moralizers, today many self-convinced intellectuals hold business and government jobs because they have managed to scare their clients into taking cognizance of some actual or imaginary veto group.

As things are today, however, most observers seem unwilling to take a straight look at the amorphous distribution of power in America. Sophisticated social scientists pin their hopes or fears on this or that elite, echoing the bottom dogs who feel there is a boss somewhere. Yet people fail to see that, while it may take leadership to start things running, or to stop them, very little leadership is needed once things are under way—that, indeed, things can get terribly snarled up and still go on running. If one studies a factory, an army group, or other large organization, one wonders how things get done at all, in view of the lack of leadership and the extensive featherbedding. Perhaps they get done because we are still trading on our reserves of inner-direction, especially in the lower ranks. At any rate, the fact they do get done is no proof that there is someone in charge. Power in America seems to me situational and mercurial; it resists attempts to locate it the way a molecule, under the Heisenberg principle, resists attempts simultaneously to locate it and time its velocity.

There are, of course, still some veto groups that have more power than others and some individuals who have more power than others. But the determination of who these are has to be made all over again for our time: we cannot be satisfied with the answers given by Marx, Mosca, Michels, Pareto, Weber, Veblen, or Burnham, though we can learn from all of them. Paradoxically, it may be that while the mesas of the veto groups have replaced the mountain peaks of class in the United States, power has nevertheless become more concentrated in another respect, namely in the decline of the older separations of power, both constitutional and social-psychological. Most of the constitutional separations—executive, legislative, and judicial; upper chamber and lower chamber; federal and state—are of diminishing importance. So are the social-psychological separations that formerly buttressed the political ones: the separations between those who sought power through wealth and wealth through power; between those locally oriented and those nationally oriented; between those who looked to business models and those who looked to agrarian ones.

We see the consequences of this loss of older divisions in a number of ways. One example is the immense power, both political and economic, possessed by Artie Samish, allegedly the veto-group boss of California. Samish is a new-type lobbyist, who represents not one but scores of interests, often competing ones, from truckers to chiropractors, and who plays one veto group off against others to shake them down and strengthen his own power: he has learned how the other-orientation of the established veto groups will lead them to call still other groups into being through his auspices. Since the old-line parties have little power in California, there is no way of reaching a clear-cut decision for or against a particular veto group through the party system; instead, the state officials have become dependent on Samish for electoral support, or at least nonopposition, through his herded groups of voters and their cash contributions; moreover, he knows how to go directly to the people through the "democratic" plebiscite machinery. Thus, one might argue that Samish has *more* power than did, on the one hand, the Southern Pacific in the days of its California hegemony or, on the other hand, Hiram Johnson in the days of his glory. The separations that divide politics from economics, the legislative branch from the executive, or the public at large from its representatives—these older compartmentalizations and protections do not exist for him.[6]

Carey McWilliams has seen that Samish's power rests both on the peculiar election machinery of the state and on the fact that no one industry or allied group of industries, no one union, one ethnic group or region, is dominant. The situation is very different in a state like Montana, where copper is pivotal, and one must be either for the union or for Anaconda. It is different again in Virginia where, as V. O. Key shows in *Southern Politics,* the setup of the state constitution favors control by the old courthouse crowd. In view of these divergences, rooted in local legal niceties as well as in major social and economic factors, it is apparent that any discussion of class and power on the national scene can at best be only an approximation. Yet I

6. Ironically enough, but typically enough, Samish craves the one power he does not have: social power in the society-page sense. A poor boy in origin, he can make or break businessmen and politicians but cannot get into the more exclusive clubs. And while consciously he is said to despise these social leaders whom he can so easily frighten and manipulate, he cannot purge himself of the childhood hurts and childhood images of power that make him vulnerable to their exclusion of him. In this, of course, he resembles other and better-known dictators.

I have drawn on Carey McWilliams, "Guy Who Gets Things Done," *Nation,* CLXIX (1949), 31–33; and Lester Velie, "Secret Boss of California," *Collier's,* CXXIV (August 13, 20, 1949), 11–13, 12–13.

would venture to say that the United States is on the whole more like California in its variety—but without its veto boss—than like Montana and Virginia in their particularity. The vaster number of veto groups, and their greater power, mean that no one man or small group of men can amass the power nationally that Artie Samish and, in earlier days, Huey Long, have held locally.

Rather, power on the national scene must be viewed in terms of issues. It is possible that, where an issue involves only two or three veto groups, themselves tiny minorities, the official or unofficial broker among the groups can be quite powerful—but only on that issue. However, where the issue involves the country as a whole, no individual or group leadership is likely to be very effective, because the entrenched veto groups cannot be budged: unlike a party that may be defeated at the polls, or a class that may be replaced by another class, the veto groups are always "in."

Someone who wished to challenge this view might argue that the nation's big business showed that it still retained rulership when, in return for converting to war production in 1941, it insisted on retaining its prime position and its perquisites. Two answers might be made to this. One would be that the other-directedness of the antibusiness groups prevented them from challenging the "sit-down" of the business community, as Jackson challenged the sit-down of Nicholas Biddle. The other would be that business itself became frightened of its power and put up only token resistance to the renegotiation of its war contracts and war profits. Indeed, big businessmen seemed much more afraid of antibusiness postwar investigations of the Nye sort than was warranted in a society that has lost its moralizing taste for muckraking.

A more important criticism of my analysis would not rest on detailed discussion of particular instances of power concentration but would ask whether one might not find, over a long period of time, that decisions in America favored one group or class—thereby, by definition, the ruling group or class—over others. Does not wealth, one might ask, exert its pull in the long run? In the past this has been so; for the future I doubt it. The future seems to be in the hands of the small business and professional men who control Congress: the local realtors, lawyers, car salesmen, undertakers, and so on; of the military men who control defense and, in part, foreign policy; of the big business managers and their lawyers, finance-committee men, and other counselors who decide on plant investment and influence the rate of technological change; of the labor leaders who control worker productivity and worker votes; of the black belt whites who have the greatest stake in southern politics; of the Poles, Italians, Jews, and Irishmen who have stakes in foreign policy, city jobs, and ethnic religious and cultural organizations; of the editorializers and storytellers who help socialize the young, tease and train the adult, and amuse and annoy the aged; of the farmers—themselves a warring congeries of cattlemen, corn men, dairymen, cotton men, and so on—who control key departments and committees and who, as the living representatives of our inner-directed past, control many of our memories; of the Russians and, to a lesser degree, other foreign powers who control much of our agenda of attention; and so on. The reader can complete the list.

But people are afraid of this indeterminacy and amorphousness in the power situation. Even those intellectuals, for instance, who feel themselves very much out of power and who are frightened of those who they think have the power, prefer to be scared by the power structures they conjure up than to face the possibility that the power structure they believe exists has largely evaporated. This is of course partly because if someone has power, one can always imagine taking it away from him. But inside-dopesters have nothing so practical at stake in their belief that there are insiders who have power. It is rather that they, like most people, prefer to suffer with interpretations that give their world meaning than to relax in the cave without an Ariadne's thread.

XII

The Conversation of the Classes, and Other Dialogues

In the United States the more opulent citizens take great care not to stand aloof from the people; on the contrary, they constantly keep on easy terms with the lower classes; they listen to them, they speak to them every day. They know that the rich in democracies always stand in need of the poor, and that in democratic times you attach a poor man to you more by your manner than by benefits conferred.

Tocqueville, *Democracy in America*

THE SAME process that occurs, on a small scale in the self-confirming relationships of the veto groups with each other, also occurs on a wider scale in the relationship among the social classes in America. In certain respects each class, or ascertainable segment of that elusive concept, may be thought of as a loosely linked veto group. Politics is an aspect of a "conversation" among these class groups, a conversation increasingly conducted according to the inside-dopester's tolerant style. Similarly, if we look at recent international conferences in which Americans have participated, we find that the "conversation" of American diplomacy seems to be increasingly concerned with the securing of approval both for the individual participants and for the country that they represent. Even more clearly, the leadership in American domestic politics tries to carry on a conversation with the public in the intimate, ingratiating mood of the other-directeds. Indeed, even where the leaders appeal beyond the public to the "verdict of history," they are today still engaged in the endless search for approval: the anticipation of the verdict becomes a form of conversation.

I. CONVERSATIONS ACROSS THE RAILROAD TRACKS

In this section we do not consider the cross-class conversations carried on by individuals, although these are part of the picture; rather, we view the mass media, the public opinion polls, and our political institutions, generally, as the principal forums where the discourse goes on. The conversation is complex and continuous; and though its mood is tolerance, it has different meanings for the several class participants. The richer classes, for instance, have in the Roosevelt era used the conversation to sustain alternate illusions of power and powerlessness; the poorer classes, too, find variant images of power reflected in their share of the talk.

In recent years, conversing both across the class line and within it, many vocal members of the comfortable classes have talked as if they felt politically frustrated, as if they could make no headway against "that man in the White House" or, indeed, against politicians in general. The premise of calling attention to this frustration, however, has been that the speakers are not really powerless but feel only temporarily out of the seats of power. They have illusions of political omnipotence that descend from the power and competence of the late nineteenth-century captains of industry, or perhaps from earlier heritages still.

The mass media help sustain these illusions by reacting to them, just as the New Dealers took the opposition of these relicts as evidence, sometimes, that they, the New Dealers, were actually running the country and changing the location of power in America and, sometimes, that the New Dealers were being prevented from doing this by the "interests." But these illusions are also sustained by the life situation of the well-to-do. People in these groups have been brought up to make choices and to consider their opinions significant: on what to do for a living, on whether to buy a Packard or a Cadillac, on what summer resort or salad dressing is "best." That is to say, they have been brought up to consider themselves as individuals—an individuality constantly reinforced by ability to make tastes, preferences, and opinions count in daily life situations.

Moreover, voicing their opinions to others increases their feeling of potency, in a way akin to the uses of word magic by children; they reassure themselves that they grasp their world and that it is theirs, by having and expressing opinions about those aspects of reality they have been brought up to attend to. Though more likely to be moralizers than inside-dopesters, they are in social contact with political "insiders"; this helps them to identify with the political world and to feel that, except for the unfortunate temporary situation, that world still belongs to them. However, as these residual conservatives become more and more isolated, their ability to communicate across the class lines diminishes; they shout at people but cannot bring themselves to listen.

More typical of the trend toward other-direction are the men and women of the upper middle and middle classes who, while aware of their class position, see politics and popular culture in terms of an interchange among the classes in which they listen quite as much as they talk. This conversation is more than mere politeness, although it is reflected in the politeness of the up-to-date personnel relations and public relations which form part of this conversation. It is an attempt to hide, on both sides, the residual realities of the power situation; that is, the differences in wealth and status that are still important. The attempt to conceal these realities of power operates most openly in the movies and popular fiction, where a taxi driver's attitudes may change the life of a bank president. It would be a mistake to see this fantasy, perhaps in any case a disappearing one, as a conscious effort to fool the people. If the movies could make money without tangling with the veto groups by "subverting" America, they would do so—in a way, by promoting other-direction, they do. Nor is the participation by the upper middle class in the conversation of the classes a consciously exploitative device for the most part, for this class in America is by no means as powerful, as psychologically secure, or, indeed, as ruthless, as predecessor ruling classes have been. The seemingly powerful need to be reassured by contact with the seemingly less powerful, by hearing their voices, by exchange of signals.

This is not, we may suppose, what Tocqueville had in mind when he made the observation quoted at the head of this chapter. He was describing behavioral opportunism, while opportunism has now become embedded in character: the rich "speak to them [the poor] every day" because today they need their smiles and approval and cannot psychologically afford their frowns.

Often enough, this need is coupled with a genuine sensitivity to the poor-as-others, quite different from the inner-directed boss-man's paternalism. Typically, however, the other-directed person wishes to appear to himself and others as realistic and hard boiled; hence, he must overestimate the power of the weak in order to rationalize paying so much attention to them, listening so carefully and, on occasion, making more concessions than might be objectively required by the *Realpolitik* he professes as an inside-dopester. The consequence of his anxious attention to the indexes of political opinion is that the socially weak are encouraged to overestimate their power, as of course they are only too ready to do.

Consequently, we arrive at the paradoxical situation in which the veto groups who actually wield so much power today are not, in terms of the classic interpretations of power, as strong as they appear nor as strong as those who placate them think they are. Their strength arises partly from an illusion that mislocates power and powerlessness on the American scene. To be sure, power and illusion about power are not strangers historically speaking—we saw a less pronounced disparity operating in Tocqueville's age—but their merger in what seems to be a rational conversation of the classes seems to be something new.

However, as the Roosevelt-hating conservatives at the top of the social scale, far from taking part in such a conversation, conduct a monologue, so the people at the very bottom of the social scale either do not listen, or when forced to listen, do not believe what is said. Genevieve Knupfer in her "Portrait of the Underdog" has documented from public opinion polls how little receptivity these people have for information, balloting, opinion exchanging, and other modes by which the conversation of the classes is conducted.[1] Among people in these poorer classes the image of a ruling class is very strong. Like some of the very rich, they believe the political world is a manageable one—but not by them: the "insiders," the "sixty families," or just plain "they" are in easy control of events. The feeling of impotence in these lower strata is often based less on their own incompetence than on a fear of overcompetence on the side of the higher strata. This is a type of barbershop cynicism and sophistication which frequently turns up in underdog replies to public opinion polls: "What do *they* want to know for; they run their own show anyway."

1. Genevieve Knupfer, "Portrait of the Underdog," *Public Opinion Quarterly,* XI (1947), 103.

These lower-class people have so little confidence in themselves that they cannot believe that their own amiability or hostility could mean anything to the distant and mysterious "they."

In a sense this is only another way of saying that America is a middle-class country and that middle-class values and political styles of perception reach into all levels except the fringes at the very top and the very bottom. But it must be added that America is increasingly a country of the "new" middle class, bureaucratized in situation and other-directed in character; a country in which the class gradients, so clear even in the days of *The Great Gatsby,* are now too confused to be really impressive save for a few laggard snobs and would-be snobs; a country in which, perhaps, people will soon wake up to the fact that there is no longer a "we" who run things and a "they" who don't, or a "we" who don't run things and a "they" who do, but rather that all "we's" are "they's" and all "they's" are "we's."

II. CONVERSATIONS ACROSS THE SEA

Study of war and postwar international conferences reveals interesting differences in American and Russian attitudes.[2] From the evidence of newspaper reports and published memoirs it appears that the American delegations, regardless of the issues at stake, entered each of these conferences placing much glad-handed emphasis on the emotional value of conference moods. The Americans were pleased, far more than other groups, by the turns and changes of discussion that produced an atmosphere of harmony and agreement—even if the mood was represented only by a joke and even if the mood had no contractual results. As a last gambit the Americans hoped—and who has not heard a similar phrase in a meeting?—that people could at least "agree to disagree."

The attitude of the Russians was quite different. They appear to have entered the negotiations with no interest in the feeling of the occasion or any stake in the upward or downward shifts of the emotional barometer. They kept their eyes on the trading position, and even used the playful sallies of their adversaries, intended in the joking spirit of American mood-relievers, as hooks in negotiation.

2. A more systematic study of conference behavior is under way in the Social Science Division of the Rand Corporation.

Obviously, there are differences in the situation of the two sets of negotiators, and these may be more important in interpreting conference behavior by a kind of administrative anthropology than analysis of the character structure of the participants. Of course, the Americans must be concerned with domestic public opinion far more than the Russians. That opinion influences and is influenced by the emotional tone of international relations. Possibly Americans find it harder than other peoples to conceive of getting along with nations they dislike and who dislike them, no matter what interests may objectively unite them. At the same time Americans place great stress on international mood engineering in order to persuade other countries to like them and vice versa, and often to persuade themselves that they are liked in the face of contrary evidence. Thus not the negotiators but the public they represent may be other-directed. Nevertheless, it seems clear that the American representatives were during this period extremely anxious to be judged as good fellows; so good that they would not draw back the glad hand of international handshake unless the man across the table seemed about to chop it off.

But when that happens, when the glad hand is rebuffed, the mood of tolerance may change abruptly to a mood of hurt. The result may even be a desire *not* to reach an agreement—again, irrespective of trading advantages.

Not all American negotiators are like this; on the contrary, someone who is inner-directed and not especially interested in emotional mood may be in demand for that very reason when the going is rough. It would, moreover, be necessary to study not only current patterns of international negotiation but earlier ones, to see whether American conference practice actually has changed with the spread of other-direction.

When we consider again how other-directed is the American agenda of attention, it would appear that as on the domestic scene the veto groups are focused on what the significant others are doing, so on the international scene the focus is on what the significant others, in this case the Russians, are doing. And just as people in the veto groups are apt to exaggerate the power of other veto groups in order to justify their attention, so the Americans concerned with international affairs have tended to overestimate the monolithic and unshakable quality of the Russian social structure—and hence perhaps to overestimate Russian power (after badly underestimating it before World War II), despite the evidence from Nazism that totalitarian regimes appear more cohesive and well planned than they really are.

American attitudes toward our own world role may shed further light on this matter. If the United States possessed a large store of indignation and enthusiasm both in its political luminaries and its voting public, we might expect that it would by now be well on its way toward world-wide organization. Sporadic moves, to be sure, have been made in this direction. But the exploratory impulse of the inner-directed, the drive to find frontiers and then to capture them, has become attenuated.

With no large group favoring extension of American power and no large group favoring curtailment on moral grounds, the world actions of the United States during and since the war have been dominated neither by an inner ideal nor by a clear view of national interest but rather by a series of off-the-cuff responses to Russia. The Americans have let the Russian leaders make the moves and then have worked out a counterplay—the Acheson-Lilienthal atomic energy proposal and perhaps the Marshall Plan are notable exceptions. In a military sense we have "had the power," yet we have been on the defensive. With respect to armament and armament potential, the Americans have said in effect: "Let the Russians propose the goals for any kind of race they want; whatever goals they propose, we will beat them."

This situation resembles the attitude of the other-directed man in business. In contrast with the inner-directed man who had a plan of entrepreneurship that obsessed him so that his competitors were shadows on the edge of it or obstacles en route, the other-directed man lives with his attention dominated not so much by his enterprise plan but by what his associates and competitors are doing.

Consequently, the American political leader tends to feel lost when his competitors no longer provide what in the economic field would be called "price leadership." For instance, when the Berlin blockade was lifted, there were indications of regret, both in Military Government and in Washington. James Reston wrote, in the *New York Times* of May 5, 1949:

Western diplomats are reacting to the lifting of the Berlin blockade very much as Paul Makushak, the Brooklyn broom-closet hermit reacted to his freedom last month.

"It's no good being out," said Mr. Makushak. "I'd like to go back where I was." . . .

But the ending of the blockade, like Mr. Makushak's freedom, introduces a large element of doubt into their lives.

By pointing out these difficulties in an other-directed style of international politics, I do not mean to suggest that the inner-directed style was necessarily better. Although the inner-directed person operated according to plan, the plan was often narrow; in fact, he could have a clear-cut plan, in part, because of its narrowness. By sticking to it without attention to the others, he was occasionally in the position of the type of chess player who is so busy figuring out his own strategies that he loses sight of his opponent's strategies—indeed, there is some evidence that Soviet foreign policy, as in its blind failure to foresee Hitler's attack, has been beset with just such limitations. Moreover, the inner-directed person's plan was often insufficiently concerned with the human element, even apart from the blockages to vision that this insensitivity imposed.

On the other hand, other-direction as the basis of a political style does break down when the "others" neither lead nor cooperate. For the first time in our century America has no models to follow. As late as the 1930's many Americans saw in the Soviet Union or in the Swedish middle way or in fascism a model for their own social system. Now it is thoroughly clear that American domestic problems are more difficult and cannot be solved in imitation of these ways. Similarly, until the last war, many Americans found a foreign policy in backing or opposing Britain, as they seek one today in backing or opposing Russia. But this does not work when Britain looks to us for leadership, and when Russia, as in the Far East, seems determined not to tell us, by negation, what to do there. When we look to the response of the "others" to see whether any particular policy is working, we find that our own power and prospects have already influenced the response; many will ask us but no one will tell us. Both nationally and internationally, we are like a child who when young found other-direction quite successful (since he was always surrounded by a peer-group) but who as an adult finds himself suddenly alone with the others looking up to him. The position is frighteningly lonely and conspicuous.

III. CONVERSATIONS BY THE FIRESIDE

In the pamphlet, "Thoughts on Parliamentary Reform," I had said, rather bluntly, that the working classes, though differing from those of some other countries, in being ashamed of lying, are yet generally liars. This passage some opponent got printed in a placard which was handed to me at a meeting, chiefly composed of the working classes, and I was asked whether I had written and published it. I at once answered "I did." Scarcely were these two words out of my mouth, when vehement applause resounded through the whole meeting.

John Stuart Mill, *Autobiography*

Our conclusions on leadership point up an apparent contradiction in terms. If the other-directed person is by virtue of his character tolerant of others, why does he not anticipate a similar tolerance for his own actions when he is a leader? Why is he so driven to conform, when the others by their nature would tolerate his nonconformity? Would he not be approved of, within wide limits, whatever he did?

Certainly, his own attitude toward the deviation of others is tolerant enough, though he sometimes employs rather roundabout mechanisms to evade the problem. When confronted with an opinion or personality that differs from the peer-group standard, his mechanism will be to deny the deviation, to talk it away where this is possible. This is one way, in certain circles, of dealing with differences between whites and Negroes, or Jews and non-Jews—the differences are supposed to exist only in the eye of the prejudiced, and the actual minority deviations are glossed over. Still another, more subtle, device is for the other-directed person to admit that a deviation exists but to explain it to himself as not intended as a challenge to the peer-group. Thus a conventional businessman may explain away the Bohemianism of an associate by ascribing it to a conscious pose which may even be tomorrow's winner in the race of styles.

Yet, when it is his own action that is in question, the other-directed person does not seem to count on the same tolerance from the others that he would be willing to extend. At that point the peer-group jury with its veto power appears to him to be watching for him to get out of line. Very likely, this is partly because *he wants more from the others than mere tolerance; he wants approval.* But since he cannot admit this fully to himself, he must interpret the others as intolerant in order to justify his submission to them. And since he has defined the others for himself he comes to overestimate the need for conformity.

His anxiety for approval, then, disguised as a demand for conformity made by others on him, causes him to "lead" the group, where he is nominally the leader, by providing what he thinks is the appropriate response. Where there is competition for leadership posts, this will bring about marginal differentiation, as people seek on any political issue those positions where they can be seen—without being too visible for comfort. The leader will act not because of an inner-directed plan of action or because he is genuinely involved with politics but because of his psychological need to be continuously judged by others. This judgment—a judgment in the realm of taste and opinion—is the act that gives final validity to all of his experiences. He is in the position of an actor, looking for response from an audience, and of course the audience is trained to respond in terms of consumption preferences. Indeed, mood leadership in the topmost social and political groups in America is becoming increasingly self-conscious; it is part of the same development that has taken us from morality to morale. The spread of "group dynamics" may perhaps be used as an index of this shift; while it has many positive sides, it is sometimes little more than a skilled technique, built on an elaborate rationale, for breaking down privacies and other resistances to group mood.

In this way the men who, at an earlier historical period, were political leaders are now busy with the other-directed occupation of studying the feedback from all the others—their constituencies, their correspondents, the friends and enemies of their veto group, and their associates within the veto group. The revolution in communications makes this attention possible in ways that were not available to the equally assiduous client-cultivator of an earlier day, who could buy a few editors if he wanted favorable things said. And those who were once the followers have learned the arts of lobbying and media pressure. The roll call of nineteenth- and early twentieth-century leaders contains many men who refused to follow their flock: Gladstone and Cleveland, Robert Peel and John Stuart Mill (as M.P.), Woodrow Wilson and Winston Churchill. Even today the need to impose unpopular courses brings to the fore inner-directed types: Cripps, for instance, in England; Stimson and Robert Patterson in this country. Of course, political figures in all ages have been dependent on their following, and opportunism is not a twentieth-century discovery. The inner-directed leader, however, was quite conscious of discrepancies between his views and those of others; if he shifted his course, it was still *his* course. Moreover, since he was ambitious, he might well prefer later fame to momentary warmth of response; in any event he did not need to have everybody love him, but only those who mattered for his fortunes.

It is interesting, in this connection, to compare the incident described by Mill in the epigraph to this section with the American public figures who not only would not think of saying anything that might offend an audience but who frequently depart from a prepared text, carefully designed to please a wide audience, in order to mollify the smaller face-to-face group before whom the speech happens to be delivered. By this inability to stand the momentary hostility of this small group, the political figure sometimes cuts himself off from the possibility of influencing a much wider audience.

It would of course be unfair to compare the autonomous Mill with the more typical individual of either yesterday or today. My point is that the other-oriented leader, unable to take a stand against a particular audience, may actually fail to discover other potentials in the latter. Hearing the signals from the others as they seem to be, and not as they might with his aid become, he actually facilitates a circular process of mutual enslavement. If he were less "realistic," he might occasionally have the decisive experience that, by resisting a current trend, the trend itself would suddenly be seen as mythical.

Today, even if a leader, ambitious for fame, had a plan in which he was more interested than in approval, he would in all probability be stymied by the veto groups. With them as a buffer between him and his potential following, he could hardly get started. The veto groups present a dismaying series of barriers to action—a series, of course, that is strengthened by the institutional usages that have grown up around certain veto practices such as the filibuster or the vested rights of Congressional committee chairmen. Outside of formal politics the veto practices are hardly less entrenched: such unofficial barriers as the Hays (now Johnston) Office in Hollywood or the unspoken divisions of territory among some monopolies seem quite impermeable to change. It must be an intrepid person indeed—perhaps, in most cases, an enthusiast or an indignant unable to see some of the obstacles—who undertakes any ambitious program in contemporary America. Few people will run interference for him. Hence the leader can no longer be ambitious for great personal accomplishment but must cooperate for small competitive gains. The boy who would be senator, and few boys aim so high, no longer has clear models to imitate or clear channels to follow.

Thus character and situation combine to discourage the style of the moralizer and to spread the tolerant style of the inside-dopester. The latter accepts politics on the terms of the others and uses it as a sphere for the exercise of consumption preferences, either on the approval-giving or approval-receiving end. Actors and audience replace the leaders and the led.

IV. CONVERSATIONS ACROSS THE AGES

And shall we not call it unselfishness, when the historical man lets himself be turned into an "objective" mirror of all that is? Is it not magnanimity to renounce all power in heaven and earth in order to adore the mere fact of power? Is it not justice, always to hold the balance of forces in your hands and observe which is the stronger and heavier? And what a school of politeness is such a contemplation of the past! To take everything objectively, to be angry at nothing, to love nothing, to understand everything— makes one gentle and pliable. Even if a man brought up in this school will show himself openly offended, one is just as pleased, knowing it is only meant in the artistic sense of *ira et studium,* though it is really *sine ira et studio.*

Nietzsche, *Thoughts Out of Season*

If, however, other-directed political actors care primarily for the verdict of their contemporaries—the concentric circles of peer-groups, known and unknown, among which they live—why is it we find today so much discussion about the verdict of history? Here, I think there are a number of elements.

When people ask "What will history say of me?" they ask primarily because of the insecurity they feel as to whether the signals, even signals of approval, from the others, can be relied upon. Are the others 'sincere"? Will they stick when all the facts are out? Inside-dopesters who have themselves had the experience of finding their opinions rapidly fluctuating must be uneasy lest others' opinions about them might change. History is the best inside-dopester: it sees and decides all.

The leader of today, however, does not appeal to history as *against* his contemporaries; rather, he joins *with* his contemporaries in trying to look at himself and his actions through the eyes of future historians. This is why the discussion of history's verdict is not confined to the diaries of the great but spreads throughout the mass media; it is, in fact, an important part of the sophisticated political training in which the media engage. Actors and audience both ask themselves: how will we appear to these future others; will these others approve us; will they declare we were on the right track?

History is viewed, then, not as a kind of transcendent Justice based on the moralizer's tests of goodness and badness but rather as the verdict of the "others" of the not too distant future, based on success; the historians are the Younger Generation, telling the parents what the score is; they are, by definition, more up to date.

Beyond that, we have already observed the other-directed person's craving to be judged: he fears others' judgments, but at the same time needs them as a major consumption item in his way of life. But, like the emphasis on winning in the comics, this judgment has no directly moral significance: the historians are like the photographers at a photo finish who can tell better than the cheering touts who is the winner. What this means is that the other-directed person of this inside-dopester type is constantly changing roles, now judging the others, now judging himself through their eyes.

In all this we must differentiate between, on the one side, an Old Bolshevik, fundamentally inner-directed, who is as anxious about the verdict of History as a Calvinist about predestination but who sees History in terms of an Hegelian pattern; and on the other side, an American political figure, fundamentally other-directed, who makes no claims on history, of an Hegelian or any other sort, but who sees future historians as even better inside-dopesters than he. The Old Bolshevik might worry that he did the wrong thing, in terms of the historical forces with which he must cooperate; the inside-dopester might worry that, when the documents are out, he will be shown to have been played for a sucker. The former has an active attitude toward history: his task is to shape it in accordance with its immanent dynamic. The latter has a passive attitude: he is a consumer, not a producer, of history; his task is to bet on the right horse. The Old Bolshevik, despite a good deal of abdication to the Generalized Other of history, still retains his core of inner-directed ambition toward concrete, though not necessarily personal, goals. Indeed, it is just this quality which has led to his elimination in the Soviet Union and the satellite states in favor of more pliable types.

An additional motivation may exist for the other-directed person's recourse to the judgment of history. Because of the peculiar kind of hypocrisy we noted in Chapter IX, the inside-dopester must conceal fine and decent actions underneath a hard-boiled and "realistic" cloak. So he may justify actions, quite defensible in their own right, in terms of a future generation of even more objective and realistic inside-dopesters, the historians: they will prove him no softy. One can see in business and government the performance of an analogous ritual of deference to "the record"; good things and bad are done in fact and allegedly "for the record," even when the chances of the record's ever becoming known, let alone influential, are negligible. Likewise, "good will" and "public opinion" are frequently as vague a projection as History but are nonetheless invoked to justify what is done on other, and frequently unconscious, grounds.

Instances of this kind, where references to History or to the record are used to rationalize doing something decent, are probably far less frequent than use of these references as evasions of a moral problem. Many social conditions, as well as psychological changes, have tended to make obsolete the practice of the martyr who appeals against the present to the past and to the eschatological future. This practice depends on maintaining the sacredness of public trials (including the privilege against self-incrimination) and the right of the brave defendant to "go down in history." When books can be burned and people given trials only to accuse themselves in a prosecution show (under drugs or similar ultimate invasion of the self) and when, in any case, moral judgments have gone out of fashion, the lonely leader, even in less extreme situations, must feel that the ambitious appeal to a future conscience of mankind is slightly ridiculous, if not entirely impracticable. Neither God nor man will hear. Then, only conversation with the living seems "real"; conversation with the future is "imaginary."

Let me now summarize the argument in the preceding chapters. The inner-directed person, if he is political at all, is related to the political scene either by his morality, his well-defined interests, or both. His relationship to his opinions is close, not peripheral. The opinions are means of defending certain principles of politics. They may be highly charged and personal, as in the political discussion in the first pages of Joyce's *Portrait of the Artist As a Young Man,* or they may be highly charged and impersonal—a means of defending one's proper Bostonianship or other class position. In either case one's own opinions are felt to matter and to have some direct relationship to the objective world in which one lives.

As against this, the other-directed person, if he is political, is related to the political scene as a member of a veto group. He leaves it to the group to defend his interests, cooperating when called on to vote, to apply pressure, and so on. These pressure tactics seem to make his opinions manifest on the political level, but they actually help make it possible for him to be detached from his opinions. No longer operating as an "independent voter"—mostly an amiable fiction even in the era dependent on inner-direction—his political opinions, as such, are not felt to be related to his political function. Thus, they can serve him as a social counter in his role as a peer-group consumer of the political news-of-the-day. He can be tolerant of other opinions not only because of his characterological tolerance but also because they are "mere" opinions, interesting or amusing perhaps, but lacking the weight of even a partial, let alone a total, commitment to one's political role or action. They are "mere" opinions, moreover, because so intractable is the political world of the veto groups that opinion as such is felt to be almost irrelevant.

The inner-directed political moralizer has a firm grip—often much too firm—on the gamut of judgments that he is willing to apply anywhere and everywhere. The other-directed inside-dopester is unable to fortify any particular judgment with conviction springing from a summarized and organized emotional tone. It could be argued that the suppressed affect or emotional tone is still there, remaining hidden. Freudian doctrine would predict the return of the repressed. But it seems more likely, social habit being as powerful as it is, that the repeated suppression of such enthusiasm or moral indignation as the inner-directed man would consider natural permanently decrease the capacity of the other-directed man for those forms of response. The other-directed man may even begin as an inner-directed man who plays at being other-directed. He ends up being what he plays and his mask becomes the perhaps inescapable reality of his style of life.

XIII

Americans and Kwakiutls

Moralists are constantly complaining that the ruling vice of the present time is pride. This is true in one sense, for indeed everybody thinks that he is better than his neighbor or refuses to obey his superior; but it is extremely false in another, for the same man who cannot endure subordination or equality has so contemptible an opinion of himself that he thinks he is born only to indulge in vulgar pleasures. He willingly takes up with low desires without daring to embark on lofty enterprises, of which he scarcely dreams.

Thus, far from thinking that humility ought to be preached to our contemporaries, I would have endeavors made to give them a more enlarged idea of themselves and of their kind. Humility is unwholesome to them; what they most want is, in my opinion, pride.

Tocqueville, *Democracy in America*

THE IMAGE of power in contemporary America presented in the preceding chapters will possibly not be easily recognized by the reader. Current discussions of power in America are usually based on a search for a ruling class (for instance, Burnham's discovery of the "managers," Mills's of the labor leaders and others). And Americans themselves, rather than being the mild and cooperative people we have portrayed, are, to many observers and to themselves, power-obsessed or money-mad or concerned with conspicuous display. Or, as in the parable I shall use to illustrate my argument, Americans are felt, and feel themselves, to be more like rivalrous Kwakiutl Indian chiefs and their followers, than like peaceable, cooperative Pueblo agriculturists. Perhaps by further pursuing these images of power and personality we may be able to clarify the discrepancies between political fact and political ideology dwelt on in preceding chapters.

Ruth Benedict's book, *Patterns of Culture,* describes in vivid detail three primitive societies: the Pueblo Indians of the southwest, the people of the Island of Dobu in the Pacific, and the Kwakiutl Indians of the northwest coast of America.[1]

The Pueblo Indians are pictured as a peaceable, cooperative society, in which no one wishes to be thought a great man and everyone wishes to be thought a good fellow. Sexual relations are taken with little jealousy or other violent response; infidelity is not severely punished. Death, too, is taken in stride, with little violent emotion; indeed, emotion is, in general, subdued. While there are considerable variations in economic status, there is little display of economic power and even less of political power; there is a spirit of cooperation with family and community.

The Dobu, by contrast, are portrayed as virtually a society of paranoids in which each man's hand is against his neighbor's in sorcery, theft, and abuse; in which husband and wife alternate as captives of the spouse's kin; and in which infidelity is deeply resented. Dobuan economic life is built on sharp practice in interisland trading, on an intense feeling for property rights, and on a hope of getting something for nothing through theft, magic, and fraud. Except for nearby Alor, few pictures as grim as this are to be found in anthropological literature.

The third society, the Kwakiutl, is also intensely rivalrous. But the rivalry consists primarily in conspicuous consumption, typified by feasts called "potlatches," at which chiefs outdo each other in providing food and in burning up the blankets and sheets of copper which are the main counters of wealth in the society; sometimes even a house or a canoe is sent up in flames in a final bid for glory. Indeed, the society is a caricature of Veblen's conspicuous consumption; certainly, the potlatches of the Kwakiutl chiefs serve "as the legitimate channel by which the community's surplus product has been drained off and consumed, to the greater spiritual comfort of all parties concerned." Veblen was, in fact, familiar with these northwest-coast "coming out parties."

I have asked students who have read Ruth Benedict's book which of these three cultures in their opinion most closely resembles the obviously more complex culture of the United States. The great majority see Americans as Kwakiutls. They emphasize American business rivalry, sex and status jealousy, and power drive. They see Americans

---

1. *Patterns of Culture* (Boston, Houghton Mifflin, 1934; reprinted New York, Pelican Books, 1946).

as individualists, primarily interested in the display of wealth and station.

A minority of students, usually the more politically radical, say that America is more like Dobu. They emphasize the sharp practice of American business life, point to great jealousy and bitterness in family relations, and in terms of aggression see American politics, domestic and international, as existing almost in Hobbes's state of nature.

No students have argued that there are significant resemblances between the culture of the Hopi and Zuñi Pueblos and American culture—they wish that there were.

Yet when we turn then to examine the culture patterns of these very students, we see little evidence either of Dobu or Kwakiutl ways. The wealthy students go to great lengths not to be conspicuous—things are very different from the coon-coated days of the 20's. The proper uniform is one of purposeful shabbiness. In fact, none among the students except a very rare Lucullus dares to be thought uppity. Just as no modern Vanderbilt says "the public be damned," so no modern parent would say: "Where Vanderbilt sits, there is the head of the table. I teach my son to be rich." [2]

It is, moreover, not only in the virtual disappearance of conspicuous consumption that the students have abandoned Kwakiutl-like modes of life. Other displays of gifts, native or acquired, have also become more subdued. A leading college swimming star told me: "I get sore at the guys I'm competing against. Something's wrong with me. I wish I could be like X who really cooperates with the other fellows. He doesn't care so much about winning."

There seems to be a discrepancy between the America that students personally meet and make for themselves as students and the America they think they will move into when they leave the campus. Their image of the latter is based to a large extent on legends about America that are preserved in our literature. For example, many of our novelists and critics still believe that America, as compared with other cultures, is a materialistic nation of would-be Kwakiutl chiefs. There may have been some truth in this picture in the Gilded Age, though Henry James saw how ambiguous the issue was between America and Europe even then.

The materialism of these older cultures has been hidden by their

2. The remark is quoted by Justice Oliver Wendell Holmes, Jr., in "The Soldier's Faith," 1895, reprinted in *Speeches* (Boston, Little, Brown, 1934), p. 56. I am indebted to Carl Withers for discerning observations concerning changing campus mores.

status systems and by the fact that they had inherited many values from the era dependent on tradition-direction. The European masses simply have not had the money and leisure, until recent years, to duplicate American consumership patterns; when they do, they are, if anything, sometimes more vulgar, more materialistic.

The Europeans, nevertheless, have been only too glad to tell Americans that they were materialistic; and the Americans, feeling themselves nouveaux riches during the last century, paid to be told. They still pay: it is not only my students who fail to see that it is the turn of the rest of the world to be nouveaux riches, to be excited over the gadgets of an industrial age, while millions of Americans have turned away in boredom from attaching much emotional significance to the consumer-goods frontier.[3]

When, however, I try to point these things out to students who compare Americans with Kwakiutls, they answer that the advertisements show how much emotion is attached to goods consumption. But, when I ask them if they believe the ads themselves, they say scornfully that they do not. And when I ask if they know people who do, they find it hard to give examples, at least in the middle class. (If the advertisements powerfully affected people in the impoverished lower class who had small hope of mobility, there would surely be a revolution!) Yet the advertisements must be reaching somebody, the students insist. Why, I ask, why isn't it possible that advertising as a whole is a fantastic fraud, presenting an image of America taken seriously by no one, least of all by the advertising men who create it? Just as the mass media persuade people that other people think politics is important, so they persuade people that everyone else cannot wait for his new refrigerator or car or suit of clothes. In neither case can people believe that "others" are as apathetic as they feel themselves to be. And, while in the case of politics their indifference may make people feel on the defensive, in the case of advertising their indifference may allow them to feel superior.

In fact, I think that a study of American advertising during the last quarter century would clearly show that the advertising men themselves realize the consumer's loss of emotional enthusiasm. Where once car and refrigerator advertisements showed the housewife or husband exulting in the new possessions, today it is often only chil-

3. Mary McCarthy's fine article, "America the Beautiful," *Commentary*, IV (1947), 201 takes much the same attitude as the text.

dren in the ads who exult over the new Nash their father has just bought. In many contemporary ads the possession itself recedes into the background or is handled abstractly, even surrealistically; it no longer throws off sparks or exclamation points; and copy itself has become subtler or more matter of fact. Of course many old-fashioned enthusiasts of consumption remain in America who have not yet been affected by the spread of other-directed consumer sophistication and repression of emotional response. A wonderful example is the small-town Irish mother in the movie, *A Letter to Three Wives,* whose greatest pride and joy in her dingy railroad-side home is the big, shiny, new, not yet paid-for refrigerator. And it may be argued that even middle-class Americans have only covered over their materialism with a veneer of "good taste," without altering their fundamental drives. Nevertheless, the other-directed person, oriented as he is toward people, is simply unable to be as materialistic as many inner-directeds were. For genuine inner-directed materialism—real acquisitive attachment to things—one must go to the Dutch bourgeois or French peasant or others for whom older ways endure.

It is the other-directedness of Americans that has prevented their realizing this; between the advertisers on the one hand and the novelists and intellectuals on the other, they have assumed that *other* Americans were materialistic, while not giving sufficient credence to their *own* feelings. Indeed, the paradoxical situation in a stratum which is other-oriented is that people constantly make grave misjudgments as to what others, at least those with whom they are not in peer-group contact, but often also those with whom they spend much time, feel and think.

To be sure, the businessmen themselves often try to act as if it were still possible to be a Kwakiutl chief in the United States. When they write articles or make speeches, they like to talk about free enterprise, about tough competition, about risk taking. These businessmen, of course, are like World War I legionnaires, talking about the glorious days of yore. Students and many others believe what the businessmen say on these occasions, but then have little opportunity to watch what they do. Perhaps the businessmen themselves are as much the victims of their own chants and rituals as the Kwakiutls are.

Those few students who urge that America resembles Dobu can find little in student life to sustain their view, except perhaps a bit of cheating in love or on examinations. It is rather that they see the "capitalistic system" as a jungle of sharp practice, as if nothing had changed since the days of Mark Twain, Jack London, and Frank Norris. America is to them a land of lynchings, gangsterism, and deception by little foxes and big foxes. Yet, today, only small businessmen (car dealers or furnace repairmen, for instance) have many opportunities for the "wabu-wabu" trading, that is, the sharply manipulative property-pyramiding of the Dobuan canoeists.

If, however, these students turn to social science for their images of power in America, they will very frequently find their own view confirmed. The scattered remarks on the United States in *Patterns of Culture* are themselves an illustration. My students also read Robert Lynd's chapter on "The Pattern of American Culture" in *Knowledge for What?* [4] While noting contradictory exhortations to amity and brotherhood, Lynd emphasizes business as highly individualistic and politically ruthless; elsewhere he stresses the masterful ambition and conspicuous consumption typified by the older generation of the "X family" of Middletown—though this sedate group would hardly be equated by him with Kwakiutl chiefs. Ironically, the outlook of these and other sociological critics of business is confirmed and reflected by those neoclassical economists who construct models for the rational conduct of the firm—wittingly or unwittingly presenting businessmen as dismally "economic men."

Partly as a result of this image of the businessman, many students at privately endowed universities have become reluctant to consider business careers, and, as more and more young people are drawn into the colleges, these attitudes become increasingly widespread. The abler ones want something "higher" and look down their noses at the boys at Wharton or even at the Harvard Business School. Business is thought to be both dull and disagreeable as well as morally suspect, and the genuine moral problem involved in career choice—namely, how best to develop one's potentialities for a full existence—is obfuscated by the false choice of making money (and losing one's soul) in business versus penury (and saving one's soul) in government service or teaching. The notion that business today, especially big business, presents challenging intellectual problems and opportunities and is no more noticeably engaged in Dobuan sharp practice

4. Robert S. Lynd, *Knowledge for What?* (Princeton, Princeton University Press, 1939), pp. 54–113.

and Kwakiutl rivalry than any other career, seems not to exist even in the minds of students whose fathers are (perhaps woefully inarticulate) businessmen.

It is likely, then, that the students' image of business, and of American life generally, will have some self-confirming effects. Business will be forced to recruit from the less gifted and sensitive, who will muff their opportunities. People who expect to meet hostility and calculation in others will justify an anticipatory hostility and calculation in themselves.

To be sure, there are plenty of unlovely, vicious, and mean Americans, in and out of business life; plenty of frightening southern mobs, northern hoodlums, dead-end kids with and without tuxedoes. There are many cultural islands in the United States where Dobu ways abound, just as there are survivals of late nineteenth-century Kwakiutl patterns. But these islands and survivals do not make a system of power, nor are they linked by any conspiracy, fascist or otherwise.

Now, of course, to show that Americans are neither like Kwakiutls nor Dobuans does not prove they are like Zuñi and Hopi Indians. Obviously, in any case, the comparisons must be very rough; from the standpoint of my character types all three tribes, as long as they are in the phase of high population growth potential, would be more or less dependent on tradition-direction. My purpose is to present a parable, not a description. There is evidence, though it is perhaps somewhat understressed by Ruth Benedict, that the Pueblo Indians are actually not so bland and amiable as they seem, that they are, to a degree, antagonistic cooperators, with a good deal of repressed hostility and envy that crops up in dreams and malicious gossip. But this only strengthens the analogy with the middle-class Americans, whose other-directed cooperativeness is also not completely mild but contains repressed antagonistic elements.

Indeed the whole emotional tone of life in the Pueblos reminds me strongly of the American peer-group, with its insulting "You think you're big." While the Kwakiutls pride themselves on their passions that lead them to commit murder, arson, and suicide, the Pueblos frown on any violent emotion.[5] Ruth Benedict writes:

5. B. L. Whorf, "The Relation of Habitual Thought and Behavior to Language," *Language, Culture, and Personality*, ed. L. Spier, *et al.* (Menasha, Wisconsin, Sapir Memorial Publication Fund, 1941), pp. 75–93. In this famed and brilliant article Mr. Whorf suggests that Hopi cooperativeness is facilitated by a linguistic pattern that stresses the interconnection

A good man has . . . "a pleasing address, a yielding disposition, and a generous heart." . . . He should "talk lots, as they say—that is, he should always set people at their ease—and he should without fail co-operate easily with others either in the field or in ritual, never betraying a suspicion of arrogance or a strong emotion."

The quotation brings to mind the young Vermont new-style political indifferents whom we discussed in Chapter IX. It also is illustrative of one of the most striking findings from our interviews with young people. When we ask them their best trait they are hard pressed for an answer, though they sometimes mention an ability to "get along well with everybody." When we ask them, "What is your worst trait?" the most frequent single answer is "temper." And when we go on to ask, "Is your temper, then, so bad?" it usually turns out that the interviewee has not got much of a temper. If we ask whether his temper has gotten him into much trouble, he can cite little evidence that it has. What do these answers—of course no proper sample —mean? Perhaps the interviewee is boasting—he wishes he *did* have a temper. But on the whole, my impression is that temper is considered the worst trait in the society of the glad hand. It is felt as an internal menace to one's cooperative attitudes. Moreover, as business enterprise eliminates the men of lean and hungry look, so the peer-group regards temper as faintly ridiculous: one must be able to take it with a smile or be charged with something even worse than temper, something so terrible that no one will accuse himself of it even in an interview—lack of a sense of humor. The inner-directed man may also worry about temper, for instance, if he is religious, but his conscience-stricken inhibitions and reaction formations leave the emotion still alive, volcano-like, within him—often ready to erupt in political indignation—whereas the other-directed man allows or compels his

---

between thought and the material universe, and that, in its attitude toward time, stresses the preparatory thought steps preceding action. As compared with this, our language pattern separates space and thought in a metaphysical dualism and, in its attitude toward time, stresses the orderly sequence of time periods, thus separating felt, "human" time from clock-recorded time. In terms of linguistic channels, then, the western outlook on self, space, and time should foster what I have termed inner-direction. Whorf's article suggests that new linguistic channels will have to be cut within the given limits of, say, English, before we have a suitable linguistic uniform to fit the emerging other-directed type—or, as Whorf points out, to fit the new view of the universe that we find in relativity theory or, it might be added, in such work as that of L. L. Whyte on the "unitary principle." It would be fascinating to follow up these extremely tenuous and complex perspectives by systematic study of the relation between word use and word meaning and character type.

emotions to heal, though not without leaving scars, in an atmosphere of enforced good fellowship and tolerance.

Many young people today also set themselves an ideal in their sex lives not too different from the Zuñi norm. They feel they ought to take sex with little interpersonal emotion and certainly without jealousy. The word of the wise to the young—"Don't get involved"—has changed its meaning in a generation. Once it meant: don't get, or get someone, pregnant; don't run afoul of the law; don't get in the newspapers. Today the injunction seeks to control the personal experiencing of emotion that might disrupt the camaraderie of the peer-group.

The chief worry of the Pueblo Indians is directed not to each other's behavior but to the weather, and their religious ceremonies are primarily directed toward rain making. To quiet their anxiety the Indians go through rituals that must be letter perfect. American young people have no such single ritual to assure personal or tribal success. However, one can see a similarity in the tendency to create rituals of a sort in all spheres of life. I have found, for example, that when I ask students why they come to class so regularly day after day, why they do not take two weeks off to go somewhere or do something on their own (as they are technically free to do), I receive answers that are mainly rationalizations. For instance, I am told that they must come to class or else they will flunk. But when we examine this allegation, it turns out to be contrary to the evidence: students often get ahead just when they break through the not yet completely bureaucratized routines of university life. It is just this prospect that is frightening. The students feel safer when they are assured of a course of approval from their peers, their antagonistic cooperators, as well as from the adult authorities. They feel safer when they can engage in a common ritual of attendance. Likewise, people make a ritual out of work, out of having fun, out of political participation as inside-dopesters or as indignants, as well as out of countless private compulsions. But the rituals, whether private or public, have usually to be rationalized as necessary; and since this is not self-evident and since the sign of success is not so explicit as a downpour of rain, the American young people can hardly get as much comfort from their rituals as the Pueblo Indians do from theirs.

What does all this mean as an indicator of the way in which a group of young people sizes up the distribution of power and power practices in America? The young people have begun to pass out of the adolescent peer-groups; they have not yet taken their places in the adult patterning of American life. What will be the effect of the discrepancy in their seeing the United States as a place led by Kwakiutl chiefs, leading Kwakiutl-style followers, when they themselves have set their feet along the "Hopi Way"? Will they seek to bring about changes, through social and political action, that will make America more comfortable for the tolerant, other-directed types? Or will they seek to adopt more ruthless, Kwakiutl-like behavior as supposedly more compatible with real life? Or, perchance, will they admit that *they,* too, are Americans, after all not so unique, which might require a revision of their images of power, their images of what Americans in general are like?

Doubtless, all these things can occur, and many more. But there is perhaps one additional factor which will shape both changing ideology and changing character. The students, aware of their own repressed competitiveness and envy, think that others may try to do to them what they themselves would not dare to do to others. The society *feels* to them like Kwakiutl or even Dobu, not only because that is the ideology about America they have learned but also because their own cooperativeness is tinged with an antagonism they have not yet completely silenced. And perhaps this gives us another answer to our puzzle about tolerance in the previous chapters, when we asked why, if the other-directed person is tolerant, he is himself so afraid of getting out of line? It may be that he feels his own tolerance precarious, his dreadful temper ready to let fly when given permission; if he feels so irritable himself, no matter how mild his behavior, he must fear the others, no matter how amiable they, too, may appear.

This may be simply a way of saying that the transition from innerdirection to other-direction is not complete—possibly, can never be complete.

Perhaps neither my students nor the authorities they read are representative. Perhaps the "Zunification" of America is more widely recognized than I think. In any event it is significant that these students would prefer to live in the Pueblo culture, if they had to choose among the three described by Ruth Benedict. And, while this choice is in itself not to be quarreled with, the important fact is that they do not know that they already are living in such a culture. They want social security, not great achievements. They want approval, not fame. They are not eager for talents that might bring them into conflict; whereas the inner-directed young person tended to push himself to the limit of his talents and beyond. Few of them suffer, like youth in the earlier age, because they are "twenty, and so little accomplished." Whereas the inner-directed middle-class boy often had to learn after twenty to adjust, to surrender his adolescent dreams and accept a burgher's modest lot, the other-directed boy never had such dreams. In a profound sense he never experiences adolescence, moving as he does uninterruptedly with the peer-group, from the nursery years on. He learns to conform to the group almost as soon as he learns anything. He does not face, at adolescence, the need to choose between his family's world and that of his own generation or between his dreams and a world he never made.

Since, moreover, his adjustment to this group reality begins earlier, it becomes more a matter of conforming character and less a matter of conforming behavior. The popular song, "I don't want to set the world on fire," expresses a typical theme. The Kwakiutl wanted to do just that, literally to set the world on fire. The other-directed person prefers "love" to "glory." As Tocqueville saw, or foresaw: "He willingly takes up with low desires without daring to embark on lofty enterprises, of which he scarcely dreams."

There is a connection between the feeling these students and other young people have about their own fates and the contemporary notions of who runs the country. We have seen that the students feel themselves to be powerless, safe only when performing a ritual in approving company. Though they may seek to preserve a factitious emotional independence by not getting involved, this requirement is itself a peer-group mandate. How, then, as they look about them in America, do they explain their powerlessness? Somebody must have what they have not got: their powerlessness must be matched by power somewhere else. They see America as composed of Kwakiutls, not only because of their own residual and repressed Kwakiutl tendencies but even more because of their coerced cooperativeness. Some big chiefs must be doing this to them, they feel. They do not see that, to a great extent, it is they themselves who are doing it, through their own character.

The chiefs have lost the power, but the followers have not gained it. The savage believes that he will secure more power by drinking the blood or shrinking the head of his enemy. But the other-directed person, far from gaining, only becomes weaker from the weakness of his fellows.[6]

6. We may again raise the question whether this is exclusively an American (or twentieth-century) development by referring to some lines from Nietzsche's *Thus Spake Zarathustra:* "Lo! I show you *the last man* . . .

'We have discovered happiness'—say the last men, and blink thereby. They have left the regions where it is hard to live; for they need warmth. One still loveth one's neighbor, and rubbeth against him; for one needeth warmth.

Turning ill and being distrustful, they consider sinful: they walk warily. He is a fool who still stumbleth over stones or men! . . .

One still worketh, for work is a pastime. But one is careful lest the pastime should hurt one.

One no longer becometh poor or rich; both are too burdensome. Who still wanteth to rule? Who still wanteth to obey? Both are too burdensome.

No shepherd, and one herd! Everyone wanteth the same; everyone is equal: he who hath other sentiments goeth voluntarily into the mad-house . . .

People still fall out, but are soon reconciled—otherwise it spoileth their stomachs.

They have their little pleasures for the day, and their little pleasures for the night, but they have a regard for health."

PART III

AUTONOMY

XIV

Adjustment or Autonomy?

Among the works of man, which human life is rightly employed in per-
fecting and beautifying, the first in importance surely is man himself.
Supposing it were possible to get houses built, corn grown, battles fought,
causes tried, and even churches erected and prayers said, by machinery—by
automatons in human form—it would be a considerable loss to exchange
for these automatons even the men and women who at present inhabit the
more civilized parts of the world, and who assuredly are but starved specimens of what nature can and will produce. Human nature is not a machine
to be built after a model, and set to do exactly the work prescribed for it,
but a tree, which requires to grow and develop itself on all sides, according
to the tendency of the inward forces which make it a living thing.

John Stuart Mill, *On Liberty*

IF THE leaders have lost the power, why have the led not gained
it? What is there about the other-directed man and his life situation which prevents the transfer? In terms of situation, it seems
that the pattern of monopolistic competition of the veto groups resists individual attempts at power aggrandizement. In terms of character, the other-directed man simply does not seek power; perhaps,
rather, he avoids and evades it. If he happens to be an inside-dopester,
he creates a formula that tells him where the power exists, and he
seeks to make all the facts thereafter conform to this formula. In a
sense, this means that he would rather be right than be president. His
need to be in the know, his need for approval, his need in the upper
strata for marginal differentiation, may lead to actions that look like
a drive to get or hold power. But the fact is that the further away the
inside-dopester is from inner-direction, the less is he ambitious, exploitative, and imperialistic. He expects some "others"—some Kwakiutl or Dobuan types—to be doing the exploiting. He fits himself as
a minor manipulator, and self-manipulator, into the image he has of
them.

If the other-directed person does not seek power, then what does he seek? At the very least, he seeks adjustment. That is, he seeks to have the character he is supposed to have, and the inner experiences as well as outer appurtenances that are supposed to go with it. If he fails to attain adjustment, he becomes *anomic*—a term I shall define in a moment. At most, the other-directed man occasionally seeks to be *autonomous*.

His opportunity to become autonomous lies precisely in the disparity that exists between the actual, objective pressures for conformity that are inescapable and the ritualistic pressures that spring not from the Kwakiutl-like institutions of America but from the increasingly other-directed character of its people. In other words, I do not believe that the social character evoked by today's social structure, namely, the other-directed character, is a perfect replica of that social structure, called into being by its demands.

I. AUTONOMY AND THE CURVE OF POPULATION

Disparity between social character and adult social role—between the real and inevitable pressures for conformity and the purely imaginary pressures of other-directedness—may become one of the leverages of social change. Probably, the larger the society the more room there is for such disparity. Moreover, as we saw in Chapter I, the *social* character is not all of character. The individual is capable of more than his society usually asks of him, though it is not at all easy to determine this, since potentialities may be hidden not only from others but from the individual himself. Of course, social structures differ very much in the degree to which they evoke a social character that in the process of socialization fills up, crushes, or buries individuality.

We may take, as extreme cases, the primitive societies of Dobu or Alor. People there seem to be so crushed from infancy on by institutionalized practices that, while they manage to do what their culture asks of them in the emotional tone which the culture fosters, they cannot do much more. The Rorschach tests taken of the Alorese, for instance, indicate that there is a good deal of characterological uniformity among individuals and that few reserves of depth or breadth exist beyond the cultural norm or what Kardiner calls the basic personality type. Such a society might die out as a result of its apathy and misery, especially when further disorganized by white contact, but it is hard to conceive of an internal rejuvenation led by the more autonomous members of the group. Caught between social character and rigid social institutions, the individual and his potentialities have little scope. Nevertheless, even in such a society there will be deviants; as Ruth Benedict has pointed out, we know of no cultures without them. However, before turning to see whether the extent of deviation may be related to population phase, it is necessary to understand more precisely what is meant by deviation.

THE ADJUSTED, THE ANOMIC, THE AUTONOMOUS

The "adjusted" are those whom for the most part we have been describing. They are the *typical* tradition-directeds, inner-directeds, or other-directeds—the people who respond in their character structure to the demands of their society or social class at its particular stage on the curve of population. Such people fit the culture as though they were made for it, as in fact they are. There is, characterologically speaking, an effortless quality about their adjustment, although as we have seen the mode of adjustment may itself impose heavy strains on the so-called "normal" people. That is, the adjusted are those who reflect their society, or their class within the society, with the least distortion.

In each society those who do not conform to the characterological pattern of the adjusted may be either anomic or autonomous. Anomic is English coinage from Durkheim's *anomique* (adjective of *anomie*) meaning ruleless, ungoverned. My use of anomic, however, covers a wider range than Durkheim's metaphor: it is virtually synonomous with "maladjusted," a term I refrain from using because of its negative connotations; for there are some cultures where I would place a higher value on the maladjusted or anomic than on the adjusted. The "autonomous" are those who on the whole are *capable* of conforming to the behavioral norms of their society—a capacity the anomics usually lack—but who are free to choose whether to conform or not.

We are concerned here not with deviations in overt behavior but with conformity or nonconformity in character structure itself. The adjusted person may on occasion make mistakes that appear as deviations, though he has not in fact deviated from the requisite character —just as the society to which he belongs may not be adjusted to its material environment or neighbors: "adjustment," as we use the term, means sociopsychological fit, not adequacy in any evaluative sense. Similarly, the anomic person is a characterological nonconformist who is frequently neurotic, but he may outwardly conform most of the time, while paying so high a price for this behavioral conformity as to develop psychosomatic symptoms. The autonomous person may or may not conform outwardly, but, whatever his choice, he pays less of a price, since he decides the matter and is less driven.

These three universal types (the adjusted, the anomic, the autonomous), like our three historical types (tradition-directed, inner-directed, and other-directed) are *ideal* types, that is, constructions necessary for experimental work. Every human being will be one of these types to some degree; but no one could be completely characterized by any one of these terms. To put it in the extreme, even an insane person is not anomic in every sphere of life; nor could an autonomous person be completely autonomous, that is, not irrationally tied in some part of his character to the cultural requirements of his existence. Nevertheless, we can characterize an individual by the way in which one mode of adaptation predominates, and, when we study individuals, analysis by such a method provides certain helpful dimensions for descriptive and comparative purposes. We can also characterize a society by examining the relative frequency with which the three modes of adaptation occur in it, and the relative importance of the three types in the social structure.

About the anomics who arise as by-products, so to speak, of the attempt to create inner-direction and other-direction a good deal has been suggested in the foregoing pages. Even a society depending on tradition-direction will have a certain number of anomics, those constitutionally and psychologically unable to conform or feel comfortable in the roles such a society assigns to its regularly recurring deviants. Some of these people can exploit the kinship system to keep going, but in a society of any size there will be some who are pushed out of that tight web. To these somewhat idiosyncratic and accidental outcrops of anomic character, more complex societies add the people who, once capable of adjustment, are thrust aside by the emergence of a new dominant type. Types brought up under a familial regime of tradition-direction may later find themselves misfits in a society by then dependent on inner-direction; likewise, the rise of other-direction may drive inner-directed as well as tradition-directed types into anomie.

We referred to such people in Chapter IX, where we described the political style, or lack of style of the indifferents, many of whom have not made a successful adaptation to the characterological and social demands of modern, urban American culture. Some of these people despair of politics as they despair of themselves; they cannot understand or grapple with their life experiences. We saw in Chapter X that, nevertheless, such people have a considerable political potential; that, by drawing from the reservoir of indignation, they might be mobilized in opposition to the tolerant style of the adjusted other-directed types. The anomics, also, offer a cadre of those who are potentially willing to do the political dirty work of totalitarianism— those whom Marx called the "Lumpenproletariat" but who are at least as frequently found outside as inside the slum.

But the anomics include not only those who, in their character, were trained to attend to signals that either are no longer given or no longer spell meaning or success. They may also, paradoxically, be those who are overadjusted, who listen too assiduously to the signals from within or without. Thus we have seen that in a society dependent on inner-direction there may be oversteered children and over-steered adults, people of too tight superego controls to permit themselves even the normal satisfactions and escapes of their fellows. Likewise, among those dependent on other-direction, some may be unable to shut off their radar even for a moment; their overconformity makes them a caricature of the adjusted pattern—a pattern that escapes them because they try too hard for it.

We have seen, for example, the effort of the other-directed person to achieve a political and personal style of tolerance, drained of emotion, temper, and moodiness. But, obviously, this can go so far that deadness of feeling comes to resemble a clinical symptom. The psychoanalyst Ralph Greenson, observing soldiers hospitalized for apathy in World War II, writes of them:

The most striking characteristic of the apathetic patient is his visible lack of emotion and drive. At first glance he may seem to be depressed; closer scrutiny, however, reveals lack of affect. He appears slowed up in the psychic and motor responses; he shows an emptiness of expression and a mask-like facies . . . They behave very well in the ward, complying with all the rules and regulations. They rarely complain and make no demands . . . . these patients had no urge to communicate their sufferings and no insight into their condition.[1]

My own belief is that the ambulatory patients in the ward of modern culture show many analogous symptoms of too much compliance and too little insight, though of course their symptoms are not as sudden and severe. Their lack of emotion and emptiness of expression are as characteristic of many contemporary anomics as hysteria or outlawry was characteristic of the societies depending on earlier forms of direction.

Taken all together, the anomics—ranging from overt outlaws to "catatonic" types who lack even the spark for living, let alone for rebellion—constitute a sizable number in America. Quite a little is known about them in terms of personality type, social class, and so on. In fact, social science and psychiatry have until recently been preoccupied with understanding the anomic and suggesting therapies, just as medicine has been concerned with fighting the external agents that make people sick rather than with understanding the internal mysteries that keep them well. Indeed, it is usually not too difficult to explain why someone is anomic, since the tragedies and warpings of life, like germs, are omnipresent, and any personal disaster can be traced back to its "cause." While in our interviews with over one hundred and fifty people, only three or four have turned up who might possibly be classified as autonomous, a very considerable proportion are anomic; and it is possible not only to explain what anomie means in their case but also, within limits, to show how it might have come about.

We obviously know much less about those whom I call autonomous. Many will even deny that there are such people, people capable of transcending their culture at any time or in any respect. Those who become autonomous in our own society, for instance, seem to arise in a family background and class or regional setting that have had quite different consequences for others. In fact, under the conditions of characterological struggle in the advanced industrial countries, autonomous, adjusted and anomic types can be brothers and sisters within the same family, associates on the same job, residents in the

1. "The Psychology of Apathy," *Psychoanalytic Quarterly*, X (1949), 290; see also Leites, "Trends in Affectlessness," *American Imago*, Vol. IV (April, 1947). Robert K. Merton, "Social Structure and *Anomie*," *Social Theory and Social Structure* (Glencoe, Illinois, Free Press, 1949).

same housing project or suburb. Often constitutional factors are introduced to explain those elements of the interplay between person and environment we do not understand.

TAKING THE ROLE OF THE OTHER

Despite our very limited knowledge it is reasonable to assume that a decisive step in the road toward autonomy is connected with the social shifts that we see linked to the curve of population. To put this in the negative, it is difficult, almost impossible, in a society of high population growth potential, for a person to become aware of the possibility that he might change, that there are many roles open to him, roles other people have taken in history or in his milieu. As the philosopher G. H. Mead saw, this taking the role of the other leads to becoming aware of actual differences and potential similarities between the other and the self. That is why culture contact alone does not lead people to change when their interpretations of the contact spring out of a tradition-directed mode of life. High population growth potential, tradition-direction, and the inability of the individual to change roles—to think of himself as an individual capable of such change—these, as we saw in Chapter I, all go together.

For centuries the peasant farmers of Lebanon suffered from invasions by Arab horsemen. After each invasion the peasants began all over again to cultivate the soil, though they might do so only to pay tribute to the next marauder. The process went on until eventually the fertile valleys became virtual deserts, in which neither peasants nor nomads could hope for much. The peasants obviously never dreamed they could become horsemen; the marauders obviously never dreamed that they too might become cultivators of the soil. This epic has the quality not of human history but of animal life. The herbivores are unable to stop eating grass though they eat only to be devoured by the carnivores. And the carnivores cannot eat grass when they have thinned out the herbivores. In these societies dependent on tradition-direction there is scarcely a notion that one might change character or role.

If Arabs could imagine becoming cultivators, and vice versa, it would not necessarily follow that the symbiotic ecology of the two main groups would change. These tradition-directed types might still go on doing what they realized they need not do. Nevertheless, once people become aware, with the rise of inner-direction, that they as individuals with a private destiny are not tied to any given ecological pattern, something radically new happens in personal and social history. Then people can envisage adapting themselves not only within the narrow confines of the animal kingdom but within the wide range of alternative possibilities illustrated—but no more than illustrated—by human experience to date. Perhaps this is the most important meaning of the ever renewed discovery of the oneness of mankind as a species: that all human experience is relevant.

The Arab who can see himself as a peasant, even though he would be, for reasons of temperament or other factors, unable to make so radical a shift has already gained a new perspective on the relation: Arab-peasant. He may conceive of structuring it in some other way, by manipulation rather than by force, for instance. But if he did that, he would change, and so would the peasant: their relations could never again have the old animal-like simplicity.

The more advanced the technology, on the whole, the more possible it is for a considerable number of human beings to imagine being somebody else. In the first place, the technology spurs the division of labor, which, in turn, creates a greater variety of life experiences and human types. In the second place, the improvement in technology permits sufficient leisure to contemplate change—a kind of capital reserve in men's self-adaptation to nature—not on the part of a ruling few but on the part of many. In the third place, the combination of technology and leisure helps to acquaint people with other historical solutions—to provide them, that is, not only with more goods and more experiences but also with an increased variety of personal and social models.

How powerful such an influence can be the Renaissance indicates. Then, a richer picture of the past made it possible to live toward a more open future. Italians, newly rich and self-conscious, tried to imitate Greeks; and northern peoples, such as the Elizabethan English, tried to imitate Italians. The inner-directed character type emerged as the dominant type from the new possibilities created at this period; he built both those possibilities and the limits he put on them into his character. From the masses of the tradition-directed there arose many mobile ones who decided that they could be "horsemen" and no longer had to be "cultivators"; and the new technology and new lands beyond the sea gave them the necessary physical and intellectual store for the shift, while at the same time making it possible for the cultivators to support more noncultivators. Ever since, in the countries of transitional population growth, men have robbed the earth of its fruits and the farmer of his progeny in order to build the industrial civilization (and the lowered birth rate) of today. In this process the farmer's progeny had to learn how to become something other than cultivators.

Today again, in the countries of incipient population decline, men stand on the threshold of new possibilities of being and becoming—though history provides a less ready, perhaps only a misleading, guide. They no longer need limit their choices by gyroscopic adaptation but can respond to a far wider range of signals than any that could possibly be internalized in childhood. However, with the still further advance of technology and the change of frontiers from production to consumption, the new possibilities do not present themselves in the same dramatic form of passing from one class to another, of joining one or another side—the exploiting or the exploited—in the factory and at the barricades. In fact, those, namely the Communists, who try to structure matters according to these older images of power, have become perhaps the most reactionary and most menacing force in world politics.

In a society of abundance that has reached the population phase of incipient decline the class struggle alters as the middle class expands until it may number more than half of the whole population in occupational terms, with an even larger proportion, measured in terms of income, leisure, and values. The new possibilities opening up for the individual are possibilities not so much for entering a new class but rather for changing life style and changing character within the middle class.

Under these conditions autonomy will not be related to social class in terms of differences between the middle and the working class. Nevertheless, we might consider the autonomous as related to class in one way. Class, as Marx used the concept, referred to a polarization of society caused by the consequences for human consciousness of differing relationships to the mode of production. The historical types of character and the range of adjustment, autonomy, and anomie at any given time are, like classes, the products of differing life experiences—this would seem to hold for groups even though, in the case of individuals, idiosyncratic factors of constitution may be relevant.

In the era dependent on inner-direction, when character was largely formed for work and at work, it made a great deal of difference whether one owned the means of production or not. Today, however, the psychological advantages of ownership are very much reduced in importance; character is increasingly formed for leisure and during leisure—and both leisure and means of consumption are widely distributed. Thus, adjusted, autonomous, and anomic outcomes are often the result of very impalpable variations in the way people are treated by and react to their education, their consumer training, and, generally, their encounters with people—all within the broad status band of the middle class.

To be sure, there may be correlations, as yet unnoticed, between autonomy and occupation. Work has not completely lost its relevance for character even today. And occupational status affects leisure status. Those who are potentially autonomous may select some occupations in preference to others; beyond that, the day-by-day work experiences of members of different occupational groups will shape character. On the whole, however, it seems likely that the differences that will divide societies in the phase of incipient population decline will no longer be those between back-breaking work on the one hand and *rentier* status on the other, between misery and luxury, between long life and short life—those differences that dominated the thinking of men as varied as Charles Kingsley, Bellamy, Marx, and Veblen during the era of transitional population growth. Most people in America today—the "overprivileged" two thirds, say, as against the underprivileged third—can afford to attend to, and allow their characters to be shaped by, situational differences of a subtler nature than those arising from bare economic necessity and their relations to the means of production, understood in Marx's generalizing sense.

The autonomous person, living like everyone else in a given cultural setting, employs the reserves of his character and station to move away from the adjusteds of the same setting. Thus, we cannot properly speak of an "autonomous other-directed man" (nor of an "anomic other-directed man") but only of an autonomous man emerging from an era or group depending on other-direction (or of an anomic man who has become anomic through his conflict with other-directed and/or inner-directed patterns). For autonomy, like anomie, is a

deviation from the adjusted patterns, though a deviation controlled
in its range and meaning by the existence of those patterns.

II. THE AUTONOMOUS AMONG THE INNER-DIRECTEDS

The autonomous person in a society depending on inner-direction,
like the adjusted person of the same society, possessed clear-cut, internalized goals and was disciplined for stern encounters with a
changing world. But whereas the adjusted person was driven toward
his goals by a gyroscope over whose speed and direction he had hardly
a modicum of control and of the existence of which he was sometimes unaware, his autonomous contemporary was capable of choosing his goals and modulating his pace. The goals, and the drive toward
them, were rational, nonauthoritarian and noncompulsive for the autonomous; for the adjusted, they were merely given.

Obviously, however, as long as tight despotic or theocratic controls
of conduct existed, it was difficult to "choose oneself" either in work
or play. For, while it is possible to be autonomous no matter how tight
the supervision of behavior as long as thought is free—and thought as
such is not invaded effectively until modern totalitarian systematiza-
tion of Inquisition and witchcraft trial techniques—in practice most
men need the opportunity for some freedom of behavior if they are to
develop and confirm their autonomy of character. Sartre, I believe, is
mistaken in his notion that men—other than a few heroic individuals
—can "choose themselves" under conditions of extreme despotism.

The autonomous are not to be equated with the heroes. Heroism
may or may not bespeak autonomy; the definition of the autonomous
refers to those who are in their character capable of freedom, whether
or not they are able to, or care to, take the risks of overt deviation. The
case of Galileo illustrates both points. In order to accomplish his work,
Galileo needed *some* freedom, such as the freedom to exchange as-
tronomical texts and instruments, to write down results, and so on.
Yet, while autonomous (so far as we can determine), he did not need
to make a martyr of himself for the Inquisition. He deliberately chose
a nonheroic course. In the Soviet Union and its satellites today he
could not make even this choice, since the choice between martyrdom
or secrecy is not available under the grisly regime of the NKVD.

The four centuries since the Renaissance have seen the rise and fall of many periods when theocratic, royal, or other authoritative controls were not as tight as in Soviet Russia or Franco Spain today; periods also when economic life for many was raised above mere subsistence, thus providing opportunities for autonomy. And there were loopholes for autonomy even in the earlier despotic periods, since the despots were inefficient, corrupt, and limited in their aims. It is only modern totalitarianism that wages open and effective war on autonomy—its animating purpose, as Erich Fromm has said, is "escape from freedom." Likewise, as Fromm has also pointed out, the diffuse and anonymous authority of the modern democracies is less favorable to autonomy than one might assume. One reason, perhaps the chief reason, is that the other-directed person is trained to respond not so much to overt authority as to subtle but nonetheless constricting interpersonal expectations.

Indeed, autonomy in an era depending on inner-direction looks easier to achieve than autonomy today. Autonomy in an inner-directed mode is, however, no longer feasible. To understand why this is so requires a glance at the powerful bulwarks or defenses for autonomy that an era dependent on inner-direction provided and that are no longer so powerful today. These include, in the Protestant lands, certain attitudes toward conscience, and everywhere, the bulwarks of work, property, class, and hierarchy as well as the comforting possibilities of escape to the frontier.

In the first place, a Protestant or secular-Protestant society of adjusted inner-directed types expects people to conform, not by looking to others but by obedience to their internal gyroscopes or consciences. This affords privacy, for while society may punish people more or less for what they *do*, it lacks the interest and psychological capacity to find out what they *are*. People are like the yachts in a Bermuda race, attentive not to each other but to the goal in view and the favoring winds.

In the second place, there was always available a line of defense in the existence of frontiers of settlement and the right of asylum. The power to move around the globe in the days before passports placed limits on the tyrants' reach and gave reality to the concept of inalienable rights.[2] Roger Williams lighting out for himself; Voltaire shuttling back and forth over Europe; Karl Marx finding refuge in the

2. For fuller discussion of this now dormant freedom, see my article, "Legislative Restrictions on Foreign Enlistment and Travel," *Columbia Law Review*, XL (1940), 793–835.

British Museum; Carl Shurz fleeing to America—these are scenes from an almost vanished past.

In the third place, the autonomous in the era dependent on inner-direction had available to them the defenses provided by work itself, in a period when the adjusted people also were mainly work oriented. Though it was hard to admit that one found joy in one's work in the puritan countries, it was permissible to regard it as an end in itself, as well as a means to other ends. The "hardness of the material" attracted the autonomous, indeed—again, like their less autonomous fellows—often hardened them to all other considerations. The following passage from Claude Bernard's *Experimental Medicine,* first published in 1865, expresses this outlook:

After all this, should we let ourselves be moved by the sensitive cries of people of fashion or by the objections of men unfamiliar with scientific ideas? All feelings deserve respect, and I shall be very careful never to offend anyone's. I easily explain them to myself, and that is why they cannot stop me. . . A physiologist is not a man of fashion, he is a man of science, absorbed by the scientific idea which he pursues; he no longer hears the cry of animals, he no longer sees the blood that flows, he sees only his idea and perceives only organisms concealing problems which he intends to solve. Similarly, no surgeon is stopped by the most moving cries and sobs, because he seeks only his idea and the purpose of his operation. . . . . After what has gone before we shall deem all discussion of vivisection futile or absurd. It is impossible for men, judging facts by such different ideas, ever to agree; and as it is impossible to satisfy everybody, a man of science should attend only to the opinion of men of science who understand him, and should derive rules of conduct only from his own conscience.[3]

It is clear, moreover, that such a man as Claude Bernard looked to his scientific colleagues, not for approval of himself as a person but for the validation of his objective work. He had less need for people, for warm interpersonal response, than the autonomous man who arises among the groups dependent on other-direction.

3. Claude Bernard, *An Introduction to the Study of Experimental Medicine,* trans. Henry C. Greene (New York, Macmillan, 1927), pp. 102–103. Freud, whose attitude was remarkably similar, gives us as one of his favorite quotations, a similar passage from Ferdinand Lassalle: "A man like myself who, as I explained to you, had devoted his whole life to the motto 'Die Wissenschaft und die Arbeiter' (Science and the Workingman), would receive the same impression from a condemnation which in the course of events confronts him as would the chemist, absorbed in his scientific experiments, from the cracking of a retort. With a slight knitting of his brow at the resistance of the material, he would, as soon as the disturbance was quieted, calmly continue his labor and investigations." See Freud, *Wit and Its Relations to the Unconscious,* trans. Brill (New York, Moffat, Yard, 1916), p. 115.

In the fourth place, property and class were substantial defenses for those who strove for autonomy. They protected not only the crazy millionaire's conspicuous consumption but the irreverence of the secluded Bentham and the integrated double life of that fine horseman and industrialist of Manchester, Friedrich Engels.

The hierarchical pattern of the era dependent on inner-direction also provided certain protections for autonomy. If people could manage to fulfill their hierarchical role, what they did in their off hours was more or less up to them. They were protected then, not only by their work and their property but by their position, be it elevated or humble. Henry Adams, at least an aspirant for autonomy if not an achiever of it, could spend his days as an ambassador's secretary and his evenings in contemplation and writing. Charles Lamb as a petty official could write in his spare time. Hawthorne, and many other nineteenth-century American writers, held posts that did not require them to give much of themselves—certainly not the self-exploitations on and off the job asked of far better paid writers who hold hack jobs today. The hierarchical chain, so long as it was not too tight, held people in place with some degree of security, while permitting sufficient tether for the autonomous. Within certain given limits of property and place, one could move without arousing shocked antagonism, traumatic either in terms of one's feelings or one's worldly fate.

More subtly, in the ways also indicated in Chapter V, a hierarchical society kindled emulation in the young. The would-be autonomous were given models to follow in their chosen field, and the society, though changing, moved slowly enough so that if they caught up with their models they were not too far behind their own times.

Many of these same defenses, however, operated far more frequently as barriers to autonomy than as defenses for it. A society organized in terms of class, private property, and hierarchy resisted autonomy with all the weapons of family, wealth, religion, and political power: the complaints and protests of political and religious reformers, artists, and artisans against this type of largely bourgeois social organization, now vanishing, were true and just enough. But we must never forget that these barriers and oppressions could frequently be organized as defenses of the individual; once their flanks were turned by energy and talent, they provided the freedom in which autonomy as well as *rentier* complacency could flourish.

In biographies and memoirs of the last several hundred years we can watch individuals begin their struggle for autonomy within the despotic walls of the patriarchal family. The family operated, much more than the state, as the "executive committee" of the inner-directed bourgeois class, training the social character both of future members of that class and of future servants to it. We have seen in Chapter IV how print might succor a child in his lonely battle with parents, teachers, and other adult authorities—though a book might also disorient him and increase the pressure on him. But with good luck a book, like a sympathetic teacher or relative, might break the solid front of authority in the home:

Not until adolescence could other children be of much help, though then, especially when adolescence later took the institutional form of a youth movement, they might assist the break from home. Adolescence, in fact, was usually the period of crisis for the boy or girl who sought autonomy. While even the adjusted had to make the passage from home, they moved thence into a social system that still held them fast, finding such authoritative parent surrogates as were necessary to calibrate their already internalized parental signals. However, the would-be autonomous youth, in breaking with parents, were breaking with authority as such, internalized as well as external. One can trace this process in all its poignancy in the development of John Stuart Mill, who got out from under his father only when well along in life, or of Franz Kafka, who never did.

Once out in the world, the person struggling for autonomy faced directly the barriers of property—if he was without it; of hierarchy— if he sought to climb or oppose it; of religion—if he contravened its controls on expression. It was not thought sufficient punishment for a man that he was destined to hell-fire, but his life on this earth, too, had to be made miserable for his own good, and at times this attitude led to a good deal of theological resonance between one person and another. In strongly Protestant communities in particular, one's discreet overt behavior could not assure to oneself the freedom Erasmus or Galileo had made use of. The result was that between the oversteered and the understeered there was little room for autonomy. The struggle to turn these obstacles into defenses was often too tough, and the individual was scarred for life, as were Marx, Balzac, Nietzsche, Melville, E. A. Robinson, and many other great men of the era dependent on inner-direction. Still others, however—John Dewey, wiry Vermonter, is a magnificent example and so, in a very different way, is Bertrand Russell—more favored by fortune, could live lives of personal and intellectual collision and adventure with little inner conflict.

III. THE AUTONOMOUS AMONG THE OTHER-DIRECTEDS

The same conditions that produce conformity in the adjusted majority and force great numbers into anomie also provide for autonomous choice. We have seen how the autonomous man, emerging from an inner-directed culture, freed himself of the restrictions which that culture imposed; how he was able, in part, to convert the very barriers to autonomy—work, property, social hierarchy—into protective devices. His freedom, always a partial affair, was acquired by the process of coming to understand his society and the alternatives which it held open to him and by creating entirely new alternatives.

The character of the autonomous individual is derived from, hence in part determined by, the prevailing modes of conformity in the society in which he lives. Autonomy is never an "all or nothing" affair; it does not come about suddenly, but sometimes imperceptibly, and always as the result of a continual struggle with the forces of the culture which oppose it. I like to interpret the conception that "Man is born free; and everywhere he is in chains," to mean that man is born a slave—a slave to his biological and cultural inheritance—but that he can become, through experience and experiment, increasingly free. No one entirely lacks the capacity for autonomy and freedom, though people often willfully reject them. But even in those instances in which the struggle for freedom is abandoned, the rationalizations for denying freedom seem to testify to the pull of freedom—else why do the world's deniers of freedom argue so much and, in purely logical terms, so well? Men desire freedom through understanding and control of their ceaselessly changing and problematic inner and outer environment.

Lawyers and lawmakers have a technique called "incorporation by reference"; by means of it they can refer in one statute or document to another without full quotation. In the same way I would like to incorporate by reference here the writings of Mill which deal with individuality: the *Autobiography,* the essays *On Liberty* and *On Social Freedom,* and *The Subjection of Women.* These writings represent an extraordinary foreshadowing of the problems of the autonomous individual when, with the decline of the older barriers to freedom, the newer and far more subtle barriers of public opinion in a democracy arise. Indeed, in reading modern writers, such as Sartre, Simone de Beauvoir, Erich Fromm, José Ortega y Gasset, and Bertrand Russell, who deal with similar themes, one is struck by the degree to which, underneath differences in idiom, their philosophic outlook resembles Mill's in many important respects.

Mill wrote: "In this age the mere example of nonconformity, the mere refusal to bend the knee to custom, is itself a service." But his interest was more in the individual than in the service. He observed two tendencies that have grown much more powerful since he wrote. He saw, as many others did, that people no longer took their cues "from dignitaries in Church or State, from ostensible leaders, or from books" but rather from each other—from the peer-group and its mass-media organs, as we would say. He saw, as few others did, that this occurred not only in public matters but also in private ones, in the pursuit of pleasure and in the development of a whole style of life. All that has changed, perhaps, since he and Tocqueville wrote, is that the actions they saw as based on the fear of what people might say—on one kind of opportunism, that is—are today the more automatic outcome of a character structure governed, not only from the first but throughout life, by signals from outside. In consequence, naturally enough, a major difference between the problems of Mill's day and ours is that someone who today refuses "to bend the knee to custom" is tempted to ask himself: "Is this what I really want? Perhaps I only want it because . . ."

This comparison may overstate historical changes; the autonomous at all times have been questioners. The autonomous among the inner-directeds, however, were partially shaped by a milieu in which people took many psychological events for granted, while the autonomous among the other-directeds live in a milieu in which people systematically question themselves in anticipation of the questions of others. More important, in the upper socioeconomic levels in the western democracies today—these being the levels, except for the aristocracy, most strongly permeated by other-direction—the coercions upon those seeking autonomy are not the visible and palpable barriers of family and authority that typically restricted people in the past.

This is one reason why it is difficult, as an empirical matter, to decide who is autonomous when we are looking at the seemingly easy and permissive life of a social class in which there are no "problems" left, except for persons striving for autonomy. These latter, in turn, are incapable of defining the "enemy" with the relative ease of the autonomous person facing an inner-directed environment. Is the inside-dopester an enemy, with his sympathetic tolerance, but abysmal disinterest and inability to understand savage emotions? Are they enemies, those friends who stand by, not to block but to be amused, to understand and pardon everything? An autonomous person of today must work constantly to detach himself from shadowy entanglements with this top level of other-direction—so difficult to break with because its demands appear so reasonable, even trivial.

These demands, to be sure, are not actually demands for conformity in the sense of the term as Mill used it. The adjusted middle-class people of the era dependent on inner-direction were often aggressively unconcerned with their own feelings and tastes or those of others; for them life was not something to be tasted but something to be hacked away at. Among the autonomous, and also the anomics, of that era were the people who were very much concerned with taste, with what they liked; people who rejected the Philistine norm. In their sensuous feeling for experience, their concern for nuance, many of the Romantic poets and other artists of the nineteenth century were strikingly "modern." What they put into their poems and other works, in refinement and subjectivity, is part of the legacy to the very language and activities of the other-directeds.

In this respect the groups dependent on other-direction have made an advance over the era dependent on inner-direction—an advance already prepared by the latter's autonomous wing. But given today's style of taste and sensitivity, the ways of rebelling and finding one's own tastes and shades of feeling are much less clear cut than they were when the simple exercise of nonconformity to inner-directed standards was enough to make a person stand out as autonomous. In what spheres does autonomy exist today, when the older barriers have crumbled and can serve neither as defenses nor as obstacles for a lifelong agenda of attack?

For the other-directed person sexual life, as we have seen in Chapter VII, is perhaps the last frontier of consumption, an area of mystery in which he anxiously tests the power to attract others and to have "experience." This pursuit is accelerated by the anxiety which the other-directed brings to it; and the anxiety, in turn, is reinforced and intensified by the seemingly casual demand of the "sophisticated" peer-group that one's achievements be publicized. The tolerant inquisition multiplies the variety of possible meanings to be given to sexual life. Men compete with the image of their forefathers, who, having chaste and modest women, could retain the initiative; they may also feel compelled to compete with the Kinsey athletes who belong to their peer-group. And, as women become more knowing consumers, the question of whether or when to "assume the initiative" becomes a matter for anxious speculation. Perhaps even more difficult roles are forced upon women. Also pioneers of the sex frontier, they must foster aggressiveness and simulate modesty. They have less chance to escape the frontier even temporarily through their work, for, if they have a profession, both men and women are apt to think that their skill detracts from their sexual life or that their sexual life detracts from their skill. Many middle-class women appear to have turned back, in a futile effort to recapture the older and seemingly more secure patterns. But in doing so, they have bowed not to authority or internalized inhibitions but to a diffuse image of male expectations, female peer-group jealousies, and reactionary counseling dressed up as the psychoanalytic inside story.

By no strategy can men and women today evade the problems of their sexual life. The person who seeks to come to terms with sexual life as part of a more autonomous life style must pick his or her way, without clear models, among easy regressions and easy aggressions, in a social setting where, on the one hand, couples either degenerate into two exclusive circles, men and women separately engaged in shop talk and office gossip, or on the other hand into a mixed company, with subtle or not so subtle efforts at mutual flirtation. We are unlikely to invent the society that can escape Rilke's question: "Aren't lovers forever reaching verges in each other?" But the question of pushing back the verges by mutual growth toward autonomy cannot arise among groups that are not aware of different possible structurings of expectations or, if aware, are unable to respect them.

Another look at the changed face of Bohemia may register the kinds of novel problems faced by the would-be autonomous among the other-directeds. Among the groups dependent on inner-direction the deviant individual can escape, geographically or spiritually, to

Bohemia; and still remain an "individual." Today, whole groups are matter of factly Bohemian; but the individuals who compose them are not necessarily free. On the contrary, they are often zealously tuned in to the signals of a group that finds the meaning of life, quite unproblematically, in an illusion of attacking an allegedly dominant and punishing majority of Babbitts and Kwakiutl chiefs. That is, under the aegis of the veto groups, young people today can find, in the wide variety of people and places of metropolitan life, a peer-group, conformity to which costs little in the way of search for principle.

We saw as an example of this, in Chapter XII, the attitude of the businessman who is tolerant of the Bohemianism of an associate because he regards it as a form of marginal differentiation, an entry in tomorrow's race of styles. Now we can see, somewhat more precisely, what this sort of tolerance may mean for the individual. He may find himself in the position unanticipated by Mill, of an eccentric who must, like a movie star, accept the roles in which he is cast, lest he disappoint the delighted expectations of his friends. The very fact that his efforts at autonomy are taken as cues by the "others" must make him conscious of the possibility that the effort toward autonomy might degenerate into other-directed play-acting.

Tolerance raises other problems too. If rotten behavior is tolerated under the prevalent modern rationalization that the individual whose behavior is excused "couldn't help it" or because all standards of conduct have become relativized, the individual is prevented from finding out what ails him. Often he is in the position of the child in the other-directed home, who succeeds in pushing his parents around and regrets his success because he would really like to be told in a friendly, not overbearing, way what the limits of decent behavior are. The "humanistic conscience" which Erich Fromm describes as "man's recall to himself," is, to be sure, an inner voice. It can be silenced by external authority. But it can also be muted when other people refuse to remind the individual of how his conduct looks to them.

One frequently observes that, in emancipated circles, Negroes who have behaved badly are treated by whites in this "tolerant" fashion. Everything is forgiven them, because they are Negroes and have been put upon. This sails dangerously close to prejudice in reverse. The Negroes who are allowed and even sometimes covertly encouraged to "get away with murder" are not confronted with standards of human decency that the whites may be more ready to apply to each other. Moral issues are befogged on both sides of the race line, since neither whites nor Negroes are expected to react as individuals striving for autonomy but only as members of the tolerating or the tolerated race.

Plainly, to sort out what is valid in the mood of tolerance from what is suspect requires a high level of self-consciousness. The individual striving for autonomy also needs a great deal of self-consciousness to differentiate between actions he takes because they will be tolerated and those he takes because he really wants to. Indeed, it is just this type of heightened self-consciousness that, above all else, constitutes the insignia of the autonomous in an era dependent on other-direction.

For, as the inner-directed man is more self-conscious than his tradition-directed predecessor and as the other-directed man is more self-conscious still, the autonomous man growing up under conditions that encourage self-consciousness can disentangle himself from the adjusted others only by a further move toward even greater self-consciousness. His autonomy depends not upon the ease with which he may deny or disguise his emotions but, on the contrary, upon the success of his effort to recognize and respect his own feelings, his own potentialities, his own limitations. This is not a quantitative matter, but in part an awareness of the problem of self-consciousness itself, an achievement of a higher order of abstraction.

As we know all too well, such an achievement is a difficult thing; many of those who attain it cannot manage to mold it into the structure of an autonomous life but succumb to anomie. Yet perhaps the anomie of such processes is preferable to the less self-conscious, though socially supported, anxiety of the adjusteds who refuse to distort their culture and end by distorting themselves.

We cannot, of course, be sure whether in the future the autonomous will be able to change the culture in which they live in order to make it more hospitable for themselves. Nevertheless, it seems quite possible that, as other-direction spreads, the characterological victory of the rising other-directeds over the waning inner-directeds may become more certain, just as the opposition between the latter and their tradition-directed predecessors has diminished to the point of disappearing altogether. Thereafter, polarization will occur among the other-directeds themselves—between those who will cling to adjustment and those who will strive for autonomy. And since the latter threaten, by their very presence, the whole shaky mode of adaptation of the adjusted majority, the struggle between this saving remnant of autonomous ones and those not capable of being autonomous and not desirous of allowing others so to be can conceivably become quite fierce.[4]

The autonomous among the other-directeds face different and more subtle obstacles than the autonomous among the inner-directeds and have lost many old defenses available to the latter. With greater experience, however, the new obstacles to autonomy may in turn be made into defenses. In the preceding discussion I have emphasized the negative aspects of tolerance, because it is these aspects that create problems for the groups sufficiently privileged to have moved into the phase of other-direction. At the same time we have observed that the other-directeds often refuse to act as if *they* were tolerated. Once people can become accustomed to tolerance, they can use it to help them grow, rather than as an Alice-in-Wonderland drink with which they shrink themselves to the size of the others.

If we look at the social situation of the adjusted other-directed man, we see that not all his character resources are inevitably occupied in being, and becoming, adjusted. Indeed, his very other-direction gives him a sensitivity and rapidity of movement that may be historically new. That part of his social character which fits him for his roles at work is a smaller part of his total character than among most tradition-directed and inner-directed types. To be sure, he has been strenuously socialized and has lost much of himself in the process. But his repressions are probably less opaque than those of the adjusted inner-directed man in the Protestant lands.

We know that the inner-directeds helped to create the potentialities of the more self-conscious and in certain ways freer society which is emerging among the other-directeds today. They left us a great legacy of material abundance and scientific technique—a legacy so great that in moments of despair we act as if we would prefer to have been disinherited. But this is suicidal. Let us try to see whether American institutions actually provide a larger opportunity for the other-directed man to explore his character resources than he now realizes.

4. I have drawn here from my essay, "The Saving Remnant: An Examination of Character Structure," *Years of the Modern,* ed. John W. Chase (New York, Longmans, Green, 1949), pp. 115–147.

XV

False Personalization: Obstacles to Autonomy in Work

Only man can be an enemy for man; only he can rob him of the meaning of his acts and his life because it also belongs only to him to confirm it in its existence, to recognize it in actual fact as a freedom . . . my freedom, in order to fulfill itself, requires that it emerge into an open future: it is other men who open the future to me, it is they who, setting up the world of tomorrow, define my future; but if, instead of allowing me to participate in this constructive movement, they oblige me to consume my transcendence in vain, if they keep me below the level which they have conquered and on the basis of which new conquests will be achieved, then they are cutting me off from the future, they are changing me into a thing. Life is occupied in both perpetuating itself and in surpassing itself; if all it does is maintain itself, then living is only not dying, and human existence is indistinguishable from an absurd vegetation . . .

Simone de Beauvoir, *The Ethics of Ambiguity*

I. CULTURAL DEFINITIONS OF WORK

THE CHARACTER reserves of the other-directeds are the possible sources of increased autonomy. But it should be clear from the discussion of the work, the play, and the politics of the other-directed man that his reserves, while perhaps more flexible than those of the inner-directed man, are constantly exhausted by his social organization. These reserves are especially exhausted by our current cultural definitions of work and play and the relations between them—definitions which, as we saw in Chapters VI and VII, introduce much strenuous "play" into the glad handers' work and much group-adjustive "work" into their play. All of us are forced, to a degree, to accept these cultural definitions of work and play, just as we are forced to accept certain cultural definitions of class, sex, race, and occupational or social role. And the definitions are forced on us by the ways of the culture and by the socialization process we undergo, whether they happen to be timely or anachronistic, useful for or destructive of our character reserves and of our fundamental humanity.

In the present state of our knowledge of man it seems well-nigh impossible to give a "correct" definition of work and of play—to say precisely how society in general, or any given society, should define these spheres and how it should value them. (We are using the word "play" here, it should be noted, as a kind of extreme or limiting case of the leisure and consumption sphere, much of which is admittedly not play in any sense of playfulness.) Yet, even if it is impossible to propose universal definitions, it is possible to show that current cultural definitions are cramping and unsatisfactory. And it needs no argument that, right or wrong, these definitions are widely influential. They channel the character resources of society, and they confirm the pattern of these resources, once they have begun to be organized into the various social character types discussed in previous chapters.

Work has the greater prestige; moreover, it is thought of as alien to man—it is a sort of disciplined salvage operation, rescuing a useful social product from chaos and the disorders of man's innate laziness. The same era, that of transitional growth of population, that saw the most astounding increase in man's mastery over nature, took it as axiomatic, echoing a series of writers from Malthus to Sumner and Freud, that people had to be driven to work by economic necessity. This necessity, furthermore, had to be directed and distributed through a system of hierarchical social organization. Today, knowing more about the nature of man and of work, we still nevertheless accept the psychological premise that work and productivity are disciplines exerted against the grain of man's nature. We do not quite see, though we are close to seeing, that what looks like laziness may be a reaction against the kind of work people are forced to do and the way in which they are forced to define it—just as such a reaction as political indifference (new style) says more about the state of current politics than it does about the psychological apathy of the individual citizen.

Because work is considered more important than play, it has been traditional to take most seriously the work that looks least like play, that is, the more obviously physical or physically productive work. This is one of the reasons why, though we would rather read about the Captains of Nonindustry than the Captains of Industry, the latter are still considerably less vulnerable to veto-group attack, and why generally the prestige of the tertiary service, entertainment, education, and communication trades is low. But this ranking is probably changing, though at differing rates in the several social classes. As the older ruling class patterns wane, a reasonably glamorized service trade like medicine comes to outrank all but the very largest posts in manufacturing or railroading. And doubtless there are many people who would rather be movie stars or directors than bankers of equivalent salary.

But these alterations in cultural definition, reflecting alterations in our social structure, have not moved to the point where they help the housewife who, though producing a social work product, does not find her work explicitly defined and totaled, either as an hour product or a dollar product, in the national census. The housewife is credited with being a worker only to the degree that she and her husband agree so to define her; and this usually means that she is exhausted at the end of the day without feeling any right to be, thus adding insult to injury. In contrast, the workers in the Detroit plant who finish their day's production goal in three hours and take the rest of the day off in factory loafing, are defined as eight-hour-per-day workers by themselves, by their wives, by the census.

These cultural definitions of work have curious implications for the health of the economy as a whole and, therefore, derivatively for the chances of autonomy in living. We tend to emphasize the importance of expanding those parts of the economy that have prestige and to overlook economic opportunities in the parts closer to play. For example, in the days of the CCC camps, it was widely assumed that CCC work on fire trails was more important than CCC work on recreational areas, just as the WPA Federal Theater was considered as less important economically than the stalwart Georgian public buildings of the PWA.

All but a few of our current estimates of capital growth needs seem to rest on similarly sticky notions as to the kind of production America needs. Indeed, when one reads some economic and social screeds, one might have the impression that the consumer or the player exists primarily for the work he does in leading and controlling the economy by his one-dollar-one-vote sovereignty over production planning and investment; of course production also legitimizes itself by reference to presumed consumer wants. This tendency to define consumption as a means rather than as an end in society is one reason, of course, not the only one, we make full employment our principal economic and social goal—and then look for full employment through more production of production rather than through an increased "capital budget" of the enormous variety of recreational resources our leisure, our training in consumption, and our educational plant allow us to develop. However, by thinking of expansion of consumption in terms of the market for durable and semidurable consumer goods—with the skies eagerly scanned for such new gadgets as television to hurl into the Keynesian multiplier formula—we are left open to an antiquated set of economic habits and assumptions. By clinging to them one heavy-draft, politically feasible outlet remains for the overexpanded primary and secondary spheres: a war economy.

We can sum up both this economic specter and the characterological problem of autonomy with which we are mainly concerned by saying that the struggle for a personally productive orientation,[1] based on the human need for active participation in a creative task, has become exigent precisely because we live in a period when the solution of the technical problems of production is in sight.

In a sense this dilemma sums up all the aspects of the current cultural definitions of work we have discussed so far. The inner-directed man had to accept these definitions: his institutions and his character combined to prevent him from choosing his work, and made him accept it as a Malthusian necessity. The other-directed man does not have to accept these definitions—and cannot do so if he wishes to move toward autonomy. Both his institutions and his character give him a greater degree of flexibility in redefining and restructuring the field of work. At present, however, he uses this flexibility to go through a process of semiadjustment to the new potentialities of work which allows him at the same time to accept the old definitions and the new situation of relative abundance. He does this by throwing into work all the resources of personalization, of glad handing, of

1. The term "productive orientation" is that used by Erich Fromm in *Man for Himself* for the type of character that can relate itself to people through love and to objects and the world generally through creative work. I have drawn freely on his discussion for my concept of autonomy.

which his character is capable, and just because he puts so much energy and effort into work, he reaps the benefit of thinking it important. In short he becomes adjusted via the definition of work.

II. GLAMORIZERS, FEATHERBEDDERS, INDISPENSABLES

We turn now to examine the first of a pair of twin concepts that will concern us in this and the following chapter. The one, we call "false personalization"; the other, "enforced privatization." We have met false personalization in this book before, in the form of the spurious and effortful glad hand. I see false personalization as a principal barrier to autonomy in the sphere of work: it is this, not the technical problems of production still remaining, that exhausts the character reserves of the other-directed man. Enforced privatization is the principal barrier to autonomy but, as we shall see, by no means the only one in the sphere of play. Privatization is our generic term for the restrictions, economic, ethnic, hierarchical, familial, that keep people from adequate leisure opportunities, including friendship. To some degree those who suffer most from false personalization at work also suffer most from enforced privatization at play.

As we have seen, the other-directed man does not personalize his work in a vacuum but in a social world of others who take some of their cues from him, give him some in turn, and mirror his dilemma. For example, we can see a steady spread of other-directed work values into the white-collar lower middle class, as well as the way in which this process boomerangs on the glad-handed manager himself. We can also see an effort to inject false personalization into the relations between management and factory labor—and the resistance to this effort that takes the form of featherbedding. In general we can see how the other-directed man goes about donating his energies to the sphere of work in order to be rewarded with the badge of indispensability.

WHITE-COLLAR PERSONALIZATION: TOWARD GLAMOUR

The inner-directed manager never "saw" his secretary. The latter, as a member of a different class and, often, a different ethnic group, also seldom "saw" the boss as an individual. Brought together by the invisible hand, both were concentrated on the work, not on each other, save as a benevolent but insensitive paternalism bridged the social gap. By contrast, the other-directed manager, while he still patronizes his white-collar employees, is compelled to personalize his relations with the office force whether he wants to or not because he is part of a system that has sold the white-collar class as a whole on the superior values of personalization. The personalization is false, even where it is not intentionally exploitative, because of its compulsory character: like the antagonistic cooperation of which it forms a part, it is a manipulative and self-manipulative mandate for those in the white-collar ranks and above.

This shift toward false personalization in the white-collar class is visible in the media. For example, we can see the change from morality to morale in comparing the attitudes toward women's office work signified by two Chicago dailies. One, the *Tribune,* stands by the older values of job-mindedness; the other, the *Sun-Times,* speaks implicitly for the newer values of personalization.

The *Tribune* conducts a regular daily column called "White Collar Girl," which preaches the virtues of efficiency and loyalty. Its tone suggests that it is written for the office girl who wants a paternalistic response from a somewhat distant boss but does not expect much more. It is beamed at readers who on the whole accept the classic inner-directed pattern of office management—though just the same they would not mind if the boss personalized a bit more, while staying definitely boss.

The *Sun-Times* speaks to a presumably somewhat more liberal and progressive group in the same occupational stratum but under the general classification of the "career girl." The career girl is appealed to not in a single column focused on the employee relationship but in a variety of columns emphasizing careers, successful self-entrepreneurships by glamorous women, and articles on the psychology of office relationships. These articles project the sense of a personnel-managed economy in which most executives are dutifully other-directed and, whether male or female executives, interested in the girls as more than the "help," in fact, as glamour-exuding personalities.

The *Sun-Times* makes a much closer connection between styles of leisure sociability and styles of relationship to a working group than the *Tribune* does. It conveys the idea that the boss is personalizing all the time, and as well as he knows how, and that the problem—virtually the only problem—for the white-collar girl is to determine the style in which to respond to the boss and to make him responsive. The

Tribune, far less interested in mood engineering in the office, retains respect for the nonglamorous skills of shorthand and typing, such as one still finds in, say, the efficient head of a law office secretarial pool. But one feels that this is a passing phase in American office life and that today the sociability of the white-collar girl is not only a demand made by her own ambitions for marriage and demands made on her by others, by the constant liberalizing of employer attitudes, but also a result of the sophisticated disrepute into which her nonpersonality skills have fallen.

Where there is apathy about politics, we expect to find an appeal to glamour. So here, where there is apathy about work, the appeal is again to glamour, which depends less on the work itself than on whom one does it for. Most unpopular of all is work in a pool, which minimizes glamour, or work for a woman boss, which inhibits it. It appears that the women actually wish to throw their emotional reserves into the office situation, rather than to protect them for the play situation. And we must conclude from this that neither their work nor their play is very meaningful in itself.

This puts the boss, in effect, in the position of having to satisfy an almost limitless demand for personalization that is partly based on the unsatisfactory nature of the white-collar girls' life outside the office. There enforced privatization often prevails: despite an urban milieu, white-collar girls seldom have the resources, educational, financial, simply spatial, to vary their friendship circle and their recreations. Grasping at glamour, these women are driven to find it, as vicarious consumers in their playtime, in listening to a crooner or a presidential candidate, as they are driven in their work time to find it in the boss and in the superstructure of emotions they weave into the office situation, in which everyone becomes the personal customer of the other. That the other-directed manager helped start this chain of personalization because he, too, holds skill in disrepute and lives an inadequate leisure life is not much comfort to him when he must personalize, not only as a banker selling bonds, a statesman selling an idea, or an administrator selling a program but simply as a boss or customer surrounded by white-collar girls.[2]

2. Cf. Geoffrey Gorer, *The American People* (New York, Norton, 1948). Gorer lays all this to American child-rearing habits rather than to a high technology in which business is no longer America's business. Obviously, both child rearing and technology are relevant here, and our purpose is not to add to the plethora of Gorer's critics but to make use of his valuable concrete observations.

It is this same sort of sensitivity, moreover, that makes it difficult for people to extricate themselves from chains of false personalization by wearing a completely alien work mask. Some inner-directeds can do this without cynicism: they simply do not see the others as people, or as highly differentiated and complicated people. But the other-directed managers, professionals, and white-collar workers cannot so easily separate coercive friendliness on the job from a spontaneous expression of genuine friendliness off the job.

THE CONVERSATION OF THE CLASSES: FACTORY MODEL

The white-collar worker imitates, even caricatures, the style of the other-directed upper middle class. The factory worker, on the other hand, is from Missouri: he has to be sold on the virtues of the glad hand. To be sure, in the small open-shop plant the worker may feel an emotional tie to the boss—though this is more apt to take the older paternalistic rather than the newer personnel form. And there have been cases, as illustrated by the Jack and Heintz Company during the last war, when egregiously manipulative mood engineering seems to have carried the day in the factory. There each of several thousand workers became an associate, as eager as Mr. Jack himself to exorcise those gremlins of resentful mood that might show up in absenteeism and low productivity.[3] On the whole, however, the manager has an uphill fight in getting factory workers in large unionized plants to accept the proffered glad hand, and this very resistance furnishes him with a virtually unlimited agenda for the devouring of his own work energies. As we saw in Chapter VI, he can go on endlessly adding people to the management group—training directors, counselors, and other morale builders—and he can also become involved in arranging research on morale to test the efficacy of these men and measures.

Just as the factory worker, when he was at school, regarded the teachers as management and went on strike or slowdown against

3. In a significant study, unfortunately never published in full, Erich Fromm and Ernest Schachtel showed by means of questionnaires that there were in 1929 decisive differences in ideology, and probably in underlying character structure, between workers in small German plants (under 200) and in large plants, though both groups were unionized and both were nominally Social Democratic or otherwise leftist in party affiliation. The authors made the point that the worker in the small plant could still feel somehow related to the boss—and these workers turned out to be on the whole more authoritarian and more nationalistic—while the workers in large plants, who had no hope whatever of personal access to the boss, developed a more independent attitude. For references to this investigation see *Studien über Autorität und Familie*, ed. Max Horkheimer (Paris, Alcan, 1936); see also S. Kracauer, *Die Angestellten Aus dem neuesten Deutschland* (Frankfurt a/M, Societäts-Verlag, 1930).

their well-intentioned or class-biased efforts, so in the factory he does not take the glad hand held out by the personnel department. Indeed, while the manager believes that high production attests high morale, the opposite may be the case: high morale can coexist with low production via featherbedding. For if the workers feel united in solidarity and mutual understanding—which they would define as "high morale"—the conditions exist for facilitating slowdowns and the systematic punishing of rate-busters.

There are many managers, however, who do not content themselves with allowing top management and the personnel department to tell workers that they have a stake in the output and that their work is important and glamorous—whether it is or not. Many sincerely seek to put plans into operation that give workers an actually greater share by rearrangement of ownership, production planning, and control. One aim of these proposals is to introduce emotional vitality, or a gamelike spirit, into the factory. Both results, along with higher productivity, are often attained.

Yet an element of false personalization typically remains in the fact that these programs, in addition to their manifest aims, are also something in the nature of a catharsis for other-directed managers. The harmony of feelings among manager, worker, and work process often matters more to the manager than it matters to the worker or the work process, partly because, as we have seen, the other-directed manager cannot stand hostility and conflict and partly, as we have also seen, because trying to eliminate hostility and conflict keeps him busy. In this situation the achievement of harmony sometimes becomes not a by-product of otherwise agreeable and meaningful work but an obligatory prerequisite. The consequence in some cases may even be to slow down the work because people have been led to expect harmony of mood, and need to be persuaded and repersuaded constantly that it exists.

This does not deny that much can and needs to be done to reduce the monotony of the production line and the mood-leadership boners of the supervisors. When the morale engineers have power to move people from job to job and to change team patterns, they accomplish a great deal. But, as I have said, it is often the psychological needs of the managers that determine the emphasis and priority of factory reorganization. For the conversation of the classes goes on at the work place, too. Much of the conversation concerns, on the one hand, the "isolates" who, while doing their production job, refuse to involve themselves in the harmony of feelings of the factory workers and, on the other hand, the featherbedders who involve themselves all too well.

Both these groups seek to retain their emotional freedom against the efforts of the factory to force them to mix work and play. The isolate does not want to be involved in emotional planning and factory-group dynamics. The featherbedders, the far more numerous group, want management to stop its own featherbedding first, before agreeing to stop theirs. But featherbedding, as compared with management personalizing, puts a relatively light tax on the emotions. It requires little moral ingenuity, since it is simply regarded as resistance to the boss's exploitation—the way work is culturally defined in the larger unionized plants. Featherbedding becomes as hard work as personalizing only in the crisis situation of the planned slowdown, when teamwork is required to sabotage skill effectively. At other times it is no more demanding than the sociability of the men's room.

Obviously, in the face of such resistances from both isolates and featherbedders, it will be a long time before the factory worker follows the example of the white-collar worker and, in imitation of the boss, puts pressure on him to personalize still more and better. But perhaps we see here one source for the envy of the working class that many middle-class people feel: they envy not only its greater freedom in overt aggression but also the very refusal to get involved in the work situation and the consequent ability to save reserves for play even where the work is monotonous, physically tiring, or sweated.

THE CLUB OF INDISPENSABLES

Responding to the personalizations of the secretary or trying to give mood leadership to the factory floor—these occupations do not alone account for the manager's keeping himself busy. He is busy because he is more than busy: he is indispensable.

In earlier chapters we saw how the other-directed man clings to a picture of his social position and function which tempts him to regard himself as indispensable. He believes that America possesses a ruling hierarchy whose hands are on the controls of the economy and polity. He builds these assumptions into the manner and mood of his work and so proves himself right. In this way he clings to the notion of scarcity that was so thoroughly elaborated in the official American culture of the school, the church, and politics. He needs to combat the notion that he himself might not be so scarce—that he might be dispensable. And surely, in the world as it is now, this fear of being considered surplus is understandably frightening.

Yet the other-directed man buys his feeling of being scarce at the expense of failing to see how little work, and much less teamwork, is needed in many productive sectors to keep the society rolling.[4] It is of the very nature of false personalizing to conceal this fact. And of course the cultural definitions of work also play a part in building up the notion of indispensability—for instance, by making paid work an ideal expression of man's effortfulness—and in providing the indispensables with secondary gains, such as sympathy from wives and children and exculpation from leisure demands and possibilities.

III. THE OVERPERSONALIZED SOCIETY

There are many possibilities for opening up channels for autonomy. Among them high priority must be given to efforts to depersonalize work, to make it less strenuous emotionally, and to encourage people to decide for themselves whether and how much they want to personalize in what the culture inescapably requires in the way of work. But of course there are psychological obstacles in the way of any institutional changes. The character of the other-directed man is elicited by contemporary institutions, and then, as an adult, he demands that the institutions exploit the character he has come to assume as his. Consequently, if the institutions should no longer employ him in the way he expects to be employed, will he not feel empty emotionally?

Percival and Paul Goodman asked themselves this same question in *Communitas,* a book which includes one of the most imaginative discussions of work and play in any contemporary writing.[5] They portray a utopia in which people could earn their living by a minimum

4. Hanns Sachs, *Freud, Master and Friend* (Cambridge, Massachusetts, Harvard University Press, 1945), pp. 46–47, tells one of Freud's favorite stories, which seems as relevant to social as to individual structure: "Many years ago an old professor of medicine died who had ordered in his will that his body should be dissected. The autopsy was performed by a renowned pathological anatomist and I functioned as his assistant. 'Look here,' the anatomist said to me, 'these arteries! They are as hard and thick as ropes. Of course the man couldn't live with them.' I answered him: 'All right. But it is a fact that the man did live till yesterday with these blood vessels.' "

5. *Communitas: Means of Livelihood and Ways of Life* (Chicago, University of Chicago Press, 1947), p. 120.

of effort and would then be faced with the really shocking problem of how to get through the day:

Suddenly, the Americans would find themselves rescued from the physical necessity and social pressure which alone, perhaps, had been driving them to their habitual satisfactions: they might suddenly find the commercial pleasures flat and unpalatable, but they would not therefore suddenly find any resources within themselves.

Like that little girl in the progressive school, longing for the security of the grownup's making her decisions for her, who asks: "Teacher, today again do we have to do what we want to do?"

All these difficulties are granted. But it is necessary to make a start somewhere and, preferably, in many places at once. We can try to alleviate the psychological pressures of work while at the same time we seek to make play more inviting, and this in turn, in one of Myrdal's "virtuous circles," will reduce the use of work as therapy for other-directeds. Perhaps a real opportunity for autonomy lies in a reconsideration of the emotional space left in our society by its impersonality, and chiefly the impersonality of the productive and distributive machinery. Perhaps we must take far greater advantage than we do of the fact that industrial automatism permits the release of our attention from productive process. The failure to accept this, and the attempt instead to personalize, emotionalize, and moralize machine process at every point, appears to be a fallacy of misplaced participation.

This fallacy is characteristic of the proposals for introducing joy and meaning into modern industrialism that come from the schools of De Man, Mayo, and many other recent writers. These men, like some of the syndicalists and those who put their faith in the cooperatives, want to restore the personal relations at work characteristic of a society dependent on tradition-direction as well as of the earlier stages of inner-direction. At least in America they make the mistake of seeing our civilization as an "impersonal" society and bemoaning it. The unintended effect of many of their strictures is to lend moral support to the false personalizing of the managers. To put this in other terms, perhaps it is possible to gain from layout engineering greater results in making work more tolerable and less exhausting than are gained from the manipulative practices of the mood engineers. Pending automatization, assembly work can be rearranged to reduce monotony; plants can be relocated to reduce travel time. This means working with rather than against the grain of impersonality in modern industry.

This outlook may remind the reader of two historically earlier views of related problems. It was the belief of Alfred Marshall that man's activity as a machine tender caused him to absorb some of the rationality of the machine. The views expressed here imply none of this particular pragmatism—in fact, contact with engineers can incline one to the belief that rationality is least of all to be expected among those who are closest in their daily work to the hardness of the material as embodied in machine production. Again, it was the belief of Thorstein Veblen that man's activity as a machine tender might encourage his sense of the matter of fact, as opposed to myth and archaisms, provided that the machine tender was neither swindled by the predatory Captains and their satellites nor misled by a "parental bent"—a fatherly attitude toward his product—that may become compulsive. The views presented in this volume are closer to Veblen's than to Marshall's in assuming that cultural definitions of work can "distort" technological imperatives. But there is this important difference. I do not look to machinery as such to encourage man's sense of the matter of fact. Maybe there is some long-run effect of this sort. Americans, however, seem to be not particularly aware of the mechanical power grids by which they live. While they do not stand in animistic awe of machinery, neither do they find it a pacifier, according to the view of Veblen, or a tutor, according to the view of Marshall.

Both men lived before the really great strides made by mechanization in the last several decades; they did not live to see the bounteous possibilities of abundance in the United States today. And Veblen at least was perhaps too much of a secularized puritan to appreciate these possibilities: he wanted the producer to produce, with no nonsense about it, and the consumer to consume, guided by strenuous consumer research in the direction of functionalism. From the point of view of this book we can agree that work should not be loaded down by featherbedding either among managers or workers—but this for the sake of pleasure and consumption and not for the sake of work itself. Industrial automatism should be defined not as a tutor to man nor as a personalized, grimacing servant of the *Tootle* type but as man's increasingly successful effort to turn repetitive and boring work over to mechanical energies.

One nightmare of our contemporary situation is that the work as a machine tender, boring as it is, is often felt to be less boring than the alternatives. For many white-collar workers, as we have seen, false personalization is the only personalizing that they meet. For many factory workers featherbedding is the only sociability they get. Work, when it has these overtones for people, still remains real, important, and magnetic. This was one lure that during the last war drew many women of the middle and lower middle classes into the factories and held them there despite poor working conditions, inadequate transportation, and pressure from spouses. Escaping from domestic lives of extreme privatization, they were willing, even eager, to accept the most monotonous-seeming jobs.

Any effort, therefore, to further automatize work must take account not only of temporary technological unemployment but of the situation of those overly privatized ones who still suffer from the residual barriers of family, poverty, and hierarchy we have inherited from the era dependent on inner-direction. But surely we can think of better things for them than the factory as a refuge from home, just as we can think of better ways of giving poverty-stricken people security and good medical care than shutting them up in prison.

THE AUTOMAT VERSUS THE GLAD HAND

In the present state of our social and economic accounting, it is impossible to say where necessary personalization ends and unnecessary personalization begins. Nor can we clearly separate profitably productive effort from busy work. We cannot tell, for example, how much the slow progress toward automatization in the tertiary trades is due to low wages, as where Negro laundresses and pressers are engaged in a muscular race with existing mechanical power, how much to failure to invent the necessary machinery, how much to consumer demand to buy personalization along with a product, and how much to the needs of the work force itself to personalize, for reasons already given, whether the consumer asks for it or not.

If we look at the florist, the undertaker, the airline hostess, the carhop, or the dress-shop keeper, we must ask how much of their personalizing is the result of a measurably competitive response to a consumer demand. Is there any way of showing its relation to a product or a profit output? Or to work drives of the workers themselves? How much depends on the cultural definitions of work? We can put at one extreme the case of the chef who delights in making ice cream sculpture chiseled for each banqueteer, and at the other the salesperson who provides a "monogrammed" manner in the sale of a routine mass-produced product.

We cannot be very specific about such matters; we lack the proper social inventories. But what is clear is that there has been a historic reversal in the work effort of the different parts of the economy. Steelmaking, once a tough man's job, has been reduced in some modern rolling mills to a button-pushing process. Conversely, the growth of the consumer and luxury market in the United States, coupled with the rise of other-direction, may make the salesperson's work harder than it was in 1900. Then, for example, the salesgirl in the Fifth Avenue store sold her limited stock to the carriage trade at a pace set for her by the relative slowness of the trade itself. Indeed, "shopping" not buying was a pastime even then. But the customer was not in a hurry, nor, within the range of her class-based style, was she too anxious about her choice, though she might cavil at the price. Moreover, the salesgirl, serving only a few customers, could recall their requirements and therefore be of some assistance where assistance was in order. Today the salesgirl in the department store, a typical figure in the distributive chain of personalization, faces a mass clientele huge in size, nervous in motion, and unsure in taste. She is asked to respond in a hurry to a series of vaguely specified wants.

These observations suggest that much of the pathos of our current stage of industrialism resides in the fact that we need rapidly to expand the tertiary trades that cater to leisure, while these are the very trades which may today combine the greatest difficulty and tediousness of physical work—there is much of this, for instance, in the department store—along with the severest emotional demands. The problem of where to automatize is generally looked at by economists as a problem in investment and reinvestment, and also in labor mobility. Yet perhaps a national capital goods budget should include in its forecasts a guess as to the degree of false personalization that it may evoke or eliminate. In our recent past the development of the automobile and the oil industry was carried out without any particular sense of the employment possibilities they would create in service stations, let alone any sense of the psychology of employment there. During the depression the service-station man was bound more than ever by a discipline of false personalization. While on his own so far as the big oil companies went, he had to treat each potential customer to the "full treatment." But, perhaps, as compared to the waitress or sales-girl, entangled both with customers and with others involved in the same distributive chain, the "independent" gas station operator was not too badly off.

What we very much need is a new type of engineer whose job it is to remove psychic hazards springing from false personalization, as safety engineers now remove hazards that endanger life and limb. For in-stance, such an engineer might seek a way of making gas pumps au-tomatic like slot machines and of turning service stations into as nearly automatic form as some of the most up-to-date roundhouses for engines now are. By careful layout engineering an effort could be made to eliminate working conditions and locations that coerce the emotions—making sure meanwhile that other jobs are available for those displaced by automatization. But of course a culture that took psychic hazards, the slower menaces to character, as seriously as it takes or tries to take physical ones would look rather different from ours! Some imagination and ingenuity will be required to construct indexes by which to measure the amount of false personalization re-quired by a given job under normal conditions and to set ceilings be-yond which such personalization would not be allowed to go.

Allowing for all these difficulties of accepting and assigning respon-sibility for characterological risks in commerce and industry, it would still seem that we have lagged in the automatization of the distribu-tive trades. Bellamy saw some of the possibilities quite lucidly, and in *Looking Backward* he made consumer purchasing take the form of giving an order "untouched by human hands" to merchandising cen-ters much like the local depots in which one today can make out or-ders to Sears or Montgomery Ward. For us, too, the machine and proper organizational arrangements provide the criterion by which to judge whether any given agenda of personal attention is necessary or not. Clearly, if most vending could be made automatic, both con-sumers and salespeople would be saved from much motion and emo-tion. The Piggly-Wiggly-style grocery, the Automat, the mail order, all dependent on colorful, accurate display and advertising, are the technical inventions that widen the interstices of the distribution system where autonomy can thrive. It is a curious paradox that auto-matic vending, such as is incorporated in juke boxes and other coin machines, tends to be mixed up with rackets, as if there is something illegal in attempting to take advantage of one of the great gains made possible by the mechanical ingenuity fostered in the era of free trade and the invisible hand. It is odd, too, that advertising—which helped end that era—has done so little to eliminate the unnecessary salesperson, sales space, and sales wrapping. It is interesting to speculate on the possibilities of an institutional advertising campaign, sparked, say, by the Advertising Council, that would enhance the desirability of those products that not only were untouched by human hands but that were untarnished by false personalization. Perhaps displays of goods on TV may eliminate other sales steps. But we know from the dramatic example of the failure of savings-bank, over-the-counter life insurance how reluctant people are to buy without the interjection of the personalized touch.

IN THE MEANTIME

The restructuring of the economy to cut down false personalization by the axe of automatization will certainly not come in a day. The task of shifting our American "selves" away from jobs and job situations where we can only make a living at the expense of productivity by a regime of glad handing, featherbedding, and veto-group politicking requires great economic and still greater political ingenuity. How should we proceed pending such utopian reorganization?

It might be possible to reduce the feeling of many other-directeds that their "take" from make-work is an exploitative social dividend —a feeling that the labor featherbedder, resting on more traditional cultural definitions of his job, is less likely to have. We have lost the inner-directed justifications that protected far more unjust income distributions than we see before us today. Frequently, moreover, it is the felt antisocial character of the work itself, not of its dividends, that makes for guilt, and the feeling of what work is social is also the heritage of our antiquated cultural definitions. These tend to rank as parasitic much work that is not defined as production, whether in the distributive trades or in such auxiliary services as insurance, accounting, and law. (However, by a newer ethic, work, say, in insurance, accounting, or law, for the government is defined as productive, even when, if done for "private" interests, it would not be.)

It will be a long time—despite the work of Norbert Wiener and other builders of electronic computers!—before the Automat replaces the script writer. But the Automat could already eliminate many jobs about which people feel guilt, and we should put on the list for mechanization all work that is viewed as unnecessary by those who do it. Meanwhile, pending large-scale and difficult reorganization, such jobs help keep "the system" going. It goes without saying that people should feel free to vote against the system and to seek to change it without having to bear prematurely, in terms of their own occupational role and generous pay check, all the burdens and guilts for the system's present-day inadequacies. The guilts are all too likely to lead both to self-constriction in the leisure sphere and to expiation either in further personalizing at work or, in some cases, in a burst of political indignation.

Such redefinitions might be accelerated by drawing once more from Bellamy. His plan, requiring all youth to serve a three-year term in the "industrial army," was designed by him to facilitate national industrial organization and to guide the young in their final vocational choices. When the CCC gave us something of the same sort, it was, like so many of the good things we do, only for "relief"; the well-off were excluded. Something like a combination of Bellamy's army and the CCC would perhaps serve all of us as an initiatory alleviation of guilts about later "unproductive" work, pending the arrival of our new definitions of productiveness. Once people had done an arduous stint in the late adolescent years of strong energies and, for some, of strong idealisms, they might feel entitled to the life of Riley. Certainly, many veterans, studying or loafing in an interesting way under the GI Bill of Rights—the phrase is exceedingly important [6]— feel far less guilty about pulling down a check from Uncle Sam than they would about pulling down a scholarship, or a stipend from hard-driven parents.

Another possible stopgap solution might come not from extensive social rearrangement but from individual decision. Those seeking autonomy might simply refuse to take the cultural definitions of what constitutes "work" for granted—a kind of strike, not against work as such but against the requirement that all recruitable emotional energies be harnessed by endless reciprocal chain in work.

Thoreau was a first-class surveyor; he chose this occupation—a near-vanished craft-skill par excellence—as a well-paying one that

6. As we proceed, it will appear that we must develop a new bill of rights for the other-directed man, without relinquishing the struggle to maintain the old bill of rights that protected autonomy among the inner-directeds.

would give him a living if he worked one day a week. Dr. William Carlos Williams is a popular general practitioner in Paterson. Charles Ives "worked" by heading an agency that sold half a billion dollars' worth of insurance, and he "played" by composing some of the more significant, though least recognized, music that has been produced. Ives felt, and feels, not in the least guilty about the money he made or about the fact that he lived a "normal" American life, rather than a Bohemian one. Yet many men are unwilling to do what these men have done or what Charles Lamb or Hawthorne or many others did in the nineteenth century: to justify their work primarily by its pay check, especially if the work is short and the pay check large. Instead as we have seen they try by false personalization, by mood leadership, by notions of indispensability, and by countless similar rituals and agendas, to fill up the vacuum created by high productivity. Yet people's real "work"—the field into which, on the basis of their character and their gifts, they would like to throw their emotional and creative energies—cannot now conceivably coincide, perhaps in the majority of cases, with what they get paid for doing.

I conclude, however, with the thought that the anxieties that turn up in people's feelings about their work can perhaps not be alleviated by either the temporary or long-run expedients suggested here. For their source may not lie in the meaninglessness or inadequacy of the work itself, but deeper. It may be that the other-directed man feels guilty about being himself (or more accurately, as Erich Fromm suggests, about not being himself). No therapy at work or from work need necessarily satisfy so basic and bottomless a need for justification. Yet we should consider the possibility that, if the other-directed is to be made free, it will be not by work but by play. The first step may consist of giving play a far higher priority as a producer both of societies and character than we give it today.

XVI

Enforced Privatization: Obstacles to Autonomy in Play

I may remark . . . that though in that early time I seem to have been constantly eager to exchange my lot for that of somebody else, on the assumed certainty of gaining by the bargain, I fail to remember feeling jealous of such happier persons—in the measure open to children of spirit. I had rather a positive lack of the passion, and thereby, I suppose, a lack of spirit; since if jealousy bears, as I think, on what one sees one's companions able to do—as against one's falling short—envy, as I knew it at least, was simply of what they *were,* or in other words of a certain sort of richer consciousness supposed, doubtless often too freely supposed, in them. They were so *other*—that was what I felt; and to *be* other, other almost anyhow, seemed as good as the probable taste of the bright compound wistfully watched in the confectioner's window; unattainable, impossible, of course, but as to which just this impossibility and just that privation kept those active proceedings in which jealousy seeks relief quite out of the question.

Henry James, A Small Boy and Others

B ECAUSE THE distribution of leisure in America has been rapid as well as widespread, leisure presents Americans with issues that are historically new. At the same time part of the promise of leisure and play for the other-directed man is that it may be easier in play than in work to break some of the institutional and characterological barriers to autonomy. We can see, from our preliminary examination of autonomous possibilities in the sphere of work that play, far from having to be the residue sphere left over from work time and work feeling, can increasingly become the sphere for the development of skill and competence in the art of living. Play may prove to be the sphere in which there is still some room left for the would-be autonomous man to reclaim his individual character from the pervasive demands of his social character.

Admittedly, we know very little about play, partly as the result of the cultural definitions that give priority to work. Research has been concerned mainly with the "social character" of the producer; only recently has the same attention been paid to the consumer; we have still to discover the player. We do not know, for instance, whether we are training more group players than solitary players in America today; and if so, how this reacts on the prevailing cultural definitions of play. We do not know to what extent culturally defined "success at play" has become a more important badge of group approval than success at work; and if so, how this serves to foreclose untutored and unpublicized escape routes. Is it sensible to suggest research into play when it is possible that it would lead to increasing public and systematic interference with an area that ideally deserves privacy and lack of system? Perhaps a conspiracy of silence about leisure and play is its best protection.

We must return later to the problem of overguided play. First, let us deal with those people who are denied, or deny themselves, freedom in the realm of sociability and friendship—this may stand for denials of freedom in the sphere of play generally.

I. THE DENIAL OF SOCIABILITY

In the previous chapter we noted the excess of sociability in the form of false personalization, which is forced on many people in our economy. Such observations do not deny that for the other-directed man a deficit of sociability is even more serious than an excess. The presence of the guiding and approving "others" is a vital element in his whole system of conformity and self-justification. Depriving him of the sociability his character has come to crave will not make him autonomous, but only anomic—resembling in this the cruelty of depriving the addict of liquor or drugs by a sudden incarceration. Moreover, if the other-directed man is seeking autonomy, he cannot achieve it alone. He needs friends.

The other-directed man is socialized in a peer-group of children who resemble him in such visible indexes as age, color, and class but who may not resemble him at all in his more private temperament, interests, and fantasies. He has learned, if he is adjusted, to look like those others with whom he has been brought up, with whom he has learned cooperation, tolerance, and restraint of temper. In this process he has learned to forget aspects of his character that are not "social," not other-directed. So long as he continues to remain in a peer-group of his happenstance neighborhood, his occupational colleagues, his status equals or would-be equals, the chances are that he may not notice, or notice only in boredom and other vague unrest, any discrepancies between his image of himself and his image of the "others." Conversely, if he should begin to find himself among people who welcome and appreciate or at least do not punish expression and exploration of these buried parts of the self, he may be able to move toward greater autonomy.

To make this move, however, requires the ability, psychological and institutional, to find one's way to the new friends, the new or overlapping peer-group.

As matters stand, however, greater freedom in friendship choice is not by any means the most fashionable remedy offered today for the sociability problems of modern urban people. Many critics of contemporary life would move in the exactly opposite direction, on the assumption that people have not too little freedom but too much. Some of these critics speak from a religious platform, others out of a preoccupation with urban anomie. Greatly troubled by the fact that Americans move their households once in every seven years, they do not seek to make this movement easier by developing, for example, trailers or Buckminster-Fuller-type houses that possess a relative freedom from their sites. Rather, they would like to freeze people into communities in which friendship will be based largely on propinquity. They are apt to share the outlook of the city planner who said that he thought the ideal communities in America were to be found among the rural Negroes of the deep South and the French Canadians of the Quebec villages. It was disclosed later in the conversation that his own friends were scattered over two continents. Here we find the classes planting roots to privatize the masses by the same kind of magical incantations the Dobuans use to keep their yam tubers in place!

We might term those critics the neotraditionalists. They seem to want to deny to others the privileges of modern society which, however, they themselves take as a matter of course. Their own choice is for French food one day and Italian the next; they select their ideas from all ages and their friends from all places; they enjoy primitive African and Renaissance Italian sculpture and read books in four languages. These are felt as advantages, not liabilities; and it is ironic that many sophisticated other-directed people, out of fear, impatience, fashion, and boredom, express nostalgia for a time in the past in which they could not have had such choices. Mark Twain's *Connecticut Yankee in King Arthur's Court* indicates a greater awareness of the irony; and Twain, with all his bitterness, expresses a sounder sentiment about the road back.

Despite such critical voices, however, American sociability or the friendship market, like the American goods market, is in many ways the freest and largest in the world. Parents can monitor their children's social relations only at the class and ethnic fringe, and this they are still free to do assiduously. In adolescence, however, the automobile frees many Americans from parentally supervised sociability. By adulthood ease of transport, unity of language, and plenty of spending money release people for vacations, parties, and trips in search of many and varied friends.

Nevertheless the friendship market is beset with many "tariffs," economic, political, and cultural. First of all, there are the grosser inequities in income distribution—often based in turn on cultural definitions of work—that limit individual access to consumer goods, leisure, and play. Although floors are built under the consumption of some farmers and workers, many of them fancy featherbedders, other farmers and workers remain unprotected by subsidies or wage contracts and are therefore excluded from the "4-H Club Culture" or "UAW Culture" variants of taste, sociability, and play. These exclusions and privatizations haves complex results for the excluders and, in general, for the more privileged groups. Especially the other-directeds may find their paths to autonomy twisted by guilt for the excluded, by the limitation of their own choices that exclusion entails, and by the over-all reduction of the play potentialities of the economy that is the consequence of such reduction in any of its subsectors.

II. GUILTY ASSOCIATIONS

Have we really considered the effects on the more privileged middle-class groups of the existence of people on the other side of the tariff walls for whom the promises of the leisure economy have not yet come true? We do know something about the social anxiety of those who become willing enforcers and prisoners of Jim Crow or the Red scare or other less definite status bogies. And we know well the mood of those inner-directeds who approach blockages in others' sociability with a relatively simple moralizing decision to demolish the barrier on grounds of social necessity or justice. But these attitudes are not our chief concern in this chapter. We deal here rather with that limited group of sensitive, upper middle-class other-directeds who experience the barriers not only in their ethical, political, or economic meaning but in terms of a personal challenge to their friendship choices.

In this latter group sociability is sometimes subtly and paradoxically limited by the very efforts undertaken, in the name of tolerance, to cross the tariff walls and to establish associations that the general culture may still call "guilty" ones. The other-directed man, moving with a tolerant peer-group, is not permitted to expand his friendships to wider social strata at his own pace. He may be asked suddenly to drop not only one barrier at a time—say, the caste barrier—but two—say, the class barrier as well. For example he may be asked to meet Negroes of a *class* position lower than his own, while the moral issue is posed for him simply in terms of *color*. This can happen to him at precisely the time when he has cut himself off from the customary sources of his morality and, thereby, from the personal forcefulness he needs in order to live up to his new equalitarian values. One possibility here is that he will feel sudden panic at the forcible dropping of tariffs on the friendship market to which his psychic economy has grown accustomed, and react violently toward his older standards.

Another, perhaps more frequent, possibility is that association with the former nonassociates may even present itself as a form of punishment that a person ought to accept as a penalty for his previous wrongheadedness. This may show up in work and politics as well as in play.

III. SOCIABILITY AND THE PRIVATIZATION OF WOMEN

So long as the woman's place is consistently that of a drudge, she is, in the average of cases, fairly contented with her lot. She not only has something tangible and purposeful to do, but she has also no time or thought to spare for a rebellious assertion of such human propensity to self-direction as she has inherited.

Veblen, *The Theory of the Leisure Class*

If, on the one hand, an American woman cannot escape from the quiet circle of domestic employments, she is never forced, on the other, to go beyond it.

Tocqueville, *Democracy in America*

As with the other "minorities," the education and partial emancipation of women puts the "majority" (in this case, the men) in an ambiguous position. They are no longer protected against women by a rigid etiquette or other formal arrangements. Moreover, as we saw in Chapter VII, women make sexual demands and offer sexual potentialities that their mothers would never have dreamed of, or would only have dreamed of. By the same token, they make demands for understanding and companionship. But men, already anxious among the antagonistic cooperators of their own sex, do not always welcome the "cooperation" and companionship from the opposite sex that the dropping of an older tariff permits and in a way requires. While the inner-directed man, who could still patronize women, complained to his mistress that his wife did not understand him, the other-directed man in effect complains that his women understand him all too well. Indeed, any man who reads such stories as "Let's Go Out Tonight" must feel wary among magazine-educated women!

These uneasinesses among the newly liberated are one source of the current attempts to reprivatize women by redefining their role in some comfortably domestic and traditional way. Many people, both men and women, are troubled by the so-called disintegration of the family and look longingly back to the family structure of societies at an early point on the curve of population. They usually fail to see that the current divorce rate is, in part, an index of the new demands for sociability and leisure freedom of sensitive middle-class couples; that these demands not only begin high, in the choice of a mate, but, as Margaret Mead has observed, include the dynamic that each partner to a marriage expects the other to grow and develop at approximately the same rate as himself.[1]

To be sure, many divorces are the result of wildcatting on the sex

1. Margaret Mead, *Male and Female* (New York, William Morrow, 1949); see also the very perceptive observations in the article by Talcott Parsons, "Age and Sex in the Social Structure of the United States," *American Sociological Review*, VII (1942), 604–616; reprinted in *Personality in Nature, Society, and Culture*, ed. Kluckhohn and Murray, pp. 269–281.

frontier that our leisure society has opened up for exploitation by others than aristocrats and bums, and by women as well as men. Doubtless, too, many women act as nonpecuniary pirates on that frontier, as if to punish men for the previous privatizations of women. Yet clearly, any effort by the neotraditionalists to close the sex frontier, while it might help restore the glamour sin had in the earlier era, would be irrelevant to the problems created by the greater demands a leisure-oriented people put upon their choice in companionship, sexual and otherwise. The autonomous, as I stated in Chapter XIV, point the way to a new model of marriage that finds its opportunity precisely in the choices that a free-divorce, leisure society opens up. Because women are less privatized than they have traditionally been, marriage offers more for millions of people than ever before in its long history.

Nevertheless, we have quite a way to go before women can associate with men at work and play on any footing of equality. Today men who find it easy and natural to get along with women and prefer mixed company both at work and play have to fight the residues of older privatizations. For one thing, they are hardly able to avoid many stag occasions, into which some men retreat from the liberations forced on them by the new intersex ethics. As the latency period in childhood gets shorter and shorter, so that boys can be boys only from six to ten, adult males try to create or retain artificial latency periods in which they will not be under pressure from women—or, worse, from male judgments as to how they are succeeding with women. Thus, both sexes experience the limits, pressures, and guilts of emancipation.

Hence, we should not be surprised to see in the social strata where other-direction prevails that very considerable privatization even of the women of higher economic status still goes on, and that these women, often compulsory players and consumers, have not solved the problems of competence in play. The heroine of "Let's Go Out Tonight," for example, is frozen into her suburban cottage, cut off from the whole friendship market of both men and women—except those she can meet socially with her husband. Many suburbanites, not to speak of farm wives, are much worse off. The husband drives to work in the only car and leaves his wife a prisoner at home with the small children, the telephone, and the radio or television. Such women can easily become so uninteresting that they will remain psychological prisoners even when the physical and economic handicaps to their mobility are removed. And this privatization in turn limits the friendship choices and increases the guilts of everyone else.

As we saw earlier, the war helped deprivatize many women who welcomed work in industry or other war work as a real increase in their sociability. Even in those cases where earnings are not vital to the established living standards of a family, the working woman frequently does find her way to an independence that would hardly be recognizable by the middle-class woman of the nineteenth century. This independence lays the groundwork for some autonomy in play, even when the work remains, as it does for most working women, routine.

Does this view neglect the unembattled leisure possibilities of certain middle- and upper middle-class women who compose an advance guard in the use of leisure? Suppose that a woman of this group has successfully passed the point where her consumption is budgeted wholly to satisfy the canons of conspicuous consumption. Suppose, too, that her leisure is not entirely controlled by the leisure habits of her husband's business-minded peer-group and that she has solved in one way or another the battle of the housework. She has decided either to do her own work, reducing the domestic production schedule to fit her capacity, or has decided to accept outside help and thus has taken up the burdens of being a labor manager and morale builder right at the frictional sore point of the class system. Suppose that she even gets credit for the variety and complication of these tasks which she must accomplish prior to play. What then?

When all this is attended to, some middle- and upper middle-class women do have time to play. Such a woman can move into the peer-groups of the bridge players, the garden clubbers, any of the other groups of pastimers. The transition sounds easy. The difficulty is that women are being driven out of many of the areas in which they formerly occupied their leisure with amateur competences. For example, they are no longer welcome as ladies bountiful; the social workers have so professionalized the field of helping people that any intrusion by benevolent amateurs is deeply resisted and resented. Likewise, amateurs can no longer help sick people, unless they are willing, as nurses' aids, to help registered nurses be professionals by doing all the dirty work for them. They cannot help others enjoy themselves, because settlement work and recreational activities have also been professional-ized.[2] While they can discuss politics and race relations in the League of Women Voters and the YWCA, they can do so only under the packaged and, in fact, quite excellent programs provided from central headquarters.

Thus everywhere they turn to put their part time energies to work, they face a veto group and its insistence that, to participate, they must "go through channels" or become slaveys and money-raisers for those who control the channels. And money-raising itself is now increas-ingly professionalized, with only the money-giving left to the "par-ticipants." Reacting to this situation, the women either sink back into indifference or conclude, like their working-class sisters, that only through a job, a culturally defined job, will they be liberated. Instead of moving toward autonomy in play, an autonomy toward which they could also help their men, they often simply add to their own domestic problems all the anxieties men endure at work.

IV. PACKAGED SOCIABILITIES

These culturally defined tariffs that crisscross the friendship mar-ket among the American peer-groups severely limit the choices any given individual has for finding those who can help him become au-tonomous. Perhaps one other example should be mentioned, namely the tendency toward self-privatization on the part of the various not quite assimilated ethnic groups. For we encounter here a rather para-doxical development, which results from a change in the meanings read into the otherwise admirable doctrine of "cultural pluralism."[3]

What has happened is that the older pressures toward forcible Americanization which we associate with the settlement house have receded. Only recent groups of poverty-stricken immigrants, like the Mexicans and Puerto Ricans, are steadily subjected to such pressures. The lower-class Negro, Italian, Jew, or Slav is permitted to approach the American middle-class norm at more or less his own mobility pace. Under the practice of cultural pluralism this means that the ethnic groups are no longer urged to accept the whole package of work and play as "the Americans" define it. On the contrary, the

2. This discussion of the effect of growing professionalization on amateur aid has profited from the work of Everett Hughes.

3. I am indebted to Judge Jerome Frank for calling to my attention some of these less than innocent meanings of the slogan of cultural pluralism.

ethnics are invited to add to the variety of the nation by retaining the colorful flavors of their "racial heritages." As we saw in discussing food in Chapter VII, these are precisely the heritages that are combed over by the dominant groups in search of gastronomical differentiations.[4] So far, so good. But at the same time the middle- and upper-class Negro, Italian, Jew, or Slav is not quite assimilated; he remains identifiably or in his own feeling an ethnic. He is kept from complete social participation in the dominant groups by subtle and not so subtle barriers. Meanwhile veto-group leaders in his own ethnic group come along to urge him to welcome the autarchy thus partially forced on him from outside, to confine his sociability "voluntarily" to his "own" group, and to obey the leisure styles of that group. This, too, is called cultural pluralism, though for the individual it operates as a monolith.

Thus, for example, while lower-class Negroes in the big northern cities are immobilized by poverty and segregation, the upper middle-class Negroes are subject to their race leaders' definitions of what it means to be a Negro, especially in those fields, like leisure, which more than the field of work, are under race control. Sociability with whites runs risks not only from the side of the newly liberated whites but from the pressures of the race leaders, who may for instance interpret friendliness as Uncle Tomism.

Other leisure pursuits may similarly become tainted by race considerations. In some circles middle-class Negroes are forbidden to like jazz because there are whites who patronize Negroes as the creators of jazz; other Negroes may be compelled to take pride in jazz or in Jackie Robinson, as Jews may be required to take pride in Israel or Einstein. Still other middle-class Negroes cannot enjoy watermelon

---

4. Food, of course, is only a symbol or instance of the way in which American play styles are greatly dependent on the post-Protestant (Jew or Catholic) and pre-Protestant (Negro) immigration. From the 1880's to the 1920's, for example, the white Protestant majority waged an increasingly unsuccessful war to maintain its dominance not only in the work sphere, where it was well skilled, but also in the play sphere, where it was constantly having to fight for a precarious competence. Hence it resisted any new consumption potentialities offered by the work-disfranchised ethnics, ranging from Italian food to the borsch-circuit comedy and the Negroid Charleston. Prohibition was the last major battle in that war. Its bad effects were blamed on the "Sicilian gangster." Now obviously the fact that Jews and Negroes could climb, and even avoid the ethnic affronts, most easily in the arts and entertainments put them in a good position of leadership when the larger society itself shifted to embrace consumption values. Thus it is that the ethnics are the ones who liberate the majority. Once their liberations succeed, as in the triumph of their cooking, this success tends to become rationalized by the dominant culture as continental style—a method of transferring a consumer value from a consumership gradient to a class gradient. Increasingly, America's play patterns may suffer from the lack of a customary though underrecognized stimulus and élan when there are no more immigrants or people close to immigrant culture.

or other foods that are part of the traditional Negro diet and certainly are not allowed to enjoy popular-culture portrayals such as those of Rochester or Amos and Andy. Similarly, while the lower-class Jew is not much bothered by metaphysical definitions of Jewishness, the almost but not wholly assimilated Jew is subservient to the Jewish cultural compartmentalizers who tell him what his leisure style and friendship practice should be. These indivisibilities, in which one must submit to the packaging of one's sociabilities by a combination of external pressure and small-time culture dictators among the marginally underprivileged, operate both through peer-group censorship and through the exhortations of the media beamed at the particular minority. Play and sociability are then consumed in guilty or anxious efforts to act in accordance with definitions of one's location on the American scene, a location which, like a surviving superstition, the individual cannot fully accept or dare fully to reject.

V. THE THREAT OF THE LONELY PLAYERS

If we sum up all these restrictions—remembering that we have been illustrating here the more impalpable varieties—we can see that a cultural bill of rights is necessary to liberate sociability for all in the United States, before any can be wholly liberated. If this is so, it means that the autonomous among the other-directeds face problems far more acute than those faced by the autonomous among the inner-directeds. We have seen this already in the sphere of work, where we noticed how widely and sensitively the other-directeds respond to their business and professional teammates, not only at their own job or skill levels but at lower levels as well. Similarly, the man who is upper middle class by either birth or achievement finds it more difficult today than fifty years ago to luxuriate in consumption goods and leisure, among other reasons because he knows that some people are privatized to the point of lacking even minimum satisfactions in a consumer-oriented economy. The advertising man, for instance, may pay heavily for the presence in society of those who cannot afford or are not allowed to consume the very commodity he advertises. In this case, the sharp contrast between the society he advertises as a utopia of efficient distribution and bountiful consumption and the facts of consumption stickiness and tariffs are apt to bother his play time.

These problems troubled few middle- and upper middle-class consumers in an era depending on inner-direction. Even those who rose through achievement might find in their farewell to former class associates far less inner perplexity than in their dismissal of former ethnic, kin, or sectarian affiliations—for this, we recall, was the era of the concern with the hardness of the material rather than with the softness of the personnel. Indeed, until the age of Taft, most consumers, whatever their blockages in escape, could remain innocently uninvolved in the lacks of others. They could easily moralize them away. Or if they were especially troubled they could assuage their consciences by personal benevolence. They did not think of the poor as people but as an abstraction, or in terms of the few they personally knew and helped. Often they could actually believe that their own consumption and sociability served the public weal in some fashion guaranteed by the invisible hand.

Moreover, as we have also seen, the inner-directed person was protected at his play by the fact that he felt himself to be a great producer; this definition of himself at work gave him a large measure of confidence in whatever pattern of sociability and consumption he chose. His right to play was supported, and of course limited as well, by his class position and his power to assure himself of moral and physical privacy. But such escapes and protections are largely closed to many other-directeds of the upper middle class today.

We can see this, for example, when we observe the kinds of sociability practiced by an other-directed father with his children, as compared with those of his inner-directed predecessor. The latter's authority easily structured the parent-child relation into one of great social distance. Play meant a sudden gift from the gods, something quite wonderful for the child happening without any reason. The father could unbend, could be sociable and gay, just because of the gratuitous nature of the move. Or in other cases he was too stiff, too withdrawn to play at all, or the forms of his play would be so remote as not to have any conceivable relationship to children.[5]

When the other-directed father plays with his children, he is re-

5. We have to watch, in many inner-directed men, for types of play hidden inside what looked very much like work. Edmund Gosse, for instance, describing his father, makes it plain that the father, a highly ascetic puritan, could not play with the son or, indeed, with anyone. But he also notes that the plates his father, a biologist, drew to illustrate his volumes were very beautiful artistic creations—really, a kind of highly sublimated play. A number of intellectual theories and chains of reasoning developed by sternly inner-directed men have been "play" of the same sort: Freud's *Moses and Monotheism*, or much of his dream theory, seem good examples.

sponding to an immediate demand, not acting as a nodding Jove. In the unstructured situation he may be very aware of his incompetence at play, of the distance that separates him from his own childhood, its tastes and pleasures, and even more from the new tastes and pleasures of youth. If he has to learn the rules of the game from the child, who is the patronizer and who is patronized? Beyond all that, the father is almost inevitably bound up in his play with morale considerations: he may view play as therapy for the children, for himself, or for their relationship. Lacking models and unwilling to grant the difficulty either of play or of contact with the alien civilization of childhood, he is as likely as not to end up wondering whether he has given too much or too little time to the children and perhaps feeling with some resentment that he has enough to do being sociable with his own peer-group, without trying to cross the barriers of age.

We may draw another quite different example of other-directed inhibitions in play by noticing how often the objects of consumption themselves can testify to misplaced guilts on the part of the privileged groups. It is quite possible that a man buying a painting may become confused in his choice by worrying as to whether he ought to patronize American artists or those of his own city or region, or perhaps a deserving refugee; or at a less conscious level he may buy a Gropper or early George Grosz to haunt him; or he may look for paintings that he can justify as "owed" to his wife, to the space on his wall, to his station in life, to his investment policy. Similarly, the consumer choice of many in the 1940's for poorly made movies with a high moralizing content (e.g., "tolerance"), rather than for well-made movies regardless of overt message, is a response of the kind I am trying to analyze here. Under these conditions play and sociability become not the area in which to refresh character reserves but the area in which one pays for one's failures or the failures of one's symbolic group in the work and political areas.

VI. FREEING THE CHILD MARKET

This is not meant to imply that autonomy in character will come about immediately by getting rid of the barriers to autonomy that false personalization and enforced privatization constitute. The individual may or may not make use of the freedoms offered him by such institutional changes, and obviously many complex factors are involved in determining whether he will welcome his freedom or seek to escape from it. Indeed, throughout this discussion I can only indicate some of the barriers to autonomy which have received inadequate recognition; to go on from there to see what are some of the positive sources of autonomy in character is another, far more difficult, undertaking.

Still proceeding, then, along the line of blockages, I want to suggest a more or less fantastic model to stimulate thinking about what might be done, here and now, this year, to reduce the amount of privatization from which people suffer. I have chosen as a paradigm a model "world's fair for children" to indicate how we might work along the lines of existing institutions once we become convinced of the importance of experience as a consumer in shaping character today.

Although small children rapidly get over the stage of passionate belief in the advertising of the box top and its radar signal rings, there is, as we have seen, one feeling they learn in that stage which they do not get over. This is the belief that they must have a reason for consuming anything—a reason acceptable in the taste-exchanging process. While the advertiser opens the children up to this kind of preference rationalization, it is the peer-groups of child and adult life which step in later to provide the "reasons." It is this support, as much as any intrinsic power of advertising itself, that makes advertising appear to many observers as a powerful barrier to or manipulator of consumer free choice. The advertisers themselves seem to be unaware of the possibilities of loosening the rules of this game, both for their own benefit, the benefit of their clientele, and the benefit of the economy.

Ideally, of course, the advertisers and their clients should see to it that all their potential consumer trainees have the wherewithal to practice bounteous consumption; quite sad is the life of the child who, while being exposed to consumer training, lacks even the minimum wherewithal. The proposal I want to make to advertisers is modest: that some of the funds reserved for national promotion and advertising of consumer goods used by children should be set aside in a fund for experimental creation of model consumer economies among children.

A number of possible patterns suggest themselves. A group of advertisers, for example, might issue scrip money to groups of children, allowing them to patronize some central store—a kind of everyday world's fair—where a variety of "luxury" goods ranging from rare foods to musical instruments would be available for their purchase. At this "point of sale" there would stand market researchers, able and willing to help children make their selections but having no particularly frightening charisma or overbearing charm or any interest on the employers' side in pushing one thing rather than another. These "experiment stations" might become the source of revealing information about what happens to childhood taste when it is given a free track away from the taste gradients and "reasons," as well as freedom from the financial hobbles of a given peer-group. In precisely such situations children might find the opportunity to criticize and reshape in their own minds the values of objects. In the "free store" they would find private alcoves where they might enjoy books and music, candy and comics, in some privacy.[6] It would be interesting to see whether children who had had the luck to express themselves freely in consumption preferences, released from ethnic and class and peer-group limitations, might develop into much more imaginative critics of the leisure economy than most adults of today are.[7]

Only the craftsmen of retailing and market research could help refine such a model and iron out the many practical problems involved. Perhaps, rather than or in addition to a world's fair, advertisers might send out "salesmen" whose purpose it was, not to sell but to give away goods. They would seek to discover reasons for blockages in choice and, again like the play therapist, try to encourage the noncash "customers" to become more free and imaginative.[8]

6. The closest existing analogy to this "commodity library" is perhaps the neighborhood librarian, who can help children find their way to books because she seems to be out of the direct line of school and home authority, because her interest often actually is in helping rather than in forcing children, and because being typically of an inner-directed background, she does not insist on personalizing the relationship with the child. Ideally, the libraries ought to provide each child with a cubicle where he would have a key and complete privacy, where he could paint, listen to music, read, or just loaf, away from the peer-group and from the adult world. Unfortunately, as we have seen, children do not have such privacy at home or at school.

7. See the stimulating contemporary attempt to build utopian models of this sort for work and play in the Goodmans' *Communitas: Means of Livelihood and Ways of Life*.

8. There is no real problem in the choice of children to enjoy these wonders. To get away from the sterile arguments of those for and against radio's giveaways the FCC might accept the giveaway merchandizing technique only if advertisers display ingenuity in making the principle do service in promoting market analysis and consumer autonomy. A model consumer economy for children selected by chance would serve just such purposes.

A more serious problem would be to prevent the children from exploiting or being exploited by a black-market type of operations, after the fashion of the soldiers who created a consumer economy from army and occupied-country "surplus."

One can conceive of other such model "economies of abundance" in which every effort would be made, on an experimental basis, to free children and other privatized people from group and media pressure. Indeed, market research has for many years seemed to me one of the most promising channels for democratic control of our economy. Market researchers know as well as anyone that their methods need not be used simply to manipulate people into buying the goods and cultural definitions that already exist or to dress them up in marginal differentiations, but can be employed to find out not so much what people want but what with liberated fantasy they might want.[9] Without "mock-ups" and pilot models people rarely enough make this leap of the imagination.

9. My emphasis throughout on the mass media and the commodities turned out by mass production should not be taken as an implicit denial of the importance of the more traditional fine arts. The values of these arts for autonomy have been thoughtfully treated—from an adult education point of view, e.g., in the work of Hughes Mearns, and from a sensitive philosophic understanding, e.g., in the work of John Dewey and Susanne K. Langer. My effort rather has been directed to the gap generally believed to exist between high culture and mass culture—a gap concealing ambiguities on both sides.

XVII

The Problem of Competence: Obstacles to Autonomy in Play (*Continued*)

For as soon as labor is distributed each man has a particular and exclusive sphere from which he cannot escape. He is a hunter, fisherman, a shepherd, or a critical critic, and must remain so if he does not want to lose his means of livelihood; while in a communist society, where nobody has one exclusive sphere of activity, but each can become accomplished in any branch he wishes, society regulates the general production and thus makes it possible for one to do one thing today and another tomorrow—to hunt in the morning, to fish in the evening, to criticize after dinner just as I have in mind, without ever becoming hunter, fisherman, shepherd, or critic.

Karl Marx, on the amateur.

I can play the lute and the pipe, the harp, the organistrum, the bagpipe and the tabor. I can throw knives and catch them without cutting myself. I can tell a tale against any man and make love verses for the ladies. I can move tables and juggle with chairs. I can turn somersaults and stand on my head.

Medieval entertainer, on the professional.

I. THE PLAY'S THE THING

THE LAST chapter, dealing largely with limitations on play, suggests that the sphere of leisure is blocked in America. As in all such situations, it is important to understand the institutional difficulties involved, if we are not to become too pessimistic about the future. If we realize that the other-directed man can hardly be expected to have done better in play than he has done, we may expect a good deal more of him once we can develop institutional means to release the American leisure society from some of its chains. There are a few signs, to be considered later, that already point in this direction.

Privatization as an obstacle to play can be thought of primarily as a relic of previous eras of status-dominated leisure. But it is by no means the only obstacle to leisure we have inherited. A whole historic spectrum of play, in sport, art, idleness, and other ceremonial escapes, was destroyed or subverted by the puritan wing of inner-direction. Today the other-directed man retains few play ceremonials, and those he has are seldom fixed and objective. They are fluctuating and innovational and demand a kind of subjectivity that is far different from the readier, perhaps less complicated, funmaking of earlier character types.

Myth and ritual are not absent from the life of modern urban, other-directed men; as we have seen, work and politics and consumption are filled with myth and ritual which are not recognized as such. But the same forces that have led us to disguise our work rituals as rational necessities have had perhaps a more disruptive impact on our play rituals, which could not so easily retreat behind the rationalizations and opacity that continue to screen the mythical and magical elements of our daily work. Thus even our holidays make work out of funmaking or gift giving which we have neither the wit to welcome nor the courage to refuse; we know holidays are calculated steps in the distributive economy and that new holidays, e.g., Mother's Day, are foisted on us—there are more commercially sponsored "Weeks" than there are weeks in the year. Here puritanism is an Indian giver: it not only gives priority to work and distribution but, what is more, takes back the niggardly holidays it gives us. The scars that puritanism has left on the American, and not only on the Philadelphian, Sunday are well known. In general our puritan heritage is obviously responsible for much of the rigidity and unimaginative use of our leisure.

It may take a long time before the damage done to play during the era depending on inner-direction can be repaired. In the meantime other-direction has added new hazards. Among these, the demand on the other-directeds that every sphere of life be attended by the responsibility for "making a group mood" (by manipulating one's own mood and often by seeing to it that everyone gets equally tight) constantly interferes with spontaneous sociability, not to mention privacy, in play. Indeed, while privatization as an obstacle to play may be thought of as an inheritance from the era depending on inner-direction, lack of privacy in play may be thought of as an obstacle especially prevalent among the other-directeds.

We have seen that children learn early in their lives that they must have no secrets from companionable peers and adults; and this includes their use of leisure. This is perhaps to be expected from the other-directeds who care more for the mood and manner of doing things than for what is done, who feel worse about an exclusion from others' consciousness than about any violation of property or pride, and who will tolerate almost any misdeed so long as it is not concealed from them. Presumably, parents who want their children to become autonomous may help them very much by letting them learn they have the right to make their choices (by lying if necessary) between those leisure situations in which they wish to be intimate with others and those in which intimacy is merely the demand of an authority, parental or groupish. Obviously an individual who needs, for the autonomous use of leisure, both play which is private, reverie filled, and fantasy rich, and play which is sociable, even ceremonial, has a hard time combating all at once the privatizations we have inherited and the personalizations we have newly elaborated.

These are very general considerations, and they must be supplemented by reminding ourselves of the continuing consequences, both for work and play, of the Great Depression. The depression did not lead to a redefinition of work but on the contrary made work seem not only precious but problematic—precious because problematic. It is significant that we have now taken full employment, rather than full nonemployment, or leisure, as the economic goal to which we cling in desperation. This is not surprising when we realize how stunted were the sociabilities and other play opportunities for the man unemployed in the depression. We could see then, in the clearest form, how often leisure is defined as a permissive residue left over from the demands of work time. Even financially adequate relief could not remove this moral blockage of play, any more than retirement pay can remove it for the forcibly retired oldsters. For the prestige of work operates as a badge entitling the holder to draw on the society's idleness fund. Even the adolescent who is engaged in "producing himself" suffers emotional discomfort if he cannot demonstrate that he is at work or training assiduously for narrowly defined work aims. In sum, taking together the young, the unemployed, the postemployment old, the housewife, and the guilty featherbedders, not to speak of the "idle rich," we may have a great number who more or less unconsciously feel some uneasiness in play—because by cultural definition the right to play belongs to those who work.

If the depression is one highly visible specter that distorts our cultural and economic thinking, with fears of recurrence leading both to frantic spending and frantic saving, to frantic working and frantic featherbedding, another specter closely related to the depression is only barely and arguably visible. This is the feeling that the consumption of what used to be called surpluses is now obligatory on a large and complex scale, both to direct the economy and keep it going. I do not mean to suggest that people eat potatoes because the Commodity Credit Corporation is glutted with potatoes; the transfer of values from production to consumption is not so simple. Rather, today's middle-class man, having lived through the depression, may be encouraged to consume as an element, a final step, in the productive and distributive process: he is made to feel he is there so that the producer will do the right thing and so that he will do the right thing by the producer. As at Christmas, he uses his play to absorb the surplus, to work it off, so to speak.

Curiously enough, he finds for himself in this way some of the fictitious indispensability we have already traced in his political and work attitudes. The images of power are built with such elaboration that every effort looks inevitable and many a nonexpensive leisure hour, just sitting, for instance, seems a waste. Everyone is reassured he has a place, and pays for this by using up much of the playfulness which he might "waste" in becoming autonomous. We seem in this way partly to have inherited, partly to have reproduced, the same sort of fetishism about leisure as a whole that Marx observed about commodities and market relations.

Many observers of the contemporary American scene, both European and domestic, believe that this fetishism is a necessary trait of capitalist culture. In their view the American distributive system makes such excessive demands for emotional involvement in the market as to exclude the possibility that the individual can make other uses of fantasy and spontaneous playfulness. These observers seem to feel that advertising and myth manipulation cannot afford to let go their grip because the whole social and economic order depends on the identifications built up by irrational appeals. Being of the opinion that there is only a limited amount of fantasy to go around, they feel that all of it must inevitably be channeled to power the mechanism of production, display, and distribution. The commercialization and alleged standardization of the media are explained, in terms of this perspective, as the other side of the mechanization and standardization of the capitalist work sphere itself. It is argued, accordingly, that only a change in the system will permit a change in the patterns of leisure and allow the now passive audience to participate actively and critically in its entertainments.

There can, of course, be no doubt that industrialism coupled with puritanism worked havoc with play along these lines; and changes in the system are overdue. Current Marxist or Weberian diagnoses of our present play shortcomings, however, seem to me to overlook a number of important problems. First, we do not yet possess a clear grasp of the work-play axis of the system today—we do not know how much actual as against alleged standardization there is in work or how much actual as against alleged standardization there is in audience uses of popular-culture materials. Whatever the system is, it is changing fast. Moreover, it is far less systematic than in our quest for certainty we like to suppose.

Second, advertising and sheer consumption no longer have their old pre-World War II magic for that sophisticated trainee-in-consumption, the other-directed man. He is not *impressed* by standardization and commercialization of leisure; he is simply *oppressed* by them. His oppression springs, in part, from the tremendous development of virtuosity that specialization and division of labor have brought to the field of play as well as to the field of work. The varied capacities of the medieval entertainer whose boast is quoted at the chapter head include some amiable virtuosities. But they would hardly get him a billing on the RKO circuit or television today, and he would certainly not be good enough for Ringling Brothers. The amateur player has to compete with professionals who are far more professional than ever before—can he tell Laurence Olivier how to play *Hamlet,* as Hamlet himself could get away with telling the professional players how *not* to do it? We saw in Part I that, while the inner-directed man held on tenaciously to his competence as a player at least in his downward escapes, the other-directed man is faced with and oppressed by virtuosity from the omnipresent media wherever he turns.

Thus it looks as if the task of restoring competence to play is almost, if not quite, as difficult as that of restoring it to work. While a change in income relations, or even in the organization of industry, might make for fairer distribution of leisure and a lessening of guilts, it could not of itself teach men how to play who have historically forgotten how and who have turned the business over to professionals. Are we right, then, in supposing that play offers any easier channels to autonomy than work; are not both equally "alienated" in Marx's sense, so much so that even the coming of socialism would mean little?

The problem is actually even more thorny than that. As we have already seen and as we shall see perhaps more clearly as we proceed, the consequences of making people more competent players can be ambivalent: the very measures taken to increase competence may result in decreasing play. Yet it is, in my opinion, largely through competence in leisure that most other-directed people can develop autonomy and political imagination. For while, as we have seen, the inner-directed man even if he could not play could feel, qualitatively, that he was a participating member of his society by virtue of his work alone, the other-directed man if he cannot play is apt to feel disqualified from participation in a society which is increasingly governed by a leisure ideology. And even apart from such cultural pressures and definitions, I believe play is of basic human importance for achieving autonomy.

The competence the other-directed man needs to attain in play is thus related both to his situational pressures and to the problems play would present in any culture. His competence need not be especially high in any virtuoso sense but it must be high enough so that the individual, faced with the mass media and the class media, does not regard himself as a helpless duffer at every point.

There is evidence that various types of competence are being built up in the play of the other-directeds, in the face of all the obstacles we have listed. Some of these skills, such as craftsmanship, have old foundations; others, such as consumership, have new aspects. Even taste exchanging, that intangible product of the play-work of the other-directed peer-groups, can be seen as a training ground for leisure skills. Perhaps there is more competence at play than meets the eye— less passivity, less manipulation, less shoddiness than is usually charged.

II. THE FORMS OF COMPETENCE

CONSUMERSHIP: POSTGRADUATE COURSE

Consumership is the most generalized and all embracing of the channels of play. While delight in a sport, a craft, or an art object may in our culture be far more than mere consumership, such delight seldom far transcends consumership when the individual's orientation is toward a "best-buy," peer-oriented ideal. Success in play in this style of consumption becomes little more than felt approval from the peers, real and imagined, with whom one associates oneself. In Chapter IV we identified the mass media, whose influences are in turn reshaped by the peer-groups' opinion leaders, as the main tutors in this kind of consumership. We saw there an audience structure in which the peers and the media provide overlapping images of appropriate consumption.

Now we can carry this analysis one step further, by noting that it is only for the characterologically adjusted that peers and media provide a felt unity. For the anomic, peers and media diverge so sharply that, if the media are comprehensible at all, it is only as a savage critique of the peers or the self or both. For the autonomous, by contrast, the divergence of peers and media is sufficient to create a tension favorable to criticism of both, and partial escape from both. This suggests that there are situations in which the media can be set against the power of the peers; and situations in which the power of the peers can be set against the media. Let us consider the first of these possibilities.

Competent consumership in the other-directed economy is, as we have seen, no longer focused on the consumption object itself but on the internalized image of the consumer. Since for most Americans the entertainment world represents the biggest image of how consumership should be undertaken and in what spirit, show people are the most influential of our tutors in consumption style. They do this, of course, both on and off the air or screen, in a life role which is a blend of artistic illusion and social reality. In this respect café society has replaced Society. Actors and entertainers, the promoters of movies and sports, the radio and advertising men, the entrepreneurs in similarly glamorous professions, inevitably set our sportist and Bohemian styles. Surely these styles are often little more than cues for marginal differentiation among groups of fans and servile imitators. But this is not the only use made of these leisure-style models. We must acknowledge our debt to the entertainment world and defend its freedom to find new leisure patterns against the fears of the censors. The veto groups are always at work to haul the entertainers into line—to forbid their developing new models of personal dress and other items of consumership in which they have vested interests.

If a famous actor becomes too preoccupied with stamp collecting, we can be sure that the button collectors will needle him. Entertainers, setters of the lighter, brighter pace, are increasingly under the "older brother" rule: they must act as nice tutors for the "younger brother," the consumer. Jimmy Fidler and Louella Parsons crack the ruler on the actress who fails to be "sincere" on the night shift where she practices the public arts of private consumption. All these informal controls seem to be part of a structure in which the media artists are systematically limited in their impact on the existing profiles of peer-group consumption.

In spite of these pressures a few mass-media personalities manage to develop great styles—McCarthy-Bergen, for instance, finds how to be funny while operating under the proviso that, both as artist and citizen, he must offend no interest group larger than three. W. C. Fields projected a wild, fantastic resistance to amiable, smooth American ways in his "tales of norm and 'abnorm.'"

There are signs that the purely on-the-screen effects of the movie makers are beginning to deal more directly with the feelings of a middle class not yet fully aware of the extent of its play problems. A number of recent movies can be interpreted as encouraging new leisure and domestic styles among men—with the implication that freedom from their peers will help them to increase their own competence as consumers and encourage their development toward autonomy. In Letter to Three Wives and Everybody Does It the hero (Paul Douglas) is represented as a power seeker with hair on his chest who is making the "one-class jump"—the jump from lower middle class to upper middle class which still propels much of our economic and social life. The one-class jumper, caught as he is between a peer-group he has left and another he has not quite achieved, is usually too insecure, too driven, to be a good candidate for autonomy. Douglas begins with a stereotyped, inner-directed tone of toughness and insensitivity but ends up by discovering new angles in his own complex emotions when he learns (in Everybody Does It) that the singing talent being sought by his socialite would-be canary wife is actually his own. This discovery may constitute a commentary on the fact that men need no longer delegate artistic sensibilities to wives seeking culture as status or as career, but can if they wish enjoy them as part of their own competence. This is a new twist and one that James M. Cain and the scenarists must have been perfectly aware of, in the old comedy-dilemma of the man who meets and surpasses the leisure ideals of his new, upper-class peer-group.

Still other comedies of manners of recent years tackle a similar theme of peer-free competence from a different perspective. They portray with sympathy the style of a man who allows himself the luxury of being a "generalist" at life, self-educated, eccentric, near-autonomous. In the *Mr. Belvedere* series, for instance, Clifton Webb is a thinly disguised intellectual and social deviant who is an expert at anything he cares to turn his hand and brain to. Yet, like Beatrice Lillie, he attains his range of skill and competence only in situations where society permits a high degree of individualism; and he is allowed to create his breath-taking personal style only because of his astonishing dexterity. On one level the "message" of the Belvedere movies is quite different from that of the Douglas movies, where a heightened expressiveness is suggested as an attractive "extra" in life to the ordinary upper middle-class man and not to the nonconformist. But on another level the two types of pictures are very much alike. Both seem to be saying, among all the other amusing things they have to say, that the so-called power of the peers is not important. Both characterizations give the individual the right to explore and elaborate his own personality and sensitivity with a work-leisure competence that goes beyond the requirements of the peers.

Surely the great mass-media artists, including the directors, writers, and others behind the scenes who "create" and promote the artists, make an important contribution to autonomy. The entertainers, in their media, out of their media, and in the never-never land between, exert a constant pressure on the accepted peer-groups and suggest new modes of escape from them. The sharpest critics of American movies are likely to forget this too easily. They concentrate heavily, these days, on their attempts to use certain peer-group standards of "high" taste as a resistance point to be set up against admitted failures of quality in the movies. Obviously, my point here is not that we are abundantly supplied with movie criticism—we have almost none. Rather my point is that autonomy, building on an exploration of a tension between peers and media, must take advantage of both sides of the tension. The "advanced" peer-grouper who attacks the movies indiscriminately often only demonstrates his adjustment to those class media where "Hollywood" is a cuss word. He never gets the chance to see that many movies, in many conventionally unexpected ways, are liberating agents. In more general terms, this rejection of the movies often symbolizes a blanket rejection of our "passive" popular-culture consumership. By contrast, the critics are likely to place their bets on leisure activities that are individualistic and involve personal participation. For instance, craftsmanship.

CRAFTSMANSHIP: IS THE HAND QUICKER THAN THE EYE?

The "Belvedere" movies happen to be flashing satire on competence and craftsmanship, in much the way that *The Admirable Crichton* is a satire on competence and class. Today the craftsman often seems eccentric because of his fanatical devotion to his craft or hobby; Mr. Belvedere uses his various craft-skills to flaunt and enjoy his eccentricity, to rub it in. In this sense his life style is a new commentary on the question whether craft competence in leisure is on the decline in America. Certainly many people have the leisure and encouragement to pursue crafts who never did before. We are told that the employees at the Hawthorne plant of the Western Electric Company include thousands of active, eager gardeners; that they run an annual hobby show of considerable size and style; that the factory helps bring together amateur photographers, woodcarvers, model builders—the whole countless range of modern hobbyism—in addition, of course, to the usual sports, music, and dramatic groups. But there are no statistics to show whether hobbies that were once privately pursued are now simply taken over as part of the program of the active, indeed world-famous, industrial relations department. This is another way of saying that, beyond a few careful exploratory works such as the Lundberg, Komarovsky, and McInerny book, *Leisure: a Suburban Study,* we do not even begin to know whether craftsman-like leisure has developed new meanings in modern America. Are there correlations between styles of leisure and character types, and are these correlations discoverable?

It seems plausible to assume that the craftsmanlike use of leisure has certain compatibilities with the whole way of life of men dependent on inner-direction: their attention to the hardness of the material, their relative unconcern and lack of training for the more complex forms of peer-group taste exchanging. Moreover, the inner-directed man who carries into his hobby some of his surplus work impulses might find the maintenance of his technical skill playing directly back into his value on the job, making him, for instance, a better and more inventive gadgeteer. Even today, among many skilled workmen, such interchange between the home hobby shop and the plant suggestion box is not by any means a forgotten folkway. But the craft-skill is valued more than ever before for its own sake, as in the case of the Sunday painter.

The dramatic turn toward craftsmanlike hobbies in a "full-employment" postwar economy has perils of its own variety. The conservatism of the craftsman—in this aspect, part of the conservatism of play itself—finds its ideals of competence constantly threatened by a series of power tools and hobby products that make it possible for the dub to appear like a professional. The craftsman backwoods cook, for instance, is now imitated by the suburbanite with store-furnished back-yard grill and metallurgical wizardry of pots, pans, and wienie holders. True, the economic advances of the last decades have done much to enrich the older forms of mechanical hobby and craftwork: the home craftsman of real craft aspirations is better off with a power tool than without one. But how many can retain the spontaneous craft aspiration?

Some of the ambiguities of craft hobbyism dependent on a power tool are illustrated by a study of automotive hobbyists—especially the hot rodders.[1] A wide range of standards of technique and design gives room to both the green amateurs and the semi-professional car racers, while all the hobbyists have the comfort of working within an old American tradition of high-level tinkering. Competence and imagination are on the scene in force among the youths who race their quasi-Fords and quasi-Chevrolets on the Dry Lakes of the Far West, in a continuous competition with the mass-produced standards of Detroit. Among these groups there exists an active and critical attitude toward the Detroit car as it is now built, or as it was built until recently. Here, astonishingly enough, the top commercial product of the country, the Detroit car, far from driving out amateur performance, has only stimulated, perhaps even provoked it. Moreover,

1. This study was undertaken by Eugene Balsley, a student at the University of Chicago.

the individual who remakes cars according to standards of his own devising is obviously not exploiting any questionable social dividend in his pursuit of leisure but is "doing for himself" with what parts and help he can muster on a small bank roll. The very economy of his means helps give the procedure its atmosphere of high competence and high enjoyment.

But this field too is becoming professionalized and standardized. *The Hot Rod,* a magazine founded to cater to the growing number of auto hobbyists (at the same time standardizing their self-image), reports that the business of supplying the amateurs with parts and tools is becoming a big business—some $8,000,000 in 1948. In the meantime Detroit has found its way to many of the hot-rodder powerplant notions, if not stripped-down body notions.

We see looming upon the horizon of the hot rodder much the same fate that has overtaken other amateur competences, not only in the area of crafts and hobbies but, as we shall see below in the instance of jazz, in the area of taste exchange and criticism. Those who seek play autonomy in a craft must keep an eye on the peer-groups (other than their own immediate one) and on the market, if only to keep out of their way. But this in turn may involve them in a steady search for difficulties in execution and privacies in vocabulary (in some ways, like the "mysteries" of medieval craftsmen) in order to outdistance the threatening invasion of the crowd. Then what began more or less spontaneously may end up as merely effortful marginal differentiation, with the roots of fantasy torn up by a concern for sheer technique. The paradox of craftsmanship, and of much other play, is that in order to attain any importance as an enlivener of fantasy it must be "real." But whenever the craftsman has nourished a real competence he also tends to call into being an industry and an organization to circumvent the competence or at least to standardize it.

Moreover, as with any other activity, the pursuit of a severely technical competence can become an end in itself. The hobby of the replica or miniature is a striking illustration. On the one hand, it shows the paucity of imagination that finds itself capable only of literal imitation, where banality is concealed by ingenuity of means. Such an obsession may demonstrate a pathetically uncritical acceptance of the design of industrial forms as they now exist. It may also demonstrate a greater respect for the capital goods economy (the toy railroad) than for the consumer economy (the toy dollhouse), and thus exhibit a pathetically uncritical acceptance of cultural definitions. On the other hand, the ingenuity may become so technical as to call into being prefabricated parts and designs if more than a very few "craftsmen" are to be successful. The creation of a fictionally difficult craft object with the help of someone else's blueprints, factory tools, and factory parts is a last step in the disintegration of the hardness of the material as the attraction to craft hobbyism.

Nevertheless, the man whose daily work is glad handing can often rediscover both his childhood and his inner-directed residues by serious craftsmanship. An advertising man, involved all day in personalizing, may spend his week ends in the craftsmanlike silences of a boatyard or in sailboat racing—that most inner-directed pursuit where the individual racers independently move toward the goal as if guided by an invisible hand! And yet it is clear that these "players" may locate themselves in the craftsmanship pattern for reasons that have nothing to do with the search either for competence or for the more distant goal of autonomy. There may be status motives. There may be an unconscious or barely conscious desire to run away from the problems set up in the play worlds of taste exchanging and criticism. All these ambiguities are, of course, more present in the response of the middle-class person than in that of the mechanic or farmworker.

CRAFTSMANSHIP: THE MORALIZING SPECTER

It is important to see how perplexing these ambiguities are, because otherwise we may be tempted to place more stock in craftsmanship as the "best" form of play than is warranted. This temptation is particularly strong among those who try to deal with the challenge of modern leisure by filling it with play styles drawn from the past in Europe or America. Indeed, there is a widespread trend today to warn Americans against relaxing in the featherbed of plenty, in the pulpy recreations of popular culture, in the delights of bar and coke bar, and so on. In these warnings any leisure that looks easy is suspect, and craftsmanship does not look easy.

The other-directed man in the upper social strata often finds a certain appeal in moralizing about craftsmanship versus consumption. High prestige is still associated with inner-direction and with inner-directed political moralizing. Yet it is a blind alley for the other-directed man to try to adapt his leisure styles to those which grew out of an earlier character and an earlier social situation; in the process he is almost certain to become a caricature. This revivalist tendency is particularly clear in the type of energetic craft hobbyist we might term the folk dancer. The folk dancer is often an other-directed urbanite or suburbanite who, in search of an inner-directed stance, becomes "artsy and craftsy" in his recreations and consumer tastes. He goes native, with or without regional variations. He shuts out the mass media as best he can. He never wearies of attacking from the pulpit of his English bicycle the plush and chrome of the new-model cars. He is proud of not listening to the radio, and television is his bugbear.

Yet the vogue of the folk dancer is testimony to people's search for meaningful, creative leisure. The folk dancer wants something better but does not know where to look for it. He abandons the utopian possibilities of the future because, in his hatred of the American present, as he interprets it, he is driven to fall back on the vain effort to resuscitate the European or American past as a model for play. Like many other people who carry the ancestor within of an inner-directed character and ideology, he fears the dangerous avalanche of leisure that is falling down on the Americans.

In this fear the folk dancer is near-cousin to a number of other contemporary critics who, though genuinely concerned with autonomy, have no hope of finding it in play—not even, for the most part, in the hard play of crafts or sports. These critics go the folk dancer one better; they look to experiences of enforced hardship in *work,* or even to social and individual catastrophe, as the only practicable source of group cohesion and individual strength of character. They see men as able to summon and develop their resources only in an extreme or frontier situation, and they would regard my program for the life of Riley in a leisure economy as inviting psychological disintegration and social danger. Hating the "softness of the personnel"—not seeing how much of this represents a characterological advance—they want to restore artificially (in extreme cases, even by resort to war [2]) the "hardness of the material."

2. The war experience seemed to establish that there was little "practical" need for such hardship therapies in the interests of production or warmaking. It turned out that characterological other-direction and political indifference did not imply an inability to stand physical hardships. Efforts were made to treat the soldier as if he were in America, with cokes, radio programs, and entertainments from home. Certainly such "softness" did not impede fighting power. The tractability of Americans made it possible to build an army less on

That catastrophes do sometimes evoke unsuspected potentialities in people—potentialities which can then be used for further growth toward autonomy—is undeniable. A serious illness may give a man pause, a time for reverie and resolution. He may recover, as the hero, Laskell, does in Lionel Trilling's novel, *The Middle of the Journey*. He may die, as does the Russian official in Tolstoy's short story, "The Death of Ivan Ilyitch," who near death, confronts himself and his wasted life honestly for the first time. And the swath of the last war does offer repeated evidence that not only individuals but whole groups and communities can benefit from hardship, where not too overwhelming. An example is reported by R. K. Merton, P. S. West, and M. Jahoda in their study of a warworkers' housing community in New Jersey. The warworkers found themselves living in a jerry-built morass, without communal facilities, without drainage, without a store. Challenged by their circumstances, they responded by energetic improvisation and managed, against all kinds of obstacles, to make a decent, livable, even a lively community for themselves. The dispiriting sequel is familiar: the community, its major problems of sheer existence surmounted, became less interesting to live in, its cooperative store, built by so much energetic and ingenious effort, folded up.

There are many interlacing problems here. It is one thing to be able to face hardship when necessary. It is another thing to *seek* hardship. Many people will run to a war or a fire because they want threats and demands made on them and find these neither in their business-as-usual nor their play-as-usual. Others, however, seem to be able to regard as an imminent catastrophe the danger that they will not become what in character they might be; they suffer from the kind of "humanistic conscience" Erich Fromm describes in *Man for Himself*. Mere adjustment is a hardship, and at the same time a temptation, for people who can recognize potential autonomy in themselves; to become and remain autonomous is never easy.

TASTE EXCHANGING: THE NEWER CRITICISM

Craftsmanship, whatever part it may play in the leisure of an individual or a group, is obviously not a complete solution, any more

---

hierarchy than on group-mindedness. The tractability, the familiarity with machines, the widespread social skills, and the high educational level made it possible to train men quickly for the fantastically varied services and missions of modern warfare.

than consumership is, to the problems of leisure among the would-be autonomous. Often, indeed, craftsmanship is far from a creative expression but serves instead as an escape from the peer-group—an escape not into a chosen reverie or a select sociability but self-organized loneliness. We know many a man whose radar is not in very good working order who tries to shut off the signals by attaching himself fiercely to the objects of his craft or hobby, to nature, or to animals. Here anomie may be hidden under, or only barely avoided by, the hobby. While the inner-directed man could solace himself in these pursuits and even move toward autonomy through them, the other-directeds can hardly maintain such an unambiguous relation to craftsmanlike leisure. By definition the other-directeds in search of autonomy have no choice but to pass into and through taste exchanging—that characteristic process by which the other-directed person makes his temporary alignments with the peer-groups and takes the next step beyond the general consumership prevailing in the leisure economy. Once he has traversed this stage successfully he may be able to value and develop his own standards of taste, even to criticize the taste-making operations in the society as a whole.

What do we mean by contrasting the taste-exchanging use of leisure with craftsmanlike use of leisure? The contrast is really one between two worlds and two character types. Craftsmanship has its historic roots in the artisanship of the era dependent on tradition-direction, and it survives in the ways already touched on among the inner-directeds. Taste exchanging can scarcely begin until there is a surplus of goods and leisure; it has its historic roots in the connoisseurship of the era dependent on inner-direction. Now while the nineteenth-century connoisseur might exchange tastes in good cigars or Raphaels, the onset of other-direction vastly increases not only the range of consumer goods and intangibles about which one talks but also, as we have seen, the degree of involvement of the individual with the peer-group judgments and their media reinforcements. The connoisseur might feel a mistake in taste to be a reflection on his class status and aspirations. The other-directed man feels a mistake—if it goes beyond the tolerant limits of *de gustibus*—as a reflection on his most vital asset, his radar. The result is that while connoisseurship was generally leisurely, taste exchanging is often harried and desperate.

It is important to understand this transition in order to see how grave is the problem of competence that modern taste exchanging presents, how much greater its demands on the individual than mere middle-class consumership. For while connoisseurship and craftsmanship alike make their appeal to standards of judgment that are old and established, standards related by easy stages to the workmanlike impulses of work-minded economies, taste exchanging on the other hand is the rich and amorphous social by-product of the sudden stream of consumer goods provided in the incipient-decline phase of population growth. Inevitably, gradients of taste and taste exchanging have become part of the panoply by which the sensitive middle classes have sought to cope with the fluctuating values created by the impact upon them of a "luxury" mode of life. The taste exchanger is one who has been forced very quickly to make judgments on an enormous variety of novel objects over whose conditions of production he has had little control and of whose productive process he has had small knowledge. The movie audience is an example. Knowledge of the techniques of movie making has been limited, until recently, to a few well-read movie fans and to the even fewer home-movie makers who know how to cut film. Indeed, there are still some people in the movie audience who have so little understanding of the art as to be unable to distinguish between fictional and factual elements in the personality of a movie actor. Obviously to become good critics they must gain this understanding, but do they need, in addition, to have a grasp of film techniques?

While I do assert that taste exchanging can ascend to competence in criticism, I do not assert that competence depends on being able to produce the art work oneself or on being able fully to understand the techniques. It is too ascetic, too inner-directed, and not really relevant today, to ask every car driver to become a mechanic; all he needs to know is how the car looks and feels to him. One can judge movies without understanding booms, montage, or editing. There are many avenues to competence, which will differ for different people. What I want to emphasize here is the wealth of competence that the American consumer actually is able to muster, considering the novelty and magnitude of the problems he is up against.

Advertising, we must observe, was one of the first tutors in competence. By providing the images and the terms for taste exchange, it sought to reassure people that they did possess the critical talents and vocabulary necessary to distinguish between high and low quality.

One of the effects of advertising, however, is to make such distinctions increasingly difficult; it becomes necessary for the peer-group to modify or even oppose the advertisers' "critical" analysis of the flow of goods and services. How do the peers accomplish this? We have already seen something of the "talk of the town" the peer-group develops in order to confront or to evade these challenges to its critical competence. We saw, for instance, in Chapter X how contemporary audiences are likely to apply the test of "sincerity" in responding to entertainers whose virtuosity can no longer be judged.

Such rudimentary critical vocabularies do not bridge the growing gap between the advancing peer-group taste exchangers and the lagging advertisers. A new group of "culture diffusionists" or, as Russell Lynes calls them, "taste-makers," has been growing up to fill professionally the other-directed man's need to find a pedigree, a ticket, a label, and generally a way of talking, for each item or constellation of items in the flood of objects. The nineteenth-century connoisseur had his taste-makers, too—Bernard Berenson is a fine survival—but such men operated more as diffusionists of the old "high" culture of Europe than as mediators between the various "brow levels" within America. The contemporary American culture diffusionist makes a living or a reputation by diffusing the taste judgments of the peer-group he belongs to, to other peer-groups lower down on the taste gradient.

The celerity, refinement, and drive of this process should be viewed as a tremendous experiment, perhaps the really strategic one, in American adult education. The process must be seen, moreover, as going on both among the audience for goods and services and among the producers of goods and services. Thus we have already observed how the media men look up to the taste-makers in the realm of political moralizing. In this chapter, however, our concern is only with the audience, the audience which is being pushed, and is pushing itself, up the taste gradient, and, in a reciprocal process, is pushing the taste-makers in their turn toward further sophistication.

The speed with which this taste gradient is being climbed has escaped many critics of the popular arts who fail to observe not only how good American movies, popular novels, and magazines frequently are but also how energetic and understanding are some of the comments of the amateur taste exchangers who seem at first glance to be part of a very passive, uncreative audience. One of the most interesting examples of this is the criticism of jazz among the *afficionados* that grew almost as rapidly as jazz itself. I speak here not of such critics as Wilder Hobson and Panassié but of the large number of young people who, all over the country, greeted jazz affectionately and criticized it fondly, on a level of discourse far removed from the facile vocabulary of "sincerity" or "swell." These people found in jazz, as others have found in the movies or the comic strips, an art form not previously classified by the connoisseurs, the school system, or the official culture. They resisted, often violently, and occasionally with success, the effort of the popular-music industry itself to ticket its products: in the very form of their choices—preference for combos over star soloists, preference for improvisation, distrust of smooth arrangers—they set up their own *standards* in opposition to *standardization*. Much like the hot rodders, they developed their own language and culture to go with their new skill.

Here again, as with the hot rodders, the verbal craftsmanship of jazz lovers' taste exchange could not long continue to develop among isolated peer-groups. Jazz has long since been parceled out by a cult or a series of cults, in which the increasingly exacting aesthetic criteria employed by the peer-groups are no longer amiably built up by the free flow of critical energies operating on the intangibles of jazz performance. Through their very precision and almost fanatical insistence on values untainted by commercialism and showmanship, the criteria have often become ends in themselves. In the meantime jazz itself (other than subtle bop) has lost much of its vitality, and the level of popular music other than jazz has declined even more markedly.

These illustrations serve to indicate the ambiguity of the demands for active participation made by the critics of American popular culture and peer-group taste exchange. Play can easily vanish when people have to strain for competence. Many of the folk dancers and hardship lovers discussed in the preceding section seem to have formed their standards of proper and active recreation by reference to some kind of plainly strained-for pursuit: muscle building or mind building. They may be imitating much nineteenth-century (and later) recreation and fail to see that this (and not only on the supervised playground or in the YMCA) was often little more than a sublimating mobility channel for ambitious youth or an effort to divert the attention of presumptive juvenile delinquents. And they also, as we have seen, may not recognize how self-conscious and self-critical many of the popular-culture audiences have become.

Unwilling to see that taste exchanging in popular audiences often is the basis for increasing competence in criticism, they view jazz, soap opera, the movies, and television with the same horror with which the inner-directed man was urged to view the brothel and burlesque; with the result that they may add still further elements of effortfulness to the group-adjustive and work-adjustive strains already present in the peer-media context. This is an unanticipated consequence of their application of inner-directed standards to the new situations created by the flood of leisure. These critics of mass *production* often fail to observe that, while in its earlier stages mass production did drive out fine handicrafts and debase taste, we have now a situation better termed *class*-mass production where our industrial machine has become flexible enough to turn out objects of even greater variety and quality than in the handicraft era. Likewise, these critics of mass *consumption* may fail to observe that, while the first consequences of mass leisure were often destructive of older values of craftsmanship and ceremonial consumption, we have today a situation of *class*-mass consumption in which it is economically possible for the first time in history to distribute first-class novels and nonfiction, paintings, music, and movies to audiences that can fit them into leisure patterns of great individuality.

These considerations lead me to suggest that one step toward autonomy may come through the seemingly "idle" and contentless practice of taste exchanging: the other-directed man may begin to realize that he is actually a good deal more competent than he gets or gives himself credit for being. He has learned a lot, successively, from the advertisers and the culture diffusionists, as well as from the process—seemingly so aimless—of peer-group taste exchange itself. His judgments are increasingly sensitive and sharp. Provided he were more aware of the competence he has, he could move more easily and less anxiously toward new competence.

This dialectic between an externally testable competence and felt subjective competence can be seen in its simplest form among many industrial workers who have remained relatively untouched and untroubled by the increasing complexities of leisure among the other-directeds. They can assume that their competence as spectators of the sports and entertainments they follow is high, that their vocabulary is adequate not only for the peer-group but for the media beamed to the peer-group. By concentrating on certain aspects of sports and movies for instance, they can know their tastes pretty well and at the same time can come close to meeting their own self-demands for competence. They know all the things they feel they must know, and know them without a sense of strain. But the industrial worker pays a price for his occasionally undisturbed ability to find an enclave within the wider American culture. He escapes from virtuoso competition but he must be satisfied with the play package as it exists in his sub-culture, and cannot experiment with wider play horizons.

By contrast with many among the industrial workers, the middle-class other-directed man is taught by his education to accept sharp and often unexplained breaks with the tastes of his childhood. He feels obligations to abandon "trashy" books and comics, though he may allow himself to return to them as an adult, provided he returns in a new, e.g., a "sociological," way. Forced toward new peer-groups as he moves on to high school and college, he cannot retain the old taste-exchanging vocabularies of his former peer-group. And he may never feel fully in control of the taste gradients of the new peer-groups, since these in turn are under pressure from the mass media as well as from the seekers of marginal differentiation within the group itself.

There is a point, however, where the process of straddling peer-groups and climbing taste gradients may begin to be an exhilarating and liberating one, in which the golden bowl of leisure objects and their aura of critical vocabularies can at last be comfortably enjoyed. For this to happen, the other-directed person needs to become even more self-conscious than he already is of the game of taste exchange and more aware than he is of the gifts he brings to the game. To feel that one is just a working, straining member of a distributive economy of leisure is not enough.

For one thing, the other-directed man seems often to feel that he is making a judgment only when he is making a conscious effort to "make a judgment." He may thus gloss over the competence he has in those residual areas of his leisure life where he is accepting objects and fantasies directly and naturally, without continuous checking by the criteria of the taste-makers. He may for instance, be a good judge of science fiction and not know it, or a good judge of public statuary and not know it. He may be blaming himself for lapses from "realism" and not know he deserves credit for retaining his ability to have good daydreams. He may be making judgments of the qualities or "tastes" of experience much of the time and know it only some of the time. It is safe to predict that the most important developments in our leisure life in the next few decades will be influenced by the growing impact of this unrecognized virtuosity in taste. It will not be the result of inner-directed *force majeure* but of other-directed awareness.

III. THE AVOCATIONAL COUNSELORS

Despite this growing awareness the other-directed person may not be able to rescue himself, either from the peer-group or the taste-makers, all by himself. Even though he may feel aware of his competences and opportunities he still may not be able to become autonomous. Indeed, he may be swamped by his opportunities. We know that if we increase the social space within which a person can move we may only induce agoraphobia.

To bring an individual into unfrightening contact with his opportunities therefore often requires some guides and signposts. In our urban, specialized society these take the form of avocational counselors, operating at least partially through institutional channels. Let us take a look at a few of these.

"Avocational counseling" may seem like a rather clinical term to describe the activities undertaken by a number of relatively rapidly growing professions in the United States, including travel agents, hotel men, resort directors, sports teachers and coaches, teachers of the arts, including dancing teachers, and so on. But there are also many counselors who supply advice on play and leisure as a kind of by-product of some other transaction. The interior decorator, for instance, seems at first glance to belong in a different occupational group from the dude-ranch social director. To be sure, most clients of the interior decorator may be looking for the correct design for conspicuous display. Moreover, the relationship may be simply one of culture diffusion and taste exchange, concerning the relative merits of antiques and Robsjohn-Gibbings. But beyond these functions may lie a realm in which the interior decorator is looked to for more basic domestic rearrangements that can facilitate a more comfortable leisure life, more "colorful" literally and figuratively. The sale of the decorating service may conceal the sale of this significant intangible.

This function is perhaps even more evident in the work of the domestic architect for the upper middle-class client. True, like the decorator, he still counsels his clients in providing the correct public façade, and his current lesson of conspicuous retreat from display may for many be only a change in style of display and not necessarily a decline of architectural or decorative exhibitionism. But a generation ago he would not have dreamed of counseling his clients about the functional interior relationships in the dwelling in terms of anything more avocational than "gracious living." Today, however, the architect, by interior and exterior planning, can lead as well as follow the play patterns of his clients. Through him and his views there filters a variety of tastes, inclinations, social schemes (as in easily rearranged living rooms), leisure-time ecologies that scarcely existed a generation ago. The architect—and, beyond him, the city planner—brings together play opportunities that might otherwise remain subdivided among a score of specialists.

We all know how little use Americans have made in the past of the architectural avocational counselor in disguise, how they have fled into some historically standardized solution from the autonomous possibilities of designing a house to fit their individual needs. Increasingly, however, many Americans seem to feel they must build "modern" houses, without knowing whether they really like them, because it would be stuffy and reactionary to do otherwise; in other words, out of the same kind of compulsive liberation that drives many people to other guilty choices in friends and consumption goods. Nevertheless, with the architects' encouragement and help, it is possible that people are becoming willing to have a house fit them. This requires that they find out who they are.

Another set of avocational counselors is clustered around the chronological center of American leisure habits, the vacation. The vacation itself, frequently involving the meeting of others who are not members of one's own peer-group and who may be located outside one's own experience with the social structure, may be considered as dramatic a symbol of the encounters among people in the population phase of incipient decline as the market place was in the population phase of transitional growth. To be sure, with high wages millions of Americans spend their vacations hunting animals rather than people; other millions putter about that residue of earlier eras—the house-and-garden. But increasingly the vacation serves as a time and place for bringing those who have leisure and money to buy in contact with those who have a leisure skill to sell—riding, swimming, painting, dancing, and so on. But of course avocational counseling here, except perhaps for ship and shore recreational directors, is usually trying to sell a commodity or a service rather than to help the individual find what he wants and might want.

While, however, we are finding new avocational counselors, some older ones are going out of business. This is especially noticeable in the media. Thus we seem to be losing our leisurely magazines, with their essayistic tradition and their encouragement of fantasy and escape. Indeed, the disappearance of the old-style *Harper's,* the genteel *Atlantic,* the old *Life,* etc., has left us almost without any low-pressure journalism. It is significant that the principal upholder of an Addisonian tradition, *The New Yorker,* serves both as an avocational counselor of great imagination and as a consumers' union report— a weekly taste guide for those in the so-called provinces (including, of course, many New Yorkers). We need many more journals as good as *The New Yorker;* even more, we need more journals operating in a nonslick manner on still another emotional level.

What is necessary, in fact, is a new kind of institutional analysis, in which we re-examine our tertiary and service employment sectors, on the one hand to see where false personalization exists and where we can get rid of it, and on the other to make an inventory of such avocational counseling as goes on and see how this might be expanded. Certainly our rule of thumb should be that all distribution which is personalized without being individualized should be pushed rapidly toward automatization. Correspondingly, all distribution where avocational counseling accompanies the sale of a leisure commodity might be examined for possible increases in resources, personnel, and training. For instance, while the waitress in Child's might be done away with for an automat, the waiter in a Japanese restaurant who does his cooking and chromatic food arranging at the table should be kept, and certainly the waiter or waitress who, where a long à la carte exists, can unobtrusively help introduce Americans to the glory and variety of presently available fish. While the automobile salesman might sometime disappear (Americans know enough about cars not to need salesmen) the sporting-goods salesman of fish flies and golf clubs might stay. The previous chapter made some suggestions as to the changes in distributive technique that might encourage such developments. Such suggestions, for example the world's fair for children, may look simply like a shift from less expensive selling to more expensive "specialty" selling. The inference is correct; as our national income grows, this merchandising shift is needed and desirable. But over and beyond merchandising changes the urgent shift that is required, in our present state of technique, character, and culture, is a shift of service people from jobs in which they are the mere personalizing handlers of stock consumption goods to jobs in which they can maintain a closer, more craftsmanlike or critical touch with the commodities they handle and the consumers with whom they do business.

It is easy to foresee, in the next decades, a great expansion among the avocational counselors—though, obviously, there are other non-utilitarian competitors for the American surplus. The objection remains that to turn the other-directed man over to an avocational counselor to teach him competence in play is merely to increase the very dependence which keeps him other-directed rather than autonomous. Will not the virtuosity of the counselor make the tutee feel still more incompetent than he already does? Will not any effort at social inventories and planning of play rob him of such spontaneities and privacies as he may still retain? Possibly. But it is not a question of shall we or shall we not have avocational counselors. They are already here, all around us. In the field of craftsmanship and taste exchanging, as in other fields of monopoly and veto-group pressure, we have seen that the private planners are energetically at work.

It seems, therefore, that our effort should be directed toward making the avocational counselors as good and as available as possible. The other-directed man suffers from failure to realize what he is up against when he searches for competence in his leisure time, or stops searching. The avocational counselor may then help him realize, as a good golf pro does, that most American adults have no simple time learning to play and need help. For one does not become autonomous by being hard on oneself. On the other hand, the other-directed man may in a way not expect enough of himself, may not take his failures in play seriously enough, settling too easily for an adjustment that gets by with the peer-group. The avocational counselor might stimulate, even provoke, such a person to more imaginative play by helping him realize how very important for his own development toward autonomy play is.[3]

It should be plain, in view of this discussion, that we still know very little about the relations between the varieties of play and the varieties of autonomy. This chapter is merely an attempt to redefine for the individual those overindustrialized elements in himself and his environment that constitute a threat to his humanity. I believe that one major premise of any utopian society will be its recognition, as a matter of course, that failure in play is a psychic hardship of the most intolerable sort.

3. The importance of play for America's economic future has already been indicated. A good deal could also be said about its importance for the political future. To take just one example, Americans tend to judge foreign peoples from their bias of work-mindedness, somewhat mitigated by missionary influences. Since the rest of the world, save Russia, is less work-minded than we, these judgments are usually both narrow and offensive. Judgment from the standpoint of play competence would actually lead to quite a different spectrum of hospitalities to other cultures—and especially to those now in the stage of high population growth potential.

XVIII

Autonomy and Utopia

Time, events, or the unaided individual action of the mind will sometimes
undermine or destroy an opinion, without any outward sign of the change.
It has not been openly assailed, no conspiracy has been formed to make war
on it, but its followers one by one noiselessly secede; day by day a few of
them abandon it, until at last it is only professed by a minority. In this state
it will still continue to prevail. As its enemies remain mute or only interchange their thoughts by stealth, they are themselves unaware for a long
period that a great revolution has actually been effected; and in this state
of uncertainty they take no steps; they observe one another and are silent.
The majority have ceased to believe what they believed before, but they still
affect to believe, and this empty phantom of public opinion is strong enough
to chill innovators and to keep them silent and at a respectful distance.

Tocqueville, *Democracy in America*

IN these last chapters I have set forth some thoughts about the
middle-class world of work and play, in the hope of finding ways
in which a more autonomous type of social character might develop. The reader who recalls the concepts of the first chapter may ask
how my emphasis on gross ecological and economic factors, as symbolized by the curve of population, can be reconciled with my belief
in the importance of new models of leisure in implementing characterological change.

My emphasis on ecology and economy does rule out the purely ra-
tionalistic interpretations of much contemporary intellectual history,
for I believe that only certain ideas will be generated and catch on,
under any given socioeconomic conditions. Furthermore, my focus on
character structure leads me to view the role of ideas in history still
more narrowly; character, with all its intractabilities and self-
reproducing tendencies, will largely dictate the way ideas are received. In contrast to those few people who still put their faith in

some world-wide intellectual or religious revival, I do not believe any idea, no matter how noble and necessary, is likely to capture a globe that, though composed of people with the same basic humanity, still contains people at very widely differing stages on the not easily accelerated curve of character and population.

However, I have dealt in much of this book with the importance of ideas and how they take hold. I have dealt, for instance, with the part played by the storyteller who structures the world for the child and with the part played in character formation by cultural definitions of work and play structuring vital segments of experience for the adult.

Hence, despite the massed obstacles to change inherent in the relative compatibility between social structure and character structure, I believe that ideas can make a decisive historical contribution. Marx is a good example of this. While he denied that ideas are very important and argued that conditions make history, still his own writing is a series of inflammable ideas. While he dismissed the utopian speculations of his predecessor socialists, remarking that "Historical action is to yield to their personal inventive action, historically created conditions of emancipation to fantastic ones . . ." yet as we all know, he did not leave the working class to be emancipated only by events. In his alternate role as propagandist, he tried himself to shape the ideological and institutional environment in which workers would live. And since he had ruled out utopian speculation as mere idle dreams, this "environment" turned out to be much more constricting than that imposed by the capitalists; it was and is a "party" environment.[1]

Indeed, I think we need to insist today on bringing to consciousness the kind of ideas that Marx dismissed as "utopian." However, since we live in a time of disenchantment, such thinking, where it is rational in aim and method and not simply escapism, is not easy. It is easier to concentrate on programs for choosing among lesser evils. We are well aware of the "damned wantlessness of the poor"; the rich as well, for the most part, have inhibited their claims for a decent world to the "practical" point, limited to what can be mentioned in the conversation of the classes. Both rich and poor avoid any goals, personal or social, that seem out of step with peer-group aspirations. The politically operative inside-dopester seldom commits himself to aims be-

1. Harold Rosenberg has observed in an article of extraordinary brilliance that this Communist party apparatus provides a party picture of the experience the worker is supposed to have. It is hard to think of what could be more "inventive," more "fantastic"—more "utopian." "The Pathos of the Proletariat," *Kenyon Review*, XI (1949), 595.

yond those that common sense proposes to him. Actually, however, in a dynamic political context—and, as the population cycle moves unevenly throughout the world, such a context seems unavoidable—it is the modest, commonsensical goals of the insiders and the "constructive" critics that are unattainable. For example, it often seems that the retention of a given status quo is a modest hope; many lawyers, political scientists, and economists occupy themselves by suggesting the minimal changes which are necessary to stand still; yet today this hope is almost invariably disappointed; the status quo proves the most illusory of goals.[2]

Of course it does not follow that the utopian goals of the would-be autonomous are attainable. It is much more likely that, out of impatience with uncertainty and with the "sluggish masses," parties and authoritarian movements will force people toward goals which are neither commonsensical nor utopian but merely regressive.

In any case, the autonomous, insignificant in numbers, play a minor and scarcely discernible role in our politics. One might expect, a priori, that the autonomous in character would, in their political style, go beyond the intellectual limitations of the moralizer and beyond the moral limitations (and hence the intellectual ones) of the inside-dopester and would become genuinely involved with politics, intelligent about it, and emotionally committed to it. But this is not always what we find. Many people who are clearly autonomous in character are sometimes political indifferents. Other autonomous people, less adequate in politics than in other life spheres, are indignants and sometimes inside-dopesters. Conversely, some people may manage to be productive in their political roles who are anomic or adjusted in character: politics may be their most creative sphere. On reflection, this is perhaps what we should expect if we remind ourselves that such words as autonomy and adjustment are constructions, not real people.

Of course these are not the only reasons why we cannot point to a political style that is distinctively the style of the autonomous. We happen to live at a time when the older motivations for political activity —namely, clear self-interest and clear morality—are operative only among the groups I have termed the moralizers. But, for reasons we

2. For fuller discussion see my articles, "Some Observations on Community Plans and Utopia," *Yale Law Journal*, LVII (1947), 173; "A Philosophy for 'Minority' Living," *Commentary*, VI (1948), 413; and "Equality and Social Structure," *Journal of Legal and Political Sociology*, I (1942), 72.

have seen, the moralizers are able to bring sufficient pressure on many other-directeds so as to make politics for them a group-conforming and group-consuming activity. Their political participation is not based, as the moralizers would like it to be, on clear political interests and self-evident duties; it is simply another peer-group ritual and requirement.

Moreover, the moralizers are always ready to tell an individual what his political "constituency" is. He should interest himself in local affairs and know the name of his alderman. But he should also know what is going on in Burma. The moralizers would not allow him to make the decision, on the basis of his individual temperament and reflections, either to concern himself exclusively with manageably local matters (as in the decision described thoughtfully by Granville Hicks in *Small Town*) or to concern himself only with international affairs and leave it to others to put out all local fires. However, in the politically saturated strata the citizen needs a "right of nonparticipation," under cover of which to make his own decisions, quite as much as he needs the right of participation in occasional periods of threat or crisis.

Under noncrisis conditions people may find new motivations for political interest and participation, motives neither moralistic nor group conforming. They may turn to politics because it is interesting, because it is one important way of helping them to understand their environment, because of a desire to have less misery in the world. Out of such materials the autonomous may invent a new political style.

For this reason I have emphasized the industrial cornucopia rather than the shack in the slum, even though (according to Hansen's *Economic Policy and Full Employment*) we have seven million substandard houses and no "public dynamite days" to get rid of them. As against the brilliant morbidity with which community surveys have exposed the evils of industry and the banalities of our leisure, I have concentrated on some of the economic richness of our middle-class life.

In the same vein, we might ask, is it conceivable that these economically privileged Americans will some day wake up to the fact that they overconform? Wake up to the discovery that a host of behavioral rituals are the result, not of an inescapable social imperative but of an image of society that, though false, provides certain "secondary gains" for the people who believe in it? Since character structure is, if anything, even more tenacious than social structure, such an awakening is exceedingly unlikely—and we know that many thinkers before us have seen the false dawns of freedom while their compatriots stubbornly continued to close their eyes to the alternatives that were, in principle, available. But to put the question may at least raise doubts in the minds of some.

Occasionally city planners put such questions. They comprise perhaps the most important professional group to become reasonably weary of the cultural definitions that are systematically trotted out to rationalize the inadequacies of city life today, for the well-to-do as well as for the poor. With their imagination and bounteous approach they have become, to some extent, the guardians of our liberal and progressive political tradition, as this is increasingly displaced from state and national politics. If, to take a fine example, we look at Percival Goodman's plan for Queens County, we see expressed in physical form a view of life which is not narrowly job-minded. It is a view of the city as a setting for leisure and amenity as well as for work. As people, and not only oldsters, increasingly move to the frontiers of leisure and as companies, freed by electrification and trucking, increasingly ignore the older conventions for the location of industry, the future of cities may well be transformed by such planners rather than by the bomb distributionists or the doctrinaire decentralizers. But at present the local power of the local veto groups and the vicious urban circle of taxes, flight to suburbia, and more taxes put even the most imaginative of city planners under great pressure to show that they are practical, hardheaded fellows, barely to be distinguished from traffic engineers.

However, just as there is in my opinion a greater complexity of leisure response in contemporary America than appears on the surface, so also the sources of utopian political thinking may be hidden and constantly changing, constantly disguising themselves. While political curiosity and interest have been largely driven out of the accepted sphere of the political in recent years by the "crisis" mood of the press and of the more responsible sectors of public life, people may, in what is left of their private lives, be nurturing newly critical and creative standards. If these people are not strait-jacketed before they get started —by the elaboration and forced feeding of a set of official doctrines— people may some day learn to buy not only packages of groceries or books but the "larger package" of a neighborhood, a society, and a way of life.

If the other-directed people should discover how much needless work they do, discover that their own thoughts and their own lives are quite as interesting as other people's, that, indeed, they no more assuage their loneliness in a crowd of peers than one can assuage one's thirst by drinking sea water, then we might expect them to become more attentive to their own feelings and aspirations.

This possibility may sound remote, and perhaps it is. But undeniably many currents of change in America escape the notice of the reporters of this best-reported nation on earth. We have inadequate indexes for the things we would like to find out, especially about such intangibles as character, political styles, and leisure uses. America is not only big and rich, it is mysterious; and its capacity for the humorous or ironical concealment of its interests matches that of the legendary inscrutable Chinese. By the same token, what my collaborators and I have to say may be very wide of the mark. Inevitably, our own character, our own geography, our own illusions, limit our view. I must again remind the reader of the limitations of social class and region, and of observational standpoint, which frame the picture of America presented here.

But while I have said many things in this book of which I am unsure, of one thing I am quite sure: the enormous potentialities for diversity in nature's bounty and men's capacity to differentiate their experience can become valued by the individual himself, so that he will not be tempted and coerced into adjustment or, failing adjustment, into anomie. The idea that men are created free and equal is both true and misleading: men are created different; they lose their social freedom and their individual autonomy in seeking to become like each other.

Index

ADAMS, BROOKS, 206; supporter of Bryan, 236
Adams, Henry, 298
Adjustment: defined, 287–288; of inner-directed, 295; overadjustment and anomie, 289–290;
of other-directed, 306; through work, 311; unity of peer-group and mass media, 348; see also Avocational counselors; Group adjustment
Adorno, T. W., 99
Advertising: consumer training of children, 81, 100, 101, 339, 340; student interpretations of, 274, 275; and distribution system, 322, 323; consequences of, 346; and consumer competence, 358, 359
Agee, James, 99 n.
Ambition. See Goals
American capitalism, critics of, 345–346
Anderson, Sherwood, mentioned, 126
Anomic type: defined, 287–288; in tradition-directed society, 288; as result of overadjustment, 289–290; in other-directed society, 294, 348; and struggle for autonomy, 305, 327; disguised by craft or hobby, 357
Anomie, 13; see also Anomic type
"Antagonistic cooperation": within peer-group, 78, 82, 280; contrasted with inner-directed ambition, 104; reinforced by parents and teachers, 111; and goals of other-directed, 144; in sex, 163; within veto groups, 244; and monopolistic competition, 245 n.; of Pueblo Indians, 277; and false personalization, 312; see also Peer group
Anxiety: characteristic of other-directed, 26; of parents with respect to children, 50–52; with respect to work, 128–129, 325; with respect to sex, 156, 303; with respect to consumption, 158; as reflected in contemporary literature, 161; indication of need for adjustment, 161; of nineteenth-century inner-directed politicians, 195; and group leader's need of approval, 265; assuaged by rituals, 279
Apathy: political apathy and social change, 3, 4; current fears of and attacks upon, 128–129, 180; of inner-directed, 130; sex, as other-directed defense against, 154; induced by incomprehensibility of politics,
202; glamour in politics, as defense against, 214–215; induced by tolerance, 289; glamour in work, as defense against, 313
Architect, as avocational counselor, 364
Architecture. See Dwelling
Arendt, Hannah, 231 n.
Army officers, power position of, 251
Asceticism: idealization of, 172–173; in politics, 197; see Puritan
Asch, Solomon, 167 and n.
Athenian empire, illustrating correlation between character type and curve of population, 27–29
Audience: in tradition-directed society, 87–88;
in inner-directed society, effect of literacy, 91–93;
in other-directed society, as consumer, 159; in movies, 162, 358; *Medea*, 164; and consumption of politics, 211, 214; loss of stratification in radio and press, 219; demand for sincerity, 220 and n., 221, 359; as lobby group, 265; as critic of mass media, 359–360; industrial workers as, 361–362
Automat. See Distribution
Autonomy: defined, viii, 287–288, 300; and curve of population, 291–294; and choice of occupation, 294;
in tradition-directed society, 291, 292; lack of in Dobu and Alor, 286–287;
in inner-directed society, effect of technological progress and leisure, 292; description of, 295–299, 336–337; in young, 299; obstacles to, 298–299, 336–337; in crafts and hobbies, 357;
in other-directed society, opportunity for, 286, 317–319, 336; in children, 339–341, 344; obstacles to, compared with inner-directed, 302, 336–337; and tolerance, 304–305; and sex, 303; and Bohemianism, 303–304; resisted by other-directed, 305–306;
in work, the limitations of cultural definitions, 309–310; false personalization, 311–317, fiction of "indispensability," 316–317; mechanization, and the depersonalization of work, 317–319;
in play, and relation to peer-group and

48–55; by teachers, 60–64; by peer-group, 69–82; by mass media, 99–112;

see also Dwelling; Literature; Mass media; Myth; Parents; Peer-group; Teachers

Childrens' model consumer economy, 339–341

Churchill, mentioned, 265; compared with Roosevelt, 240

City planning, 204, 317, 318, 328, 364, 372

Civil War (U.S.), 30, 179, 192, 198, 236

Clark, Colin, 21

Class: upper middle class and "other-direction," 19, 52; "old" and "new" middle class, 21, 47, 48, 260; ascendency of bourgeois, 38; relation to character structure, 38, 55; in tradition-directed society, 40; and the peer-group, 72; effects upon literature, 96; and consumption, 122–124, 150, 153, 170; and popular culture, 165; and politics, 177, 195, 207, 236–238, 242, 243; politics and the lower class, 186–187; lower class attitudes toward sincerity, 223 n.; changes in structure, and attitudes toward work, 309; as defense of autonomous inner-directed character, 298; envy of working class, 316; social mobility of lower classes, 334; see also Ruling class; Status

Comics, 36–37, 168, 223–224, 268, 362; realism in, 101–106; heroism in, 105–106; see also Mass media

Commager, Henry Steele, 106 n.

Communication, nonverbal, 38, 99; see also Mass media

Communism, 116, 293; and the inside-dopester, 206

Competence. See Consumption; Play; Work

Competition: among inner-directed, 104–119; among other-directed, 82, 83, 141, 146–147; see also "Antagonistic cooperation"; Goals; Individualism

Conformity: and fear of nonconformity, 76; and characterological ideal, 129; and self-manipulation, 161; see also Character; Characterological struggle

Congress, future control of, 254

Congreve, William, mentioned, 198

Conspicuous consumption, 121–123, 170; disappearance of, 273; and avocational counseling, 363

Consumer trainee, 79, 80–82, 100–102, 110; and popular culture, 158–159; see also Mass media; Peer-group

"Consumers' Union." See Peer-group

Consumption, patterns of, 72, 78;
inner-directed, 120–126; as escape, 120, 123–126, 159; as work (acquisition), 121–

122, 147; competence, 127; and respectability, 126;
other-directed, 123, 158–159; and shopping, 140; politics as object of, 212; non-materialistic, 273–274; obligatory nature of, 345; and advertising, 346; as peer-oriented play, 348; see also Food; Leisure; Peer-group; Sex

Cookbooks, 150–152; contrasted with sex books, 155

Cooperation: inner-directed, 115; other-directed, 135; see also "Antagonistic cooperation"; Teachers; Work

Coser, Rose Laub, x

Craftsmanship, 133–134; and leisure, 351, 354; and autonomy, 353–354; moralizing aspects of, 354–355; as escape from peer-group, 357; in jazz, 360; see also Hobbies; Work

Crèvecoeur, M., mentioned, vi

Cripps, Sir Stafford, mentioned, 265

Cultural pluralism, 334, 335

Cynicism. See Politics

DAVIS, ROBERT GORHAM, 99 n.

Death rates, 18; see also Population

de Beauvoir, Simone, mentioned, 301; quoted, 307

Defoe, Daniel, literary style of, 95

De Man, Henri, 318

Denney, Reuel, ix

Depression, effect of on economic goals, 345

Deviants: in tradition-directed society, 12; characterological, 287–288; see also Anomic; Autonomy; Rebels

Dewey, John, 341 n.

Dewhurst, F. Frederick, 75 n.

Dexter, Lewis, x

Dinerman, Helen, 216 n.

Discipline, parental, 51, 54; by teachers, 58, 63; see also Children

Distribution of goods, changes in, 143; see Consumption; False personalization; Market research; Work

Distribution system, criticized, 345–346

Division of labor, 41; and opportunities to change role, 292; in play, 346

Divorce, 331

Dobuan culture, compared to American, 272, 273, 275, 277, 286; see also Power

Drucker, Peter, 21, 250

Durkheim, Emile, 129, 287

Dwelling, as agent of character formation: in tradition-directed society, 40; in inner-directed society, 43–44; in other-directed society, 49; of the lower class, 53; war